JavaScript
A Beginner's Guide

Third Edition

About the Author

John Pollock is employed as a Web Administrator during the day and works on Web sites and other projects during the evening. He runs two Web sites devoted to Web development and design—PageResource.com (www.pageresource.com) is a development tutorial site, and JavaScript City (www.javascriptcity.com) is a site that offers free JavaScript code to Web developers. John holds a bachelor of arts in English from Sam Houston State University and currently lives in New Waverly, Texas with his wife Heather.

About the Technical Editor

Scott Duffy is an author and consultant based in Toronto, Canada. He designs and develops Web sites for small and medium-sized companies.

JavaScript
A Beginner's Guide

Third Edition

John Pollock

New York   Chicago   San Francisco
Lisbon   London   Madrid   Mexico City
Milan   New Delhi   San Juan
Seoul   Singapore   Sydney   Toronto

The **McGraw·Hill** Companies

Library of Congress Cataloging-in-Publication Data

Pollock, John.
    Javascript : a beginner's guide / John Pollock. — 3rd ed.
        p.   cm.
    ISBN 978-0-07-163295-9 (alk. paper)
    1. JavaScript (Computer program language)   2. Web site development.   I. Title.
QA76.73.J39P65   2009
005.2'762—dc22   2009031734

McGraw-Hill books are available at special quantity discounts to use as premiums and sales promotions, or for use in corporate training programs. To contact a representative, please e-mail us at bulksales@mcgraw-hill.com.

JavaScript: A Beginner's Guide, Third Edition

    34567890 QFR/QFR 154321

ISBN 978-0-07-163295-9
MHID   0-07-163295-6

Sponsoring Editor Jane K. Brownlow		**Proofreader** Claire Splan	
Editorial Supervisor Janet Walden		**Indexer** Claire Splan	
Project Manager Smita Rajan, Glyph International		**Production Supervisor** Jim Kussow	
Acquisitions Coordinator Joya Anthony		**Composition** Glyph International	
Technical Editor Scott Duffy		**Illustration** Glyph International	
Copy Editor Bill McManus		**Art Director, Cover** Jeff Weeks	
		Cover Designer Jeff Weeks	

*To my wife Heather Pollock, Bruce and Joy Anderson, and
Dr. J. D. and Linda Andrews*

*In memory of James D. and Livian Anderson, John William and Edith Hopkins,
Burley T. and Aline Price, and "Doc" Flores*

Contents at a Glance

Contents

Acknowledgments

I would like to begin by thanking my wonderful wife, Heather Pollock, for all of her love, support, and encouragement in all I do. I love you!

I would like to thank my parents, Bruce and Joy Anderson, for their love and guidance, and for always supporting my endeavors.

I would like to thank Dr. J. D. and Linda Andrews for their love, guidance, and support.

In addition I would like to thank John and Betty Hopkins (grandparents), James D. and Livian Anderson (grandparents), Clifton and Juanita Idom (grandparents), Richard Pollock (brother) and family, Misty Castleman (sister) and family, Warren Anderson (brother) and family, Jon Andrews (brother) and family, Lisa and Julian Owens (aunt/uncle) and family, and every aunt, uncle, cousin, or other relation in my family. All of you have been a great influence in my life.

I would like to thank all of my editors at McGraw-Hill/Professional for their outstanding help and support throughout the writing of this book. Thanks to Jane Brownlow, Joya Anthony, Janet Walden, Smita Rajan, Bill McManus, Claire Splan, Jim Kussow, Jeff Weeks, and to all of the copy editors who worked on each edition of the book.

Thanks to my technical editor, Scott Duffy, for editing and checking over all of the technical aspects of the book, and helping me provide clear explanations of the topics that are covered.

I would like to thank my English professors at Sam Houston State University in Huntsville, Texas for guiding me toward a better understanding of the English language. Thanks to James J. Dent, Helena Halmari, Douglas Krienke, Julie Hall, Tracy Bilsing, Phillip Parotti, Ralph Pease, Paul Ruffin, and Jack Kerr. In addition, I thank all of my other professors at the university for helping me gain knowledge in so many areas.

I want to thank my friends for putting up with me and for giving me encouragement when I have needed it. Thanks to Don Sargent and family, Dwayne Lacy, Marty J. Reeder and family, Garrett Cradduck and family, and to all of my other friends for your support and guidance.

I would like to thank God for the ability He has given me to help and teach people by my writing. "In all your ways acknowledge Him, and He shall direct your paths." (Proverbs 3:6).

Introduction

Welcome to *JavaScript: A Beginner's Guide, Third Edition*! Years ago, I was surfing the Web and noticed that people were publishing pages about themselves and calling them homepages. After viewing a number of these, I decided to create a homepage myself. I had no idea where to begin but, through trial and error, I figured out how to code HTML and publish my documents on a Web server. Over time, I saw some interesting effects used on other homepages (like alert messages that popped up out of nowhere or images that would magically change when I moved my mouse over them). I was curious and just *had* to know what was being done to create those effects. Were these page creators using HTML tags I did not know about?

Eventually, one site revealed what they were using to create those effects: *JavaScript*. I went in search of information on it, and came across a few tutorials and scripts on the Web. Since I had programmed in other languages (such as a relatively obscure language called Ada), I was able to catch on to JavaScript fairly quickly by looking at these tutorials and scripts.

I learned enough that I decided to create a Web site that would teach HTML and JavaScript to beginners. As soon as I began the project, I received questions from visitors that were way over my head—forcing me to dig deeper and learn more about JavaScript. As a result, I became completely familiar with this scripting language and what it can do. Not only can you add fun effects to a Web page, you can create scripts that will perform useful tasks, like validate form input, add navigational elements to documents, or react to user events.

The goal of this book is to help you to learn the basics of the JavaScript language with as little hair pulling and monitor smashing as possible. You do not need any prior programming experience to learn JavaScript from this book. All you need is knowledge of HTML and/or XHTML, Cascading Style Sheets (CSS), and how to use your favorite text editor and Web browser (see Chapter 1 for more information).

What This Book Covers

The 16 chapters of this book cover specific topics on the JavaScript language. The first two chapters cover the most basic aspects of the language: what it is, what you need to know to begin using JavaScript, and how to place JavaScript into an HTML file. The middle of the book (Chapters 3–15) covers beginning JavaScript topics from variables all the way to using JavaScript with frames. The final chapter (Chapter 16) introduces some advanced techniques, and points you toward resources if you want to learn more about JavaScript once you have completed the book.

This book includes a number of special features in each chapter to assist you in learning JavaScript. These features include:

- **Key Skills & Concepts**   Each chapter begins with a set of key skills and concepts that you will understand by the end of the chapter.

- **Ask the Expert**   The Ask the Expert Sections present commonly asked questions about topics covered in the preceding text, with responses from the author.

- **Try This**   These sections get you to practice what you have learned using a hands-on approach. Each Try This will have you code a script through step-by-step directions on what you need to do to in order to accomplish the goal. You can find solutions to each project on the McGraw-Hill/Professional Web site at www.mhprofessional.com/computingdownload.

- **Notes, Tips, and Cautions**   Notes, Tips, and Cautions call your attention to noteworthy statements that you will find helpful as you move through the chapters.

- **Code**   Code listings display example source code used in scripts or programs.

- **Callouts**   Callouts display helpful hints and notes about the example code, pointing to the relevant lines in the code.

- **Self Test**   Each chapter ends with a Self Test, a series of 15 questions to see if you have mastered the topics covered in the chapter. The answers to each Self Test can be found in the back of the book in the appendix.

That is it! You are now familiar with the organization and special features of this book to start your journey through JavaScript. If you find that you are stuck and need help, feel free to get online and visit the JavaScript discussion forums on the Web Xpertz Web site at www .webxpertz.net/forums. The forums will allow you to interact with other JavaScript coders who may be able to help you with your questions.

Now it is time to learn JavaScript. Get ready, get set, and have fun!

Chapter 1

Introduction to JavaScript

Key Skills & Concepts

● Using Text Editors, WYSIWYG Editors, and Web Browsers

● Defining JavaScript

● Differences Between JavaScript and Other Languages

Welcome to *JavaScript: A Beginner's Guide, Third Edition*! You're obviously interested in learning JavaScript, but perhaps you're not sure what you need to know to use it. This chapter answers some basic questions about what JavaScript is, discusses its advantages and limitations, explains how you can use it to create more dynamic and inviting Web pages, and provides a brief history of the language.

JavaScript is ubiquitous on the World Wide Web. You can use JavaScript both to make your Web pages more interactive, so that they react to a viewer's actions, and to give your Web pages some special effects (visual or otherwise).

JavaScript often gets thrown in with Hypertext Markup Language (HTML) as one of the recommended languages for beginning Web developers (whether you build Web sites for business or pleasure). Of course, you can build a Web page by using only HTML, but JavaScript allows you to add additional features that a static page of HTML can't provide without some sort of scripting or programming help.

What You Need to Know

Before you begin learning about JavaScript, you should have (or obtain) a basic knowledge of the following:

● HTML and Cascading Style Sheets (CSS)

● Text editors

● Web browsers

● The different versions of JavaScript

If you have this basic knowledge (the different versions of JavaScript will be discussed in this chapter), then you'll do just fine as you work through this book. Knowing another programming/scripting language or having previous experience with JavaScript isn't required. This book is a beginner's guide to JavaScript.

If you think you don't have enough experience in one of the aforementioned areas, a closer look at each one may help you decide what to do.

Basic HTML and CSS Knowledge

While you don't need to be an HTML guru, you do need to know where to place certain elements (like the head and body elements) and how to add your own attributes. This book will reference scripts in the head section (between the <head> and </head> tags) and the body section (between the <body> and </body> tags).

Occasionally, you will also need to add an attribute to a tag for a script to function properly. For example, you may need to name a form element using the id attribute, as shown in the following code:

```
<input type="text" id="thename" />
```

If you know the basics of using tags and attributes, the HTML portion shouldn't pose any problems to learning JavaScript.

If you don't have a basic knowledge of HTML, you can learn it fairly quickly through a number of media. For example, you can buy a book or look for some helpful information on the Web. A good book is *HTML: A Beginner's Guide, Fourth Edition* by Wendy Willard (McGraw-Hill Professional, 2009). To find information about HTML on the Web, check out these sites: www.pageresource.com/html and www.w3schools.com/html/default.asp.

Occasionally, you will need to use CSS to add or change presentation features on a Web page. We will mainly use CSS for the purposes of dynamically changing CSS properties via JavaScript in this book. A good place to learn CSS is www.w3schools.com/css/css_intro.asp.

Basic Text Editor and Web Browser Knowledge

Before jumping in and coding with JavaScript, you must be able to use a text editor or HTML editor, and a Web browser. You'll use these tools to code your scripts.

Text Editors

A number of text editors and HTML editors support JavaScript. If you know HTML, you've probably already used an HTML editor to create your HTML files, so you might not have to change.

However, some HTML editors have problems related to adding JavaScript code (such as changing where the code is placed or altering the code itself when you save the file). You may need to use a simpler editor or look for an HTML editor that handles the addition of your own JavaScript code easily (such as Adobe Dreamweaver). Some examples of text editors are Notepad, TextPad, and Simple Text.

Web Browsers

Again, if you've been coding in HTML, you probably won't need to change your browser. However, some browsers have trouble with the newer versions of JavaScript. The choice of Web browser is ultimately up to you, as long as it's compatible with JavaScript. I recommend one of the following browsers to test your JavaScript code:

- Microsoft Internet Explorer version 6.0 or later
- Mozilla Firefox version 1.0 or later
- Opera version 6.0 or later

New versions of these browsers continue to be produced. At the time of this writing, nonbeta versions of Internet Explorer 8, Firefox 3, and Opera 9 are available.

To give you an idea of what some browsers look like, Figure 1-1 shows a Web page when viewed in Microsoft Internet Explorer, and Figure 1-2 shows the same page when viewed in Mozilla Firefox.

If you have an older browser and you can't upgrade, a number of features (mostly discussed later in the book) may not work in that browser. Even so, the book can still help you learn the JavaScript language itself, so you don't need to give up if you have an older browser. The three browsers mentioned and the versions of JavaScript they support are shown in Table 1-1.

The next section, "Which Version?," explains what the version numbers mean in more detail. Once you've determined that you meet the basic requirements, you're ready to begin learning the language.

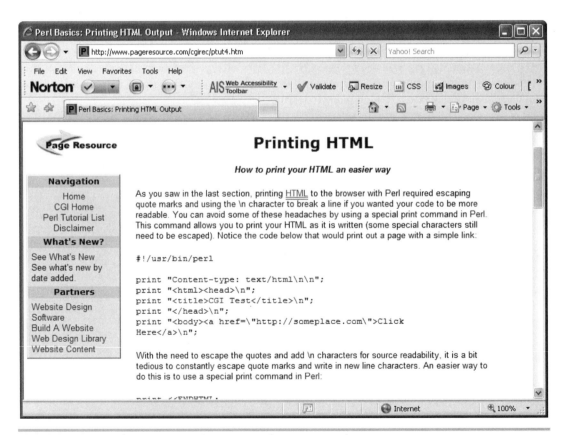

Figure 1-1 A Web page viewed in Microsoft Internet Explorer

Microsoft Internet Explorer Version	Mozilla Firefox Version	Opera Version	JavaScript Version Supported
–	3	–	1.8
–	2	–	1.7
–	1.5	–	1.6
5.5–8	1	6–9	1.5
4	–	–	1.3

Table 1-1   JavaScript Versions Supported by the Three Major Browsers

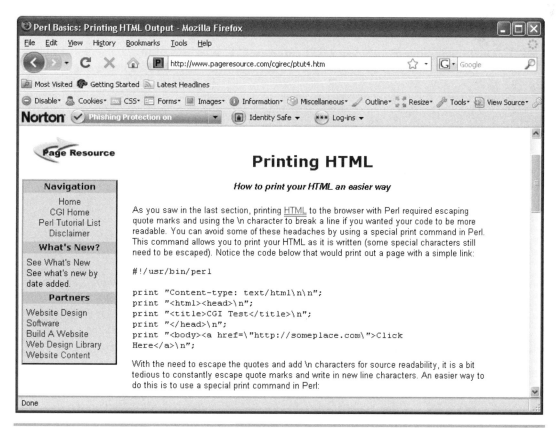

Figure 1-2   A Web page viewed in Mozilla Firefox

Which Version?

At the time of this writing, the browsers recommended earlier in this chapter should support at least JavaScript 1.5. (The newest version of Firefox supports JavaScript 1.8.)

You may also see or hear about JScript or ECMAScript. JScript is the version of JavaScript that Microsoft Internet Explorer uses (which has additional features because it is implemented as a Windows Script engine; it can use server-side languages to perform more complex tasks like updating databases). For more information on JScript, see http://msdn.microsoft.com/en-us/library/hbxc2t98.aspx.

ECMAScript is the international standard name and specification for the JavaScript language, so it's not a new language but a standard that is set for JavaScript and JScript. For more on ECMAScript, see www.ecma-international.org/publications/standards/Ecma-262.htm.

Ask the Expert

Q: You mentioned that I could use a text editor or HTML editor of my choice, but I'm not quite sure what that means. What is a text editor and where can I find one?

A: A text editor is a program that you can use to save and edit written text. Text editors range from simple to complex, and a number of choices are available: Notepad, WordPad, Simple Text, and Corel WordPerfect X4, to name a few. You can also purchase and download some from the Web, like NoteTab or TextPad.

An HTML editor is either a more complex text editor or an editor that allows you to add code by clicking buttons or by other means—often called a What You See Is What You Get (WYSIWYG) editor. I recommend a plain text editor or an HTML editor that doesn't change any code you add to it manually. Some examples of HTML editors are Adobe Dreamweaver and Softpress Freeway.

Q: What exactly do I need to know about using a text editor?

A: Basically, you only need to know how to type plain text into the editor, save the file with an .html or .htm extension, and be able to open it again and edit it if necessary. Special features aren't needed because HTML files are made up of plain text.

Q: What do I need to know about using a browser?

A: All you absolutely need to know is how to open a local HTML file on your computer (or on the Web) and how to reload a page. If you don't know how to open an HTML file from your own computer, open your browser and go to the File menu. Look for an option that says something like Open or Open File, and select it. You should be able to browse for the file you want to open like you would with other programs. The following illustration shows where the option is in Microsoft Internet Explorer:

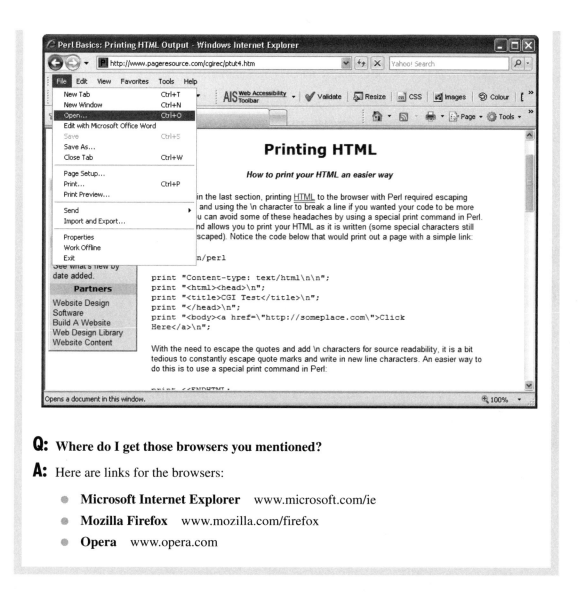

Q: Where do I get those browsers you mentioned?

A: Here are links for the browsers:

- **Microsoft Internet Explorer**   www.microsoft.com/ie
- **Mozilla Firefox**   www.mozilla.com/firefox
- **Opera**   www.opera.com

Remember, It's Not Java

JavaScript and Java are two different languages. Java is a full programming language that must be compiled (running a program through software that converts the higher-level code to machine language) before a program (often called a Java *applet*) can be executed. Java is more powerful but also more complex. JavaScript doesn't need a compiler and is more lenient in a number of areas, such as syntax.

Similarities to Other Languages

JavaScript does have similarities to other programming and scripting languages. If you have experience with Java, C++, or C, you'll notice some similarities in the syntax, which may help you to learn more quickly. Because it's a scripting language, JavaScript also has similarities to languages like Perl—it, too, can be run through an interpreter rather than being compiled.

If you have programming or scripting experience in any language, it will make learning JavaScript easier—but it isn't required.

Beginning with JavaScript

JavaScript came about as a joint effort between Netscape Communications Corporation and Sun Microsystems, Inc. The news release of the new language came on December 4, 1995, back when Netscape Navigator 2.0 was still in its beta version. JavaScript version 1.0 became available with the new browser. (Before its release as JavaScript, it was called LiveScript.)

JavaScript is an object-based, client-side scripting language that you can use to make Web pages more dynamic. To make sense of such a definition, let's look at its important parts one by one.

Object Based

Object based means that JavaScript can use items called *objects*. However, the objects are not *class based* (meaning no distinction is made between a class and an instance); instead, they are just general objects. You'll learn how to work with JavaScript objects in Chapter 8. You don't need to understand them in any detail until you know a few other features of the language.

Client Side

Client side means that JavaScript runs in the *client* (software) that the viewer is using, rather than on the Web server of the site serving the page. In this case, the client would be a Web browser. To make more sense of this, let's take a look at how a server-side language works and how a client-side language works.

Server-Side Languages

A server-side language needs to get information from the Web page or the Web browser, send it to a program that is run on the host's server, and then send the information back to the browser. Therefore, an intermediate step must send and retrieve information from the server before the results of the program are seen in the browser.

A server-side language often gives the programmer options that a client-side language doesn't have, such as saving information on the Web server for later use, or using the new information to update a Web page and save the updates.

However, a server-side language is likely to be limited in its ability to deal with special features of the browser window that can be accessed with a client-side language (like the content in a particular location on a Web page or the contents of a form before it's submitted to the server).

Client-Side Languages

A client-side language is run directly through the client being used by the viewer. In the case of JavaScript, the client is a Web browser. Therefore, JavaScript is run directly in the Web browser and doesn't need to go through the extra step of sending and retrieving information from the Web server.

With a client-side language, the browser reads and interprets the code, and the results can be given to the viewer without getting information from the server first. This process can make certain tasks run more quickly.

A client-side language can also access special features of a browser window that may not be accessible with a server-side language. However, a client-side language lacks the ability to save files or updates to files on a Web server like a server-side language can.

NOTE

Using the XMLHttpRequest object allows JavaScript to request data from the server. This will be covered briefly in Chapter 16.

A client-side language is useful for tasks that deal with parts of the browser or that allow information to be validated before it is sent to a server-side program or script. For instance, JavaScript can open a new window with specific dimensions, specific features (such as a location bar or status bar), and a specific point of placement on the screen.

JavaScript can also be used to check the information entered into a form before the form is sent to a server-side program to be processed. This information check can prevent strain on the Web server by preventing submissions with inaccurate or incomplete information. Rather than running the program on the server until the information is correct, that data can be sent to the server just once with correct information.

Scripting Language

A scripting language doesn't require a program to be compiled before it is run. All the interpretation is done on-the-fly by the client.

With a regular programming language, before you can run a program you have written, you must compile it using a special compiler to be sure there are no syntax errors. With a scripting language, the code is interpreted as it is loaded in the client. Thus, you can test the results of your code more quickly. However, errors won't be caught before the script is run and could cause problems with the client if it can't handle the errors well. In the case of JavaScript, the error handling is up to the browser being used by the viewer.

Putting It All Together

With all this in mind, you might wonder how JavaScript is run in a browser. You might wonder where to write your JavaScript code and what tells the browser it is different from anything else on a Web page. The answers are general for now, but the next chapter provides more details.

JavaScript runs in the browser by being added into an existing HTML document (either directly or by referring to an external script file). You can add special tags and commands to the HTML code that will tell the browser that it needs to run a script. Once the browser sees these special tags, it interprets the JavaScript commands and will do what you have directed it to do with your code. Thus, by simply editing an HTML document, you can begin using JavaScript on your Web pages and see the results.

For example, the following code adds some JavaScript to an HTML file that writes some text onto the Web page. Notice the addition of <script> and </script> tags. The code within them is JavaScript.

```
<html>
<body>
<script type="text/javascript">
document.write("This writes text to the page");
</script>
</body>
</html>
```

This tag tells the browser that JavaScript follows

This line writes the text inside the quote marks on the page

This line tells the browser that this is the end of the script

The next chapter looks at how to add JavaScript in an HTML file by using the <script> and </script> HTML tags. This will be your first step on the road to becoming a JavaScript coder!

Online Resources

To find additional information online to help you with JavaScript, here are some useful resources:

- A place to find tutorials with working examples of the results: www.pageresource.com/jscript

- An excellent tutorial site that includes cut-and-paste scripts: www.javascriptkit.com

- A place where you can address questions about JavaScript to fellow coders: www.webxpertz .net/forums

Try This 1-1 Use JavaScript to Write Text

pr1_1.html

This project shows you JavaScript in action by loading an HTML document in your browser. The script writes a line of text in the browser using JavaScript.

Step by Step

1. Copy and paste the code shown here into your text editor:

```
<html>
<body>
<script type="text/javascript">
document.write("This text was written with JavaScript!");
</script>
```

```
</body>
</html>
```

2. Save the file as **pr1_1.html** and open it in your Web browser. You should see a single line of text that was written with JavaScript.

Try This Summary

In this project, you copied and pasted a section of code into a text editor and saved the file. When you opened the saved file in your Web browser, a line of text was displayed in the browser. This text was written in the browser window using JavaScript. You will see more about how this type of script works in Chapter 2.

 ## Chapter 1 Self Test

1. You must know which of the following to be able to use JavaScript?

　A　Perl

　B　C++

　C　HTML

　D　SGML

2. Which of the following is something you should have to use JavaScript?

　A　A Web browser

　B　A C++ compiler

　C　A 50GB hard drive

　D　A CD-RW drive

3. The choice of a Web browser is up to you, as long it's compatible with _____.

　A　Flash MX

　B　VBScript

　C　JavaScript

　D　Windows XP

4. JavaScript and Java are the same language.

    A True

    B False

5. JavaScript is more _____ than Java in a number of areas, such as syntax.

    A complex

    B powerful

    C compiled

    D lenient

6. JavaScript has similarities to other programming and scripting languages.

    A True

    B False

7. Before its release as JavaScript, JavaScript was called _____.

    A Java

    B JavaCup

    C LiveScript

    D EasyScript

8. JavaScript is _____.

    A object based

    B object oriented

    C object deficient

    D not a language that uses objects

9. A client-side language is run directly through the _____ being used by the viewer.

    A server

    B client

    C monitor

    D lawyer

10. How can a client-side language help when using forms on a Web page?

    A It can save the information on the server.

    B It can validate the information before it is sent to the server.

    C It can update a file and save the file with the new information.

    D It can't help at all.

11. A _____ language doesn't require a program to be compiled before it is run.

    A programming

    B server-side

    C scripting

    D computer

12. With a scripting language, the code is interpreted as it is loaded in the client.

    A True

    B False

13. In JavaScript, what handles errors in a script?

    A The Web server

    B A compiler

    C A program on the Web server

    D The Web browser

14. How is JavaScript added to a Web page?

    A It is written into a special editor in the browser.

    B It is taken from a compiled program on the server.

    C You place the code in a file by itself and open that file.

    D It is added to an HTML document.

15. What is added to a Web page to insert JavaScript code?

    A <script> and </script> HTML tags

    B The JavaScript code word

    C <javascript> and </javascript> HTML tags

    D <java> and </java> HTML tags

Chapter 2

Placing JavaScript in an HTML File

Key Skills & Concepts

- Using the HTML Script Tags

- Creating Your First Script

- Using External JavaScript Files

- Using JavaScript Comments

Now that you have been introduced to JavaScript, you're ready to start coding. Since JavaScript code is run from HTML documents, you need to know how to tell browsers to run your scripts. The most common way to set off a script is to use the HTML <script> and </script> tags in your document. You can place your script tags in either the head or body section of an HTML document.

This chapter first shows you how to use the script tags to begin and end a segment of JavaScript code. Then, you will get started creating and running your first scripts. At the end of the chapter, you will learn how to add JavaScript comments to document your scripts.

Using the HTML Script Tags

Script tags are used to tell the browser where some type of scripting language will begin and end in an HTML document. In their most basic form, script tags appear just like any other set of HTML tags:

```
<script>◄──────────────── Tells the browser where script code begins
JavaScript code here
</script>◄──────────────── Tells the browser where script code ends
```

As you can see, there is the opening <script> tag, the JavaScript code, and then the closing </script> tag. When you use just the basic opening and closing tags like this, many browsers will assume that the scripting language to follow will be JavaScript. However, some browsers may need to be told which scripting language is being used.

Besides distinguishing where a script begins and ends for the browser, script tags can also tell the browser which scripting language will be used and define the address for an external JavaScript file. These additional functions are achieved through the type and src (source) attributes.

Identifying the Scripting Language

The scripting language between the opening and closing script tags could be JavaScript, VBScript, or some other language. Even though JavaScript is usually set as the default scripting language in browsers, there may be some browsers that do not default to JavaScript.

To be safe, it is a good idea to explicitly identify the language as JavaScript. You do this by adding the type attribute with the value of "text/javascript" to the opening script tag:

```
<script type="text/javascript">          Tells the browser the scripting
JavaScript code here                      language will be JavaScript
</script>
```

The type attribute in the opening script tag is also required in XHTML in order for the Web page to validate.

In older versions of HTML, the script tag was not case sensitive. However, with XHTML, the script tag must be in lowercase. JavaScript is case sensitive in all versions, so you will need to be more careful with it. In this book, I will use XHTML 1.0 Transitional for the HTML code (all tag and attribute names will be in lowercase). For the JavaScript code, I will use the case that is needed for it to function correctly.

Calling External Scripts

Script tags are also useful if you wish to call an external JavaScript file in your document. An *external JavaScript file* is a text file that contains nothing but JavaScript code, and it is saved with the .js file extension. By calling an external file, you can save the time of coding or copying a long script into each page in which the script is needed. Instead, you can use a single line on each page that points to the JavaScript file with all of the code.

You can call external scripts by adding an src (source) attribute to the opening script tag:

```
<script type="text/javascript" src="yourfile.js"></script>
```

This example calls a JavaScript file named yourfile.js from any page on which you place the line. Be sure there are no spaces or code between the opening and closing script tags, as this may cause the script call to fail.

If the script is extremely long, using the src attribute to add the script to multiple pages can be much quicker than inserting the entire code on each page. Also, the browser will cache the external JavaScript file the first time it is loaded, making subsequent Web pages that use the script render faster. Using an external script is also helpful when dealing with page validation and when trying to keep script code separated from markup (HTML) code.

Using <noscript></noscript> Tags

One way of providing alternate content for those viewers without JavaScript (or with JavaScript turned off) is to use the noscript tag. The <noscript></noscript> tags may be placed anywhere in the HTML document and can contain any content needed for those viewers browsing without JavaScript (such as viewers using mobile browsers like the ones on a Blackberry or iPhone). For example:

```
<script type="text/javascript">
  document.write("The color is red.");      Displays for those viewers with JavaScript
</script>
<noscript>                        Begins noscript content for those
  The color is red.               viewers without JavaScript
</noscript>                        Ends noscript content
```

Ask the Expert

Q: Do I always need to use script tags to add JavaScript to a page?

A: It's possible to use *event handlers* that allow you to write short bits of script within the event-handling attribute of an HTML tag. You'll learn about event handlers in Chapter 7.

Q: What about the language attribute?

A: With XHTML, the language attribute has been replaced with the type attribute. Using the language attribute may cause a Web page to fail XHTML validation (in XHTML strict) and is no longer recommended.

Q: My page won't validate in XHTML strict (or transitional) when I add a script to it. How do I get the page to validate?

A: If the script contains characters used in XHTML such as < (which is used for "less than" in JavaScript but is seen as the beginning of a new tag in XHTML), then the page won't validate with the script directly in the document without adding a CDATA section:

```
<script type="text/javascript">
<![CDATA[◄─────────────────── Begins the CDATA section
var x  = 5;
var y = 10;
if (x < y) {
   window.alert("x is less than y");
}
]]>◄─────────────── Ends the CDATA section
</script>
```

This will allow the page to validate, but because the <![CDATA[and]]> characters are in the script, the script will no longer work. To fix this, you need JavaScript comments (/* and */) around those characters when they are within the script tags:

```
<script type="text/javascript">
/*<![CDATA[*/◄─────────────── Opening and closing JavaScript comments
var x  = 5;                    are placed around <![CDATA[
var y = 10;
if (x < y) {
   window.alert("x is less than y");
}
/*]]>*/◄─────────── Opening and closing JavaScript
</script>         comments are placed around ]]>
```

As you can see, this can get quite tedious very quickly! Typically, the better option is to use an external script file, which eliminates this problem because only the script tags themselves are needed in the XHTML document.

This example displays the phrase "The color is red." to the viewer either through JavaScript or through the text within the <noscript></noscript> tags.

CAUTION
Some older browsers may not handle the noscript tag correctly and won't display the content in either section. If your users have older browsers, another alternative is to display the content on the page and then use JavaScript to enhance the content for those who are able to display it with JavaScript on.

Creating Your First Script
Now that you know how to use the HTML script tags to tell browsers about the JavaScript in a document, you're ready to learn how to add the actual JavaScript code between those script tags. The first coding example often given to teach any language is one that writes some sort of text to the default output area, commonly known as a basic "Hello World" script. Following that convention, your first script will write a string of text to a Web page.

Writing a "Hello World" Script
Rather than write "Hello World," you'll use another line of text for this script: "Yes! I am now a JavaScript coder!" This requires only a single line of code, using the document.write() method, which writes a string of text to the document:

```
<script type="text/javascript">
  document.write("Yes! I am now a JavaScript coder!");
</script>
```

Notice the parentheses and the quotation marks around the text. The parentheses are required because the document.write() method is a JavaScript *function*, which takes an *argument* contained in parentheses. You will learn more about JavaScript functions in Chapter 4.

The quotation marks denote a *string* of text. A string is a type of variable that is defined in JavaScript by placing it inside quotation marks. Chapter 3 provides details on strings and other types of JavaScript variables.

The last thing to notice about your script is the semicolon at the end of the line. The semicolon signals the end of a JavaScript statement. A *statement* is a portion of code that does not need anything added to it to be complete in its syntax (its form and order). A statement can be used to perform a single task, to perform multiple tasks, or to make calls to other parts of the script that perform several statements. Most JavaScript statements end with a semicolon, so it is a good idea to get in the habit of remembering to add one.

NOTE
In later chapters, you will see various lines that do not end in semicolons because they open or close a block of code. Also, many scripts you encounter may not end statements with semicolons. JavaScript is lenient about the use of a semicolon in most cases; however, it is best to use the semicolon to end a statement because it can prevent possible errors and aid in debugging (removing errors from) the script later.

So, to write a text string to the page, you use the document.write() method, followed by the text, surrounded by quotation marks and enclosed in parentheses. End the line (the statement) with a semicolon. JavaScript will handle the rest of the job.

Creating an HTML Document for the Script

In order to make this example complete and test the script, you need to insert it into an HTML document. First, create the following HTML document with the basic tags (using any text editor you prefer):

```
<!DOCTYPE html PUBLIC "-//W3C//DTD XHTML 1.0 Transitional//EN"
"http://www.w3.org/TR/xhtml1/DTD/xhtml1-transitional.dtd">
<html xmlns="http://www.w3.org/1999/xhtml">
<head>
<title>Untitled Document</title>
</head>
<body>
</body>
</html>
```

Save the document as test1.html in your text editor. You will call it later with a Web browser to see the results of the script. Next, you'll add the script to this HTML document, so leave the file open.

Inserting the Script into the HTML Document

Now you need to insert the script in the document. Where should it go? You can place a script between the <head> and </head> tags, or between the <body> and </body> tags. Since this example writes a text string directly to the page, you want to insert the script between the <body> and </body> tags, wherever you want the text string to appear. It can come before, after, or between any HTML code on the page.

To make it clear how the script results appear, you'll add HTML code to write lines of text before and after the script. The script tags and the script itself are inserted between those lines. Add the lines shown next between the <body> and </body> tags:

```
This is the first line, before the script results.
<br />
<script type="text/javascript">
  document.write("Yes! I am now a JavaScript coder!");
</script>
<br />
This line comes after the script.
```

Save the test1.html document again. You should now be able to open the document in your Web browser to see the results of the script. Figure 2-1 shows how the text should look in your browser when you load the Web page.

Congratulations, you have now finished your first script!

NOTE

The example code in this section uses the entire HTML document and all of its tags. In order to keep things as relevant as possible, from this point on the example code will use only the HTML tags involved with the scripts rather than the entirety of its tags. Project code may use entire HTML documents as needed.

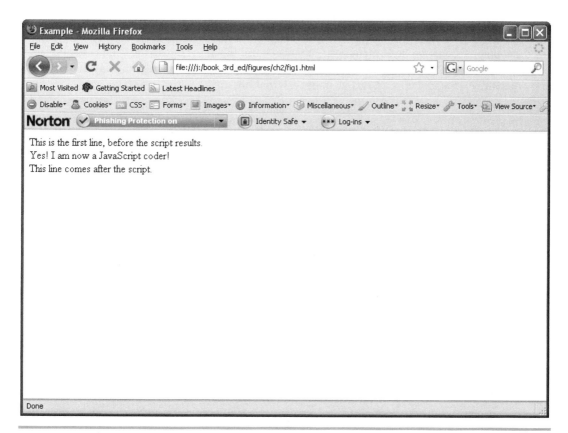

Figure 2-1 The test.html file in a Web browser

Ask the Expert

Q: **Why is there a dot (.) in the document.write() command?**

A: Document is one of JavaScript's predefined objects, and write() is a predefined method of the document object. The dot puts the object and the method together to make the function work. Chapter 8 explains JavaScript objects, and Chapter 9 is devoted to the document object.

Q: **How do I know when to add the script inside the head section and when to add it inside the body section?**

A: The main situation in which to add a script to the body section of a document is when you are writing something directly to the page. In many cases, most of the scripting can be accomplished in the head section, since you can use functions to call the code in the body section. We will often use external scripts in this book, which will eliminate much of the dilemma since all the code will be in the external file.

Try This 2-1 ## Insert a Script into an HTML Document

`pr2_1.html`

This project gives you practice adding a script to your page. You will create an HTML document and insert a script that displays a short sentence in the browser window when the page loads.

Step by Step

1. Set up an HTML document so that you have a simple file with nothing between the <body> and </body> tags yet.

2. Put the following line of text into the Web page:

   I am part of the HTML document!

3. Insert a <br /> tag after this line (to insert a line break on the page).

4. After the <br /> tag, insert a script that will write the following line on the page:

   This came from my script, and is now on the page!

5. After the script, add another <br /> tag.

6. Put the following line of text into the Web page after the last <br /> tag, and make it emphasized:

   I am also part of the HTML document, after the script results!

7. Here is what your HTML document should look like:

```
<!DOCTYPE html PUBLIC "-//W3C//DTD XHTML 1.0 Transitional//EN" "http://
www.w3.org/TR/xhtml1/DTD/xhtml1-transitional.dtd">
<html xmlns="http://www.w3.org/1999/xhtml">
<head>
<title>JavaScript Project 2-1</title>
</head>
<body>
I am part of the HTML document!
<br />
<script type="text/javascript">
  document.write("This came from my script, and is now on the page!");
</script>
<br />
<em>I am also part of the HTML document, after the script results!</em>
</body>
</html>
```

8. Save the file as pr2_1.html and view the page in your browser to see the results.

Try This Summary

In this project, you created an HTML file. Using the knowledge that you acquired thus far in this chapter, you inserted within the HTML file a script that writes a specific line of text on the page. When the HTML page is opened in a Web browser, the result of the script is displayed between two lines of text.

Using External JavaScript Files

Now suppose that you want to use your "Hello World" script (the one you created earlier in this chapter) on more than one page, but you do not want to write it out on each page. You can do this by putting the script in an external script file and calling it with the src attribute of the script tag. For this method, you need to create a JavaScript text file to hold your script. You also need one or more HTML files into which you will place the script tags to call your external script file.

Creating a JavaScript File

For this example, you will create a JavaScript file that contains only one line. For practical applications, you would use this approach for lengthier scripts—the longer the script is, the more useful this technique becomes (especially if you are trying to validate your Web pages or you are separating your script code from your markup).

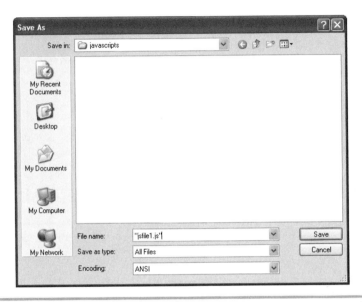

Figure 2-2 An example of saving a file with a .js extension using quote marks so it will save with the correct file extension

Open a new file in your text editor and insert only the JavaScript code (the document. write() statement) itself. The script tags are not needed in the external JavaScript file. The file should appear like this:

```
document.write("Yes! I am now a JavaScript coder!");
```

Save the file as jsfile1.js in your text editor. To do this, you may need to use the Save As option on the File menu and place quotation marks around your filename, as shown in Figure 2-2 (using Notepad with Windows).

Once the file has been saved, you can move on to the next step, which is to create the HTML files in which to use the script.

Creating the HTML Files

You will create two files in which to place your script. The technique should work for any number of HTML files, though, as long as you add the required script tags to each file.

For the first file, create your base HTML document and insert the script tags into the body section of the document, using the src attribute to point to the jsfile1.js file, and add some HTML text to the body of the page to identify it as the first HTML document:

```
<body>
<script type="text/javascript" src="jsfile1.js"></script>
<p>
  This is page 1, and the script works here!
</p>
</body>
```

Save this file as jsext1.html in your text editor. Be sure to save it in the same directory as your jsfile1.js file.

The second HTML document looks the same as the first one, except that the HTML text says that it's page 2:

```
<body>
<script type="text/javascript" src="jsfile1.js"></script>
<p>
  This is page 2, and the script also works here!
</p>
</body>
```

Save this file as jsext2.html in your text editor. Again, be sure to place it in the same directory as the other files.

Viewing the Pages in Your Browser

Open the jsext1.html file in your Web browser. It should appear as shown in Figure 2-3, with the JavaScript inserted in the page from the external script file.

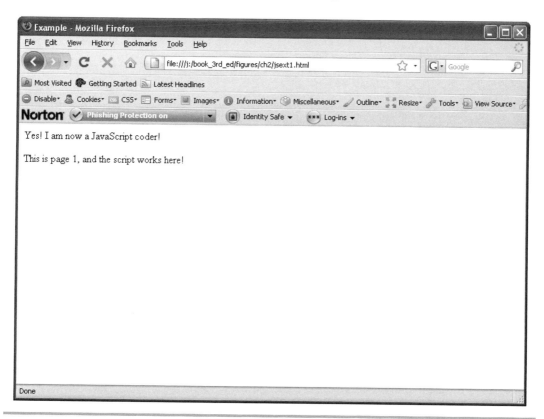

Figure 2-3   The result of calling the script in the jsext1.html file, the first HTML page

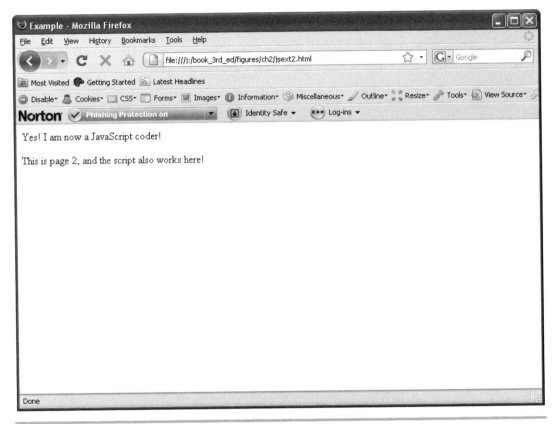

Figure 2-4 The result of calling the script in the jsext2.html file, the second HTML page

Next, open the jsext2.html file in your Web browser. It should appear as shown in Figure 2-4, with only the small difference of the text you added to the HTML file to say that this is page 2. The JavaScript should write the same text to this page as it did to the first HTML page.

Although we used a short script in this example, it should give you an idea of how using an external file could be a great time-saver when you have a large script.

Try This 2-2 Call an External Script from an HTML Document

```
pr2_2.html
prjs2_2.js
```

This project will allow you to practice creating external JavaScript files and using them to insert a script into a Web page.

Step by Step

1. Set up a simple HTML document with nothing between the <body> and </body> tags.

2. Place the following line of text between the body tags of the page:

   This text is from the HTML document!

3. Place a <br /> tag after this text. If you need to save this file now, save it as pr2_2.html.

4. Create an external JavaScript file that will write the following line when it is executed:

   I love writing JavaScript and using external files!

5. Here is how your JavaScript file should look:

   ```
   document.write("I love writing JavaScript, and using external files!");
   ```

6. Save the JavaScript file as prjs2_2.js.

7. Go back to the HTML document. Place the script tags after the <br /> tag in the document so that the external JavaScript file will write its sentence on the page.

8. The body of your HTML document should look like this:

   ```
   <body>
   This text is from the HTML document!
   <br />
   <script type="text/javascript" src="prjs2_2.js"></script>
   </body>
   ```

9. Save this file as pr2_2.html and view the results in your browser.

Try This Summary

In this project, you created an HTML page. Using your knowledge of external JavaScript files from the previous section, you created an external JavaScript file and placed the necessary code into the HTML file to include the external JavaScript file. When the HTML file is displayed in a Web browser, a line of plain text is shown, followed by the results of the external JavaScript file.

Using JavaScript Comments

You may need to make notes in your JavaScript code, such as to describe what a line of code is supposed to do. It's also possible that you will want to disable a line of the script for some reason. For instance, if you are looking for an error in a script, you may want to disable a line in the script to see if it is the line causing the error. You can accomplish these tasks by using JavaScript comments. You can insert comments that appear on one line or run for numerous lines.

Inserting Comments on One Line

If you want to add commentary on a single line in your code, place a pair of forward slashes before the text of the comment:

```
// Your comment here
```

In this format, anything preceding the two slashes on that line is "live" code—code that will be executed—and anything after the slashes on that line is ignored. For example, suppose that you wrote this line in your code:

```
document.write("This is cool!"); // writes out my opinion
```

The document.write() method will be run by the browser, so the text "This is cool!" will be written to the page. However, the comment after the slashes will be ignored by the browser.

If you place the forward slashes at the beginning of a line, the browser will ignore the entire line. Suppose that you move the slashes in the previous example to be the first items on the line:

```
// document.write("This is cool!"); writes out my opinion
```

In this format, the entire line is ignored, since it begins with the two slashes that represent a JavaScript comment. The text will not be written to the page, since the code will not be executed by the browser. In effect, you are disabling the document.write() statement. You may wish to do this if the script containing this line has an error and you want to know whether or not this line is causing the problem.

Adding Multiple-Line Comments

Comments denoted by a pair of forward slashes apply only to the line on which they appear; their effects are cut off at the end of the line. To add comments that span any number of lines, you use a different comment format: a forward slash followed by an asterisk at the beginning of the comment, then the text of the comment, and then an asterisk followed by a forward slash at the end of the comment. Here's an example:

```
/*
My script will write some text into my HTML document!
All of this text is ignored by the browser.
*/
document.write("You can see me!");
```

Using this format, you can begin the comment on one line and end it on another line.

Multiple-line comments can be handy when you want to insert lengthier descriptions or other text, but you need to be careful when you use them. Look at this example to see if you can find a problem with it:

```
<script type="text/javascript">
/*
This code won't work for some reason.
```

```
document.write("I want someone to see me!");
</script>
```

Did you notice that the closing JavaScript comment symbols are missing? When you use multiple-line comments, you need to be careful to close them. Otherwise, you might accidentally comment out code you need executed! In this example, the comment just keeps going on with no end in sight. To fix this, you need to close the JavaScript comments before the document.write() method is used:

```
<script type="text/javascript">
/*
The JavaScript code is now working! This text is hidden.
*/
document.write("Now everyone can see me!");
</script>
```

In the preceding examples, you saw how comments can be used to provide some documentation of what to expect from each script. In Chapter 16, you will learn how using comments can help you debug your JavaScript code. For now, you should get in the habit of adding comments to your scripts as short documentation or instructions.

Chapter 2 Self Test

1. What is the purpose of the <script> and </script> tags?

   A To tell the browser where a script begins and ends

   B To let the browser know the scripting language to be used

   C To point to an external JavaScript file

   D All of the above

2. Why should you use the type attribute in the opening script tag?

   A To let the browser know what type of coder you are

   B To be sure the browser does not interpret your JavaScript as another scripting language and to ensure the Web page validates in XHTML

   C To create a typing script

   D To make sure the script does not make a grammatical error

3. Is JavaScript code case sensitive?

   A Yes

   B No

4. The noscript tag provides _____ for those without _____.

5. An external JavaScript file commonly uses a filename extension of _____.

    A .js

    B .html

    C .jav

    D .java

6. Which of the following correctly points to an external JavaScript file named yourfile.js?

    A <extscript type="text/javascript" src="yourfile.js"></extscript>

    B <script type= "text/javascript" src="yourfile.js"></script>

    C <script language="yourfile.js"></script>

    D <script type="text/javascript" link="yourfile.js"></script>

7. In older versions of HTML, the script tag is not case sensitive. However, with XHTML, the script tag must be in _____.

8. The _____ signals the end of a JavaScript statement.

    A colon

    B period

    C question mark

    D semicolon

9. To write a string of text on a Web page, the _____ method is used.

    A document.write()

    B document.print()

    C document,type()

    D window.print()

10. When would it be a good idea to use an external JavaScript file?

    A When the script is short or going to be used in only one HTML document

    B When your Web site viewers have older browsers

    C When the script is very long or needs to be placed in more than one HTML document

    D External files are not a good idea

11. JavaScript comments can be very useful for the purpose of _____ or _____ your code.

12. Which of the following indicates that a single line of commentary will follow it within JavaScript code?

   A /*

   B /-

   C //

   D <!--

13. Which of the following indicates that more than one line of commentary will follow it within JavaScript code?

   A /*

   B /-

   C //

   D <!--

14. Which of the following indicates the end of a multiple-line JavaScript comment?

   A \\

   B -->

   C /*

   D */

15. When you use multiple-line JavaScript comments, you need to be careful to _____ them.

   A close

   B read

   C program

   D compile

Chapter 3

Using Variables

Key Skills & Concepts

- Understanding Variables

- Why Variables Are Useful

- Defining Variables for Your Scripts

- Understanding Variable Types

- Using Variables in Scripts

Now that you have learned the basics of adding JavaScript to a Web page, it is time to get into the inner workings of the language. Since variables are an important part of JavaScript coding, you will need to know as much as possible about what they are and why they are useful in your scripts. Once you have an understanding of how variables work and what they can do, you will be able to move on to other topics that build on the use of the various types of variables.

In this chapter, you will begin by learning what variables are and why they are useful. You will then move on to find out about the methods that are used to declare variables and how to assign a value to a variable. Finally, you will see how to use variables in your scripts.

Understanding Variables

A *variable* represents or holds a value. The actual value of a variable can be changed at any time. To understand what a variable is, consider a basic statement that you may recall from algebra class:

```
x=2
```

The letter x is used as the name of the variable. It is assigned a value of 2. To change the value, you simply give x a new assignment:

```
x=4
```

The name of the variable stays the same, but now it represents a different value.

Taking the math class example one step further, you probably had to solve a problem like this one:

```
If x=2, then 3+x=?
```

To get the answer, you put the value of 2 in place of the variable x in the problem, for $3+2=5$. If the value of x changes, so does the answer to the problem. So, if $x=7$, then the calculation turns into $3+7$, and now the result is 10.

Variables in JavaScript are much like those used in mathematics. You give a variable a name, and then assign it values based on your needs. If the value of the variable changes, it will change something that happens within the script.

Why Variables Are Useful

Using variables offers several benefits:

- They can be used in places where the value they represent is unknown when the code is written.

- They can save you time in writing and updating your scripts.

- They can make the purpose of your code clearer.

Variables as Placeholders for Unknown Values

Oftentimes, a variable will hold a place in memory for a value that is unknown at the time the script is written. A variable value might change based on something entered by the viewer or may be changed by you later in the script code.

For instance, you might have a function that takes in certain values based on user input (functions will be discussed in Chapter 4). Since the value of user input is unknown at the time the script is written, a variable can be used to hold the value that will be input by the user. This is true for any sort of user input, whether it be in the form of a JavaScript prompt/confirm box, input fields in a form, or other methods of input.

Variables as Time-Savers

Variables speed up script writing because their values can change. When you assign a value to a variable at the beginning of a script, the rest of the script can simply use the variable in its place. If you decide to change the value later, you need to change the code in only one place—where you assigned a value to the variable—rather than in numerous places.

For instance, suppose that back in math class, you were asked to solve this problem:

```
If x=2, then 3+x-1+2-x=?
```

You know that you need to substitute the value of 2 for each x that appears, for 3+2–1+2–2=4. Now if the teacher wants you to do this problem again with a different value for x, the whole problem does not need to be rewritten. The teacher can just give you the following instruction:

```
Solve the above problem for x=4.
```

The longer and more complex the problem gets, the more useful the variable becomes. Rather than rewriting the same thing over and over, you can change one variable to offer an entirely new result.

Variables as Code Clarifiers

Since variables represent something, and you can give them meaningful names, they are often easier to recognize when you read over (and debug) your scripts. If you just add numbers, you may forget what they stand for. For example, consider this line of code:

```
TotalPrice=2.42+4.33;
```

Here, the numbers could mean almost anything. Instead, you might assign 2.42 as the value of a variable named CandyPrice and 4.33 as the value of a variable named OilPrice:

```
TotalPrice=CandyPrice+OilPrice;
```

Now, rather than trying to remember the meaning of the numbers, you can see that the script is adding the price of some candy to the price of some oil. This is also useful in debugging, because the meaningful variable names make it easier to spot errors.

Defining Variables for Your Scripts

Now that you understand what variables are and why you want to use them, you need to learn how to make them work in your scripts. You create variables by *declaring* them. Then you assign values to them using the JavaScript *assignment operator*. When you name your variables, you need to follow the rules for naming variables in JavaScript, as well as consider the meaningfulness of the name.

Declaring Variables

To declare text as a variable, you use the var keyword, which tells the browser that the text to follow will be the name of a new variable:

```
var variablename;
```

For example, to name your variable coolcar, the declaration looks like this:

```
var coolcar;
```

In this example, you have a new variable with the name coolcar. The semicolon ends the statement. The variable coolcar does not have a value assigned to it yet. As described in the next section, you can give your new variable a value at the same time that you declare it or you can assign it a value later in your script.

The code for giving a variable a name is simple, but there are some restrictions on words that you can use for variables and the cases of the letters. You'll learn more about JavaScript naming rules after you see how to assign a value to a variable.

Assigning Values to Variables

To assign a value to a variable, you use the JavaScript assignment operator, which is the equal to (=) symbol. If you want to declare a variable and assign a value to it on the same line, use this format:

```
var variablename=variablevalue;
```

For example, to name your variable paycheck and give it the numeric value 1200, use this statement:

```
var paycheck=1200;
```

The statement begins with the keyword var, followed by the variable paycheck, just as in the plain variable declaration described in the previous section. Next comes the assignment operator (=), which tells the browser to assign the value on the right side of the operator to the variable on the left side of the operator. To the right of the assignment operator is 1200, which is the numeric value being assigned to the variable paycheck. The line ends with a semicolon to mark the end of the statement.

CAUTION

Be careful not to think of the assignment operator (=) as having the meaning "is equal to." This operator only assigns a value. The operator for "is equal to" is two equal signs together (==), as you'll learn in Chapter 5.

To declare and assign another variable, you use the same format, placing the statement on a new line. For example, to set up a variable named spending to track the amount of money you are spending from the paycheck variable, use these statements:

```
var paycheck=1200; ◄──────────── Assigns a value of 1200 to the variable paycheck
var spending=1500; ◄──────────── Assigns a value of 1500 to the variable spending
```

Of course, you will also notice that this financial situation is headed for trouble, since the money being spent in the spending variable is more than what is being brought in with the paycheck variable. Oddly, it is starting to look like the budget for my Web site!

The examples you've seen illustrate the proper and safe way to code variable declarations and assignments. However, the truth is that JavaScript allows a certain amount of flexibility when it comes to variables. In many cases, the code will work without using precise coding syntax. For example, you may see some scripts written without using the var keyword the first time a variable is used. JavaScript will often declare the variable the first time it is used even if it is previously undeclared. An example is shown here:

```
paycheck=1200;
```

This works since the variable is being assigned a value (JavaScript will simply declare the variable and assign it the value of 1200). However, if you were trying to declare the variable without an assignment, the following would not be valid:

```
paycheck;
```

This declaration would still require the var keyword to be valid, as in the following code:

```
var paycheck;
```

You may also see a script that leaves off the ending semicolon:

```
var paycheck=1200
```

And in some scripts, both features are left out of the variable assignment:

```
paycheck=1200
```

All of these shortcuts may seem handy, but it is best to go ahead and define each variable before using it, use the var keyword, and include the semicolon. Not doing so can cause errors in some browsers and may give people the impression the code was not written well. Also, any of these omissions can be really troublesome if you need to debug the script. Giving variables the correct declarations and assignments will avoid problems, and your code will be easier to read and understand.

Naming Variables

Before you start naming your own variables, you need to be aware of JavaScript's naming rules. The factors you need to consider when choosing names are case sensitivity, invalid characters, and the names that are reserved by JavaScript. Additionally, you should try to give your variables names that are both easy to remember and meaningful.

Using Case in Variables

JavaScript variables are case sensitive—paycheck, PAYCHECK, Paycheck, and PaYcHeCk are four different variables. When you create a variable, you need to be sure to use the same case when you write that variable's name later in the script. If you change the capitalization at all, JavaScript sees it as a new variable or returns an error. Either way, it can cause problems with your script.

Here are a couple of suggestions for using case in your variable names:

- If you are using a variable name that consists of only one word, it is probably easiest to use lowercase for the entire name. It will be quicker to type, and you will know when you use it later to type it all in lowercase.

- For a variable name with two words, you might decide to capitalize the first letter of each word. For example, you may name a variable MyCar or My_Car (you will see more on the underscore character, _, in the next section).

The capitalization of variables is entirely up to you, so you should use whatever style you are most comfortable with. It is best that you adopt a convention and continue to use it. For instance, if you name a variable using lowercase characters only, you should do the same throughout the script to avoid accidentally switching the case when using the variable later. In this book, I use only lowercase characters for variable names, to keep the code clear.

Using Allowed Characters

An important rule to remember is that a variable name must begin with a letter or an underscore character (_). The variable name cannot begin with a number or any other character that is not a letter (other than the underscore). The other characters in the variable name can be letters, numbers, or underscores. Blank spaces are not allowed in variable names. So, the following variable names would be valid:

- paycheck
- _paycheck
- pay2check
- pay_check
- pay_245

However, the following variable names are not valid:

- #paycheck
- 1paycheck
- pay check
- pay_check 2
- _pay check

The hardest rule to remember may be that you cannot begin the name with a number (it's the one I forget most often). While such a name seems reasonable, JavaScript doesn't allow it.

Avoiding Reserved Words

Another rule to keep in mind when naming your variables is to avoid the use of JavaScript reserved words. These are special words that are used for a specific purpose in JavaScript. For instance, you've learned that the reserved word var is used to declare a JavaScript variable. Using it as a variable name can cause numerous problems in your script, since this word is meant to be used in a different way.

Table 3-1 lists the reserved words in JavaScript. Note that all of these words are in all lowercase letters. In later chapters, you will learn how these reserved words are used, so they will become more familiar over time.

Giving Variables Meaningful Names

Although *x* is an acceptable variable name, it is unlikely that you will be able to remember what it stands for if you need to debug the program later. Also, if someone else is trying to help you debug the code, their job will be even harder.

You should try to give your variables names that describe what they represent as clearly as possible. Suppose that you want to use a variable to hold a number of an example on a page. Rather than use *x*, *ex*, or another short variable, use something more descriptive:

```
var example_number=2;
```

abstract	delete	goto	null	throws
as	do	if	package	transient
boolean	double	implements	private	true
break	else	import	protected	try
byte	enum	in	public	typeof
case	export	instanceof	return	use
catch	extends	int	short	var
char	false	interface	static	void
class	final	is	super	volatile
const	finally	long	switch	while
continue	float	namespace	synchronized	with
debugger	for	native	this	
default	function	new	throw	

Table 3-1 JavaScript Reserved Words

The variable example_number will be easy for you to recognize later, and other coders will be more likely to understand its use quickly.

The more variables you use in a script, the more important it becomes to use meaningful and memorable names.

Understanding Variable Types

So far, you've seen examples of variable values that are numbers. In JavaScript, the variable values, or *types*, can include number, string, Boolean, and null.

Unlike stricter programming languages, JavaScript does not force you to declare the type of variable when you define it. Instead, JavaScript allows virtually any value to be assigned to any variable. Although this gives you flexibility in coding, you need to be careful because you can end up with some unexpected results—especially when adding numbers.

Number

Number variables are just that—numbers. JavaScript does not require numbers to be declared as integers, floating-point (decimal) numbers, or any other number type. Instead, any number is seen as just another number, whether it is 7, –2, 3.453, or anything else. The number will remain the same type unless you perform a calculation to change the type. For instance, if you use an integer in a variable, it won't suddenly have decimal places unless you perform a calculation of some sort to change it (dividing unevenly, for instance).

As you've seen, you define a number variable by using the keyword var:

```
var variablename=number;
```

Here are some examples:

```
var paycheck=1200;
var phonebill=29.99;
var savings=0;
var sparetime=-24.5;
```

If you need to use a particularly long number, JavaScript has exponential notation. To denote the exponent, use a letter *e* right after the base number and before the exponent. For example, to create a variable named bignumber and assign it a value of 4.52×10^5 (452,000), put the letter *e* in place of everything between the number and the exponent (to represent the phrase "times 10 to the power of"):

```
var bignumber=4.52e5;
```

NOTE

JavaScript may return an answer to a calculation using exponential notation (like many calculators).

String

String variables are variables that represent a string of text. The string may contain letters, words, spaces, numbers, symbols, or most anything you like. Strings are defined in a slightly different way than numbers, using this format:

```
var variablename="stringtext";
```

Here are some examples of string variables:

```
var mycar="Corvette";
var oldcar="Big Brown Station Wagon";
var mycomputer="Pentium 3, 500 MHz, 128MB RAM";
var oldcomputer="386 SX, 40 mHz, 8MB RAM";
var jibberish="what? cool! I am @ home 4 now. (cool, right?)";
```

As you can see, strings can be short, long, or anything in between. You can place all sorts of text and other characters inside of string variables. However, the quotation marks, some special characters, and the case sensitivity of strings need to be considered.

Matching the Quotation Marks

In JavaScript, you define strings by placing them inside quotation marks (quotes, for short), as you saw in the examples. JavaScript allows you to use either double quotes or single quotes to define a string value. The catch is that if the string is opened with double quotes, it must be closed with double quotes:

```
var mycar="Red Corvette";
```

The same goes for single quotes:

```
var myhouse='small brick house';
```

Trying to close the string with the wrong type of quotation mark, or leaving out an opening or closing quotation mark, will cause problems.

```
var mycar="Red Corvette';
var myhouse= 'small brick house";
var mycomputer="Pentium 3, 500 mHz, 128MB RAM;
```

Incorrect, string is opened with double quotes and closed with a single quote

Incorrect, string is opened with a single quote and closed with double quotes

Incorrect, string does not have a closing quote

These mistakes will result in an "Unterminated String" error in the Web browser.

Watching the Case

JavaScript strings are case sensitive. This may not seem important now, but it matters when you need to compare strings for a match. It only takes one character having a different case to make the strings different:

```
"My car is fun to drive!"
"my car is fun to drive!"
```

You'll learn more about string comparisons in Chapter 5.

Using Special Characters

Special characters enable you to add things to your strings that could not be added otherwise. For example, suppose that you need a tab character between each word in a string. If you press the TAB key on the keyboard, JavaScript will probably see it as a bunch of spaces. Instead, use the special character \t, which places a tab in the string, as in this example:

```
var mypets="dog\tcat\tbird";
```

In each spot where the special character \t appears, JavaScript interprets a tab character.

The special characters all begin with a backslash character (\). Thus, if you want a single backslash character in your string, you need to use the special code for a backslash: \\.
For instance, suppose you wish to write the following sentence on a Web page: "Go to the directory c:\javascript on your computer." If you use the string as it is written, your code would look like this:

```
<script type="text/javascript">
  document.write("Go to the directory c:\javascript on your computer.");
</script>
```

The single backslash won't be printed to the browser

The problem is that the single backslash would not be printed on the Web page. It would appear as

```
Go to the directory c:javascript on your computer
```

Unless the backslash is followed with the code for a special character, JavaScript prints the character after the slash as it appears (you will see this in the escape technique discussed in the next section). To fix this, use the \\ special code to print a single backslash on the page:

```
<script type="text/javascript">
  document.write("Go to the directory c:\\javascript on your
computer.");
</script>
```
Using the special code for the backslash character allows it to be printed to the browser

Now you get the sentence you want printed to the browser, like this:

```
Go to the directory c\:javascript on your computer.
```

The special characters used in JavaScript are shown in Table 3-2.

Suppose that you want to print a sentence on a Web page with strong emphasis. JavaScript allows you to print HTML code to the page as part of a string in the document.write() method (which you used for your first scripts in Chapter 2). To print in bold type, you could just add in the <strong> and </strong> tags from HTML, as in this sample code:

```
<script type="text/javascript">
  document.write("<strong>JavaScript Rules!</strong> This is fun.");
</script>
```
Note the HTML <strong> and </strong> tags within the JavaScript string

Output Character	Special Code to Use
Backslash (\)	\\
Double quote (")	\"
Single quote (')	\'
Backspace	\b
Form feed	\f
Newline	\n
Carriage return	\r
Tab	\t
Vertical Tab	\v

Table 3-2 Special JavaScript Characters

Now suppose that you want the code itself to appear on two lines when it is viewed, like this:

JavaScript Rules!
This is fun.

You might try this by adding the newline special character to the code:

```
<script type="text/javascript">
  document.write("<strong>JavaScript Rules!</strong>\n This is fun.");
</script>
```

The \n special code is only a newline in JavaScript; it will not result in an HTML line break. The JavaScript newline code does not add a new line to the result of the code shown in the browser display. So, the end result of the preceding code is a sentence like this one:

JavaScript Rules! This is fun.

If you want to add a line break in the browser display, you need to use the HTML <br /> tag to produce it.

Keep in mind that the JavaScript newline affects only the appearance of the source code; it does not play a factor in the end result. However, it does help later when you want to format the output of JavaScript alert boxes and various other JavaScript constructions.

Escaping Characters

JavaScript allows you to *escape* certain characters, so that they will show up correctly and avoid causing errors. Like special characters, escape sequences use the backslash character (\), which precedes the character that needs to be escaped.

As noted earlier, JavaScript checks each string for the presence of special characters before rendering it. This is useful if you want to have a quote within a string. For example, suppose that you want to print the following sentence on a Web page:

John said, "JavaScript is easy."

What would happen if you just threw it all into a document.write() command?

```
<script type="text/javascript">                 The extra set of quote marks here will cause an error
  document.write("John said, "JavaScript is easy."");
</script>
```

If you look near the end of the document.write() line, you will see that the two double quotes together could cause trouble, but the browser will actually get upset before that point. When the double quote is used before the word *JavaScript*, the browser thinks you have closed the string used in the document.write() command and expects the ending parenthesis and semicolon. Instead, there is more text, and the browser gets confused.

To avoid problems with quotes, use the backslash character to escape the quotation marks inside the string. By placing a backslash in front of each of the interior double quote marks,

you force them to be seen as part of the text string, rather than as part of the JavaScript
statement:

The backslashes allow the inner quote
marks to become part of the string

```
<script type="text/javascript">
  document.write("John said, \"JavaScript is easy.\"");
</script>
```

This fixes the problem with the string, and the sentence will print with the quotation marks.

CAUTION

Also watch for single quotes and apostrophes within strings. Escaping these is required
for strings enclosed within single quotes.

The escape technique also works for HTML code in which you need quotation marks.
For instance, if you want to put a link on a page, you use the anchor tag and place the URL in
quotes. If you escape the quotes in the anchor tag, JavaScript allows you to write the HTML
code to the page within the document.write() method, as in this example:

```
<script type="text/javascript">
  document.write("<a href=\"http://someplace.com\">Text</a>");
</script>
```

This does the job, but there is also an easier way to make this work if you do not want to
escape quotation marks all of the time.

To avoid escaping the quotes in the preceding code, you could use single quotes around the
URL address instead, as in this code:

Single quotes within double quotes are okay

```
<script type="text/javascript">
  document.write("<a href='http://someplace.com'>Text</a>");
</script>
```

You can also do this the other way around if you prefer to use single quotes on the outside,
as in this example:

Double quotes inside single quotes are also okay

```
<script type="text/javascript">
  document.write('<a href="http://someplace.com">Text</a>');
</script>
```

The important point to remember here is to be sure that you do not use the same type of
quotation marks inside the string as you use to enclose the string. If you need to go more than
one level deep with the quotes, you need to start escaping the quotes; this is because if you
switch again, it will terminate the string. For example, look at this code:

```
document.write("John said, 'Jeff says, \"Hi!\" to someone.'");
document.write("John said, 'Jeff says, "Hi!" to someone.'");
```

The first one would work, since the quotes are escaped to keep the string going. However,
the second line only switches back to double quotes when inside the single quotes within the

string. Placing the double quotes there without escaping them causes the string to terminate and gives an error.

As you can see, quotation marks can be a real pain when you need to use a large number of them within a string. However, remembering to use the backslash to escape the quotes when necessary will save you quite a few headaches when you are looking for a missing quote. I've had to look for missing quotes in my code a number of times, and my head was spinning after a few of those encounters! Later in this chapter, you will see that you can add strings together, which can simplify the use of quotes for you.

Boolean

A *Boolean* variable is one with a value of true or false. Here are examples:

```
var JohnCodes=true;
var JohnIsCool=false;
```

Notice that the words *true* and *false* do not need to be enclosed in quotes. This is because they are reserved words, which JavaScript recognizes as Boolean values.

Instead of using the words true and false, JavaScript also allows you to use the number 1 for true and the number 0 for false, as shown here:

```
var JohnCodes=1; ◄————— Using the number 1 is the same as using the value of true
var JohnIsCool=0; ◄————— Using the number 0 is the same as using the value of false
```

Boolean variables are useful when you need variables that can only have values of true and false, such as in event handlers (covered in Chapter 7).

NOTE

When we talk about the concept of a Boolean variable, the first letter of the word *Boolean* is capitalized (because it is derived from the name of the mathematician George Boole). However, the JavaScript reserved word boolean is written in all lowercase letters when you use the keyword in a script.

Null

Null means that the variable has no value. It is not a space, nor is it a zero; it is simply nothing. If you need to define a variable with a value of null, use a declaration like this:

```
var variablename=null;
```

As with the Boolean variables, you do not need to enclose this value in quotation marks as you do with string values, because JavaScript recognizes null as a keyword with a predefined value (nothing).

Null variables are useful when you test for input in scripts, as you'll learn in later chapters.

Ask the Expert

Q: Why do I need to learn about variables? Couldn't I just put in the number or text I want to use right where I'm going to use it?

A: You can do that; however, it will make longer scripts much harder to write, read, and debug. It also makes it much more difficult to update your scripts because, in order to change that number or text, you would need to change every line where it appears. When you use variables, you can modify just one line of code to change the value of a variable every place it is used. As you gain more experience with JavaScript, you will see just how useful variables are.

Q: Why don't I need to define the type of number I am using (such as float or integer) when I declare a numeric variable?

A: JavaScript doesn't require this, which can be a good or bad feature depending on your perspective. To JavaScript, any number is just a number and can be used as a number variable.

Q: Why do I need to put quotation marks around the text in a string?

A: This is done so that JavaScript knows where a string begins and ends. Without it, JavaScript would be unsure what should be in a string and what should not.

Q: But doesn't a semicolon end a statement? Why not use that and lose the quote marks?

A: A variable declaration or any command involving strings can become more complex when the addition operator is used to add two strings and/or variables together. When this happens, JavaScript needs to know when one string stops and another begins on the same line.

Q: What does the backslash (\) character do, in general?

A: If the backslash is followed by a code to create a special character, the special character is rendered in its place. Otherwise, the first character after a single backslash is seen "as-is" by JavaScript and treated as part of the string in which it resides.

Try This 3-1 # Declare Variables

`pr3_1.html`

This project gives you the opportunity to practice declaring variables with various values. It also prints a short line of text on the page.

(continued)

Step by Step

1. Create an HTML page, leaving the space between the <body> and </body> tags open.

2. Between the <body> and </body> tags, add the <script> and </script> tags as you learned in Chapter 2.

3. Create a numeric variable named chipscost and give it the value 2.59.

4. Create a Boolean variable named istrue and give it the value false.

5. Create a variable named nada and give it the value null.

6. Create a JavaScript statement to write to the Web page the string value that follows. Remember to escape quotation marks when necessary:

   John said, "This project is fun!"

7. The body section of the HTML document should look like this when you are finished:

```
<body>
<script type="text/javascript">
  var chipscost=2.59;
  var istrue=false;
  var nada=null;
  document.write("John said, \"This project is fun!\"");
</script>
</body>
```

8. Save the file as pr3_1.html and view it in your Web browser.

   You should see only the text that you output with the document.write() command. The variable definitions won't be printed on the browser screen. You can view the page source code to see how the variable definitions look in the code.

Try This Summary

In this project, you were able to use your skills to declare different types of variables in a script. This project included a numeric variable, a Boolean variable, and a variable with a value of null. You were also able to use skills learned in Chapter 2 to write a line of text to the page with JavaScript.

Using Variables in Scripts

To make a variable useful, you need to do more than just declare it in the script. You need to use it later in the script in some way, perhaps to print its value or even just to change its value. To use a variable, you make the call to a variable after it has been declared.

Making a Call to a Variable

The following code shows how to write the value of a variable to a Web page using the document.write() method:

```
<script language="JavaScript">
  var mycar="Corvette";
  document.write(mycar);◄——————— Prints the value of the mycar variable to the browser
</script>
```

The script begins by declaring a variable mycar and giving it a value of "Corvette". Then, in the document.write() command, you see that just the variable name mycar is enclosed within the parentheses. The result of this script is simply to write "Corvette" to the browser.

There are no quotation marks around the mycar variable that is being written to the page. The reason for this is that the mycar variable has already been given a string value, so it does not need to be within quotes to print its value to the page in the document.write() command. Already, you can see how using a variable has the advantage of making a short document.write() command easier to code.

Adding Variables to Text Strings

The preceding code just prints the value of the variable in the browser. If you want that variable to print along with some other text in a string, the document.write() command becomes more complex. The text string needs quotes around it if it has not been defined as a variable, and the variable needs to be on its own. You use the addition operator (+) to add the value of the variable to the string, as shown in this example:

```
<script type="text/javascript">
  var mycar="Corvette";
  document.write("I like driving my "+mycar);◄—— A variable is added to the string
</script>                                           that is written to the browser
```

This code prints the following sentence in the browser window:

```
I like driving my Corvette.
```

Notice the space after the word "my" in the code. This ensures that a space appears before the variable is added to the string. If you used the line

```
document.write("I like driving my"+mycar);
```

the result would be

```
I like driving myCorvette.
```

When adding strings, you need to be careful to add the spaces that you want to appear in the output.

The addition operator enables you to place a variable before, after, or even into the middle of a string. To insert a variable into the middle of a string (so that it shows with text on both sides of it), just use another addition operator to add whatever you need to the right of the variable, as in this example:

```
<script type="text/javascript">
  var mycar="Corvette";
  document.write("I like driving my "+mycar+" every day!");
</script>
```

The variable is added between two strings

Now the variable sits inside two text strings, putting a single string together from three pieces. This code prints the following sentence to the browser:

```
I like driving my Corvette every day!
```

When using the variable, you need to make sure that the variable and addition operators are not inside the quotation marks of a string. If they are, you will not get the results you intended. For example, look at this code:

```
<script type="text/javascript">
  var mycar="Corvette";
  document.write("I like driving my +mycar+ every day!");
</script>
```

The addition operator must also be outside the quote marks to work

JavaScript will not recognize the operators and variables here; they are seen only as part of the text string because they are inside the quotes. Instead of using the variable, JavaScript takes everything literally and prints this sentence in the browser:

```
I like driving my +mycar+ every day!
```

To make this code easier to write, you could place every string involved into a variable, so that you only need to add the variable values together rather than dealing with the quotes, like this:

```
<script type="text/javascript">
  var firstString= "I like driving my ";
  var mycar="Corvette";
  var secondString= " every day!";
  document.write(firstString+mycar+secondString);
</script>
```

Three variables are added together and printed to the browser

This prints the same sentence but allows you to change its parts later without needing to edit the document.write() command.

The techniques you've learned in this section will become useful as your strings become more complex, especially when you use HTML code within the strings.

Writing a Page of JavaScript

Now that you know how to use variables and write basic HTML code to the page using JavaScript, you will create a page that is almost entirely written with JavaScript (everything inside the <body> and </body> tags), as a way to reinforce the techniques you have learned up to this point.

Creating the Framework

The first thing you need is a basic framework for the page so that you know where to insert your script. Since you are writing information onto the page, the script tags will be placed within the <body> and </body> tags. In this case, an external script file named ch3_code.js will be used. The body section of your HTML document will look like this:

```
<body>                          The script tags are inserted here to call the external JavaScript file
<script type="text/javascript" src="ch3_code.js"></script>
</body>
```

The code you place in the ch3_code.js file will determine what shows up in the browser when you have finished.

Defining the Variables

To begin your script file, use some JavaScript code to write an HTML heading. You could write the code as a string directly into the document.write() command, as shown here:

```
document.write("<h1>A Page of JavaScript</h1>");
```

On the other hand, you could place the string inside a variable and use the variable inside the document.write() command later in the script:

```
var headingtext="<h1>A Page of JavaScript</h1>";
Other code may be placed here...
document.write(headingtext);
```

For this example, you will go with the second method, since it uses a variable. You will see how this can be a handy feature as you get further into the script.

In fact, along with the headingtext variable, you'll create a bunch of variables to hold the strings of HTML code to add to the page. The next one will add a short sentence of introduction to the page. The variable declaration for the introduction will look like this:

```
var myintro="Hello, welcome to my JavaScript page!";
```

Next, you'll add a link to the page. The variable declaration for the link looks like this:

```
var linktag="<a href=\"http://www.pageresource.com\">Link to a Site</a>";
```

Next, you'll put in some red text to add a little color. Here's the redtext variable definition:

```
var redtext="<span style=\"color:red\">I am so colorful today!</span>";
```

Finally, you'll add in some variables that give you just the opening and closing strong tags and paragraph tags:

```
var begineffect="<strong>";
var endeffect= "</strong>";
var beginpara="<p>";
var endpara="</p>";
```

The code for all of the variables in the ch3_code.js file is as follows:

```
var headingtext="<h1>A Page of JavaScript</h1>";
var myintro="Hello, welcome to my JavaScript page!";
var linktag="<a href=\"http://www.pageresource.com\">Link to a Site</a>";
var redtext="<span style=\"color:red\">I am so colorful today!</span>";
var begineffect="<strong>";
var endeffect= "</strong>";
var beginpara="<p>";
var endpara="</p>";
```

Adding the Commands

Now, following the variable declarations, you can add some document.write() commands to the ch3_code.js file to write the contents of the variables back to the HTML document:

```
document.write(headingtext);
document.write(begineffect+myintro+endeffect);
document.write(beginpara);
document.write(linktag);
document.write(endpara);
document.write(beginpara);
document.write(redtext);
document.write(endpara);
```

This writes the heading at the top of the page. Adding the begineffect and endeffect variables to the left and right of the myintro variable writes the introductory text in bold under the heading. After that is a new paragraph, followed by a link, and then another new paragraph, followed by the red text message.

Here is the entire code for the ch3_code.js file up to this point:

```
var headingtext="<h1>A Page of JavaScript</h1>";
var myintro="Hello, welcome to my JavaScript page!";
var linktag="<a href=\"http://www.pageresource.com\">Link to a Site</a>";
var redtext="<span style=\"color:red\">I am so colorful today!</span>";
var begineffect="<strong>";
var endeffect= "</strong>";
var beginpara="<p>";
var endpara="</p>";
```

All of the variables are declared and assigned values here

```
document.write(headingtext);
document.write(begineffect+myintro+endeffect);
document.write(beginpara);
document.write(linktag);
document.write(endpara);
document.write(beginpara);
document.write(redtext);
document.write(endpara);
```

The values of the variables are printed to the browser here

Save the ch3_code.js file and then load your HTML document. The end result of this code in the browser is shown in Figure 3-1. Note the strong introduction text and the use of paragraphs between sections.

Modifying the Page

Now suppose that you do not like the layout as it appeared on the Web page. Instead, you want the strongly emphasized introduction to be normally emphasized. If you had written the document.write() commands with plain strings rather than variables, you would need to search through the code to find the <strong></strong> tags and change them to <em></em> tags.

However, since you used the variables, all you need to do is change the values of the appropriate variables at the top of the script file. You only need to change the values of the variables, and you don't need to look for the strong tags inside a bunch of code.

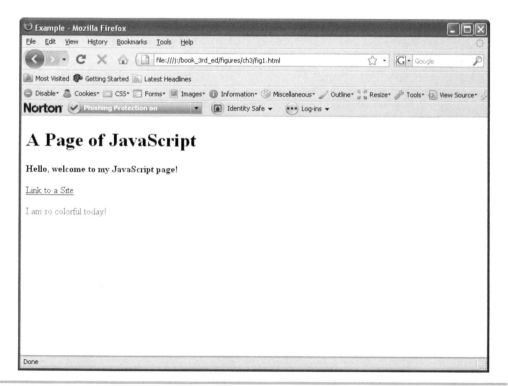

Figure 3-1   The result of the JavaScript code in a Web browser

The code that follows shows the changes that you could make to the script file to get the new effect. Notice how you only need to change the values of the begineffect and endeffect variables to change the format of the text on the page:

```
var headingtext="<h1>A Page of JavaScript</h1>";
var myintro="Hello, welcome to my JavaScript page!";
var linktag="<a href=\"http://www.pageresource.com\">Link to a Site</a>";
var redtext="<span style=\"color:red\">I am so colorful today!</span>";
var begineffect="<em>";        Changed to <em>
var endeffect= "</em>";        Changed to </em>
var beginpara="<p>";
var endpara="</p>";
document.write(headingtext);
document.write(begineffect+myintro+endeffect);
document.write(beginpara);
document.write(linktag);
document.write(endpara);
document.write(beginpara);
document.write(redtext);
document.write(endpara);
```

Save the ch3_code.js file and reload your HTML document. Figure 3-2 shows how these changes affect the display of the page in a Web browser.

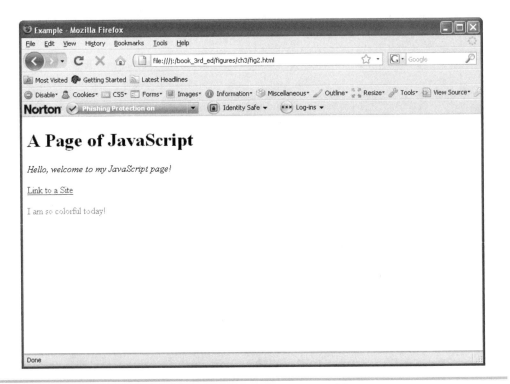

Figure 3-2 The page after changing some JavaScript variables

Try This 3-2   Create an HTML Page with JavaScript

pr3_2.html
prjs3_2.js

In this project, you will create an HTML page with JavaScript, similar to the one you created in this chapter. The variables will be given new values, and the differences should be noticeable.

Step by Step

1. Create an HTML page, leaving the space between the <body> and </body> tags open.

2. Between the <body> and </body> tags, add the <script> and </script> tags to link to a file named prjs3_2.js. Save the HTML file as pr3_2.html.

3. Open a file to use as your JavaScript file. Save it with the filename prjs3_2.js. Use this file to add the JavaScript code in steps 4–10.

4. Create a variable named myheading and give it this value:

   This is My Web Page!

5. Create a variable named linktag and give it this value:

   <a href=\"http://www.javascriptcity.com\">Web Site Link!</a>

6. Create a variable named sometext and give it this value:

   This text can be affected by other statements.

7. Create a variable named begineffect and give it the value .

8. Create a variable named endeffect and give it the value .

9. Create a variable named newsection and give it the value <br />.

10. Write the value of each variable back to the HTML document in this order:

    myheading
    newsection
    begineffect
    sometext
    endeffect
    newsection
    linktag
    newsection
    sometext

(continued)

When you have finished, save the prjs3_2.js file. It should look like this:

```
var myheading="<h1>This is My Web Page!</h1>";
var linktag="<a href=\"http://www.javascriptcity.com\">Web Site
Link!</a>";
var sometext="This text can be affected by other statements.";
var begineffect="<em>";
var endeffect="</em>";
var newsection="<br />";
document.write(myheading);
document.write(begineffect);
document.write(sometext);
document.write(endeffect);
document.write(newsection);
document.write(linktag);
document.write(newsection);
document.write(sometext);
```

11. Open the pr3_2.html page in your Web browser and view the results.

12. Reopen the prjs3_2.js file and make the changes in steps 13–14.

13. Change the value of begineffect to .

14. Change the value of endeffect to .

15. When you have finished, save the prjs3_2.js file. It should look like this:

```
var myheading="<h1>This is My Web Page!</h1>";
var linktag="<a href=\"http://www.javascriptcity.com\">Web Site
Link!</a>";
var sometext="This text can be affected by other statements.";
var begineffect="<strong>";
var endeffect="</strong>";
var newsection="<br />";
document.write(myheading);
document.write(begineffect);
document.write(sometext);
document.write(endeffect);
document.write(newsection);
document.write(linktag);
document.write(newsection);
document.write(sometext);
```

16. Reload the pr3_2.html page in your Web browser. Notice the differences resulting from the changes in the variable values in the JavaScript file.

Try This Summary

In this project, you combined your new skills on using variables with earlier skills on writing to a Web page with JavaScript. You created a Web page with a script that uses variables to write the HTML code on the page. You then changed the values of two variables and resaved the script file. The changes to the variables made visible changes to the page.

Chapter 3 Self Test

1. A variable _____ or _____ a value.

2. What are two of the benefits of using variables?

   A They can save you time in writing and updating your scripts, and they can make the purpose of your code clearer.

   B They make the purpose of your code clearer, and they make it harder for noncoders to understand the script.

   C They can save you time in writing and updating your scripts, and they make it harder for noncoders to understand the script.

   D They offer no advantages whatsoever.

3. To declare a variable, you use the _____ keyword.

4. What symbol is used as the assignment operator in JavaScript?

   A +

   B −

   C :

   D =

5. Which of the following declares a variable named pagenumber and gives it a value of 240?

   A var PageNumber=240;

   B pagenumber=220;

   C var pagenumber=240;

   D var integer named Pagenumber=240;

6. Variable names are not case sensitive.

   A True

   B False

7. A variable name must begin with a(n) _____ or a(n) _____ character.

8. You should avoid using JavaScript reserved words as variable names.

   A True

   B False

9. Which of the following variable declarations uses a variable with a valid variable name in JavaScript?

   A var default;

   B var my_house;

   C var my dog;

   D var 2cats;

10. In JavaScript, the variable values, or _____, can include numbers, strings, Booleans, and nulls.

11. To denote an exponent in JavaScript, you use a letter _____ right after the base number and before the exponent.

12. Which of the following string declarations is invalid?

   A var mytext="Here is some text!";

   B var mytext='Here is some text!';

   C var mytext= "Here is some text!';

   D var mytext= "Here is \n some text!";

13. Which of the following statements would be valid in JavaScript?

   A document.write("John said, "Hi!"");

   B document.write('John said, "Hi!"");

   C document.write("John said, "Hi!"");

   D document.write("John said, \"Hi!\"");

14. _____ characters enable you to add things to your strings that could not be added otherwise.

15. Which of the following successfully prints a variable named myhobby by adding it to a set of strings?

   A document.write("I like to +myhobby+ every weekend");

   B document.write("I like to " +myhobby+ " every weekend");

   C document.write("I like to myhobby every weekend");

   D document.write("I like to 'myhobby' every weekend");

Chapter 4

Using Functions

Key Skills & Concepts

- What a Function Is

- Why Functions Are Useful

- Structuring Functions

- Calling Functions in Your Scripts

As a JavaScript coder, you need to know how to use functions in your scripts. Functions can make your scripts more portable and easier to debug.

This chapter covers the basics of using functions. First, you will find out what a function is and why functions are useful. Then, you will learn how to define and structure functions. Finally, you will learn how to call functions in your scripts.

What a Function Is

A *function* is basically a little script within a larger script. Its purpose is to perform a single task or a series of tasks. What a function does depends on what code you place inside it. For instance, a function might write a line of text to the browser or calculate a numeric value and return that value to the main script.

As you may recall from math class, a function can be used to calculate values on a coordinate plane. You may have seen calculations like these:

```
f(x)=x+2
y=x+2
```

Both are commonly used to calculate the *y* coordinate from the value of the *x* coordinate. If you need the *y* coordinate when *x* is equal to 3, you substitute 3 for *x* to get the *y* value: 3+2=5. Using the function, you find that when *x*=3, *y*=5.

The function itself is just sitting on the paper (or, in our case, the script) until you need to use it to perform its task. And you can use the function as many times as you need to, by calling it from the main script.

Why Functions Are Useful

Functions help organize the various parts of a script into the different tasks that must be accomplished. By using one function for writing text and another for making a calculation, you make it easier for yourself and others to see the purpose of each section of the script, and thus debug it more easily.

Another reason functions are useful is their reusability. They can be used more than once within a script to perform their task. Rather than rewriting the entire block of code, you can simply call the function again.

Consider the simple function $y=x+2$. If you use it only once, the function doesn't serve much purpose. If you need to get several values, however, the function becomes increasingly useful. Rather than writing out the formula for each calculation, you can just substitute the x values each time you need to get the y value. So, if you need the y value when x is 3, 4, and 5, you can use the function three times to get the y values. The function will calculate 5, 6, and 7, respectively. Instead of writing the content of the function three times, it only needs to be written once to get three answers.

Functions can perform complex tasks and can be quite lengthy. In the examples in this and later chapters, you'll see just how useful and time-saving they are in JavaScript.

Structuring Functions

Now that you understand what functions are and why you want to use them, you need to learn how to structure them in your scripts. A function needs to be declared with its name and its code. There are also some optional additions you can use to make functions even more useful. You can import one or more variables into the function, which are called *parameters*. You can also return a value to the main script from the function using the *return* statement. You will start by looking at how the function begins.

Declaring Functions

On the first line of a function, you declare it as a function, name it, and indicate whether it accepts any parameters. To declare a function, you use the reserved word function, followed by its name, and then a set of parentheses:

```
function functionname()
```

The reserved word function tells the browser that you are declaring a function and that more information will follow. The next piece of information is the function's name. After that, the set of parentheses indicates whether the function accepts any parameters.

For example, to name your function reallycool and indicate that it does not use any parameters, the first line looks like this:

```
function reallycool()
```

Because the function does not use any parameters, the parentheses are left empty. As with variable names, there are some special considerations for naming functions. You'll learn about those considerations after the discussion of the function structure.

You may have noticed that this line does not end with a semicolon, as do the other code lines you've seen so far in this book. The semicolon is absent because you use a different technique to show where the function's code begins and ends, as described next. However, each of the separate lines of code within the function does end with a semicolon, as you will see in the examples in this chapter.

Defining the Code for Functions

Curly brackets ({ }) surround the code inside the function. The opening curly bracket marks the beginning of the function's code; then comes the code; and, finally, the closing curly bracket marks the end of the function, in this format:

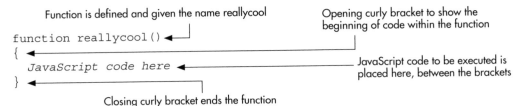

The browser will execute all of the code inside the curly brackets when the function is called (as you will learn later in this chapter). When the browser gets to the closing curly bracket, it knows the function has ended. The browser will move to the next line of code or continue whatever it was doing before the function was called.

You have some flexibility in formatting the curly brackets. There are several common ways to place the curly brackets into a script. The format shown in the preceding example "lines up" the brackets so that the opening and closing of the function are seen on the left margin of the code. This method is handy if you use other statements that need curly brackets (you will see some other statements that use curly brackets in later chapters). By indenting each set of brackets, you make it easy to see which brackets are nested within the function and which ones begin and end the function itself.

Another common format is to put the opening bracket on the same line as the function declaration, rather than on the next line:

```
function reallycool() {          Opening bracket is on the first line
    JavaScript code here         with the declaration of the function
}
```

In this format, the opening brackets of code blocks are seen to the right, and closing brackets appear on the left. This can be a useful technique if you wish to count how many brackets have been opened and/or closed within a segment of code.

Of course, if you have a particularly short function, you can even place the entirety of the function on a single line, like this:

```
function reallycool() { JavaScript code here }
```

The curly brackets are flexible in this way because white space, tabs, and line breaks that appear between tokens in JavaScript are ignored (tokens are such things as variable or function names, keywords, or other parts of the code that must remain intact). Thus, the following code would be valid:

```
function reallycool() {
var
         a
          =
             5; var b = 3; var c = 6; }
```

Though it may be more difficult to read, JavaScript will still see it as valid code since the proper syntax is otherwise in place.

The format you choose for the curly brackets will likely depend on your background in programming and how you like to see the code. All the styles are acceptable to the JavaScript interpreter, so use the one that you feel most comfortable viewing and editing. In the examples in this book, I will place the opening bracket on the same line as the function declaration (as in the second example format from this section) and may occasionally place the entirety of a function on one line if it is particularly short (as in the third example format in this section).

Naming Functions

As with variables, functions need to be named carefully to avoid problems with your scripts. The same basic rules that applied to variables apply to the naming of functions: case sensitivity, using allowed characters, avoiding reserved words, and giving functions memorable and meaningful names.

NOTE
If you already know the rules for naming variables, you may wish to skip this section, since the function-naming rules are essentially the same. However, there are some details about choosing names for functions that you may find useful.

Using Case in Function Names
Function names are case sensitive, just like variable names. This means that reallycool, REALLYCOOL, and ReallyCool represent different functions. Remember that you need to call your functions using the same letter cases as you used in their declarations.

Using Allowed Characters and Avoiding Reserved Words
The characters that are allowed for function names are the same as those you can use for variable names:

- The function name must begin with a letter or an underscore character (_).

- The function name cannot contain any spaces.

Also as with variable names, you cannot use JavaScript reserved words for function names. Doing so can cause the function to fail, which can cause real problems within a script. Refer to the section "Avoiding Reserved Words" in Chapter 3 for a complete list of JavaScript reserved words.

Giving Functions Meaningful Names

Your functions will be easier to remember and to debug if you choose names that reflect their purpose. As you learned in Chapter 3, for a variable, you should use a name that represents its value, such as example_number to stand for the number of an example on a page. A function name should tell you something about what the function will do. For example, suppose that you create a function that writes some text to the page. It could contain the following line of code:

```
document.write("<strong>This is a strong statement!</strong>");
```

You could just name the function *text*, but that might not be descriptive enough, because you could have other functions that also write text to the page. Instead, you might name it something like print_strong_text, so that you know that the function is used to print a piece of strongly emphasized text to the browser. The full function is shown here:

This name helps describe the purpose of the function

```
function print_strong_text() {
   document.write("<strong>This is a strong statement!</strong>");
}
```

This line is the code that will be executed when the function is called

As with variables, the more functions you use in a script, the more important it becomes to use meaningful and memorable names for them.

Adding Parameters to Functions

Parameters are used to allow a function to import one or more values from somewhere outside the function. Parameters are set on the first line of the function inside the set of parentheses, in this format:

```
function functionname(variable1, variable2)
```

Any value brought in as a parameter becomes a variable within the function, using the name you give it inside the parentheses.

For example, here is how you would define a function reallycool with the parameters (variables) coolcar and coolplace:

Parameters are added to the first line within the parentheses

```
function reallycool(coolcar, coolplace) {
   JavaScript code here
}
```

Notice that in JavaScript, you do not use the var keyword when you set the parameters for a function. JavaScript declares the variables automatically when they are set as parameters to a function, so the var keyword is not used here. For example, a line like this one is invalid:

```
function reallycool(var coolcar, var coolplace)
```

Where do the parameters come from in the first place? They are obtained from outside the function when you make the function call. You will see how this works later in this chapter. For now, you just need to know how they are used as parameters to JavaScript functions.

NOTE
In other languages, it is often required that a variable have a declaration when set as a parameter, but JavaScript will do this for you. However, when you declare variables anywhere else, you need to use the var keyword.

Using Function Parameter Values
When you assign parameters to a function, you can use them like any other variables. For example, you could give the coolcar variable value to another variable by using the assignment operator, as in this example:

```
function reallycool(coolcar,coolplace) {
   var mycar=coolcar;
}
```

The value of the coolcar variable is assigned to the mycar variable

This assigns the value of the coolcar parameter to a variable named mycar.

Instead of assigning its value to another variable, you could just use the coolcar parameter in the function, as in this example:

```
function reallycool(coolcar,coolplace) {
   document.write("My car is a "+coolcar);
}
```

The value of the coolcar variable is used in a document.write() command

If the value of coolcar is Corvette, then the function would print this line to the browser when it is called:

```
My car is a Corvette
```

The coolcar parameter is given a value out of the blue here. In actual use, the value must come from somewhere in the main script or another function, or else the variable will have no value.

Using Multiple Parameters
You may have noticed that the previous example had two parameters but used only one parameter. A function can have as few or as many parameters as you wish. When you assign multiple function parameters, the function doesn't need to use all of them. It can use one parameter, a few, or none. How many are used depends on what the function does and how it is called.

The only rule is that if you have more than one parameter, you need to separate each parameter with a comma, so that the browser knows what to do.

In the previous example, the second parameter was not used. Here is how you could change the function to use both parameters:

Both parameters are used as variables in this document.write() command

```
function reallycool(coolcar,coolplace) {
   document.write("My car is a "+coolcar+" and I drive it to "+coolplace);
}
```

Now, if the value of coolcar is Corvette and the value of coolplace is Las Vegas, the function would print the following line to the browser when it is called:

```
My car is a Corvette and I drive it to Las Vegas
```

You can place as many parameters as your function needs within the parentheses on the first line of the function. Here is an example with four parameters:

```
function reallycool(coolcar,coolplace,coolfood,coolbreeze)
```

Remember to separate each parameter with a comma when you have more than one.

Adding Return Statements to Functions

A return statement is used to be sure that a function returns a specific value to the main script, to be used in the main script. You place the return statement as the last line of the function before the closing curly bracket and end it with a semicolon. Most often, the value returned is the value of a variable, using the following format:

```
return variablename;
```

For example, to return the value of a variable cooltext, the return statement looks like this:

```
return cooltext;
```

This returns the value of cooltext to the place in the main script where the function was called.

Suppose that you want to write a function that returns the result of adding two strings together. You could use a return statement, as in this example:

First string to be added is assigned to a variable   Second string to be added is assigned to a variable

```
function get_added_text() {
  var textpart1="This is ";
  var textpart2="fun!";
  var added_text=textpart1+textpart2;
  return added_text;
}
```

The strings are added together to combine them and assigned to a variable

The variable with the result of the string addition is returned to the script

In this function, the first two variables are assigned string values, and the added_text variable is given the value of the addition of those two strings. The new value is sent back to the script where it was called. It returns this string:

```
This is fun!
```

This returned value is then used in the main script. In its current form, this function is not very useful, because the strings were just defined in the function rather than being brought in as parameters.

In addition to returning a variable value, you can return a simple value or even nothing. All of the following would be valid return statements:

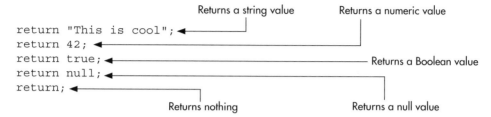

All of these return the control back to the first JavaScript statement after the function call. Returning nothing does this without sending back a value.

You can also return an expression, such as the addition of numbers or strings (or any other expression you decide to build). The following would also be valid return statements:

```
Return "This is "+"cool";  ───────── Returns the result of the addition of two strings
return 21+20+1;  ───────── Returns the result of the addition of three numbers
```

These would return the values "This is cool" and 42, respectively.

You will see examples of more useful functions that use parameters and return statements in the next section.

Calling Functions in Your Scripts

Now that you know how the function itself works, you need to learn how to call a function in your script. A call to a function in JavaScript is simply the function name along with the set of parentheses (with or without parameters between the opening and closing parentheses), ending with a semicolon, like a normal JavaScript statement:

```
functionname();
```

You can call functions anywhere in your script code. You can even call a function inside of another function. A good rule to follow is to have the function definition come before the function call in the script. The easiest way to be sure that your function definition comes before your function call is to place all of your function definitions as close to the beginning of the script as possible.

Defining a function before calling it is a suggestion for good coding practice, not a strict rule. A function can be called anywhere in JavaScript, but the function code must be loaded by the browser before the function will work. This is why it is suggested that you define your functions before calling them. If you were to call a function that is defined near the bottom of a script, there is a chance it would not load in time to be executed. Thus, it is normally best to define a function before it is called.

Script Tags: Head Section or Body Section

When adding scripts directly to a Web page rather than using an external file, making sure that variable and function declarations are in the head section often helps to ensure they are available when the script calls them in the body section. However, since JavaScript often uses information from the document that may not have loaded yet, this could become problematic. On the other hand, having a lot of JavaScript code in the body section can also be troublesome when you need to edit your HTML code (and if the JavaScript code is in the body section it needs to be after the element(s) that have the information JavaScript needs to use to ensure the necessary information is loaded). It is preferable to place all of your code into an external JavaScript file. Then, you can decide whether you want to place the script tags in the head section or in the body section.

If a script needs no information from the document, placing the script tags in the head section works very well. As an example, you will create a script that sends an alert message to the viewer as soon as the page is opened in the browser. To have a message pop up in a small message box, you use a JavaScript method called window.alert.

First, you'll learn how to create a JavaScript alert, and then you'll see how to build a function that uses that method and call the function in a script.

Creating a JavaScript Alert

Rather than writing something to the screen with the document.write() method, you can create a JavaScript alert that pops up in a message box by using the window.alert method. Like the document.write() method, the window.alert method takes the text string for the alert as a parameter, using this format:

```
window.alert("alert_text");
```

The string of text will be displayed in the alert pop-up box.

For example, suppose that you want to display "This is an alert!" in the pop-up box. You would write the command in your external JavaScript file (we will use the filename js_alert.js for this example) like this:

```
window.alert("This is an alert!");
```

Now you know how to make the alert pop up, but how can you get it to appear right as the page is opened? You can do this by making sure the script is called before the body section of the Web page is loaded. By placing the script tags inside the <head> and </head> tags of the document, as shown next, you ensure that it will be executed before the rest of the page is loaded:

```
<head>                                          This line calls the external JavaScript file
<title>Functions - Alert!</title>
<script type="text/javascript" src="js_alert.js"></script> ◄──┘
</head>
<body>
HTML code here ◄─────────────────────────── The HTML for the page would be here
</body>
```

Save the HTML file as js_alert.html and view it in your Web browser. As you can see, this would certainly be an easy way to show an alert when the page opens. However, because you are learning about functions, you will take another approach.

Using a Function for a JavaScript Alert

The following code uses a function in your external JavaScript file to pop up an alert box. In your js_alert.js file, change the code to the following:

```
                        Names and begins the function
                                      |
function show_message() {◄──────────┘
  window.alert("This is an alert!");◄──────────  The window.alert() command
}                                                 is used in the function
show_message();◄──────────── The function is called and executes, causing the alert to pop up
```

This example creates a function named show_message() to do the job of showing the alert. The alert will be shown only if you call the show_message() function somewhere after it is defined. In this case, the function is called right after its definition. The result is a small alert box with the message "This is an alert!"

NOTE

When an alert box appears, you may see the page pause until you click the OK button, or it may continue to load while waiting for you to click OK. This depends on your browser.

Even though the function is defined first, it doesn't mean it will be executed first. A function is not executed until it is called; in other words, JavaScript will not use the function until it gets to the function call in the script.

Any commands that come before the function call (and that are not part of the function definition) will be executed before the function. For instance, we could change the code in the JavaScript file as follows:

```
               The function is defined          This alert doesn't happen
                          |                      until the function is called
function show_message() {◄──────┘                        |
  window.alert("This is an alert!");◄──────────────────┘
}
window.alert("I am first, ha!");◄────────────────────This alert shows up first
window.alert("I am second, ha ha!");◄────────────┐
show_message();◄──────┐                           |
              |                         This alert is second
This finally calls the function so that the alert inside it can display
```

This example defines the same function, show_message(), on the first line. The function is followed by two lone window.alert commands, and then the line that calls the function. Save the js_alert.js file with this new code and then reload the js_alert.html file in your Web browser. You should see an interesting result!

The two lone alert commands are the first executable statements JavaScript sees, and they come first. The call to our function is seen last, so the function is executed last. The result is three alerts, in this order:

● The user gets an alert, saying "I am first, ha!" and needs to click the OK button to get rid of it.

● Then the alert that displays "I am second, ha ha!" appears, and the viewer needs to click OK again.

● Finally, the function is executed, and the viewer sees the alert "This is an alert!" and needs to click OK a third time to end the alert frenzy.

Although this example goes overboard with its alerts, it helps you understand how a function call works.

If you are not worried about how soon the alerts display, the script can be called in the body section as well. As you gain more experience coding, choosing whether to place script tags in the head or body section will become easier. When scripts use information from the body of the HTML document, the script tags typically either are placed in the head section with a function set up to initialize variables and other functions when the page has loaded (this uses event handling, which will be discussed in Chapter 7) or are placed in the body section (often just before the ending </body> tag). I will use the latter method in this book.

Calling a Function from Another Function

Calling a function within another function can be a useful way to organize the sequence in which your events will occur. Usually, the function is placed inside another function that has a larger task to finish.

When you place a function call within a function, you should define the function that will be called before you define the function that calls it, per the earlier suggestion that a function should be defined before it is called.

Here is an example of two functions, where the second function calls the first one:

This function does the work of displaying the alert

```
function update_alert(){ ◄─────────────┘
  window.alert("Welcome! This site is updated daily!");
}
function call_alert() { ◄───────────── This function just calls the previous function
  update_alert();
}
call_alert(); ◄───────────── This calls the call_alert() function to get things started
```

Notice that the update_alert() function is where all the real action happens. Everything else is a function call. The call_alert() function does nothing more than call the update_alert() function so that it is executed. Finally, you see the command that starts the entire sequence, which is the call to the call_alert() function. Since this is the first JavaScript statement outside a function, it is executed first. When it is executed, it just calls the update_alert() function, which does the work of displaying the alert.

NOTE

Most browsers would execute the preceding example without a problem even if you defined the update_alert() function after you called it. However, there is a chance that some older browsers may not be as lenient and will want the function defined before it is called. Also, if the function definition is too far down in the code to be loaded in time, it will not work correctly. Thus, it is normally best to define a function before it is called.

Now suppose that you want to create three functions to perform three tasks. To make sure that they occur in the correct sequence, you can call them in order from within another function. Here is an example of this technique with three functions that call alerts for various purposes:

```
function update_alert() {                                    This function pops up
    window.alert("Welcome! This site is updated daily!");    an alert when called
}
function section_alert() {                                   This function also pops
    window.alert("Please visit the picture section!");       up an alert when called
}
function links_alert() {                                     This function also pops up
    window.alert("Also, check out my links page!");          an alert when called
}
function get_messages() {
    update_alert();                          This function calls the other three
    section_alert();                         functions into action when called
    links_alert();
}
get_messages();                              Calling the get_messages() function starts the process
```

The code begins by defining the three functions to show each alert. Then it defines the get_messages() function, which just calls the previous three functions. Of course, the get_messages() function must be called to actually put this into action. This call happens as the first statement outside of a function.

Of course, creating a script that pops up message after message is not something you typically want to do. Although the example demonstrates the correct use of function calls, a script that does this would likely annoy your viewers! You'll see examples of practical uses of functions in later chapters.

Calling Functions with Parameters

The previous example used three different functions to show three alerts. Although it works, it would be nice if you did not need to write a new function for each alert. You can avoid doing this by using parameters. You can create a function to be used multiple times to do the same thing, but with the new information from the parameters each time.

As mentioned earlier in the chapter, variables are commonly used as parameters. However, you can also use a value as a parameter. You'll learn about the different types of variable parameters first, and then take a look at value parameters.

If you want to send the values of certain variables to the function, you must first declare the variables and then be sure that they have the values you need before you send them. Here, the *scope* of a variable becomes important. The scope of a variable determines where it is and is not valid. JavaScript has global and local variables.

Using Global Variables

Global variables are the variables that you learned about in Chapter 3. Because they are defined outside any functions, they can be changed anywhere in the script—inside or outside of functions. A global variable is declared anywhere outside a function, as in the following code:

```
var mycar="Honda";
var paycheck="1200";
```
These are global variables being declared

The variables in this example can be changed anywhere in the script. This means that they can even be accidentally overwritten or changed by a function.

To understand how global variables can be affected by a function, consider an example that shows two alerts. You want one alert to tell you how much money you need to get a certain car, and you want the other one to tell you how much money you currently have and what type of car you now own. What would happen if you used the following code?

```
var mycar="Honda";
var paycheck=1200;
function new_car() {
    mycar="Ferrari";
    paycheck=3500;
    window.alert("You need $"+paycheck+" to get a "+mycar);
}
new_car();
window.alert("You make $"+paycheck+" and have a "+mycar);
```
These are being declared as global variables

Oops! The function assigns the variables new values

The alert here is what you expect

The alert here is not what you expect, since the variables were accidentally changed

It may look as if you created new variables inside the function, even though they had the same name. However, the script would output the following text in the two alerts:

```
You need $3500 to get a Ferrari
You make $3500 and have a Ferrari
```

Obviously, this isn't right.

This example demonstrates why you need to use the var keyword when declaring variables. Without the var keyword, you are not creating new variables inside the function (which would make them local). Instead, you are changing the value of your global variables—you are issuing a reassignment command rather than a new variable command. To clear this up, you need to either change one set of variable names or use local variables, as described in the next section.

Using Local Variables

A *local variable* can be used only within the function in which it is declared. It does not exist outside that function, unless you pass it along to another function by using a parameter.

The key to creating a local variable in a function is to be sure that you declare it using the var keyword. Otherwise, any global variables by that name could be changed, as you saw in the previous example. To declare a local variable, you must place it inside a function and use the var keyword, as shown in this code:

```
function new_car() {
   var mycar="Ferrari";            These variables are declared as local variables,
   var paycheck="3500";            using the var keyword inside a function
}
```

The mycar and paycheck variables are now local variables, which can only be seen and changed by the new_car() function.

Therefore, to correct the script in the previous section, you just need to add the var keyword to declare the local variables inside the function, like this:

```
var mycar="Honda";
var paycheck=1200;
function new_car() {                   Adding the var keyword ensures that variables
   var mycar="Ferrari";                are declared locally and do not change the
   var paycheck=3500;                  global variables by the same name
   window.alert("You need $"+paycheck+" to get a "+mycar);
}
new_car();
window.alert("You make $"+paycheck+" and have a "+mycar);
```

Now the alerts should appear as you intended:

```
You need $3500 to get a Ferrari
You make $1200 and have a Honda
```

As you can see, the scope of a variable may be important when you send certain variables as parameters to a function.

Using Variables As Function Parameters

The following example uses variable parameters. It sends a global variable along to the function. It then assigns its value to a local variable to avoid any accidental changes.

The function accepts a parameter

The parameter value is
assigned to a local variable

```
function check_alert(paycheck) {
  var pcheck=paycheck;
  window.alert("You make $"+pcheck);
}
var paycheck=1200;
check_alert(paycheck);
```

The local variable is used inside
the function for the alert

The variable is
assigned a value

The value is passed to the function as a parameter

The script begins with the check_alert() function, which takes in the parameter paycheck. The line of code in the function assigns the value of paycheck to a local variable, pcheck. This way, you can use pcheck within the function to avoid changing the global paycheck variable. The function is then used to display an alert that uses the value of pcheck. After the function, in the outside script, the global variable paycheck is assigned a value of 1200. Then the code calls the check_alert() function and sends it the value of the paycheck variable.

The previous example shows a rather long way to keep from changing a global variable. Since function parameters are sent as values of variables, you can change the variable name the function accepts inside the parentheses in the function definition. This creates a local variable from the parameter that is sent to the function. Here is an example:

```
function check_alert(pcheck) {
  window.alert("You make $"+pcheck);
}
var paycheck=1200;
check_alert(paycheck);
```

The function takes in a parameter
and gives it a local variable name

The local variable is used for the alert

When this code calls the check_alert() function, it sends that function the value of the paycheck variable. The value is pulled in from the function itself. Rather than naming the value "paycheck" here and assigning it to another variable, you simply use another name within the parentheses: pcheck. The pcheck variable becomes a local variable inside the check_alert() function. Since the code sends paycheck a value of 1200, pcheck will be 1200, unless you change it later in the function.

Using Value Parameters

You can also send a value as a parameter directly. Instead of needing to declare a global variable in order to send a parameter, you can just send a value that will be turned into a local variable inside the function. This allows you to send a value on the fly and eliminates the need to have a global variable handy.

The important thing to remember is that if you send a string value, you need to enclose it in quotes. The following function call sends a string value of "something" to a function named text_alert():

```
text_alert("something");
```

For example, the last example in the previous section can be modified to add more information while using one less line by using value parameters:

```
function check_alert(pcheck,car) {
  window.alert("You make $"+pcheck+" and have a "+car);
}
check_alert(1200,"Corvette");
```

The function is sent a numeric value and a string value instead of variable values

In this example, the function call sends two parameters to the function. The first one is a numeric value and does not need quotes. The second value is a string and needs to be enclosed in quotes. These values are then sent to the function, where they are read in as the local variables pcheck and car, respectively. They can now be used in the function to display this sentence in an alert:

```
You make $1200 and have a Corvette
```

Parameters can also be sent using expressions, such as the following:

```
check_alert(500+700, "Cor"+"vette");
```

JavaScript will evaluate each expression and send the results as parameters to the function. Thus, the preceding code would have the same end result (adding 500 and 700 gives 1200, and adding "Cor" and "vette" gives "Corvette"):

```
You make $1200 and have a Corvette
```

Parameters Are Optional

Another thing that should be mentioned is that sending parameters to a function is optional. The function will do its best to do its work without the parameter values that are not sent. You could call the function check_alert() without any parameters:

```
function check_alert(pcheck,car) {
  window.alert("You make $"+pcheck+" and have a "+car);
}
check_alert();
```

Your result would be something like the following text:

```
You make $undefined and have a undefined
```

Thus, it is a good idea to set up some code to handle a situation where a parameter is not sent. This can be done using conditionals. Here is one way to check if the parameters were sent to check_alert():

```
function check_alert(pcheck,car) {
  if (pcheck && car) {
    window.alert("You make $"+pcheck+" and have a "+car);
  }
```

```
else {
    window.alert("My parameters are missing!");
  }
}
check_alert();
```

This essentially tells JavaScript to see if the parameters exist before writing the statement to the page. If they do exist, the statement is written on the page with the parameter values. If they do not exist, then the viewer gets an alert that says "My parameters are missing!" The logical operator && will be discussed in more detail in Chapter 5 and the if/else statement will be discussed in more detail in Chapter 6.

Calling Functions with Return Statements

To call a function and use a return statement in the function, you can assign the result of the function to a variable. In this way, the variable gets the value returned from the function and can be used later in the script. This is the format for declaring a variable that has the value returned by a function:

```
var variablename=functionname();
```

Consider the previous example, which had a function that returned the value of two text strings added together. You can modify it so that the function result is assigned to a variable, as follows:

```
function get_added_text() {
    var textpart1="This is ";
    var textpart2="fun!";
    var added_text=textpart1+textpart2;
    return added_text;  ◄——————————— The result of the added text is returned to the script
}
var alert_text=get_added_text();  ◄——— The result of the function is assigned to a variable
window.alert(alert_text);  ◄—————————┐
                 The value of the variable is used as the text for the alert
```

As you can see, the function returns the value of the added text variable to the script. By assigning the result of the get_added_text() function to the alert_text variable, you can use the added text later in the script. The variable is used to send an alert to the user with the result of the added text. The alert message reads

```
This is fun!
```

Now, isn't this fun? You'll see some more practical applications of return methods when you learn about form validation in Chapter 14.

Other Ways to Define Functions

There are several ways to define functions that you may come across while looking at scripts or may find useful in coding new scripts: the function declaration (already discussed), the function constructor, and the function expression.

The Function Declaration

This is the method you have been using up to this point and one that will be used often in this book. As you will recall, you simply declare the function as follows:

```
function functionname() {
  Code for function here
}
```

You can also add parameters and/or return statements as mentioned earlier in this chapter.

The Function Constructor

The function constructor creates a function object in the same way you would create a new instance of an object (this will be discussed in Chapter 8):

```
var functionname = new Function (arguments, code for function) ;
```

This will work like other functions, but the main drawback to this method is that it has poorer performance than the other methods (it is evaluated every time it is used rather than only being parsed once). More often than not, you will use one of the other two methods for defining functions.

The Function Expression

The function expression (also called the function operator) uses the same syntax as a function declaration. The main difference between this and a function declaration is that a function declaration creates a variable with the same name as the function name that can be used outside the function, while the function expression can only access the variable by its name within the function itself. For instance, the following code uses a function declaration and can output an alert using the function name as a variable (the value of the variable will be all of the function's code):

```
function send_alert() {
  var my_num = 1;
}
window.alert(send_alert);
```

On the other hand, the following code would give an error when run:

```
var get_func = function send_alert() {
  var my_num = 1;
}
window.alert(send_alert);
```

As seen in the preceding code, the function expression also uses a function name. However, the function name cannot be used as a variable outside of the function.

CAUTION

This use of the function expression in Internet Explorer 7 (as of the time of this writing) did not give an error, but gave the same result as the function declaration. To test for this difference, Mozilla Firefox may be used.

Anonymous Functions   One effective use of the function expression is to use it without a function name to create an anonymous function. An anonymous function is one that is created and called at the same time, and is helpful when you wish to call a function in only one place in your code (rather than declaring the function elsewhere in the code and reusing it by calling it more than once). The following is the general format for an anonymous function:

```
var varname = function(parameters) {
  Code for function
};
```

This uses the function keyword but does not name the function.

Anonymous functions are quite useful when dealing with JavaScript events. For example, to react to a user clicking the mouse while on a Web page, you could write a simple function for a click event on the document and then call it, as in the following code:

```
function do_not_click() {
  window.alert("Do not click on my page!");
}
document.onclick = do_not_click;
```

This declares the function, then calls it afterward (without parentheses) to handle the click event.

However, you could combine these two steps into one using an anonymous function, as follows:

```
document.onclick = function() {
  window.alert("Do not click on my page!");
};
```

Since the reaction to this event will only be in one place in the JavaScript code, the anonymous function is a handy way to handle the event without the need to declare the function elsewhere and then call it. This technique and the type of code used for event handling (such as in the code listings above) will be discussed in more detail in Chapter 7.

Ask the Expert

Q: What if I put a function into my script but decide not to call it in the script? Will it matter?

A: The function won't be executed unless it is called. However, having unused functions makes the code more difficult to maintain and will increase the download time for viewers (which could make a difference on a slow connection such as dial-up or in situations where optimization of the download time of the code is desired). Also, if the function contains syntax errors, it could send the viewer JavaScript errors and keep other things on the Web page from working correctly.

Q: **What happens if I decide to remove a function from my script later?**

A: This can cause trouble if you do not also remove any calls you made to the function. The script may cause a JavaScript error; or it may run but give you unexpected results. Also, before you remove a function, make sure that it does not perform a necessary task someplace in the script.

Q: **So, what happens if I call a function that doesn't exist?**

A: Either you will get a JavaScript error or the browser will do nothing when the function is called, since it cannot find the function.

Q: **What is the best way to determine when to use a function and when to just code what I want right into the script?**

A: For the most part, you want to use a function if the code within the function will be reusable in some way. For instance, a function that performs a specific calculation might be useful in more than one spot in the script. Also, if you just like the idea of organizing the code a little more, a function helps with that. If you decide the code will be used just once in the script, you may just want to put the code right into the script as it is or use an anonymous function for it.

Try This 4-1   Create an HTML Page with Functions

```
pr4_1.html
prjs4_1.js
```

In this project, you create an HTML page with two JavaScript functions. One function uses parameters sent to it to pop up an alert box with a message. The other function uses a return statement to send a value back to the script. That returned value then is used in an alert message to the viewer.

Step by Step

1. Create an HTML page, leaving the space between the <body> and </body> tags.

2. Create an external JavaScript file and save it as prjs4_1.js.

3. Add the script tags necessary between the <body> and </body> tags of the HTML document to include the external JavaScript file. Save the HTML file as pr4_1.html.

4. Open the prjs4_1.js external JavaScript file and do steps 5–10.

(continued)

5. Create a function named car_cost() that takes two parameters, mycar and paycheck. Create a window.alert command that will display an alert with the following message:

```
You have a <mycar variable here> and make $<paycheck variable here>
```

6. Create a function named get_added_text() that returns the value of two strings added together inside the function. The two strings to add are these two separate lines:

```
This project<space here>
is almost fun!
```

7. In the main script (after the function definitions), call the car_cost() function, and send it the values of "Mustang" and 1500 as parameters.

8. In the main script (after the function definitions), assign the result of the get_added_text() function to a variable named alert_text. Create an alert that pops up with the value of that variable.

9. When you have finished, your external JavaScript file should look like this:

```javascript
function car_cost(mycar,paycheck) {
   window.alert("You have a "+mycar+" and make $"+paycheck);
}
function get_added_text() {
   var textpart1="This project ";
   var textpart2="is almost fun!";
   var added_text=textpart1+textpart2;
   return added_text;
}
car_cost("Mustang",1500);
var alert_text=get_added_text();
window.alert(alert_text);
```

10. Save the external JavaScript file.

11. Open the pr4_1.html file and view it in your browser to see the result.

When you open the Web page, you should see two alert messages:

```
You have a Mustang and make $1500
This project is almost fun!
```

Try This Summary

In this project, you created a script that uses two JavaScript functions. The first function uses parameters and creates an alert box with a message based on the parameters that are sent to the function. The second function returns a value to the script after adding two strings together. The result of the script in the browser is two alert messages based on the information sent to the first function and the information returned to the script from the second function.

Putting It All Together

Now that you have learned the basics of using functions, take a look at the rather long page that follows. This page has some JavaScript added to the HTML document. Try to follow it through to see how it works and what it will do.

```
<body>
<h1>"Welcome to my Function Page," I said.</h1>
<script type="text/javascript">
function get_added_text(textpart1,textpart2) {
  var added_text=textpart1+" "+textpart2;
  return added_text;
}
function print_text() {
  var myfood=get_added_text("cheese","bread");
  document.write(myfood);
}
var alert_text=get_added_text("soup","crackers");
window.alert(alert_text);
print_text();
</script>
<p style="color:red">I'm seeing red!</p>
</body>
```

First, you see that there are two functions defined. The get_added_text() function is used to add two pieces of text, put a space between them, and return that value to where it was called. The print_text() function is used to send some text as parameters to the get_added_text() function, assign the result to a variable named myfood, and print the result to the page itself.

The first command executed is the one right after all the function definitions. It is this line:

```
var alert_text=get_added_text("soup","crackers");
```

This line is declaring a variable named alert_text and assigning it the value that is returned from the get_added_text() function when the function receives "soup" and "crackers" as the parameters. The result will be the two parameter values with a space between them. The returned string of "soup crackers" is now assigned to the alert_text variable.

The next line executed is the line directly afterward, shown here:

```
window.alert(alert_text);
```

The alert has the text assigned to the alert_text variable, which is the added string returned from the get_added_text() function.

Next, there is the call to put the print_text() function into action.

The first thing the print_text() function does is declare a variable named myfood and assign it the value returned from the get_added_text() function. It is sent the values of "cheese" and "bread" as parameters. So, the value returned is the string "cheese bread", which will be assigned to the myfood variable. The print_text() function then takes that value and writes it to the screen using the document.write() method.

Figures 4-1 and 4-2 show the results of this script when run in a browser. Figure 4-1 shows the alert box that pops up first, and Figure 4-2 shows the page the viewer sees after clicking OK in the alert box.

This example shows how you can use the different techniques you learned in this chapter to structure functions, add parameters to function, call functions within other functions, and use return statements. These can all be used in a single script to perform their assigned tasks when necessary.

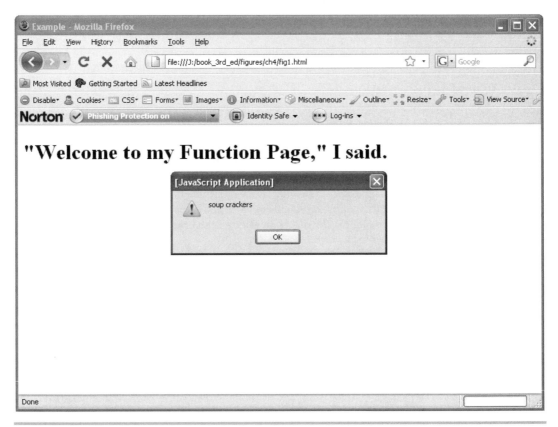

Figure 4-1 The alert box that appears before or while the page loads

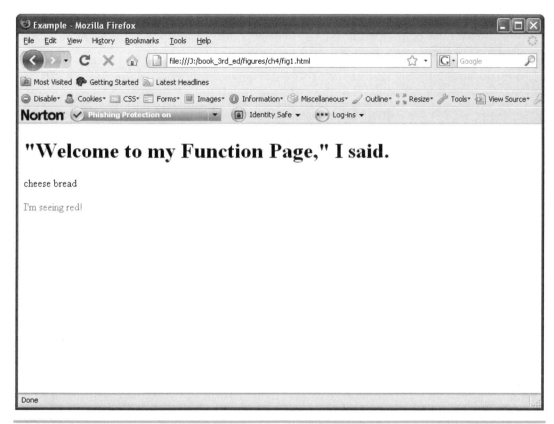

Figure 4-2   The page that appears after the OK button in the alert box is clicked

---

Try This 4-2   Write Your Own Functions

    pr4_2.html
    prjs4_2.js

In this project, you again create an HTML page with two JavaScript functions, but for this project, you use your own variable and function names and create your own version of the script.

Step by Step

1. Create an HTML file and save it as pr4_2.html.

2. Create an external JavaScript file and save it as prjs4_2.js. Use this file for steps 3–6.

3. Create one function that takes in two strings as parameters. Have it return the value of the two strings added together, but with a space between them.

(continued)

4. Create a second function that gets the result of the first function and assigns it to a variable. Write the value of this variable directly into the HTML document. The parameters to send to the first function are the strings "Hi" and "there!".

5. In the main script, create a new variable and assign it the result of the first function. This time, send the function the two strings "Regular" and "text!".

6. Create an alert that will display the value of this variable in an alert box.

7. In the body section of the HTML page, place the script tags in the document (pointing to the prjs4_2.js file) so that the script will write the result of the second function after a line of strong text reading "This is some strong text."

8. When you have finished, save the HTML and JavaScript files and view the HTML page in your browser to see how it works.

The results should be an alert that says "Hi there!" followed by the page opening when OK is clicked in the alert box. The page should display a strong line of text reading "This is some strong text." On the next line, there should be text reading "Regular text!"

Try This Summary

In this project, you used your knowledge of functions, parameters, and returning values to create a script. The result of the script is that the HTML page you created pops up an alert box and writes text to the page based on the results of the two functions that you created.

✔ Chapter 4 Self Test

1. In general, a function is a little _____ within a larger _____ that is used to perform a single _____ or a series of _____.

2. What are two reasons why a function can be useful?

   A They make simple scripts more complex, and they make it harder for noncoders to read the script.

   B They provide a way to organize the various parts of the script into the different tasks that must be accomplished, and they can be reused.

   C They make simple scripts more complex, and they can be reused.

   D They provide a way to organize the various parts of the script into the different tasks that must be accomplished, and they make it harder for noncoders to read the script.

3. On the first line of a function, you _____ it as a function, _____ it, and indicate whether it accepts any _____.

4. To declare a function, you use the reserved word _____.

   A var

   B switch

   C function

   D for

5. What surrounds the code inside a function?

   A Curly brackets – { }

   B Colons – ::

   C Square brackets – []

   D Nothing

6. Function names are case sensitive.

   A True

   B False

7. JavaScript reserved words can be used as function names.

   A True

   B False

8. Which of the following would be a valid function name in JavaScript?

   A function my function()

   B function if()

   C function get_text()

   D function 24hours()

9. _____ are used to allow a function to import one or more values from somewhere outside the function.

10. Parameters are set on the first line of a function, inside a set of _____.

   A curly brackets – { }

   B parentheses – ()

   C square brackets – []

   D nothing

11. Multiple parameters are separated by what symbol?

    A Period

    B Colon

    C Semicolon

    D Comma

12. Which of the following is a valid use of the window.alert() method?

    A win.alt("This is text");

    B window.alert("This is text);

    C window.alert('This is text");

    D window.alert("This is text");

13. Which of the following correctly calls a function named some_alert() and sends it two string values as parameters?

    A some_alert();

    B some_alert("some","words");

    C some_alert("some","words);

    D SOME_alert("some","words");

14. Which of the following correctly assigns the result of a function named get_something() to a variable named shopping?

    A var shopping=get_something();

    B var shopping="get_something";

    C var Shopping=get_Something;

    D shopping=getsomething;

15. A _____ variable can be used only within the function in which it is declared.

Chapter 5

JavaScript Operators

Key Skills & Concepts

- Understanding the Operator Types

- Understanding Mathematical Operators

- Understanding Assignment Operators

- Understanding Comparison Operators

- Understanding Logical Operators

- Understanding Order of Operations

Operators do much of the work in scripts. In the previous chapters, you have seen examples of the use of the assignment (=) and addition (+) operators. JavaScript offers many other types of operators to perform various operations.

This chapter begins by giving you an introduction to the different types of JavaScript operators. Then, you will learn about each operator and its use in scripts. Finally, you will learn about the order of precedence for operators, which determines which operations are performed before others.

Understanding the Operator Types

An *operator* is a symbol or word in JavaScript that performs some sort of calculation, comparison, or assignment on one or more values. In some cases, an operator provides a shortcut to shorten the code so that you have less to type.

Common calculations include finding the sum of two numbers, combining two strings, or dividing two numbers. Some common comparisons might be to find out if two values are equal or to see if one value is greater than the other. A shortcut assignment operator might be used to assign a new value to a variable so that the variable name does need to be typed twice.

JavaScript uses several different types of operators:

- **Mathematical**   These operators are most often used to perform mathematical calculations on two values. The mathematical operators will probably be the most familiar to you. They use symbols such as +, −, and *.

- **Assignment**   These operators are used to assign new values to variables. As you learned in Chapter 3, one of the assignment operators is the symbol =.

- **Comparison**   These operators are used to compare two values, two variables, or perhaps two longer statements. They use symbols such as > (for "is greater than") and < (for "is less than").

- **Logical** These operators are used to compare two conditional statements (or to operate on one statement) to determine if the result is true and to proceed accordingly. They use symbols such as && (returns true if the statements on both sides of the operator are true) and || (returns true if a statement on either side of the operator is true).

- **Bitwise** These are logical operators that work at the bit level (ones and zeros). They use symbols like ≪ (for left-shifting bits) and ≫ (for right-shifting bits).

- **Special** These are operators that perform other special functions of their own.

In this chapter, you will learn about each of these types of operators. This will be a general overview of the function of each type of operator, so that you will better know the purpose of all the operator types when you put them to use later. To begin, you'll look at the mathematical operators in JavaScript.

Understanding Mathematical Operators

For a mathematical calculation, you use a mathematical operator. The values that you use can be any sort of values you like. For instance, you could use two variables, two numbers, or a variable and a number. A few of these operators are able to perform a task on a single variable's value.

As a quick example, you will remember that you used the addition operator (+) to add two strings together in previous chapters. Here is an example of two string values being combined with the addition operator:

```
window.alert("I begin and "+"this is the end.");
```

You can also use the addition operator when one of the values is a variable, as in this example:

```
var part2="this is the end."
window.alert("I begin and "+part2);
```

The addition operator also works when both values are variables, as in the next example:

```
var part1="I begin and ";
var part2="this is the end."
window.alert(part1+part2);
```

These examples illustrate how you can use many of the mathematical operators with a number of values and/or variables. This allows you some flexibility in the way you code your scripts.

The three operators that work on single values are the increment, decrement, and unary negation operators. The increment and decrement operators are actually shortcuts to adding or subtracting 1, so learning how to use them could save you some coding time.

The mathematical operators and their functions are summarized in Table 5-1. The following sections discuss each operator in more detail.

Operator	Symbol	Function
Addition	+	Adds two values
Subtraction	–	Subtracts one value from another
Multiplication	*	Multiplies two values
Division	/	Divides one value by another
Modulus	%	Divides one value by another and returns the remainder
Increment	++	Shortcut to add 1 to a single number
Decrement	– –	Shortcut to subtract 1 from a single number
Unary negation	–	Makes a positive negative or a negative positive

Table 5-1 The Mathematical Operators

The Addition Operator (+)

As you have seen, the addition operator can be used to combine two strings. It is also used to add numbers in mathematical calculations.

Variables for Addition Results

One use of the addition operator is to add two numbers to get the mathematical result. When adding numerical values, you often assign the result to a variable and use the variable later to make use of the result. For example, to calculate the value of 4 plus 7 and show the result, you could code it like this:

```
var thesum=4+7;          ◀————————Two numbers are added with the addition operator
window.alert(thesum);    ◀———————— The result of the addition is shown as an alert to the viewer
```

The result is an alert that says 11.

To make the example a little more complex, you could change one of the numbers to a variable:

```
var num1=4;              ◀———————— A number is assigned to a variable
var thesum=num1+7;       ◀———————— A number is added to the variable and
window.alert(thesum);             the total is assigned to a new variable
```

The result is the same as the previous example's code: an alert that says 11.

Taking the example one step further, you could make both of the numbers variables:

```
var num1=4;
var num2=7;
var thesum=num1+num2;    ◀———— Two variables are added using
window.alert(thesum);         the addition operator
```

This example allows for the most flexibility, since you can change the values of the two number variables and get a new result without needing to dig deeper into the script to make the change.

Type Conversions in Addition Calculations

It is important to note how JavaScript performs type conversion when working with the mathematical operators. When you use the addition and other mathematical operators, you need to be aware that JavaScript automatically converts different values, like an integer (a nondecimal numeric value) and a float (a decimal numeric value) to the appropriate type. For instance, you might have the following code:

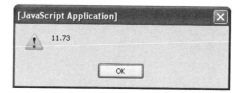

```
var num1=4.73;  ◄──────────── This variable has decimal places
var num2=7;  ◄──────────── This variable is an integer
var thesum=num1+num2;  ◄──────────── The two variables are added, and JavaScript
window.alert(thesum);                will show the answer with the decimal places
```

When the script is run, you will see an alert with the result.

[JavaScript Application]

11.73

OK

JavaScript added the integer and the float together and gave back a float: 11.73. JavaScript does this often, so you need to make sure that you have the right sort of values when you begin adding.

For example, if you add a number and a string, the result will come out as though you had added two strings. Look at this example:

```
var num1=4;  ◄──────────── This variable is a number
var num2="7";  ◄──────────── Oops! This variable is a string, not a number
var thesum=num1+num2;  ◄──────────── When they are added, they are added like strings
window.alert(thesum);
```

This looks as if it would be adding the numbers 4 and 7, since they both appear to be numbers. The trouble is that the 7 is a string in this case, not a number, because it has quotes around it. This causes the 4 to be converted to a string, and then the two strings are added (combined). The result that appears in the alert box may surprise you.

[JavaScript Application]

47

OK

Rather than the expected answer of 11, you get 47. When the two values are added as strings, they are strung together rather than added mathematically. With strings, "4"+"7"=47.

NOTE
Outside of the addition operator (+), the other mathematical operators only work on numbers and will not work on string values.

The other mathematical operators also do conversions, much like the addition operator. You'll see how this can be important later, when you learn how to take user input in your scripts.

The Subtraction Operator (−)

The subtraction operator is used to subtract the value on its right side from the value on its left side, as in mathematics. Here is an example:

```
var theresult=10-3;        ←——————— Two numbers are subtracted
window.alert(theresult);              using the subtraction operator
```

This code simply subtracts 3 (the number on the right of the operator) from 10 (the number on the left of the operator). The result is an alert that says 7.

As with the addition operator, you can use variables to hold the numbers you are working with, as in this example:

```
var num1=10;
var num2=3;
var theresult=num1-num2;    ←——————— Two variables are subtracted
window.alert(theresult);              using the subtraction operator
```

The result is the same as the previous example: an alert that says 7.

The use of variables with mathematical operators also works with the multiplication, division, and modulus operators, which are described in the next sections.

The Multiplication Operator (*)

The multiplication operator is used to multiply the value on its right side by the value on its left side. Again, this is just like mathematical multiplication. The next example shows this operator in action:

```
var num1=4;
var num2=5;
var thetotal=num1*num2;    ←——————— Two variables are multiplied
window.alert(thetotal);              using the multiplication operator
```

Here, you get an alert that says 20, the result of 4 times 5. This operator shouldn't give you too many surprises, so move on to the division operator.

The Division Operator (/)

The division operator is used to divide the value on its left side by the value on its right side. For example, the code 4/2 means 4 divided by 2 and gives the result of 2.

For a JavaScript example of this in action, take a look at this code:

```
var num1=10;
var num2=2;
var theresult=num1/num2;  ◄————————— Two numbers are divided
window.alert(theresult);               using the division operator
```

This gives you an alert that says 5, the result of dividing 10 by 2.

Division by Zero

When you use the division operator, you need to be careful that you do not end up dividing by zero in some way. If you do, the result is going to be either infinity or undefined, depending on your browser. The code that follows shows an example of this happening (although it is unlikely to occur exactly in this way):

```
var num1=10;
var num2=0;
var theresult=num1/num2;  ◄——————————Oh no! On this line you are dividing by zero
window.alert(theresult);  ◄——————————This alert won't be a number
```

If you placed this code in a document, you might see an alert box like this:

To avoid dividing by zero, be careful about what numbers or variables you place on the right side of the division operator.

Type Conversions in Division Calculations

Another thing to remember with division is that if you have two values that do not divide evenly, the result is converted into a float, and thus will have decimal places. The code that follows shows an example:

```
var num1=3;
var num2=4;
var theresult=num1/num2;
window.alert(theresult);
```

The result in this case is 0.75, which is what you see in the alert box. Some browsers may not show the 0 before the decimal, and display just .75 in the alert box instead.

This example shows a simple calculation; but the result can get much longer, depending on the numbers used. In later chapters, you will learn some techniques for formatting the output, so that the viewer doesn't end up seeing something like .75664421004.

The Modulus Operator (%)

The modulus operator is used to divide the number on its left side by the number on its right side, and then give a result that is the integer remainder of the division. Think back to when you learned long division and used remainders as part of the answer rather than converting to decimals or fractions. Dividing 11 by 2 gives 5 with a remainder of 1. The remainder of 1 is what the modulus operator gives you when you write 11%2.

The following is an example in JavaScript:

```
var num1=11;
var num2=2;
var theresult=num1%num2;          Two variables using the modulus
window.alert(theresult);          operator to get the remainder
```

The result is an alert box that shows the value of the remainder, which is 1. If the calculation had no remainder, the result would be 0.

This is the last of the mathematical operators that work on two values at the same time. The next operators work on only one value at a time.

The Increment Operator (++)

The increment operator can be used on either side of the value on which it operates. It increases the value it is operating on by 1, just like adding 1 to the value. The actual result depends on whether the operator is used before or after the value it works on, called the *operand*. This operator is often used with variables, and often within loops (covered in Chapter 6).

The Increment Operator Before the Operand

When the increment operator is placed before the operand, it increases the value of the operand by 1, and then the rest of the statement is executed. Here is an example:

```
var num1=2;
var theresult=++num1;
```

In this case, the variable num1 begins with a value of 2. However, when the code assigns the value to the variable theresult, it increments the value of num1 before the assignment takes place. The increment occurs first because the increment operator is in front of the operand. So, the value of num1 is set to 3 (2+1) and is then assigned to the variable theresult, which gets a value of 3.

The Increment Operator After the Operand

If you place the increment operator after the operand, it changes the value of the operand after the assignment. Consider this example:

```
var num1=2;
var theresult=num1++;
```

As in the previous example, num1 begins with the value of 2. On the next line, the increment operator is used after the operand. This means that the code assigns the current value of num1 to the variable theresult, and *after* that is done, it increments the value of num1. So, only after this assignment is complete do you have a new value for num1. The variable theresult is given a value of 2, and then num1 is changed to 3. If you use num1 after this, it will have a value of 3.

Another way to see how the increment operator works before and after the operand is to run the following script in your browser. Notice what the values are in the first alert and what they are in the second alert.

```
<script type="text/javascript">
num1=2;
result= ++num1;
alert("num1= "+num1+" result= "+result);
num1=2;
result= num1++;
alert("num1= "+num1+" result= "+result);
</script>
```

In the first alert box, you will see num1= 3 result= 3. Since the ++ operator is used before the operand here, the value of num1 is increased by 1 and then assigned to the result variable. In the second alert box, you will see num1= 3 result= 2. This is because the ++ operator is used after the operand, so the value of num1 is increased after it has been assigned to the result variable. The result variable gets a value of 2, but num1 will be increased to 3.

NOTE

Don't worry if the difference between using the increment operator before and after the operand is still not clear to you. When you learn how to use loops in Chapter 6, you will see how the placement of this operator can be quite important.

The Decrement Operator (– –)

The decrement operator works in the same way as the increment operator, but it subtracts 1 from the operand rather than adding 1 to it. As with the increment operator, its placement before or after the operand is important.

If you place the decrement operator before the operand, the operand is decremented, and then the remainder of the statement is executed. Here is an example:

```
var num1=2;
var theresult=--num1;
```

Here, the variable num1 is given a value of 2. In the next line, the code subtracts 1 from num1 and then assigns the result to the variable theresult. Thus, the variable theresult ends up with a value of 1 (2–1).

When you place the operator after the operand, as in the next example, the rest of the statement is executed and the operand is decremented afterward:

```
var num1=2;
var theresult=num1--;
```

This time, the variable theresult is assigned a value of 2, and then num1 is decremented to 1. If you use num1 after this line, it will have a value of 1.

As with the increment operator, the decrement operator becomes important when you work with loops, as you will learn in later chapters.

The Unary Negation Operator (–)

Unary negation is the use of the subtraction sign on only a single operand. This operator creates a negative number or negates the current sign of the number (positive or negative).

Here is an example of assigning a negative value to a number:

```
var negnum=-3;
```

This defines a variable with a value of negative 3. Basically, the operator tells the browser that the 3 is "not positive," because it negates the default sign of positive by placing the negation operator ahead of the number.

You can also use the unary negation operator to help show the addition or subtraction of a negative number, as in this example:

```
var theresult=4+(-3);
```

Notice the parentheses around the –3 portion of the statement. As in math, you can use parentheses to set the order of operations (as you'll learn later in this chapter) or just to clarify the order visually. Here, the parentheses aren't necessary, but they help organize that code so that you can see that it is adding –3 to 4. You could have written this code as well:

```
var theresult=4+-3;
```

This doesn't look as nice, but it still works.

You may be thinking that an even easier way to write the same thing looks like this:

```
var theresult=4-3;
```

You're right, this is the simplest way to write it; but it uses subtraction rather than unary negation.

To make it appear more clearly, you could use this operator on a variable value, which simply negates the sign on the number represented by the variable:

```
var x=4;
var y=3;
var z=-y;
```

This assigns the variable z the unary negated value of y, which is –3.

Now that you've learned about the mathematical operators, it's time to turn to the assignment operators.

Understanding Assignment Operators

Assignment operators assign a value to a variable. They do not compare two items, nor do they perform logical tests.

When you learned about variables in Chapter 3, you saw how the basic assignment operator, the single equal sign (=), is used to give an initial value or a new value to a variable, as in this example:

```
var mytime=0;
```

As you know, this assigns a value of 0 to a variable mytime.

The other assignment operators also give new values to variables, but they do so in slightly different ways because they perform a simple calculation as well. These operators are particularly useful within loops, as you'll learn in later chapters.

Table 5-2 summarizes the assignment operators, which are discussed in more detail in the following sections.

The Assignment Operator (=)

You have been using the direct assignment operator since Chapter 3. It assigns the value on the right side of the operator to the variable on the left side, as in this example:

```
var population=4500;
```

This assigns the value of 4500 to the variable population.

Operator	Symbol	Function
Assignment	=	Assigns the value on the right side of the operator to a variable
Add and assign	+=	Adds the value on the right side of the operator to the variable on the left side, and then assigns the new value to the variable
Subtract and assign	−=	Subtracts the value on the right side of the operator from the variable on the left side, and then assigns the new value to the variable
Multiply and assign	*=	Multiplies the value on the right side of the operator by the variable on the left side, and then assigns the new value to the variable
Divide and assign	/=	Divides the variable on the left side of the operator by the value on the right side, and then assigns the new value to the variable
Modulus and assign	%=	Takes the integer remainder of dividing the variable on the left side by the value on the right side, and assigns the new value to the variable

Table 5-2   The Assignment Operators

The Add-and-Assign Operator (+=)

The += operator adds the value on the right side of the operator to the variable on the left side and then assigns to the variable that new value. In essence, it is a shortcut to writing the type of code shown here:

```
var mymoney=1000;
mymoney=mymoney+1;
```

Here, the variable mymoney is created and assigned a value of 1000. The code then changes the value by assigning it a value of itself plus 1. The value assigned to the mymoney variable is 1001.

Instead of writing the variable name an extra time, you can use the add-and-assign operator to shorten the code. The following code gives the same result as the previous example, but saves a little typing:

```
var mymoney=1000;
mymoney+=1;
```

Using the add-and-assign operator, this code adds 1 (the value on the right) to mymoney (the variable on the left), assigning the new value of 1001 to the variable mymoney.

This operator can be used to add any value, not just 1. For example, you could add 5 in the assignment, as in this example:

```
var mymoney=1000;
mymoney+=5;
```

This time, mymoney ends up with a value of 1005.

You can even use a variable rather than a plain number value on the right side, as in this example:

```
var mymoney=1000;
var bonus=300;
mymoney+=bonus;
```

Here, bonus has a value of 300, which is added to the variable mymoney, and then mymoney is assigned the result of 1300. In this way, the value of the bonus variable can be changed to affect the result of the assignment.

This assignment operator, like the addition mathematical operator, also works with strings. Thus, you could add on to the end of a string value using this operator:

```
var myname="Bob";
myname+="by";
```

This adds the string "by" to the end of the string "Bob", which yields the string "Bobby".

The Subtract-and-Assign Operator (−=)

The −= operator works like the += operator, except that it subtracts the value on the right side of the operator from the variable on the left side. This value is then assigned to the variable. Here is an example of this operator in action:

```
var mymoney=1000;
var bills=800;
mymoney-=bills;
```

This example subtracts the value of the bills variable (800) from the mymoney variable and assigns the result to mymoney. In the end, mymoney has a value of 200. Since this is so similar to the add-and-assign operator, let's move on to the next one (which is also very similar).

The Multiply-and-Assign Operator (*=)

The *= operator multiples the value on the right side of the operator by the variable on the left side. The result is then assigned to the variable. The next example shows this operator at work:

```
var mymoney=1000;
var multby=2;
mymoney*=multby;
```

Here, the variable mymoney is multiplied by the value of the multby variable, which is 2. The result of 2000 is then assigned to the variable mymoney.

The Divide-and-Assign Operator (/=)

The /= operator divides the variable on the left side of the operator by the value on the right side. The result is then assigned to the variable. Here is an example:

```
var mymoney=1000;
var cutpayby=2;
mymoney/=cutpayby;
```

In this example, the variable mymoney is divided by the value of the variable cutpayby, which is 2. The result of 500 is then assigned to the mymoney variable.

The Modulus-and-Assign Operator (%=)

Like the other assignment variables that also perform math, the %= operator does a calculation for the variable assignment. It divides the variable on the left side of the operator by the value on the right side, takes the integer remainder of the division, and assigns the result to the variable. Here is how you might assign a value to the mymoney variable using the modulus-and-assign operator:

```
var mymoney=1000;
var cutpayby=2;
mymoney%=cutpayby;
```

Here, the variable mymoney is divided by the value of the variable cutpayby, which is 2. The result of that is 500 with no remainder, meaning that the end result of the calculation is 0. Thus, 0 is the value that gets assigned to the variable mymoney. (If they start cutting pay like this anyplace, it is probably time to leave!)

Try This 5-1 Adjust a Variable Value

```
pr5_1.html
prjs5_1.js
```

In this project, you create a page that uses some of the mathematical and assignment operators and writes the results on an HTML page.

There is more than one solution that can be used for many of these steps, so feel free to use the method you prefer. You can also try to see which method requires the least typing. Be sure to write the results of each change to the page by using the document.write() command.

Step by Step

1. Create an HTML page and save it as pr5_1.html. Place script tags inside the body section to point to a script named prjs5_1.js.

2. Create an external JavaScript file and save it as prjs5_1.js. Use this file for steps 3–10.

3. Create a variable named paycheck and give it an initial value of 2000.

4. Using only an assignment operator, increase the value of paycheck to 4000.

5. Using a mathematical operator, decrease the value of paycheck to 3500.

6. Using a mathematical operator, decrease the value of paycheck to 0.

7. Using a mathematical operator, increase the value of paycheck to 500.

8. Finally, using an assignment operator, decrease the value of paycheck to 420.

9. After you perform each action, write the value of the paycheck variable on the page.

10. Save the HTML and JavaScript files and view the HTML file in your browser to see the results.

11. A possible solution for the JavaScript file is shown in the following code, but keep in mind there are several ways to achieve the same results:

```
var paycheck=2000;
document.write(paycheck+"<br />");
paycheck+=2000;
document.write(paycheck+"<br />");
paycheck=paycheck-500;
document.write(paycheck+"<br />");
paycheck=paycheck*0;
```

```
document.write(paycheck+"<br />");
paycheck=paycheck+500;
document.write(paycheck+"<br />");
paycheck-=80;
document.write(paycheck+"<br />");
```

Try This Summary

In this project, you were able to use your knowledge of mathematical and assignment operators to display the results of several calculations on a Web page. This project could have been completed in numerous ways, depending on your preferences on the use of the various operators.

Understanding Comparison Operators

Comparison operators are often used with conditional statements and loops in order to perform actions only when a certain condition is met. Since these operators compare two values, they return a value of either true or false, depending on the values on either side of the operator. In later chapters, you will learn how to create a block of code to be performed only when the comparison returns true.

Table 5-3 summarizes the comparison operators, which are discussed in more detail in the following sections.

Operator	Symbol	Function
Is equal to	==	Returns true if the values on both sides of the operator are equal to each other
Is not equal to	!=	Returns true if the values on both sides of the operator are not equal to each other
Is greater than	>	Returns true if the value on the left side of the operator is greater than the value on the right side
Is less than	<	Returns true if the value on the left side of the operator is less than the value on the right side
Is greater than or equal to	>=	Returns true if the value on the left side of the operator is greater than or equal to the value on the right side
Is less than or equal to	<=	Returns true if the value on the left side of the operator is less than or equal to the value on the right side
Strict is equal to	===	Returns true if the values on both sides are equal and of the same type
Strict is not equal to	!==	Returns true if the values on both sides are not equal or not of the same type

Table 5-3 The Comparison Operators

The Is-Equal-To Operator (==)

For the == operator to return true, the values or statements on each side must be equal. They cannot just be close; they must return as equal. If the values do not return as equal, the == operator returns false. Note that a statement such as "4"==4 will return true because JavaScript will convert the number 4 to the string "4" for you. If you want this statement to return false, you should use the strict is-equal-to operator (===), discussed later in this chapter.

The following table shows examples of statements that use the is-equal-to operator, their return values, and the reason why they return true or false.

Comparison	Return Value	Reason
4==4	True	Two equal numbers
(4+2)==(3+3)	True	Result on both sides is 6, and 6 is equal to 6
"my socks"=="my socks"	True	Both strings are exactly the same
("my "+"socks")==("my"+ " socks")	True	Results of string additions return equal string values
4==5	False	4 and 5 are not equal numbers
(4+3)==(2+2)	False	Result on left is 7, result on right is 4, and these are not equal
"My socks"=="my socks"	False	Strings are not exactly alike (capitalization)
("my"+ "socks")==("my " +"socks")	False	Result on left has no space character; result on right does, causing the strings to be unequal

NOTE

You will notice the addition of parentheses around some of the statements in the previous table, as well as in some of the tables that come later. Here, they are used mainly for readability. You will learn more about parentheses and the order of operations near the end of this chapter.

As with the other operators, you can use variables with comparison operators. If the values of the variables are equal, the comparison will return true. Otherwise, it will return false. Suppose that you have declared the following variables:

```
var num1=2;
var num2=5;
var num3=5;
```

The following comparison would return true:

```
num2==num3
```

The next comparison would return false:

```
num1==num3
```

CAUTION

Remember that the is-equal-to operator (==) is for comparison. Be careful not to accidentally use the assignment operator (=) in its place, because it can cause your scripts to work incorrectly.

The Is-Not-Equal-To Operator (!=)

The != operator is the opposite of the == operator. Instead of returning true when the values on each side of the operator are equal, the != operator returns true when the values on each side of it are *not* equal. The only way this operator returns a false value is if it finds that the values on both sides of the operator are equal. The following table shows some examples of statements that use the != operator, their return values, and the reason they return true or false.

Comparison	Return Value	Reason
4!=3	True	4 and 3 are not equal numbers
"CooL"!="cool"	True	Strings do not have the same capitalization, so they are not equal
4!=4	False	4 is equal to 4
"cool"!="cool"	False	Strings are exactly alike, so they are equal

The Is-Greater-Than Operator (>)

When the is-greater-than operator is used, the comparison returns true only if the value on the left side of the operator is greater than the value on the right side. Like the other operators, the > operator works with string values as well as numeric ones. But how can one string be greater than another string?

In the case of strings, a lowercase letter is greater than an uppercase letter, and an uppercase letter is greater than a number. When comparing strings, JavaScript first checks the first letter of the string for a difference. If there is no difference, it moves on to the next character, then the next one, and so on, until it finds a difference or reaches the end of the string. If the two values on each side of the > operator are equal, it returns false. If the value on the right side is greater, this also returns false. The following table shows some examples of statements that use the is-greater-than operator.

Comparison	Return Value	Reason
5>2	True	5 is greater than 2
0>−2	True	0 is greater than negative numbers, such as −2
"a">"A"	True	Lowercase letters in strings are greater than uppercase letters in strings
"A">"1"	True	Letters in strings are greater than numbers in strings
5>7	False	5 is less than 7, not greater
−1>0	False	Negative numbers are less than 0, not greater
"Q">"q"	False	Uppercase letters in strings are less than lowercase letters in strings
"3">"B"	False	Letters are greater than numbers, not less than numbers
2>2	False	These are equal, so the value on the left is not greater

The Is-Less-Than Operator (<)

The is-less-than operator works in reverse from the is-greater-than operator. Rather than returning true when the value on the left is greater, the is-less-than operator returns true when the value on the left side of the operator is less than the value on the right side of the operator. This comparison operator returns false if the value on the left side of the operator is greater than or equal to the value on the right side. Again, you can see how this works by looking at the examples in this table.

Comparison	Return Value	Reason
2<10	True	2 is less than 10
"A"<"a"	True	Uppercase letters in strings are less than lowercase letters in strings
10<2	False	10 is greater than 2, not less
"a"<"A"	False	Lowercase letters in strings are greater than uppercase letters in strings, not less
10<10	False	These are equal, so the value on the left is not less

The Is-Greater-Than-or-Equal-To Operator (>=)

The >= operator is slightly different from the comparison operators you've read about so far. This operator adds an option for the values on both sides to be equal and still have the comparison return true. So, to return true, the value on the left side of the operator must be greater than or equal to the value on the right side. An is-greater-than-or-equal-to comparison will return false only if the value on the left side is less than the value on the right side. The following table shows some examples of statements that use the is-greater-than-or-equal-to operator.

Comparison	Return Value	Reason
5>=2	True	5 is greater than 2
2>=2	True	2 is equal to 2
"a">="A"	True	Lowercase letters are greater than uppercase letters
"A">="A"	True	The strings are equal
1>=2	False	1 is less than 2
"A">="a"	False	Uppercase letters are less than lowercase letters, not greater or equal to

The Is-Less-Than-or-Equal-To Operator (<=)

Much like the >= operator, the <= operator adds the possibility for the values on each side to be equal. With the is-less-than-or-equal-to operator, a value of true is returned if the value on the left side of the operator is less than or equal to the value on the right side of the operator. The following table shows examples of statements that use the is-less-than-or-equal-to operator.

Comparison	Return Value	Reason
2<=5	True	2 is less than 5
2<=2	True	2 is equal to 2
"A"<="a"	True	Uppercase letters are less than lowercase letters
"A"<="A"	True	The strings are equal
5<=2	False	5 is greater than 2, not less than or equal to
"a"<="A"	False	Lowercase letters are greater than uppercase letters, not less than or equal to

The Strict Is-Equal-To Operator (===)

This operator was added in JavaScript 1.5, so in order for it to work, your browser needs to support JavaScript 1.5 (refer to Chapter 1, Table 1-1). For the === operator to return true, the values or statements on each side must be equal and must be of the same type. This means that if you use a statement such as 3==="3", the operator will return false because the value on the left is a number and the value on the right is a string; the values are of different types. Whereas the is-equal-to (==) operator first attempts to convert the values on each side of the operator to the same type and then determines if they are equal, the strict is-equal-to operator automatically returns false if the values are not of the same type. The following table shows examples of statements that use the === operator.

Comparison	Return Value	Reason
4===4	True	Two equal numbers
(4+2)===(3+3)	True	Result on both sides is 6, and both values are numbers
"my socks"==="my socks"	True	Both values are strings, and are exactly the same
("my "+ "socks")===("my"+" socks")	True	Results of string additions return equal string values
4===5	False	4 and 5 are not equal numbers
(4+3)==="7"	False	Result on left is 7, but the 7 on right is a string, so the values are of different types and thus are not equal
"My socks"==="my socks"	False	Strings are not exactly alike (capitalization)
"2"===(1+3)	False	The values are of different types, and 3+1 does not equal 2

The Strict Is-Not-Equal-To Operator (!==)

This operator was added in JavaScript 1.5, so in order for it to work, your browser needs to support JavaScript 1.5 (refer to Chapter 1, Table 1-1). For the !== operator to return true, the values or statements on each side must not be equal or must not be of the same type. This means that if you use a statement such as 3!=="3", the operator will return true because the value on the left is a number and the value on the right is a string; the values are of different types (and thus not strictly equal). Whereas the is-not-equal-to (!=) operator first attempts to convert the values on each side of the operator to the same type and then determines if they are not equal, the strict is-not-equal-to operator (!==) automatically returns true if the values are not of the same type. The following table shows some examples of statements that use the !== operator.

Comparison	Return Value	Reason
4!==3	True	4 and 3 are not equal numbers
"4"!==4	True	Values on each side are of different types
4!==4	False	4 is equal to 4
"cool"!=="cool"	False	Strings are exactly alike, so they are equal

You'll get some practice using this and the other comparison operators when you learn about conditional statements and loops in Chapter 6. Next up are the logical operators, which are also used to check conditions.

Operator	Symbol	Function
AND	&&	Returns true if the statements on both sides of the operator are true
OR	||	Returns true if a statement on either side of the operator is true
NOT	!	Returns true if the statement to the right side of the operator is not true

Table 5-4   The Logical Operators

Understanding Logical Operators

The three logical operators allow you to compare two conditional statements to see if one or both of the statements is true and to proceed accordingly. The logical operators can be useful if you want to check on more than one condition at a time and use the results. Like the comparison operators, the logical operators return either true or false, depending on the values on either side of the operator.

Table 5-4 summarizes the logical operators, which are discussed in the following sections.

The AND Operator (&&)

The logical operator AND returns true if the comparisons on both sides of the && operator are true. If one or both comparisons on either side of the operator are false, a value of false is returned. Some statements that use the AND operator are shown in the following table.

Statement	Return Value	Reason
(1==1)&&(2==2)	True	Comparisons on both sides are true: 1 is equal to 1, and 2 is equal to 2
(2>1)&&(3<=4)	True	Comparisons on both sides are true: 2 is greater than 1, and 3 is less than 4
("A"<="A")&&("c"!="d")	True	Comparisons on both sides are true: "A" is equal to "A", and "c" is not equal to "d"
(1==1)&&(2==3)	False	Comparison on the right is false
("a"!="a")&&("b"!="q")	False	Comparison on the left is false
(2>7)&&(5>=20)	False	Comparisons on both sides are false

The OR Operator (||)

The logical operator OR returns true if the comparison on either side of the operator returns true. So, for this to return true, only one of the statements on one side needs to evaluate to true.

To return false, the comparisons on both sides of the operator must return false. The following table shows some examples of comparisons using the OR operator.

Statement	Return Value	Reason
(2==2)||(3>5)	True	Comparison on the left is true
(5>17)||(4!=9)	True	Comparison on the right is true
(3==3)||(7<9)	True	Both comparisons are true
(4<3)||(2==1)	False	Both comparisons are false
(3!=3)||(4>=8)	False	Both comparisons are false

The NOT Operator (!)

The logical operator NOT can be used on a single comparison to say, "If this is not the case, then return true." Basically, it can make an expression that would normally return false return true, or make an expression that would normally return true return false. The following table shows some examples of this operator at work.

Comparison	Return Value	Reason
!(3==3)	False	3 is equal to 3 is true, but the NOT operator makes this statement false
!(2>5)	True	2 is greater than 5 is false; the NOT operator makes the statement true

Now that you have the regular logical operators down, take a quick look at the bitwise logical operators.

The Bitwise Operators

Bitwise operators are logical operators that work at the bit level, where there is a bunch of ones and zeros. You will not be using them in the examples presented in this book, but you may see them in some scripts on the Web. The following table lists some of the bitwise operators and their symbols. This list is by no means complete, but it should help you spot a bitwise operator if you see one.

Operator	Symbol
AND	&
XOR	^
OR	|
NOT	~
Left Shift	<<
Right Shift	>>
Right Shift (Zero-Fill)	>>>

Operator	Symbol	Purpose
Conditional	?:	Often used as a short if/else type of statement. A condition is placed before the question mark (?) and a value is placed on each side of the colon (:).
Comma	,	Evaluates the statements on both sides of the operator, and returns the value of the second statement.
Delete	delete	Used to delete an object, a property, or an element in an array.
In	in	Returns true if a property is in a specified object.
Instanceof	instanceof	Returns true if an object is of a specified object type.
New	new	Creates an instance of an object.
This	this	Refers to the current object.
Typeof	typeof	Returns a string that tells you the type of the value being evaluated.
Void	void	Allows an expression to be evaluated without returning a value.

Table 5-5   Special Operators

Special Operators

There are a number of special operators in JavaScript that are used to perform specific tasks, or to aid in shortening code. Table 5-5 lists the special operators and their purposes.

Don't be discouraged if many of the terms used in this table look unfamiliar. Objects, arrays, and other unfamiliar terms are discussed in later chapters. Many of these operators will be reintroduced at the appropriate point in the later chapters, where their purpose can be expressed more clearly.

Ask the Expert

Q: Why are there so many assignment operators? If I can write x=x+1 instead of x+=1, why do I need to know about the extra assignment operators?

A: They are provided as shortcuts, so that you don't need to type the variable name a second time in the same line. They also cut down the overall size of the script a bit, which helps with the loading time of the Web page. You can use either method; it just depends on how much you want to trim the script size or avoid extra typing. Also, it is good to know what these assignment operators do, so that you can recognize their purpose in scripts.

Q: Can I use more than one operator at a time in a statement? What will happen if I do that?

A: Yes, you can use multiple operators in a single statement. The operators will be executed according to their precedence in the order of operations, which is covered in the next section.

(continued)

Q: What is with all of the parentheses? Why are they used in some cases but not in others? Is there a reason for them?

A: The parentheses used so far have been added for the readability of the statements. In some cases, it is necessary to use parentheses to get a desired result. This is something else that is covered in the next section.

Q: Are there any common typos that are made with all of these operators?

A: Often, the assignment operator (=) gets used in place of the comparison operator (==) because the second equal sign is left off by accident. Also, forgetting to use && and typing just & is another common typo that can cause trouble in a script. The same sort of mistake can occur with the logical OR (||) and bitwise OR (|) operators.

Understanding Order of Operations

In JavaScript, the operators have a certain order of precedence. In a statement with more than one operator involved, one may be executed before another, even though it is not in that order in the statement. For instance, look at this example:

```
var answer=8+7*2;
```

If you remember how this works in mathematics, you will know that the multiplication is performed first on the 7*2 part of the statement, even though it does not look like that is the right order when you read from left to right. The reason the multiplication is performed first is that the multiplication operator has a higher precedence in the order of operations than the addition operator. So, any multiplication done within a statement will be performed before any addition, unless you override it somehow.

As with math problems, in JavaScript, the way to override the order of operations is through the use of parentheses to set off the portion of the statement that should be executed first. Thus, if you wanted to be sure the addition was performed first in the preceding example, you would write it as shown here instead:

```
var answer=(8+7)*2;
```

If you use more than one set of parentheses or operators of the same precedence on the same level, then they are read from left to right, as in this example:

```
var answer=(8+7)-(4*3)+(8-2);
```

Since the parentheses are all on the same level (not nested), they are read from left to right. The addition and subtraction operators outside the parentheses have the same precedence, and thus are also read from left to right.

Type of Operator	Example of Operators
Parentheses (overrides others)	( )
Unary (mathematical, logical, or bitwise)	− ++ −− ! ~ typeof void delete
Multiplication, division, modulus	* / %
Addition, subtraction	+ −
Shifts (bitwise)	>>> >> <<
Relational comparison	> >= < <= in instanceof
Equality comparison	== != === !==
AND (bitwise)	&
XOR (bitwise)	^
OR (bitwise)		
AND (logical)	&&
OR (logical)			
Conditional	?:
Assignment	= += −= *= /= %= <<= >>= >>>= &= ^= |=
Comma	,

Table 5-6 Operator Precedence, from Highest to Lowest

The precedence of the JavaScript operators is shown in Table 5-6, ranked from highest precedence (done first) to lowest precedence (done last).

As you can see in Table 5-6, parentheses override the other operators. Parentheses are handy when you are unsure of the precedence of various operators or if you want to make something more readable.

Try This 5-2 True or False?

pr5_2.html
prjs5_2.js

This project will allow you to experiment with some of the comparison operators to see how they work. You will create a script that shows an alert stating whether or not a statement or comparison will return true. The script will use a conditional if/else statement, which is explained in detail in the next chapter.

(continued)

Step by Step

1. Create an HTML file and save it as pr5_2.html.

2. Create an external JavaScript file and save it as prjs5_2.js. Use this file for editing in steps 3–13.

3. Insert the code that follows into your JavaScript file:

```
var num1=0;
var num2=0;
if(num1==num2) {
  window.alert("True");
}
else {
  window.alert("False");
}
```

4. Open the HTML page in your browser. You should instantly see an alert saying "True."

5. Change the value of the variable num1 to 5. Resave the JavaScript file and refresh your browser. You should now get an alert saying "False."

6. In the following line of code, change the == operator to the > operator:

```
if(num1==num2) {
```

7. Resave the JavaScript file and refresh your browser. You should get "True" again.

8. Change the value of the variable num2 to 7.

9. Resave the JavaScript file and refresh your browser. You should now get "False" again.

10. In the following line (which you changed in step 4), change the operator to the < operator:

```
if(num1>num2) {
```

11. Resave the JavaScript file and refresh your browser. You should get "True" again.

12. Try to change the value of the num1 variable so that you get an alert that says "False" instead.

13. Try your own tests with the other comparison operators to see what the results will be.

Try This Summary

In this project, you were able to use your knowledge of the comparison operators to create an alert that displayed "True" or "False" depending on whether the comparison statement would return true or false. You were also able to try testing your own variations of values and operators if you desired.

Chapter 5 Self Test

1. A(n) _____ is a symbol or word in JavaScript that performs some sort of calculation, comparison, or assignment on one or more values.

2. _____ operators are most often used to perform mathematical calculations on two values.

3. The _____ operator adds two values.

4. When the increment operator is placed _____ the operand, it increases the value of the operand by 1, and then the rest of the statement is executed.

5. Which of the following is not a JavaScript operator?

   A =

   B ==

   C &&

   D $#

6. What does an assignment operator do?

   A Assigns a new value to a variable

   B Gives a variable a new name

   C Performs a comparison

   D Nothing, because assignment operators are useless

7. The add-and-assign (+=) operator adds the value on the _____ side of the operator to the variable on the _____ side and then assigns to the variable that new value.

8. What does a comparison operator do?

   A Performs a mathematical calculation

   B Deals with bits and is not important right now

   C Compares two values or statements, and returns a value of true or false

   D Compares only numbers, not strings

9. Which of the following comparisons will return true?

   A 4!=3

   B 4==3

   C 4<3

   D 4<=3

10. Which of the following comparisons will return false?

    A 4!=3

    B 3==3

    C 4>3

    D 4<=3

11. The _____ operators allow you to compare two conditional statements to see if one or both of the statements are true and to proceed accordingly.

12. Which of the following statements will return true?

    A (3==3)&&(5<1)

    B !(17>=20)

    C (3!=3)||(7<2)

    D (1==1)&&(2<0)

13. Which of the following statements will return false?

    A !(3<=1)

    B (4>=4)&&(5<=2)

    C ("a"=="a")&&("c"!="d")

    D (2<3)||(3<2)

14. _____ operators are logical operators that work at the bit level.

15. In JavaScript, the operators have a certain order of _____.

Chapter 6

Conditional Statements and Loops

Key Skills & Concepts

- Defining Conditional Statements
- Using Conditional Statements
- Defining Loops
- Using Loops

Now that you have seen how the various operators work in JavaScript, this chapter will instruct you in how to put them to good use. Conditional statements and loops enable you to make use of the mathematical, comparison, and logical operators because they enable you to specify in your code that an action should occur only when a condition is met (conditional statements) or should occur repeatedly (loops).

This chapter begins by introducing you to conditional statements. You will discover what they are and why they are useful to you in scripts. Then, you will learn about all the conditional statement blocks and how to use them. After that, you will learn what loops are and why they are useful to you in scripts. Finally, you will find out about each type of loop and learn how to use it within your scripts.

Defining Conditional Statements

In order to use conditional statements, you need to know what they are and why they are useful to you in your scripts.

What Is a Conditional Statement?

A conditional statement is a statement that you can use to execute a bit of code based on a condition or to do something else if that condition is not met. You can think of a conditional statement as being a little like cause and effect. Perhaps a good way to parallel it would be to use something a parent might say, as in the following text:

```
"If your room is clean, you will get dessert. Otherwise, you will go
to bed early."
```

The first cause would be a clean room, which would have the effect of getting dessert. The second cause would be an unclean room, which would have the effect of an early bedtime.

In your scripts, you may want to create a similar statement. Perhaps something more like the following line:

```
"If a variable named mymoney is greater than 1000, send an alert that
says my finances are OK. Otherwise, send an alert saying I need more
money!"
```

In this case, the first cause would be a variable having a value greater than 1000, which would have the effect of an alert that says things are OK. The second cause is the variable being 1000 or less. If this happens, you get an alert saying you need more money.

As you can see, if you can create statements like these in your scripts, you will be able to do quite a bit more than you have with your scripts in the past.

Why Conditional Statements Are Useful

As you saw in the previous section, a conditional statement can be quite useful to you. Rather than executing every single line of code in the script as is, you could have certain sections of the script only be executed when a particular condition is met. You could even expand that single condition into a combination of conditions that need to be met for parts of the code to run.

With conditionals, you can tell JavaScript to do things such as the following:

- If a variable named yourname is equal to John, then write a line to the page that says hello to John. Otherwise, write a line to the page that says hello to Unknown Surfer and have it be in bold type.

- If a variable named mycar is equal to Corvette or Mustang, then send an alert saying "Cool Car" to the browser. Otherwise, send an alert that says "My car is cooler" to the viewer.

- If a variable named yourname is equal to John and a variable named mycar is equal to Corvette or Mustang, then send an alert that says "John drives a cool car" to the browser. Otherwise, send an alert that says "Unknown Surfer drives a car of some sort" to the viewer.

I don't really drive a Corvette or a Mustang, so that leaves me out of the cool crowd here; however, these examples do show how you can make your scripts more useful by adding a way to check for certain conditions before an action takes place in the script.

You can make statements (such as the preceding statements) as simple or complex as you need them; however, the trick is in how to code all these statements so that JavaScript will interpret them as you intend them to be interpreted. You will learn how to do this shortly, when you read about the various types of conditional statements you can use in your scripts.

Using Conditional Statements

Now that you know what conditional statements are, it's time to look at them in more detail and learn how to code them. You will be looking at the two types of conditional statement blocks used in JavaScript: the if/else statement blocks and the switch statement blocks. To begin, you will look at the if/else statement blocks, which are used quite often in JavaScript.

Using if/else Statement Blocks

While using conditional statements, you will see that they are similar to functions in some ways. Most notable are the curly brackets ({ }) that surround the sections of code that will be executed given a condition. To give you a better understanding of how this works, I will explain the basic structure of an if/else statement block: its block structure, block nesting, and complex comparisons.

The if/else Statement Block Structure

The first thing you must deal with in an if/else statement is the first line, which tells the browser to continue or move along. You begin an if/else statement with the JavaScript keyword if, followed by a comparison in parentheses. The following line shows a sample of the format of the first line:

```
if (comparison here)
```

You replace the *comparison here* text with an actual comparison. To do this, you need to remember the comparison operators from the previous chapter. Suppose you want to see if a variable named boats is equal to 3. The following is how you write the first line of the if/else block:

```
if (boats==3)
```

Remember that a comparison will return a value of true or false. This is where the return value becomes useful. If the comparison of boats==3 returns true, the browser can go on to the next line. If it returns false, the browser begins looking for the else keyword, or the first line of script after the block following the if line is completed.

   If the comparison returns true, you need to make a block of statements after the if line that will be executed. To do this, you use the curly brackets similarly to the way you enclose commands for a function. The following code shows how to add the brackets to enclose the code that will execute if the comparison returns true:

```
if (boats==3) {◄——————————————— The comparison is on the first line
   JavaScript Statements Here ◄——————— This is where JavaScript code will be added
}
```

   If the comparison of boats==3 returns true, the code you place within the brackets will be executed. If it returns false, the code inside the brackets is ignored and the line of code after the closing curly bracket is executed.

   If you wish to use an else block to execute a certain bit of code when the comparison returns false, you place the else keyword on the next line and then follow it with its own set of curly brackets, as in the following code:

```
if (boats==3) {◄————————    The if block begins with the if
   JavaScript Statements Here    keyword and the comparison
}
else {◄———————————————— The else block begins with the else keyword
   JavaScript Statements Here
}
```

   Now you can see the entire if/else block and how it works to execute one of the two blocks of code within curly brackets. If the comparison returns true, the block of code following the if statement is executed. If the comparison returns false, the block of code following the else keyword is executed.

You can now create an entire block with code. Suppose you want to send an alert that says "You have the right number of boats" if the variable boats is equal to 3. If it is not, you want to send an alert that says "You do not have the right number of boats" instead. The code for this is shown in the following example:

```
                                    This alert is executed if the comparison on the first line returns true
if (boats==3) {
   window.alert("You have the right number of boats");◄──┘
}
else {
   window.alert("You do not have the right number of boats");◄──┐
}
                     This alert is executed if the comparison on the first line returns false
```

Now that you have the statements set up, you need to know whether or not the comparison returns true so that you can determine which block of code is executed. To do so, you need to declare the boats variable and assign it a value before the comparison takes place. This will give you the value to determine what happens in the script. See if you can guess which block of code is executed (first or second) if you use the following code:

```
var boats=3;
if (boats==3) {
   window.alert("You have the right number of boats");
}
else {
   window.alert("You do not have the right number of boats");
}
```

If you guessed the first code block would be executed, you got it! Since the variable boats is equal to 3, the comparison boats==3 returns true. Since it returns true, the first code block is executed and the code block after the else keyword is ignored. You get the alert that says "You have the right number of boats" and nothing else.

CAUTION

Be careful when typing the variable assignments (=) and the is-equal-to comparisons (==), as they can be easily reversed by accident and cause problems with your scripts.

Now take look at how to set up the statement so that you have the opposite result. The following code will cause the comparison to return false:

```
var boats=0;◄──────────  Assigning the variable a value of 0 will
if (boats==3) {          cause the comparison to return false
   window.alert("You have the right number of boats");
}
else {
   window.alert("You do not have the right number of boats");
}
```

With the value of the variable boats at 0, the comparison boats==3 will return false; thus, the first code block is ignored and the code block after the else statement is executed instead. This time you get the alert that says "You do not have the right number of boats," while the alert in the first block is ignored.

Now that you know the basic structure of the if/else statement block, you are ready to look at the technique of nesting one block within another.

Block Nesting

If you *nest* something, you are basically putting one structure inside another structure of the same or a similar nature. With the if/else statement blocks, you are able to nest other if/else statements within the first block after the comparison (the "if block") or within the second block after the else keyword (the "else block").

For example, maybe you would like the browser to execute a statement such as the following: "If a variable named have_cookbook is equal to yes, and if a variable named meatloaf_recipe is equal to yes, send an alert that says 'Recipe found' to the browser. If have_cookbook is equal to yes, but meatloaf_recipe is not equal to yes, then alert 'Have the book but no recipe' to the viewer; otherwise, send an alert that says 'You need a cookbook' to the browser."

This is a somewhat long and complex statement, but you can accomplish what you are after by nesting an if/else statement within the if block of another if/else statement.

To see how this works, consider the following example, which puts the previous statement into JavaScript form:

```
if (have_cookbook=="yes") {
  if (meatloaf_recipe=="yes") {
    window.alert("Recipe found");
  }
  else {
    window.alert("Have the book but no recipe");
  }
}
else {
  window.alert("You need a cookbook");
}
```

This if/else block is nested within an outside if block

Oh no, nesting an if block requires curly brackets all over the place! To help you figure out what is going on with this piece of code, I will break it down into its individual parts.

The first thing you get is the main (first, or outermost) if block. You use it to find out whether the variable have_cookbook is equal to yes or not. If this comparison returns true, you move along into the if block; however, the next thing you find is another if block! This is the nested if block, which means it is inside the outside if block. In the nested block, you check whether the variable meatloaf_recipe is equal to yes or not. If this returns true, you finally are able to do something, which is to send the "Recipe found" alert.

When the nested if block is finished, you see that it has an else block to go with it in case the comparison meatloaf_recipe=="yes" returned false. If it had returned false, the browser would then go to this else block and execute the code within it. In the preceding code example, the comparison on the outside block (have_cookbook=="yes") returned true, but the comparison on the nested block (meatloaf recipe=="yes") returned false. So, the nested else block is executed, sending the "Have the book but no recipe" alert.

After this nested else block, you see what looks like an extra closing curly bracket; however, this closing bracket is actually used to close the outside if block that contains all of this nested code. Looking at how the code is indented will help you see which brackets are closing which blocks. This is where using indentions or tabs can be helpful in your code, because—as opposed to the code being all in a straight line up and down—indentions can make the code easier to read.

Finally, you get to the outside else block. This is the block that is executed only if the first comparison (have_cookbook=="yes") returns false. If that comparison returns false, all the code within that outside if block is ignored (you never get to the nested if/else block) and the browser moves on to this outside else block. In this case, you get the "You need a cookbook" alert sent to the viewer.

The following example uses the same if/else code used in the preceding code example, but this time the variables are defined that will be used by the conditional statements. Both variables are given a value of yes. See if you can follow the code and name the alert that will show up on the screen when it is executed.

```
var have_cookbook="yes";
var meatloaf_recipe="yes";

if (have_cookbook=="yes") {
  if (meatloaf_recipe=="yes") {
    window.alert("Recipe found");
  }
  else {
    window.alert("Have the book but no recipe");
  }
}
else {
  window.alert("You need a cookbook");
}
```

The alert you should have chosen is the "Recipe found" alert. When the first comparison returns true, you are sent to the nested if block. Since the comparison for the nested if block also returns true, you execute the code within that block, which sends the "Recipe found" alert to the browser.

You can nest if/else statements within the outside else block, or you can even nest statements inside both the outside if block and the outside else block. If you want nested statements inside both blocks, you could expand your script a bit. The following example code expands on the code you already have, but adds an additional nested if/else statement within the outside else block:

```
if (have_cookbook=="yes") {
   if (meatloaf_recipe=="yes") {
     window.alert("Recipe found");
   }
   else {
     window.alert("Have the book but no recipe");
   }
}
else {
   if (have_web_access=="yes") {
     window.alert("Find the recipe on the Web");
   }
   else {
     window.alert("You need a cookbook");
   }
}
```

This if/else block is nested within an outside if block

This if/else block is nested within an outside else block

Although it hasn't been declared, you will notice the addition of a new variable: have_web_access. This is used to determine whether the script should tell the viewer to find the recipe on the Web or to buy a cookbook. Keep in mind that in a live script, all the variables need to be declared before being used.

This time, if the first comparison (have_cookbook=="yes") returns false, you are sent to the outside else block; however, the outside else block now has a nested if/else statement within it, so the browser now goes to the inside if block and looks at that comparison (have_web_access="yes"). If it returns true, the code within the nested if block is executed and you get the "Find the recipe on the Web" alert. If the comparison returns false, the browser moves on to the nested else block and executes that code instead. In that case, you would get the "You need a cookbook" alert.

The last thing you should know about nesting is that you can nest as many blocks as you want inside of other blocks. Rather than just nesting one if/else statement inside another, you could have a second nesting inside that statement, a third, or as many as you can track without going insane. To keep the example from getting out of hand, the following code just nests one more time within the if block of the previous code:

```
if (have_cookbook=="yes") {
   if (meatloaf_recipe=="yes") {
     if (is_moms_meatloaf=="yes") {
       window.alert("Recipe found");
     }
     else {
       window.alert("Recipe found, but not like what mom makes");
     }
   }
}
```

This if/else block is nested within a nested if block

```
    else {
      window.alert("Have the book but no recipe");
    }
  }
}
else {
  if (have_web_access=="yes") {
    window.alert("Find the recipe on the Web");
  }
  else {
    window.alert("You need a cookbook");
  }
}
```

Now there is an if/else block within an if block within an if block. As you can see, yet another variable, is_moms_meatloaf, was added to check for an even more specific recipe. You could keep going on and on like this, until you cannot take it anymore; however, this should be enough to allow you to build on it later if you need to do so.

Now that you know a bit about nesting, you need to look at one more detail before you leave the if/else topic in this section. You need to learn about making more complex comparisons in your if/else statements.

Complex Comparisons

In addition to making a simple comparison such as $x==2$ or $y<3$, you can also build more complex comparisons using the logical operators discussed in Chapter 5. As you may recall, that chapter presented some of these comparisons in a form similar to the following example:

```
(2==2)||(3<5)
```

In Chapter 5, the only concern was whether the comparison would return true or false, and not with how to add it to an if/else statement. Notice the parentheses around each comparison. They are there mainly for organization; but given the order of operations, you could write the comparison as

```
2==2||3<5
```

The problem here is that this is harder to read, so it would be difficult to determine whether there is a problem with the code if you need to debug it later.

Recall that the first line of the if/else statement uses parentheses to enclose the comparison. If you write your complex comparisons without the organizational parentheses, as in the previous example, you could have the first line look like the line of code shown here:

```
if (2==2||3<5)
```

Although this is easy to type, it's pretty difficult to read because you are not sure if it should be read as "if 2 is equal to 2 or 3 and is less than 5" or as "if (2 is equal to 2) or (3 is less than 5)." If you add the parentheses for organization, it becomes easier to read; but you must be careful that you nest them correctly. The following example code shows the addition of parentheses for organization:

```
if ((2==2)||(3<5))
```

Which form you use will come down to personal preference. For now, this chapter uses the method with the extra parentheses for organization. It should make reading the code from the book easier for you.

Now you can create scripts that allow for more values to be included or allow a specific range of values that will return true. Suppose you want to show an alert when a variable named num1 is greater than 2 but less than 11, and another alert when num1 is not in that range. You could use the following code:

```
if ((num1>2)&&(num1<11)) {          This complex comparison allows a
   window.alert("Cool number");      specific range of values to return true
}
else {
   window.alert("Not a cool number");
}
```

Your comparison is saying, "If num1 is greater than 2 and num1 is less than 11." If that comparison returns true, then you see the "Cool number" alert. If it returns false, you get the "Not a cool number" alert instead.

Of course, you can make the comparison line as complex as you want it to be. You can add *and* and *or* logical operators in one long line until you get what you need…or have a nervous breakdown. The following example adds an extra stipulation to the comparison to see if num1 is equal to 20:

```
if ((num1>2)&&(num1<11)||(num1==20)) {    This complex comparison adds an
   window.alert("Cool number");            additional number that would cause the
}                                           comparison to return true
else {
   window.alert("Not a cool number");
}
```

Now, the comparison allows the numbers greater than 2, the numbers less than 11, and the number 20 to give the "Cool number" alert. The comparison now reads, "If num1 is greater than 2 *and* num1 is less than 11 *or* num1 is equal to 20." You could keep adding information to create more numbers that will return true, or even additional number ranges that will return true.

Of course, to see the preceding code in action, you would need to declare the num1 variable and assign it a value. See if you can figure out which alert will show up if the following code is used:

```
var num1=1;
if ((num1>2)&&(num1<11)||(num1==20)) {
   window.alert("Cool number");
}
```

```
else {
  window.alert("Not a cool number");
}
```

Yes, you are stuck with the "Not a cool number" alert because the number 1 just doesn't cut it here (1 is not within the accepted range of numbers for the condition to return true). Of course, you can change it to something that fits to get the "Cool number" alert instead.

CAUTION
Complex expressions using && and || can cause unintended results in your script if not grouped correctly. For instance, the comparison ((u==v && w==x) || y==z) is going to be different than if it were grouped as (u==v && (w==x || y==z)). The first one will return true if u is equal to v and w is equal to x, or if y is equal to z. The second one will return true if u is equal to v and if either w is equal to x or y is equal to z.

Now that you have the if/else statement down, take a look at another conditional block you can use to make some things a bit easier.

Using the switch Statement
The switch statement allows you to take a single variable value and execute a different block of code based on the value of the variable. If you wish to check for a number of different values, this can be an easier method than the use of a set of nested if/else statements.

The first line of a switch statement would have the following syntax:

```
switch (varname)
```

You replace *varname* with the name of the variable you are testing. You could also replace it with some other sort of expression, such as the addition of two variables or some similar calculation, and have it evaluate. For now, you will just use a variable that has been assigned a value before the switch statement begins. In your later scripts, you may use some more complex switch statements.

Now, you need to see the general syntax for a full switch statement. The following code is an example of how a switch statement looks:

```
var thename="Fred";                    The switch statement begins based on
switch (thename) {◄───────────── the value of the thename variable
  case "George" :◄──────────────────────────────── A case is given with code to
    window.alert("George is an OK name");           execute below it if it is true
    break;
  case "Fred" :◄─────────── This is the case that is true and will be executed
    window.alert("Fred is the coolest name!");
    window.alert("Hi there, Fred!");                The break statement tells the browser
    break;◄──────────────────────────────────────── to leave the switch code block
  default :◄──The default is used when none of the cases is true
    window.alert("Interesting name you have there");
}
```

First, this example declares and assigns a variable named thename; it is given a value of Fred. Next, the switch statement begins, using the variable thename as the basis for comparison. Then, the block is opened with a curly bracket, followed by the first case statement. Written like this, it is saying, "If thename is equal to George then execute the commands after the colon at the end of this line." If thename were equal to George, you would get an alert.

Next you see the break statement, which tells the browser to exit the code block and move on to the next line of code after the block. You use the break statement in the switch block to be sure only one of the case sections is executed; otherwise, you run the risk of having all the cases executed following the one that returned true, because, by default, the browser would continue to the next statement rather than exit the block entirely even though it finds one of the cases to be true. To be sure that the browser exits the block, you add the break statement.

If you get back to the script, you see that thename is not equal to George, so this case is skipped; however, the next comparison returns true because thename is equal to Fred in the script. Thus, the set of statements in this case block will be executed. Note that two lines of JavaScript code appear before the break statement here. This shows that you could have any number of lines within a case, as long as you remember to end with the break statement.

Finally, you see the keyword default. This is used in the event that none of the case statements returns true. If this happens, the default section of code will be executed. Notice that you don't need the break statement after the default section of code, because it is at the end of the switch block anyway, so the browser will exit the block afterward, eliminating the need for the break statement.

Sometimes you want the browser to execute the statement afterward. A common use is to have multiple case statements before the code to be executed:

```
case "Fred":
case "Frederick":
case "Freddie":
alert("Fred is an OK name");
break;
```

This use of the break statement allows you to execute several cases before breaking, rather than being limited to a single case and then breaking.

Now that you have learned how to use the switch statement, take a look at the conditional operator (which was introduced in Table 5-5, "Special Operators," in Chapter 5 and will make more sense now that you have experience with if/else blocks).

Using the Conditional Operator

The conditional operator (often called the ternary operator) is one that can be used as a short way to assign a value based on a condition. For instance, you might decide you want to assign a value to a variable based on the result of a conditional statement. You could do it using the following code:

```
var mynum=1;
var mymessage;
if (mynum==1) {
  mymessage="You win!";
```

```
}
else {
  mymessage="Sorry! Try again!";
}
```

This works, and gives mymessage a value of "You win!" since mynum is equal to 1. However, the conditional operator allows you to shorten the amount of code required for this type of test. It allows you to place a condition before the question mark (?) and place a possible value on each side of the colon (:), like this:

```
varname = (conditional) ? value1 : value2;
```

JavaScript evaluates the conditional statement and if the statement returns true, the value on the left side of the colon (*value1* here) is assigned to the variable. If the statement returns false, the value on the right side of the colon (*value2* here) is assigned to the variable.

To apply this to our previous example, we could rewrite the entire piece of code as follows:

```
var mynum=1;
var mymessage;
mymessage = (mynum==1) ? "You win!" : "Sorry! Try Again!";
```

This works the same way as the previous if/else block, but allows you to write the code with a lot less typing (lessening the size of the script).

It should be noted that you can also use another method to shorten the script if using the conditional operator is not comfortable for you. Since JavaScript is lenient, you can omit the curly braces anytime you have only one statement to execute in a code block.

For instance, the following code could also be used as a shorter version of the script:

```
var mynum=1;
var mymessage;
if (mynum==1)
  mymessage="You win!";
else
  mymessage="Sorry! Try again!";
```

Also, since JavaScript is not concerned with white space or line breaks between tokens, you can also further shorten this to have the entire if/else block on one line:

```
var mynum=1;
var mymessage;
if (mynum==1) mymessage="You win!"; else mymessage="Sorry! Try again!";
```

For now, you will want to use the method that you feel most comfortable using. As you gain scripting experience, the conditional operator will be a handy way to shorten your code and help you optimize the size of your scripts when this type of comparison is needed.

The conditional statements you have used in this chapter will allow you to do much more with your scripts now that you know how to use them. You will be using these extensively in later chapters, because they can help you code more complex scripts that perform more tasks than you could without them.

Ask the Expert

Q: Do I need to use curly brackets on every if/else block? I have seen them used in code on the Web without the brackets. Why?

A: There is a shortcut that allows you to omit the curly brackets if you are only going to execute a single JavaScript statement in the if block and the else block. If you are going to execute more than one statement, the curly brackets should be used. For example, look at the following code:

```
if (x==2) {
   window.alert("Hi");
}
else {
   window.alert("Bye");
}
```

Since only one JavaScript statement is used inside the code blocks, you can use a shortcut that allows you to omit the brackets:

```
if (x==2)
   window.alert("Hi");
else
   window.alert("Bye");
```

As you can see, it can save you some typing (which is why you see this technique often in scripts on the Web). Keep in mind, however, that if you decide to add more statements within one of the blocks, you will need to add the brackets back around the code in that block.

Q: Why I am bothering with conditional statements if all I can do is assign the variable a value and then test it? If I already know what the value of the variable is, why use a conditional?

A: In later chapters, you will get to the point where you are getting information from the viewer. This information can vary depending on the viewer (for example, if the viewer needs to enter his/her name into a text box or a prompt), thus making the conditional blocks more useful since you will be able to perform one action for one viewer, and another task for a different user. With user input, you won't know the value of the variable beforehand, and you will need to handle the possibilities using conditional blocks.

Q: Why is the conditional operator often referred to as *the* ternary operator?

A: The conditional operator is the only JavaScript operator that takes three operands. Because of this, it is often called *the* ternary operator rather than one of several ternary operators. If JavaScript makes changes to add new operators in the future, this reference to the conditional operator may change.

Q: I don't like the idea of nesting one block inside of another. Can I just forget about it and never nest anything?

A: You could do that, but it will severely limit the scripts you code later because you won't be able to use one comparison statement within another (which is sometimes necessary in more complex scripts). Nesting allows you to perform more complex tasks, as you will see in later scripts. It is best to learn nesting so that you can make use of it when you need to.

Try This 6-1   Construct an if/else Block

```
pr6_1.html
prjs6_1.js
```

This project will help you learn how to construct an if/else block of your own. You will be given some variables to test, but you will need to write the if/else block.

Step by Step

1. Create an HTML page and save it as pr6_1.html. Add script tags to point to an external JavaScript file named prjs6_1.js.

2. Create an external JavaScript file and save it as prjs6_1.js. Use this file for steps 3–6.

3. Create a variable named thesport and assign it the following string value: Golf

4. Create a variable named myfood and assign it the following string value: Pizza

5. Based on the thesport variable, create a block of code that will send an alert saying "Cool Sport!" if the variable is equal to "Football"; otherwise, it will send an alert that says "That sport might be cool."

6. Based on the myfood variable, create a block of code that will send an alert saying "My favorite food!" if the variable is equal to "Pizza"; otherwise, it will send an alert that says "That food sounds OK I guess."

7. Save the JavaScript file and the HTML file and view the HTML page in your browser.

8. You should get an alert saying "That sport might be cool." When you click OK, you should then get another alert saying "My favorite food!"

(continued)

Try This Summary

In this project, you used your new skills with if/else conditional statements to create a script that pops up different alerts based on the value of a variable. You did this with two different variables: the first conditional returns false and gives the alert in the else statement, while the second conditional returns true and gives the alert in the if statement.

Defining Loops

To begin using loops, you will want to know what loops are, what they can do, and why they can be useful to you in your scripts.

What Is a Loop?

A loop is a block of code that allows you to repeat a section of code a certain number of times, perhaps changing certain variable values each time the code is executed. By doing this, you are often able to shorten certain tasks into a few lines of code, rather than writing the same line over and over again within the script and tiring your fingers.

Why Loops Are Useful

Loops are useful because they allow you to repeat lines of code without retyping them or using cut and paste in your text editor. This not only saves you the time and trouble of repeatedly typing the same lines of code, but also avoids typing errors in the repeated lines. You are also able to change one or more variable values each time the browser passes through the loop, which again saves you the time and trouble of typing a line that is only slightly different than the previous line.

As a simple example, suppose you wanted to write a sentence onto a Web page ten times in a row using JavaScript. To do this normally, you might have to write something like the following:

```
document.write("All this typing gets tiring after a while!<br />");
document.write("All this typing gets tiring after a while!<br />");
document.write("All this typing gets tiring after a while!<br />");
document.write("All this typing gets tiring after a while!<br />");
document.write("All this typing gets tiring after a while!<br />");
document.write("All this typing gets tiring after a while!<br />");
document.write("All this typing gets tiring after a while!<br />");
document.write("All this typing gets tiring after a while!<br />");
document.write("All this typing gets tiring after a while!<br />");
document.write("All this typing gets tiring after a while!<br />");
```

Ouch! Cut and paste can make the task easier, but it would still be a bit tedious, especially if you decide to write the sentence 50 times instead. With a loop, you could write that document.write() statement just one time and then adjust the number of times you want it to be written. It would be something like the following example. This is not actual code, but you will see the actual code needed to repeat a statement multiple times when you look at the loop structures in more detail in the next section, "Using Loops."

```
Do this block 10 times {
   document.write("I only had to type this once!<br />");
}
```

Of course, you will replace the "Do this block 10 times" text with an actual statement that JavaScript will understand. You will see what statements you can use to form loops in the following section.

Using Loops

In order to see how loops can really be helpful to you, you need to take a look at the different loop structures that you can use in JavaScript. The loop structures covered in this section are the *for*, *while*, and *do while* loops.

for

To use a for loop in JavaScript, you need to know how to code the basic structure of the loop and how to nest a for loop within another for loop. To begin, take a look at the basic structure of a for loop.

Structure of a for Loop

The structure of a for loop is very similar to that of the conditional blocks. The only major differences are that a loop serves a different purpose and, as a result, the first line is different. After that, you use the familiar curly brackets to enclose the contents of the loop.

The first line of a for loop would look similar to the following line:

```
for (var count=1;count<11;count+=1)
```

The first thing you see is the for keyword. This is followed by a set of parentheses with three statements inside. These three statements tell the loop how many times it should repeat by giving it special information.

The first statement (*var count*=1) creates a variable named *count* and assigns it an initial value of 1. This initial value can be any number. This number is used as a starting point for the number of times the loop will repeat. Using the number 1 will help you see more easily the number of times the loop will repeat. The preceding code begins the loop with *count* having a value of 1. Note that if the count variable had been initialized earlier in the script, the var keyword would not be needed here.

The next statement (*count*<11) tells the loop when to stop running. The loop will stop running based on this conditional statement. The condition here is to stop only when the variable *count* is no longer less than 11. This means that if you add 1 to the value of *count* each time through the loop, the loop's last run-through will be when *count* is equal to 10. When 1 is added to 10, it becomes 11; and that doesn't pass the conditional test, so the loop stops running.

The last statement in the set (*count* +=1) determines the rate at which the variable is changed and whether it gets larger or smaller each time. In the preceding code, you add 1 to the variable each time you go back through the loop. Remember, the first time through, the variable has been set to 1. Since you add 1 each time, the variable will have a value of 2 the second time through, 3 the third time through, and so on, until the variable is no longer less than 11.

To finish the structure, you insert the curly brackets to enclose the code that you wish to use within the loop. An example of the full structure of a for loop is shown in the following code:

```
for (count=1; count<11; count+=1) {      This line determines how many
                                          times the loop will run
   JavaScript Code Here          The JavaScript code for the loop
}                                 will be inside the brackets here
```

Now, you just need to add a real variable and some JavaScript code to be executed, and you will have a full for loop put together. To do this, you'll begin with a script to write a sentence to the page ten times. Now that you can use a loop, you need to write the sentence itself only once, rather than ten times in a row. The following example code shows how this can be done using a for loop:

```
for (var count=1;count<11;count+=1) {
   document.write("I am part of a loop!<br />");      This line of code is looped
}                                                      through ten times
```

The *count* variable is going to begin counting at 1, since it is assigned an initial value of 1. You are adding 1 to it each time through the loop. When the *count* variable has a value that is no longer less than 11, the loop will stop. In this case, the *count* will run from 1 to 10, thus running the loop ten times.

When 1 is added the next time the for statement is hit, the value of the *count* variable is 11, which is no longer less than 11; thus, the browser will skip over the loop and continue to the next line of code after the closing curly bracket for the loop. The <br /> tag is used in the document.write command to be sure that each sentence will have a line break after it and will not write the next sentence on the same line.

To see this work on a page, you can add the script tags and insert an external JavaScript file into the body section of an HTML page. Create a JavaScript file named loops01.js, add the following code, and save the file. Add the necessary script tags to an HTML document and save it as loops01.html.

```
document.write("Get ready for some repeated text.<br />");
for (var count=1;count<11;count++) {
   document.write("I am part of a loop!<br />");      This loop will display the text
}                                                      repeatedly in the HTML document
document.write("Now we are back to the plain text.");
```

Here, a slight change was made to increment the *count* variable. Rather than typing count+=1, the increment operator (++) was used. When simply adding one to the variable, the increment operator can be a handy way to shorten the code. However, if you wanted to increment the variable by 2 or more, the add-and-assign operator would still need to be used (that is, count+=2).

The page represented by the preceding code has a short line of text that is followed by your repeating line of text. The page ends with a note, "Now we are back to the plain text." Figure 6-1 shows how this will appear in the browser window when viewed. Notice that the sentence "I am part of a loop!" is repeated ten times.

Now that you can do a basic loop, you are ready to add something to it that will make the loop even more useful. Within the loop, you can use the value of the count variable (or whatever variable is used) to do various things.

One thing you can do (this will become more apparent when you get to arrays later) is to make use of the fact that the variable is changing each time. With the variable going up by 1

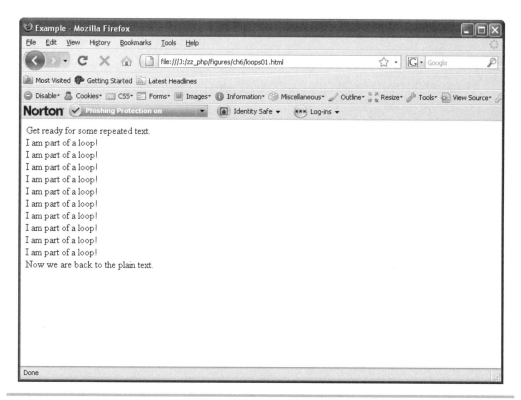

Figure 6-1 The loop displays the line of text ten times

each time through, you could use a loop to number the sentences from 1 to 10 and make the lines more readable. The following code does this:

```
document.write("Get ready for some repeated text.<br />");
for (var count=1;count<11;count++) {
  document.write(count+". I am part of a loop!<br />");
}
document.write("Now we are back to the plain text.");
```

Now the variable is used to add line numbers each time the code is repeated

In the preceding code, you just added the value of the count variable to your string at the beginning. The period before the sentence will make the line of text appear with a period after the number, a space, and your sentence on each line. Figure 6-2 shows how the script would look in the browser with this addition.

Before you move on to the while loop, you need to learn one more thing about the for loop. Just as with the if/else blocks, a for loop can be nested within another for loop.

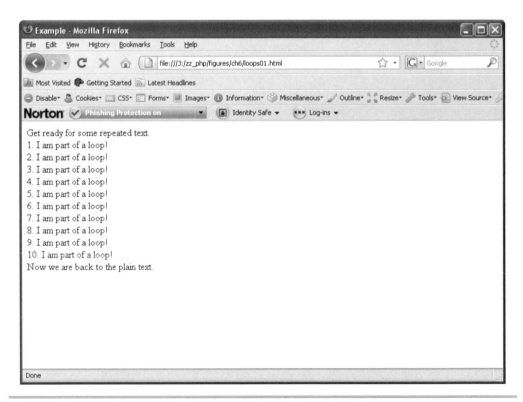

Figure 6-2 Now the repeated lines are numbered from 1 to 10

Block Nesting

Yes, you now have to deal with nested loops. As with if/else blocks, you can nest as many levels deep as you can handle. For now, you will just nest one loop within another. The following example shows a for loop within a for loop:

```
for (var count=1;count<11;count++) {
  document.write(count+". I am part of a loop!<br />");
  for (var nestcount=1;nestcount<3;nestcount+=1) {
    document.write("I keep interrupting in pairs!<br />");
  }
}
```

This nested loop interrupts the outside loop

CAUTION

Be careful when you nest loops to be sure that each nested loop has its own counter on its first line, such as for(count=1;count<11;count+=1). A counter will need to be unique to its own loop in most cases. Also, many errors may occur if the curly brackets are not included or paired correctly.

Now you get a loop that interrupts your outer loop text with text of its own. Each time you go through the outer loop, you write out the "I am part of a loop!" line. Then, you encounter another loop that writes out "I keep interrupting in pairs!" to the screen.

The inner loop is set up to repeat twice; so each time you have one sentence from the outside loop, it is immediately followed by two sentences from the inside loop. In order to see this more clearly, consider the following example, which updates the code you used earlier in the loops01.js file:

```
document.write("Get ready for some repeated text.<br />");
for (var count=1;count<11;count++) {
  document.write(count+". I am part of a loop!<br />");
  for (var nestcount=1;nestcount<3;nestcount++) {
    document.write("I keep interrupting in pairs!<br />");
  }
}
document.write("Now we are back to the plain text.");
```

Figure 6-3 illustrates how this nested loop affects the appearance of the page in the browser. You can now see how nested loops are useful to add even more information along the way if you need to do so.

To further complicate matters, you can also nest different types of blocks inside one another. For example, you can put an if/else statement block inside a loop, or a loop inside the if block or the else block of an if/else statement. The following example creates an if/else block within a for loop:

```
for (var count=1;count<11;count++) {
  if (count==5) {
    document.write("The loop is halfway done!<br />");
```

```
    }
    else {
        document.write("I am part of a loop!<br />");
    }
}
```

In this case, the browser will check whether or not the count variable has a value of 5. If it does, the browser will print a different message to the screen than the browser would otherwise. You can best see the effects of this by adjusting your JavaScript file to have the following code:

```
document.write("Get ready for some repeated text.<br />");
for (var count=1;count<11;count++) {
    if (count==5) {
        document.write("The loop is halfway done!<br />");
    }
    else {
        document.write("I am part of a loop!<br />");
    }
}
document.write("Now we are back to the plain text.");
```

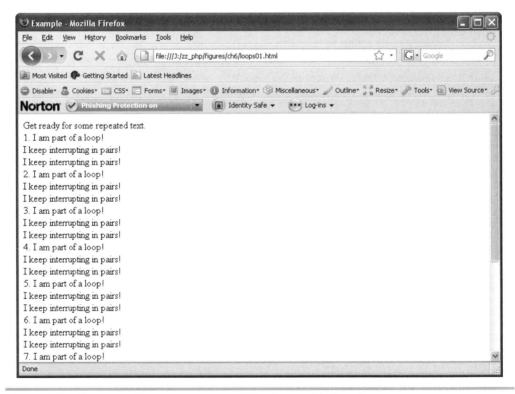

Figure 6-3 The nested loop inserts text within the outside loop's text

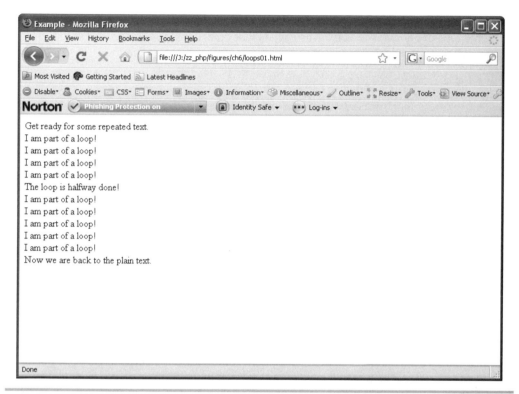

Figure 6-4   The nested if/else block causes the fifth line to be different from the other lines

Figure 6-4 shows the result of this code when run in the browser. Notice how the fifth line is different based on the conditional statement within the loop.

As you can see, you can do quite a bit with nesting. Using the same techniques you just learned, you can nest all the other statement blocks covered in this book; therefore, I won't be as detailed about the nesting techniques with the rest of the statements that are covered.

Now that you have seen how to use a for loop, take a look at how you can loop a little differently using a while loop.

while

A while loop just looks at a short comparison and repeats until the comparison is no longer true. To begin, take a look at the general syntax for the first line of a while loop:

```
while (count<11)
```

The while statement does not create a variable the way a for statement can. When using a while loop, you must remember to declare the variable you wish to use and assign it a value before you insert it into the while loop.

Although the less-than comparison is probably the most common, you can use any other type of comparison you wish. This includes the complex comparisons with the logical operators. So, you could have a first line like the following example:

```
while ((count>4)&&(count<11))
```

This time, the loop runs only while the variable is greater than 4 and less than 11. For the loop to run at all, the initial value of the variable would need to be within that range; otherwise, the loop would be skipped entirely.

The following code shows the general structure of a full while loop so that you can see how it looks:

```
var count=1; ◄———————— A variable is assigned a value to count the loop
while (count<6) { ◄———————— The while statement begins with a comparison
   JavaScript Code Here
   count++; ◄———————— The count variable is adjusted so that
}                       you do not have an endless loop
```

First, notice that the value of 1 is assigned to the variable count before the loop begins. This is important to do so that the loop will run the way you expect it to run. This loop is set up to repeat five times, given the initial value of the variable and the increase in the value of the variable by 1 each time through (count++).

In a while loop, you must also remember to change the value of the variable you use so that you do not get stuck in a permanent loop. If the previous sample loop had not included the count++ code, the loop would have repeated indefinitely, and you do not want that to happen. So, the main things you must remember with a while loop are to give the variable an initial value before the loop and to adjust the value of the variable within the loop itself.

For an example of the while loop in action, you can recode your sentence-repeat script to work with a while loop:

```
document.write("Get ready for some repeated text.<br />");
var count=1;                          This line is written on the page ten times, just as with the for loop
while (count<11) {
   document.write(count+". I am part of a loop!<br />"); ◄————┘
   count++;
}
document.write("Now we are back to the plain text.");
```

The preceding code will produce the same result as your for loop did, just with a different look, as shown in Figure 6-5. In many cases, you can choose to use a for loop or a while loop based on personal preference, since they can perform many of the same tasks.

As far as nesting with while loops, it works the same as with the for loops. You can insert another while loop, a for loop, or an if/else block within a while loop. You can also insert a while loop within the other statement blocks if you wish.

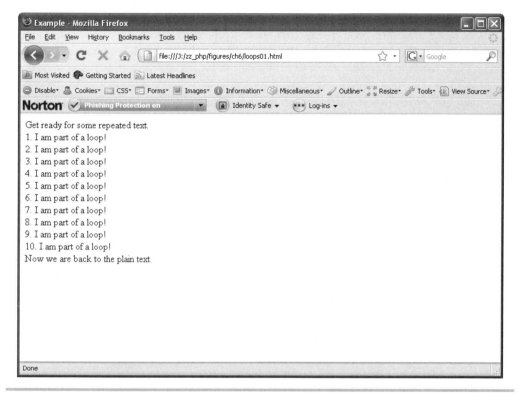

Figure 6-5   A line of text is repeated ten times using a while loop

Now that you know how while loops work, take a look at a loop that has a special feature added to it.

do while

The do while loop is special because the code within the loop is performed at least once, even if the comparison used would return false the first time. A comparison that returns false in other loops on the first attempt would cause them never to be executed. In the case of a do while loop, the loop is executed once, and then the comparison is used each time afterward to determine whether or not it should repeat.

The following is an example of a do while loop that will run five times:

```
var count=1;
do {                        The do keyword begins the do while loop
    document.write("Hi!");
    count++;                The while statement runs the comparison
} while (count<6);          each time after the first run-through
```

Notice the keyword do and the opening curly bracket are the only things on the first line of the block in the preceding code. Then, when the block is complete, you see the while statement and comparison. The do keyword is how you ensure the code block is executed at least once.

After that, the browser checks to see that the comparison returns true before repeating. In this case, the loop repeats five times since the variable count starts at 1 and is increased by 1 each time through. When the value of count reaches 6, the loop is skipped and no longer executed.

To see an example of a do while loop that gets executed at least once even though the initial comparison would return false, look at the following example code:

```
var count=11;
do {
    document.write("Hi!");          This is only written to the page once,
    count++;                        since the comparison will return false
} while (count<10);
```

Since the count variable has an initial value of 11, the loop in the preceding code will only run the first time through. When the comparison is checked (count will be 12 by this time, since 1 is added to it in the execution of the loop), it returns false and the loop is no longer run.

A do while loop is most useful when you have some code that you need to have executed at least once but need repeated only if certain conditions are met; otherwise, one of the other two loops would be sufficient for the task.

for in

The for in loop allows you to loop over all the names of the properties of an object and execute statements for each property using a variable to hold the name of the property. The general format for a for in loop is shown here:

```
for (varname in objectname) {
    JavaScript Code Here
}
```

Since you have not looked at JavaScript objects, this won't be useful to you yet. The for in loop will be covered in more detail in Chapter 8.

for each in

The for each in loop is very similar to the for in loop, but rather than looping through the name of each property it allows you to loop through the value of each of the properties. It is only supported in JavaScript 1.6 and higher. Again, this will be covered in more detail when objects are introduced in Chapter 8.

Using break and continue

The break and continue statements allow you to stop what a loop is currently doing, but work in different ways. As you will recall from the use of a break statement within a switch block earlier in the chapter, the break statement stops the loop at that point and completely exits the loop, moving on to the next JavaScript statement after the loop. For instance, break could be used in this manner:

```
for (count=1;count<11;count++) {
  if (count==5) {
    document.write("The loop is halfway done, and I am done with
it!<br />");
    break;  ◄──────────── This will end the loop when count is equal to 5,
  }                        rather than allowing the loop to complete
  else {
    document.write("I am part of a loop!<br />");
  }
}
```

This loop will go through normally until count is equal to 5. When this happens, a special message is written to the page and the break statement is used to end the loop entirely. Thus, rather than going through the loop ten times, the loop will only be executed five times.

If you decided that you did not want to completely leave the loop when that condition occurs, you could modify the loop to use the continue statement. The continue statement will stop the loop from executing any statements after it during the current trip through the loop. However, it will go back to the beginning of the loop and pick up where it left off, rather than exiting the loop entirely. For example, you could use the following code:

```
for (count=1;count<11;count++) {
  if (count==5) {
      continue;
  }
    document.write(count+". I am part of a loop!<br />");
}
```

This time, nothing is written to the page when count is equal to 5. Instead, the loop is told to go back to the beginning and continue from there. The result is that the "I am part of a loop!" message will be written to the page only nine times (since nothing happens when count is equal to 5). The loop is allowed to continue where it left off, rather than being left completely.

The break and continue statements will prove helpful to you when special situations come up that require you to stop the loop entirely or to stop the loop and restart it at the beginning.

Ask the Expert

Q: Are loops useful for anything other than writing a line of text to the page repeatedly?

A: Yes, you will see their usefulness more as you progress through the chapters. You will see that they can be useful when dealing with arrays and for repeating various actions that, in turn, create certain effects on the page.

Q: Is it really okay to use inside the loop the variable I have counting the loop? Couldn't that lead to problems?

A: It is okay to use that variable within the loop, as long as you do not somehow assign it a new value when using it. If you are worried that you might do this, assign its value to another variable and use that one in the code instead. For example, take a look at the following code:

```
for (count=1;count<11;count++) {
  var thenum=count;
  document.write(thenum+". I am part of a loop!<br />");
}
```

Here, you assign the value of the count variable to a variable named thenum. You then use the thenum variable in the code instead of the count variable.

Note, however, that it is okay to assign a new value to a count variable if that is what you intend to do. The preceding idea is only a method you can use if you do not intend to change the count variable and want to be sure you don't accidentally do so.

Q: Should I use a for loop or a while loop when I want to use a loop? Which one is better?

A: Use the type of loop you personally prefer. Often, the type of loop used depends upon the situation at hand. One type of loop might seem to make more sense than the other type under different circumstances.

A for loop is more common, though, simply because the risk of an infinite loop exists with a while loop—which is one of the worst things that can happen in JavaScript. A while loop is more useful when you don't know in advance how many times you need to loop.

Q: Will the do while loop ever be useful to me?

A: Although the do while loop does have its usefulness, it is unlikely that you will use it often unless you use scripts that need to have a loop run at least once before it is checked. You will not encounter any such scripts in this book. However, the knowledge you gained about the do while loop in this chapter will help you if you should encounter a script that uses it on the Web or elsewhere.

Try This 6-2 Work with for Loops and while Loops

pr6_2.html
prjs6_2.js

In this project, you work with for loops and while loops to see how they can perform similar tasks.

Step by Step

1. Create an HTML page and save it as pr6_2.html. Add the script tags to point to a script named prjs6_2.js.

2. Create an external JavaScript file and save it as prjs6_2.js. Use it to complete steps 3–5.

3. Using a for loop, create some code that will write the following sentence to the page 15 times (be sure to number each line from 1 to 15):

   This is getting way too repetitive.

4. Save the JavaScript file and view the HTML page in the browser. You should see the sentence 15 times, numbered from 1 to 15.

5. Edit the code so that it will do the same thing as in step 3, but use a while loop instead.

6. Save the JavaScript file again and view the HTML page in the browser. It should appear the same as before.

Try This Summary

In this project, you used your new skills to build two different HTML pages using two different types of loops. The first page used a for loop, and the second page used a while loop. Since both loops perform the same task, the page appeared the same both times when viewed in a browser.

Chapter 6 Self Test

1. A conditional statement is a statement that you can use to execute a bit of code based on a _____, or do something else if that _____ is not met.

2. You can think of a conditional statement as being a little like _____ and _____.

3. Rather than executing every single line of code within the script, a conditional statement allows certain sections of the script to be executed only when a particular condition is met.

   A True

   B False

4. Which of the following would be valid as the first line of an if/else statement?

   A if (*x*=2)

   B if (*y*<7)

   C else

   D if ((*x*==2 &&)

5. What do you use to enclose the blocks of code in conditionals and loops?

   A Parentheses

   B Square brackets

   C Curly brackets

   D Less-than and greater-than characters

6. The _____ statement allows you to take a single variable value and execute a different line of code based on the value of the variable.

7. A _____ is a block of code that allows you to repeat a section of code a certain number of times.

8. A loop is useful because it forces you to type lines of code repeatedly.

   A True

   B False

9. Which of these would be valid as the first line of a for loop?

   A for (*x*=1;*x*<6;*x*+=1)

   B for (*x*==1;*x*<6;*x*+=1)

   C for (*x*=1;x=6;*x*+=1)

   D for (*x*+=1;*x*<6;*x*=1)

10. A _____ loop looks at a comparison and repeats until the comparison is no longer true.

11. Which of these would not be valid as the first line of a while loop?

   A while (*x*<=7)

   B while (*x*=7)

   C while (*x*<7)

   D while (*x*!=7)

12. A do while loop is special because the code within the loop is performed at least once, even if the comparison used would return false the first time.

   A True

   B False

13. The first line of a do while block contains the keyword do and a comparison.

   A True

   B False

14. The last line of a do while block contains only a curly bracket.

   A True

   B False

15. How many times can you nest a code block within another?

   A None

   B Once

   C Three times, but no more

   D As many times as you like (though enough nesting could run the browser out of memory)

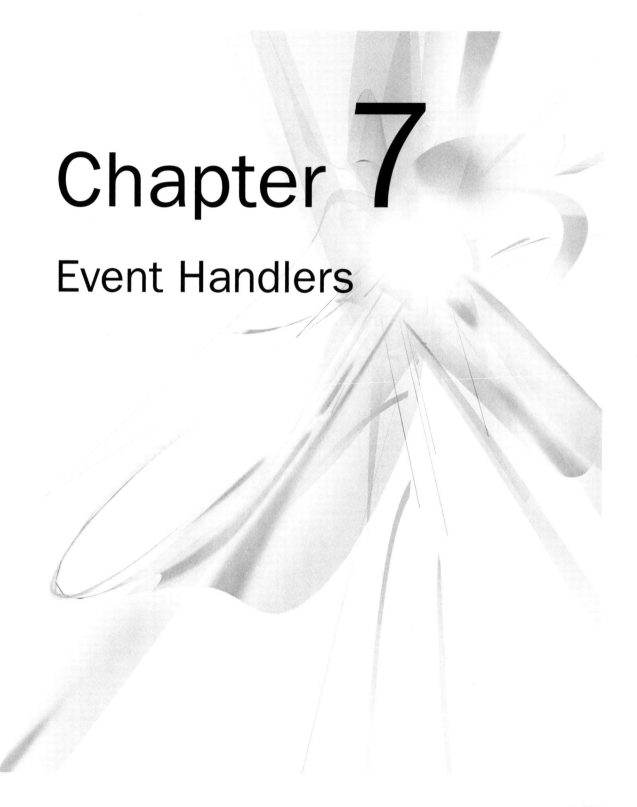

Chapter 7

Event Handlers

Key Skills & Concepts

- Understanding Event Handler Locations and Uses

- Learning the Event Handlers

- Creating Scripts Using Event Handlers

- Other Ways to Register Events

When creating scripts, you will often find that there are user "events" (such as a user moving a mouse over a certain element or clicking a particular element) to which you want your script to react. The way you do this is through the use of event handlers.

To learn how the event handlers work, you need to learn what they are and why they are useful to you. You will then learn where event handlers are placed in a document and how to use them. Finally, you will see the various events in JavaScript and the event handlers that take care of each event. To get started, this chapter presents a general overview of event handlers.

What Is an Event Handler?

An event handler is a predefined JavaScript property of an object (in most cases an element in the document) that is used to handle an event on a Web page.

You may ask the question "What is an event?" An event is something that happens when the viewer of the page performs some sort of action, such as clicking a mouse button, clicking a button on the page, changing the contents of a form element, or moving the mouse over a link on the page. Events can also occur simply by the page loading or other similar actions.

When events occur, you are able to use JavaScript event handlers to identify them and then perform a specific task or set of tasks. JavaScript enables you to react to an action by the viewer and to make scripts that are interactive, and more useful to you and to the viewer.

Why Event Handlers Are Useful

Event handlers are useful because they enable you to gain access to the events that may occur on the page. For instance, if you wanted to send an alert to the viewer when he or she moves the mouse over a link, you could use the event handler to invoke the JavaScript alert you have coded to react to the event. You are now making things happen based on the actions of the viewer, which enables you to make more-interactive Web pages.

Creating this interactivity is where many people find that JavaScript starts to become a little more fun to code and to use. With event handlers, you can create some surprises for the viewer or make some scripts that will simply add more functionality to the page. JavaScript can make a number of things happen on a Web page that will make the page more interesting than a static HTML document.

Understanding Event Handler Locations and Uses

To see how event handlers work, you need to know where you can place them in a document and how to use them to add JavaScript code for an event.

Event handlers can be used in a number of locations. They can be used directly within HTML elements by adding special attributes to those elements. They can also be used within the <script> and </script> tags or in an external JavaScript file.

To understand better where event handlers are located, you need to learn how to add event handlers to your script.

Using an Event Handler in an HTML Element

To use an event handler directly in an HTML element, you need to know the keyword for the event handler and where to place the event handler within the HTML code. To give you an example, I will introduce the onclick event handler, which is used to make something happen when the viewer clicks a specific area of the document.

One element that can be clicked is a form button. So, suppose you want to alert the viewer to something when the user clicks a form button. You would write something similar to the following code:

```
<input type="button" value="Click Me!" onclick="JavaScript code here" />
```

To use an event handler, you add it as an additional attribute to an HTML tag. The only difference between an event handler "attribute" and an HTML attribute is that you can add JavaScript code inside an event handler attribute rather than just an attribute value. In the previous code, you would replace the *JavaScript code here* text with some actual JavaScript code.

So, to make an alert pop up when the user clicks the button, you can add the necessary JavaScript code right inside your onclick attribute, as shown in the following example:

When the viewer clicks this plain button, an alert will pop up with a greeting. Notice that the rules on the quote marks apply here. Using the onclick event handler as an attribute requires you to use double quotes around all of your JavaScript code, so when you need quote marks for the alert, you use single quotes in order to avoid possible errors.

Also notice that the alert command ends with a semicolon. This enables you to add additional JavaScript code after the alert, which enables you to perform multiple actions on the click event rather than just a single JavaScript statement.

You could code in two alerts if you wanted to do so. All you have to do is remember to include the semicolons to separate the alert commands. This will be a little different because all of the code will be on one line rather than separate lines, as you normally see:

```
<body>
<form>
<input type="button" value="Click Me!"
 onclick="window.alert('Hi!');window.alert('Bye!');" />
</form>
</body>
```

Notice how the semicolons separate the JavaScript statements

This example is able to perform two JavaScript statements on the same event by using semicolons to separate them. When using event handlers, you can execute multiple commands this way. It is important, however, to keep everything between the event handler keyword (in this case, onclick) and the ending set of quotes (in this case, after the last semicolon in the code) on one line in your text editor; otherwise, a line break in the code could cause it not to run properly or to give a JavaScript error.

If the code you want to use becomes really long, you may wish to put the code in a function instead. The event handler can be used for any JavaScript code, so you can use it to call a function you have defined elsewhere. For example, you could place your two alerts within a function inside an external JavaScript file, and call the function from an event handler in the HTML code. First, code the external JavaScript file (here it will be saved as js_event_01.js) as follows:

```
function hi_and_bye() {
  window.alert('Hi!');
  window.alert('Bye!');
}
```

Next, add the script tags and the event handler to your HTML code:

Notice how the function is called using the event handler

```
<body>
<form>
<input type="button" value="Click Me!" onclick="hi_and_bye();" />
</form>
<script type="text/javascript" src="js_event_01.js"></script>
</body>
```

Notice how the function is called using the event handler just like a normal function call within a script. This enables you not only to shorten the code within the event handler, but also to reuse the function on another button click or event later in the page instead of writing the two alerts out again. The use of a function can help you quite a bit, especially when the code you want to use becomes extremely long.

Using an Event Handler in the Script Code

You can also use an event handler within the script code (whether using the script tags in the HTML document or using an external JavaScript file). One way to do this is to give the element an id attribute and then use the JavaScript method document.getElementById() to access the element. Once that is done, you can tie an event to the element.

Add the id Attribute

To use the previous script in this way, you will first add an id attribute to the HTML tag for the input button, as shown here:

```
<body>
<form>
<input type="button" value="Click Me!" id="say_hi" />
</form>
<script type="text/javascript" src="js_event_01.js"></script>
</body>
```

Notice that the button input element was given an id of say_hi. You will use this to access the button and tie it to an event in your script.

Access the Element

The document.getElementById() method allows you to access any element in the HTML document that has an id attribute using the value of its id attribute. In order to access the button input element you have been using with an id of say_hi, you could use the following code:

```
document.getElementById("say_hi");
```

This simply tells the browser you want to access the element with the id of say_hi in the HTML document. This method could be used directly in the script to access the element, but oftentimes you will want to assign this expression to a variable to save typing if you use it repeatedly. Thus, you could use the following code:

```
var hi_button = document.getElementById("say_hi");
```

Now, grab the rest of the code from the JavaScript file (js_event_01.js) and add the new line of script to it, as shown here:

```
function hi_and_bye() {
    window.alert('Hi!');
    window.alert('Bye!');
}
var hi_button = document.getElementById("say_hi");
hi_button.onclick = hi_and_bye;
```

The function and its statements

The button input element is accessed via its id (say_hi) and assigned to a variable (hi_button)

The onclick event handler is used to assign the function (hi_and_bye) to the onclick event for the button input element

There is now also an additional line of code. The last line of code takes the variable used for the input button element and gives it the onclick event handler by adding it after the variable name and a dot (.). The function hi_and_bye (which displays the two alerts) is assigned to handle the click event on the input button. Thus, when the button is clicked, the viewer will see the two alerts!

NOTE
Some of these statements (such as the use of dots (.) in the code and the document. getElementById() method) will be explained in more detail in Chapter 8 and Chapter 9.

To help make more sense of this, the last two lines could also be written in the following manner:

```
document.getElementById("say_hi").onclick = hi_and_bye;
```

Both achieve the same result, but the first method is helpful when you need to deal with the same element more than once in the code (perhaps to add other events such as onmouseover, onmouseout, or others).

You will also notice that when the function is assigned to handle the event, the parentheses are not used after the function name. This is because you want to assign the execution of the function to the event rather than the result of the function (which is what you did when you used the return statement to assign the result of a function to variables in previous chapters—this particular function would not return anything). Rather than just assigning a value, you want the function to be executed, so the whole function is assigned to the event by using just the function name.

Ask the Expert

Q: Is there a JavaScript event for everything a viewer could do on a Web page?

A: No, but many of the actions a viewer may take are covered by one of the events in JavaScript. It would be difficult to cover every possibility.

Q: You mean I can just write some JavaScript by using an event handler like an HTML attribute?

A: Yes, but keep in mind that giving an element an id attribute and responding to the event in the JavaScript code will help keep your HTML code cleaner.

Q: If I add the event as an HTML attribute, how do I decide when to use a function and when to just add the code directly into the event handler?

A: If your JavaScript code is short and you won't be repeating it multiple times with other tags and/or events, then you'll probably want to add the code straight into the event handler as an attribute. If your code is really long or you will be repeating it numerous times, you'll probably want to use a function instead to make things easier to read and to make the code reusable.

This method of handling events allows you to place all of your JavaScript code outside of your HTML elements, which keeps your HTML code cleaner and (especially if an external JavaScript file is used) more likely to validate. Later in this chapter, you will see that newer methods with particular differences are also available to handle events (but may not work cross-browser). For now, you will use the method described in this section when reacting to events within the script code.

Try This 7-1   Create a Button

```
pr7_1.html
prjs7_1.js
```

In this project, you create a button that will send the viewer three alerts when it is clicked. This project will help you to master calling a function to handle an event in the JavaScript code.

Step by Step

1. Create an HTML page and save it as pr7_1.html. Add the necessary script tags to point to an external JavaScript file named prjs7_1.js.

2. Create an external JavaScript file and save it as prjs7_1.js. Use this for step 3 and step 5.

3. Write a function named send_alerts() that will send three alerts to the viewer. The following are the three alerts:

   Alert 1: Hi there, and welcome to my page!
   Alert 2: Please sign the guest book before you leave!
   Alert 3: Are these alerts annoying you yet? Ha, Ha!

4. In the HTML document, create a button with an id of get_alerts. Add a value="Click Me" attribute to the button tag so that it has text.

5. In the JavaScript file, write the code so that the send_alerts function will execute when a click event occurs on the input button element.

6. Save the HTML and JavaScript files, and load the HTML page in your browser. You should have a button that says "Click Me" on it. Click the button, and you should get the three alerts—one after another.

Try This Summary

In this project, you used your new skills with the onclick event handler to create a script that reacts to the viewer. When the viewer clicks a button, the script uses that event to send three alerts to the viewer.

Learning the Event Handlers

Now that you know what event handlers are and how to use them, you need to see which event handlers are used for various events on a page. Begin by looking at Table 7-1, which lists the most common events, their event handlers, and samples of what actions might trigger each event.

Event	Event Handler	Event Trigger
Abort	onabort	An image is stopped from loading before loading has completed
Blur	onblur	Viewer removes focus from an element
Change	onchange	Viewer changes the contents of a form element
Click	onclick	Viewer clicks an element
ContextMenu	oncontextmenu	Viewer opens the context menu
Copy	oncopy	Viewer uses the copy command on part of a page
Cut	oncut	Viewer uses the cut command on part of a page
Dblclick	ondblclick	Viewer double-clicks the mouse
Error	onerror	Viewer's browser gets a JavaScript error or an image that does not exist
Focus	onfocus	Viewer gives focus to an element
Keydown	onkeydown	Viewer presses down a key on the keyboard
Keypress	onkeypress	Viewer presses a key on the keyboard, and releases or holds the key down
Keyup	onkeyup	Viewer releases a key on the keyboard
Load	onload	Web page finishes loading
Mousedown	onmousedown	Viewer presses the mouse button
Mousemove	onmousemove	Viewer moves the mouse (moves the cursor)
Mouseout	onmouseout	Viewer moves the mouse away from an element
Mouseover	onmouseover	Viewer moves the mouse over an element
Mouseup	onmouseup	Viewer releases the mouse button
Paste	onpaste	Viewer uses the paste command on part of the page
Reset	onreset	Viewer resets a form on the page
Resize	onresize	A window is resized
Scroll	onscroll	Viewer scrolls an area which is scrollable
Select	onselect	User makes a selection
Submit	onsubmit	Viewer submits a form on the page
Unload	onunload	Viewer leaves the current page

Table 7-1 The Events and Event Handlers

NOTE

Some of these events, such as the copy event, will only work with certain browsers (which may need to be running in their latest versions). There are also events that work only in Internet Explorer (see http://msdn.microsoft.com/en-us/library/ms533051(VS.85).aspx) or that are not necessarily cross-browser as of yet (see www.w3.org/TR/DOM-Level-3-Events/events.html#Events-EventTypes-complete).

Now that you have a general idea about event handlers, you will take a look at some of the most often used ones in detail to see how they work.

The Abort Event (onabort)

The abort event occurs when a viewer stops (aborts) the loading of an image. The event handler used for this is onabort. For example, if you wanted to display a message when the viewer stopped an image from loading, you could use the following code:

```
<img src="myimage.jpg" alt="my picture"
  onabort="window.alert('Why don\'t you want to see my picture?');" />
```

This will ask the viewer why your picture wasn't loaded. It probably would not convince the user to load the image anyway, but it lets the user know that you intended for that image to be loaded.

The Blur Event (onblur)

The blur event is the opposite of the focus event, and it occurs when the viewer takes the focus away from a form element or a window. To take the focus off something, the viewer usually gives focus to something else. For instance, the viewer could move from one form element to another, or from one window to another.

The onblur event handler is used to handle this event, and it can be used in such places as a form element's tag or in the opening body tag (for windows). The onblur event handler also has a related method called blur(), which will be covered in Chapter 10 and Chapter 14.

NOTE

The blur event is triggered only when the viewer gives focus to another area, which is the only way the browser will know the viewer released the focus from the first area. For example, when the viewer presses the ENTER key in an input field, the focus goes from the input field to the document window.

To see the blur event in action, you can also use a text box. The following example uses two text boxes: clicking the first text box gives it focus, and clicking the second text box invokes the blur event in the first text box.

```
<form>
Give this box focus:<br />
<input type="text" onblur="window.alert('Hey! Come back!');" /><br />
then give this box focus to blur the first one:<br />
<input type="text" />
</form>
```

The onblur event in a text box

Clicking this text box after giving the focus to the first one will trigger the blur event on the first text box

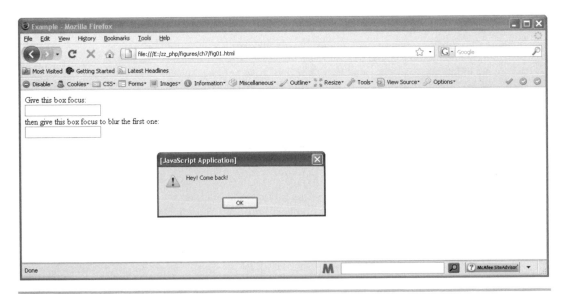

Figure 7-1 This alert pops up when the viewer takes the focus off a text box

When viewers click the second text box, they get the alert from the first one telling them to come back.

Figure 7-1 shows the result of the preceding code when run in the browser. Notice that the focus is in the second text box when the alert pops up. By clicking the second text box, the viewer invoked the blur event in the first text box.

The Change Event (onchange)

The change event occurs when a viewer changes something within a form element. For instance, the viewer might change the text in a text box or make a selection from a select box. You handle this event with the onchange event handler.

You can see how this works by setting up a select box. You can give the viewer some choices within the select box. If the user changes the default option by choosing a new one, you send an alert to ask why it was changed, as shown in the following example:

```
<form>
Are you cool?<br />
<select onchange="window.alert('Why did you change that?');">
<option selected="selected">Yes</option>
<option>No</option>
<option>Undecided</option>
</select>
</form>
```

Making a new selection from the list will invoke the onchange event handler here

If the viewer tries to change the default answer of Yes, an alert pops up and gives the viewer a message. If the select box is left alone or the viewer chooses the default option, nothing will happen.

The Click Event (onclick)

The click event occurs when a viewer clicks on an element in a Web page. Often, these are form elements and links. In modern browsers, the click event also works for more general areas, such as within a table cell or within a set of <div> and </div> tags. This chapter concentrates on the form elements and links, as they are commonly used.

The easiest way to see the click event in action is to use a form button. When the button is clicked, you want an event to occur. To make this happen, you can place the onclick event handler inside the button input tag, as shown in the following example:

```
<body>
<form>
<input type="button" value="Do not Click Here"
 onclick="window.alert('I told you not to click me!');">
</form>
</body>
```

The onclick event handler is used on a button

This will send the viewer an alert once the button has been clicked. Figure 7-2 shows the result of this code when the viewer clicks the button.

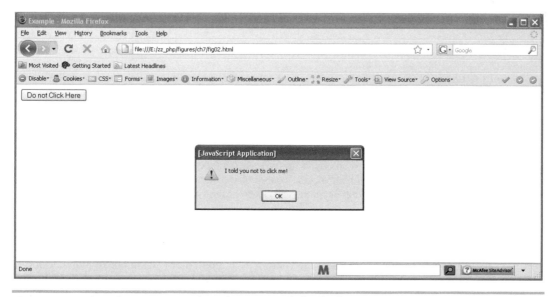

Figure 7-2   This alert pops up when the viewer clicks the button

To use this event handler to do the same thing with a link, you might be tempted to do something similar to the following:

Oh no! This will give you problems because the browser will try to follow the link

```
<body>
<a href="http://none" onclick="window.alert('Hey! You clicked me!');">
Don't Click Me</a>
</body>
```

The problem with this code is that the alert will work, but the browser will try to continue the original action of the link tag and attempt to go to http://none. This would probably cause a "Server not found" error in the browser.

One way you can avoid a "Server not found" error is to link to an actual page (which is good for accessibility); however, it may take a viewer with JavaScript on away from the current page. To keep the link from being followed (if JavaScript is on), you need to add an extra statement to the JavaScript in the click event. You need to tell the browser not to continue after you have shown the viewer your alert. To do this, you will add a return statement.

Recall from Chapter 4 on functions that you used a return statement to return a needed value to a script. Here, you are going to do essentially the same thing. You are going to return the Boolean value of false, which tells the browser that the event has been handled and no further action is required for the event. This will keep the browser from following the link after the alert has been shown. The following code shows how to add in the return statement:

```
<body>
<a href="http://none"
  onclick="window.alert('Hey! You clicked me!'); return false;">
Don't Click Me</a>
</body>
```

The return false statement keeps the browser from trying to follow the link

With this code in place, the click event will be taken care of by the onclick event handler, and the browser will not need to worry about attempting to follow the link in the hypertext reference (href) attribute.

NOTE
You can also code JavaScript for a link by using the javascript: command—for example, `<a href="javascript:window.alert('Hi');">Click</a>`—but this method is not recommended for accessibility reasons (if JavaScript is off the link doesn't go anywhere).

The Focus Event (onfocus)
The focus event occurs when the viewer gives focus to an element on a Web page. A viewer gives focus to something by clicking somewhere within the item, by using the keyboard to move to the item (often via the TAB key), or via a script. For instance, a viewer who clicks a text input box (before entering anything) gives that text box the focus. Also, clicking an inactive window and making it the active window gives the window the focus.

The event handler used with this event is onfocus, and it can be used in places such as a form element or in the opening body tag on a Web page (for focus on a window). The onfocus event handler also has a related method called focus(), which is covered in Chapter 10 and Chapter 14.

To see the focus event in action, you can create a text input box, which is one of the form elements that will enable you to give the element focus. The following example shows how to do this, as well as how to code a reminder alert to pop up when the viewer gives focus to the text box:

```
<form>                                              The onfocus event in a text box
Enter Your Name:
<input type="text" onfocus="window.alert('Don\'t forget to capitalize!');" />
</form>
```

This code will give the viewer an alert before he or she can begin typing. The alert serves as a reminder to capitalize the name. Figure 7-3 shows the result of the preceding code in the browser when the viewer gives focus to the text box.

Later chapters will examine better uses for the focus event, but this gives you an idea of how it works.

The Keydown Event (onkeydown)

The keydown event occurs when the viewer presses down a key on the keyboard. To handle this event, you use onkeydown. You can place this event handler in almost any HTML tag on a Web page.

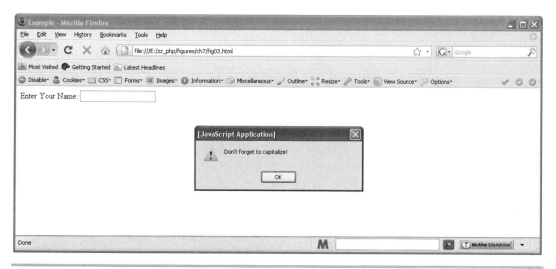

Figure 7-3   This alert pops up when the text box receives focus from the viewer

The Keypress Event (onkeypress)

The keypress event occurs when a viewer presses down a key on the keyboard and the corresponding character is typed. This occurs between the kedown and the keyup events. To take care of this event, you use the onkeypress event handler, which can be placed in almost any HTML tag on a Web page.

The Keyup Event (onkeyup)

The keyup event occurs when the viewer lets go of a key on the keyboard, releasing the key. The event handler for this is onkeyup, and it can be placed in almost any HTML tag on a Web page.

NOTE

For more information on the keydown, keypress, and keyup events, go to www.quirksmode.org/js/keys.html. This will give you a better idea of how the events work in different browsers and the type of coding you will need to use to work with keystrokes cross-browser. Since these are supported somewhat inconsistently from browser to browser, they will not be covered in detail in this book at this time.

The Load Event (onload)

The load event occurs when a Web page finishes loading. To handle this event, you use the onload event handler.

Keep in mind the load event occurs at a slightly different time than the alert scripts you placed in your pages in earlier chapters. Those started your tasks before the remainder of the page began loading. With the load event, however, your tasks will be executed as soon as the page finishes the loading process.

If you want an alert to be shown when the page has finished loading, you could use the following code:

Notice that the onload event handler is added in the body tag

```
<body onload="window.alert('I\'m done loading now!');">
Text for the body of the page...
</body>
```

When the page has finished loading, viewers will get an alert that tells them it is finished. It will be hard to distinguish the timing of the load event from the preceding code from the timing of the instant alerts in earlier scripts because the page will load very quickly, since it is all text. Figure 7-4 shows how the preceding code example would appear in the browser.

If you want to use the onload event handler in the script code rather than in the body tag, you could write this code into an external JavaScript file (save it as load_alert.js):

```
window.onload = function() {
  window.alert('I\'m done loading now!');
};
```

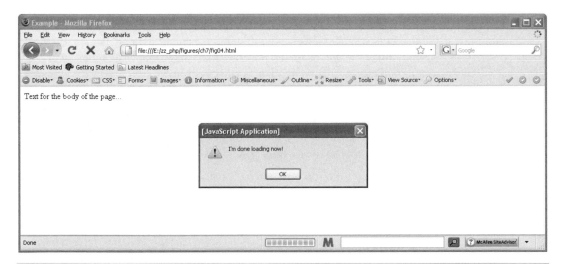

Figure 7-4   This is displayed in the browser window after the page has finished loading

This will capture the load event for the current window (the window object will be explained in more detail in Chapter 10). Notice the use of the anonymous function here to combine the steps of creating a function and assigning it to the event (for further information on functions, refer to Chapter 4). You can now point the Web page to the JavaScript file without the need to alter the body tag in the HTML code, as shown here:

```
<body>
<script type="text/javascript" src="load_alert.js"></script>
Text for the body of the page...
</body>
```

In order to see the difference in timing between an alert executed immediately and one executed in the onload event handler, you may want to add some images to the body of the page and then put the page and images on the Web. This way, the page will take some time to load, and you will see that the alert pops up when the page has finished loading instead of showing up instantly.

The Mousedown Event (onmousedown)

The mousedown event occurs when a viewer presses the mouse button down but before the click is complete (doesn't need to be released). To handle this event, you use the onmousedown event handler, which can be placed within almost any HTML tag on a Web page.

The Mousemove Event (onmousemove)

The mousemove event occurs when the viewer moves the mouse cursor. The event handler for this is onmousemove, and it can be placed within almost any HTML tag on a Web page.

The Mouseover Event (onmouseover)

The mouseover event occurs when a viewer moves the mouse cursor over an element on the page such as a text link, linked image, or linked portion of an image map. The mouseover event will also work in numerous other areas such as table cells and <div> and </div> tags. The mouseover event is handled with the onmouseover event handler.

The quickest way to use an onmouseover event handler is to set up a text link. When you add the onmouseover event handler to the link, you have the option to perform JavaScript commands when the viewer passes the cursor over the link. Thus, if you want an alert to pop up when the viewer moves the mouse over a link, you could code something like the following:

The onmouseover event handler in a link tag

```
<a href="http://www.pageresource.com"
 onmouseover="window.alert('I told you not to try to click me!');">
Don't Try Clicking Me!</a>
```

This time the visitor doesn't even get to click the link before being greeted with an alert. Keep in mind that a script like this could annoy your visitors if it is overused. Figure 7-5 shows the result of this script in a browser. The alert pops up as soon as the mouse cursor moves over the link.

Since there is no need to click the link for something to happen, the browser won't try to follow the link afterward. In fact, with this script in place, it is quite difficult to click the link at all because the alert keeps popping up when you move your mouse over to click it!

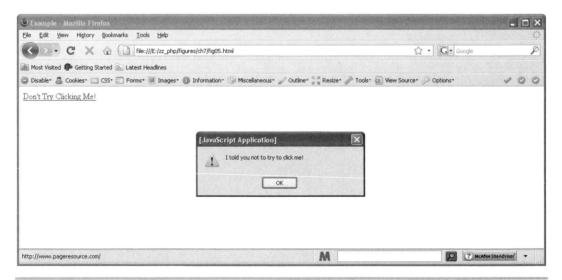

Figure 7-5 This alert pops up when the mouse cursor moves over the link

The mouseover event will become much more useful to you in later chapters when you learn more things about what you can do with the various parts of a page.

The Mouseout Event (onmouseout)

The mouseout event occurs when a viewer moves the mouse cursor away from an area on the page such as a link, linked image, or linked area of an image map. As with the mouseover event, most browsers will support the mouseout event in numerous areas. You take care of a mouseout event by using the onmouseout event handler.

Again, you can see the mouseout event most easily by setting up a link and adding the onmouseout event handler to the link. This time, you can make an alert pop up once the user moves the mouse away from the link after passing over it (assuming it has not been clicked). To do this, you could use the following code:

The onmouseout event handler in a link tag

```
<a href="http://www.pageresource.com"
 onmouseout="window.alert('What, you didn\'t like my link?');">
Click Me!</a>
```

This time the alert pops up when the viewer moves the mouse off the link and asks the viewer a question. Notice also the escaped quote mark (\') used in the word *didn't*, which keeps you from getting a string error. Figure 7-6 shows this script in action.

The mouseout event will become more useful for you as you progress, especially when used in tandem with the mouseover event.

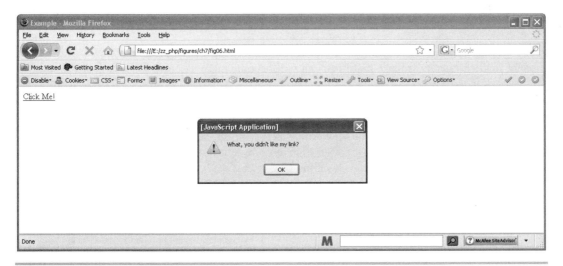

Figure 7-6   This alert pops up when the mouse is moved off the link

The Mouseup Event (onmouseup)

The mouseup event occurs when the viewer releases the mouse button after pressing it down. The onmouseup event handler is used for this event, and it can be placed within almost any HTML tag on a Web page.

The Reset Event (onreset)

The reset event occurs when a viewer uses a form reset button to reset the form fields in a form. To take care of this event, you use the onreset event handler, which can be added to the opening form tag in a form. The onreset event handler also has a related method called reset(), which is covered in Chapter 14.

The Submit Event (onsubmit)

The submit event only occurs when the viewer submits a form on a Web page. This event uses the onsubmit event handler, which can be called from an opening form tag in a document. The onsubmit event handler also has a related method called submit(), which will be covered in Chapter 14.

To see the submit event at work, you have to create a form that can be submitted with a submit button. You will then add the onsubmit event handler to the opening form tag. The following code will give a "Thank You" alert to the viewer once the submit button is clicked:

```
<form onsubmit="window.alert('Thank You');">          onsubmit used in the
What's your name?<br />                               opening form tag
<input type="text" id="thename" /><br />
<input type="submit" value="Submit Form">            The submit button triggers the
</form>                                               submit event when it is clicked
```

The submit event doesn't do you much good now (especially with the contents of the form not really going anywhere), but this event will become more useful when you get to form validation in Chapter 14.

The Unload Event (onunload)

The unload event occurs when a viewer leaves the current Web page. The viewer could leave by clicking a link, typing another address in the browser, or closing the window. The event handler used for the unload event is onunload.

This event is known to annoy viewers, because it enables the site owner to do something while visitors are trying to move on to another page or another Web site (forcing them to wait). To have an alert pop up when the user leaves the page, you could write the following code:

The onunload event handler is added to the body tag

```
<body onunload="window.alert('Be sure to come back, OK?');">
Other HTML code goes here...
</body>
```

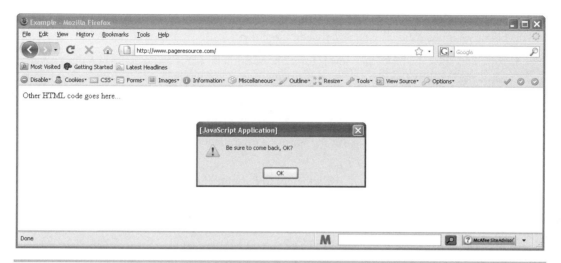

Figure 7-7   This alert pops up when the viewer tries to leave the page

Figure 7-7 shows the result of the preceding script. As viewers try to leave the page that contains this script, an alert pops up telling them to be sure to come back. Of course, this could cause a viewer to become quite inconvenienced if it is used on an index page or on a number of pages within a Web site.

As with the onload event handler, you can use the onunload event handler in the script code rather than as an attribute of the body tag by using window.onunload.

Overall, be sure to think twice before using the unload event on a live page. There can be good uses for it, but be careful because it does annoy most Web users.

Try This 7-2   Use Events to Send Out Alerts

pr7_2.html

This project enables you to practice using a few of the event handlers you have learned so far in this chapter. You will be creating a page with various links and form elements that will use events to send out alerts.

Step by Step

1. Create an HTML page and save it as pr7_2.html.

2. Add a link to the page that links to the URL http://www.yahoo.com. Add an event handler to the link tag so that when the viewer moves the mouse cursor over the link, an alert pops up that says, "Sorry, I'm not in the mood for you to leave yet!"

3. Add a <br /> tag after the link.

(continued)

4. Add the <form> and </form> tags to the page below the <br /> tag, and then add the form elements in the following steps between these tags.

5. Add a text box that asks the viewer for a phone number. Set it up so that when the viewer gives the text box focus, an alert pops up that says, "Format is *xxx-xxxx*."

6. Add a second text box that asks for the viewer's name. Set it up so that when a blur event occurs, an alert pops up that says, "Thanks, if that is your real name!"

7. Add a third text box that asks for the viewer's e-mail address. Don't set it to react to any events.

8. Add a submit button that says, "Click Here to Submit." Set it up so that when the viewer clicks it, an alert pops up that says, "Hey! I'm just a button. Leave me alone!"

9. Save the file, and open it in your browser.

10. Move your mouse over the first link. You should get the first alert.

11. Click inside the text box that asks for a phone number. You should get an alert.

12. Click the text box that asks for your name, and type in a name if you'd like.

13. Click the text box that asks for an e-mail address. You should get an alert about your name since you gave focus to this new text box, taking it away from the previous one. Note that if you have not clicked the text box for the name, you won't be removing focus from it; so be sure to give the name box focus, and then give this box focus right afterward.

14. Click the submit button so that it gives you an alert letting you know it doesn't want any company.

Try This Summary

In this project, you used your skills with several of the event handlers outlined in this chapter. You created an HTML page that reacts to a number of possible actions of the viewer, such as a mouseover, a click, or giving focus to something on the page.

Ask the Expert

Q: Why are there so many events?

A: There are so many things that a viewer (or the browser itself) can do while on a Web page that you end up with a bunch of events. The events in this chapter are only a small subset of all the events.

Q: Do I need to memorize all of these events?

A: You probably only need to memorize them if you have a test, are doing this for a job and need to know things quickly, or if you just like knowing the events off the top of your head; otherwise, you can just refer to Table 7-1 in this chapter if you are not sure which event needs to be used.

Q: Will I be using every single event in this book?

A: Since this book is a beginner's guide, you will not get to the point where you use every single event.

Creating Scripts Using Event Handlers

Now that you have tackled the long list of event handlers, it's time to have a little fun. In this section, you are going to learn two new properties that will do things other than write to the page and send an alert.

After you have seen all of those examples with alerts, the alert is probably a little stale now. Thus, you are going to try two new scripts. One will place a message inside a text box and the other will make a form button into a button that acts like a link. To begin, try placing a message in a text box.

The Text Box Message

Since you have learned the mouseover and mouseout events, you can use them in addition to other knowledge you have acquired in this chapter to build a script that will display a message in a text box when you move your mouse over a link located above the text box (it could be located anywhere you like, but for this example the link will be placed above the text box).

First, you will need to create an HTML document (save it as textbox_message.html). In this document, you will set up a link and give its anchor tag an id. Then, you will set up a text box and give its input tag an id. For example, you could use the following code:

```
<body>
<a href="message.html" id="msg_link">Get Message</a>
<br /><br />
<form>
<input type="text" id="msg_box" />
</form>
<script type="text/javascript" src="textbox_message.js"></script>
</body>
```

From this little bit of HTML code, you can use JavaScript to make this simple page go from static to interactive.

For accessibility purposes, it is good to point all hyperlinks to an actual URL with content (in this case, you might simply have the message text). This allows those without JavaScript to access the content in the script, while allowing those with JavaScript to simply use the mouseover event to access the message.

Since the text box is going to display a message when the mouse moves over the link, you'll first need to set up some variables in your JavaScript file (save it as testbox_message.js as referenced in the script tag in the preceding code). You will set up variables for the message text, the link element, and the text box element, as follows:

```
var message_text = "Help! I'm in a box!";
var message_link = document.getElementById("msg_link");
var message_box = document.getElementById("msg_box");
```

The message_text variable holds the text for the message you will display on the mouseover event, the message_link variable grabs the link element by its id (msg_link), and the message_box variable grabs the text box element by its id (msg_box).

Now that you have this information set up, you can use it along with the onmouseover event handler to display the message to the viewer in the text box:

```
var message_text = "Help! I'm in a box!";
var message_link = document.getElementById("msg_link");
var message_box = document.getElementById("msg_box");
message_link.onmouseover = function() {          ◄————— The onmouseover event handler is
  message_box.value = message_text;  ◄——————┐        assigned an anonymous function
};                                          │
```
The value of the text box is changed to display the message text

Most everything should be familiar here. The onmouseover event handler is assigned an anonymous function that handles the event. The function tells the browser to change the value of the text box so that it displays the message text. You'll notice the use of message_box.value. The value property holds the current value of an element. In the case of a text box, it holds the value of whatever is currently displayed in the text box (if it is empty, its value would be an empty string). Using this property, you can change the value to something of your choosing, as was done here.

If you save the HTML and JavaScript files and load the HTML file in your browser, you will see the result. Move your mouse over the "Get Message" link and the "Help! I'm in a box!" message should display in the text box.

Now, if you don't want that message to remain in the text box indefinitely, you can use another event to clear the text box of the message. You could use any event of your choice (on any element of your choice). One solution is to simply clear the message when the viewer moves the mouse off the link using the onmouseout event handler. Thus, you could now use the following code in your JavaScript file:

```
var message_text = "Help! I'm in a box!";
var message_link = document.getElementById("msg_link");
var message_box = document.getElementById("msg_box");

message_link.onmouseover = function() {
  message_box.value = message_text;
};
message_link.onmouseout = function () {
  message_box.value = "";
};
```

Notice that in the function for the onmouseout event handler, the message_box.value is changed to an empty string, which clears the message from the text box.

Save the JavaScript file and then refresh the HTML page in your browser. You should now be able to move the mouse over the link to receive the message and move your mouse off the link to have the message disappear. Figures 7-8 and 7-9 show the completed script in action.

The next script will make form buttons act like hyperlinks.

The Button Link

Using JavaScript, you can send the viewer to another URL. To do this, you need to use another new property: window.location. This property enables you to change the URL address of the window in which you use it. The following is the general syntax for the command:

```
window.location="http://someplace.com";
```

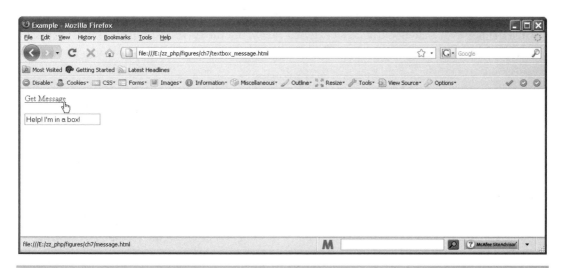

Figure 7-8   The script will display the message when the mouse moves over the link

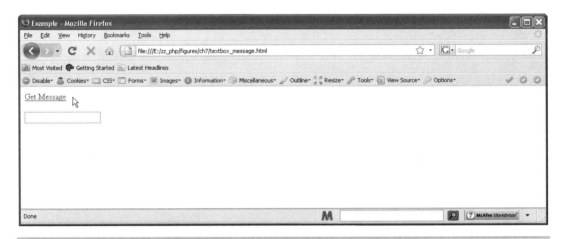

Figure 7-9 The message will go away when the mouse moves off the link

You replace the URL *http://someplace.com* with the address you wish to use in its place, such as http://www.yahoo.com or some other Web address.

To get started, you will again need to create an HTML document (save it as button_link. html). In this page, you will create an input button and give it an id, as shown here:

```
<form>
<input type="button" value="Go Searching!" id="btn1" />
</form>
```

Now, to make a button work like a link, all you need to do is use the location property with the onclick event handler. Create an external JavaScript file (save it as button_link.js) and use the following code:

The URL to go to is assigned to the web_page1 variable

```
var web_page1 = "http://www.yahoo.com";
var b1 = document.getElementById("btn1");
```

The input button element is assigned to the b1 variable

```
b1.onclick = function() {
  window.location = web_page1;
};
```

The location of the viewer is changed to the new URL

A function is assigned to the onclick event handler for the input button

Much like the previous script, this grabs the necessary values and then uses an anonymous function to execute a JavaScript command. When the viewer clicks the button, the browser goes to the new Web page.

Of course, you can do this for any number of buttons. If you want three buttons to link to three places, you could use the following HTML and JavaScript code:

```
<form>
<input type="button" value="Go Searching!" id="btn1" /><br /><br />
<input type="button" value="HTML Help" id="btn2" /><br /><br />
<input type="button" value="JavaScripts" id="btn3" />
</form>
```

With the extra buttons, add the necessary code and events for each element:

```
var web_page1 = "http://www.yahoo.com";
var web_page2 = "http://www.pageresource.com";
var web_page3 = "http://www.javascriptcity.com";
var b1 = document.getElementById("btn1");
var b2 = document.getElementById("btn2");
var b3 = document.getElementById("btn3");

b1.onclick = function() {
  window.location = web_page1;
};
b2.onclick = function() {
  window.location = web_page2;
};
b3.onclick = function() {
  window.location = web_page3;
};
```

This code creates three buttons that link to three different sites. Of course, if you decide to use a large number of these, it might be easier to work with arrays. Arrays will be discussed in Chapter 11.

CAUTION

This type of button link is an accessibility issue (since those without JavaScript will have the button do nothing). If you need to make accessible pages, you will need to provide the links with normal anchor tags in addition to having the buttons to ensure they are available to all users. Some additional scripting can handle this, and you will see how this can be done in Chapter 16.

Now you can do a few more things and have a little more fun with your examples. The window.location property will become quite useful to you as you move through the later chapters.

Other Ways to Register Events

There are two other methods for registering events in addition to the method you have used. As of the time of this writing, neither of these methods works cross-browser (which is a bit of a drawback since using them requires you to register the same event multiple times, but if certain parts of their functionality are needed they can be helpful to achieve the task at hand). These methods allow you to more easily add multiple functions for handling the same event and to more easily remove event handling functions that are not needed for a particular script. For now, you will just get a brief introduction to their use, which may prove helpful if they are needed or if one of the methods begins to work in all the major browsers.

First, you will look at the model from the World Wide Web Consortium (W3C). Next, you will look at the model from Microsoft.

The addEventListener() Method

The addEventListener() method is the one from W3C. It allows you to specify an event, a function to execute for the event, and a value of true or false depending on how you want the event handler function to be executed in the capturing (true) or bubbling (false) phase. The general format looks like this:

```
element.addEventListener('event_type', function_name, true_or_false);
```

Thus, if you want to create a linked input button as you did earlier in this chapter, you could adjust the JavaScript code to look like this:

```
var web_page1 = "http://www.yahoo.com";
var b1 = document.getElementById("btn1");
b1.addEventListener('click', function() { window.location = web_page1;
}, false);
```

Notice that rather than using the event handler, this method uses the name of the event (instead of onclick you simply use click). Also, this method will accept a function name without parentheses, or allows you to use an anonymous function (as shown above).

The capturing and bubbling matter when you have elements inside other elements that both have the same event type registered to them. Which event occurs first will depend on which method is used. If capturing is used, then the outermost element's event occurs first and the innermost element's event will occur last. If bubbling is used, the opposite is the case. The capturing phase occurs before the bubbling phase, so keep that in mind when using both phases in a script.

To remove an event, you would use the removeEventListener() method:

```
element.removeEventListener('event_type', function_name, true_or_false);
```

The attachEvent() Method

The attachEvent() method works in a similar way to addEventListener(). However, it only works with event bubbling and does not currently (as of the time of this writing) have a way to use event capturing. It is used like this:

```
element.attachEvent(event_handler, function_name);
```

Thus, if you want to use the same script you have been using, you could write it like this:

```
var web_page1 = "http://www.yahoo.com";
var b1 = document.getElementById("btn1");
b1.attachEvent(onclick, function() { window.location = web_page1; } );
```

Notice that this method does use the name of the event handler (onclick). Also, it does not have the third option; it just uses event bubbling.

To remove an event, you would use the detachEvent() method:

```
element.detachEvent(event_handler, function_name);
```

For the time being, you will continue to use in your scripts the method you have used previously in this book.

✓ Chapter 7 Self Test

1. An event handler is a predefined JavaScript property of an object that is used to handle an event on a Web page.

    A True

    B False

2. Event handlers are useful because they enable you to gain _____ to the _____ that may occur on the page.

3. To use an event handler, you need to know the _____ for the event handler and where to place the event handler in the HTML code.

4. Which of the following correctly codes an alert on the click event?

    A <input type="button" onclick="window.alert("Hey there!");">

    B <input type="button" onClick="window.alert('Hey there!");">

    C <input type="button" onclick="window.alert('Hey there!');">

    D <input type="button" onChange="window.alert("Hey there!");">

5. The _____ event occurs when a Web page has finished loading.

6. A mouseover event occurs when:

    A The viewer clicks the mouse while the cursor is over a button.

    B The viewer moves the mouse cursor away from a link.

    C The viewer clicks a link, linked image, or linked area of an image map.

    D The viewer moves the mouse cursor over an element on the page.

7. A mouseout event occurs when a viewer clicks an element on the page.

   A True

   B False

8. The _____ event occurs when the viewer leaves the current Web page.

9. The blur event is the opposite of the _____ event.

10. Which of the following correctly calls a function named major_alert() inside the onfocus event handler?

   A <input type="text" onfocus="major_alert();">

   B <input type="text" onfocus="major alert();">

   C <input type="text" onfocus="major_alert();'>

   D <input type="text" onFocus='major_alert()">

11. The _____ event occurs when a viewer changes something within a form element.

12. The submit event occurs when the viewer _____ a _____ on a Web page.

13. The keydown event occurs when a viewer presses down a key on the keyboard.

   A True

   B False

14. The mousedown event uses what keyword as its event handler?

   A onmouseout

   B onmousepress

   C onmousedown

   D mousedown

15. The _____ method and the _____ method are two new ways to register events.

Chapter 8

Objects

Key Skills & Concepts

● Defining Objects

● Creating Objects

● Understanding Predefined JavaScript Objects

Since JavaScript is an object-based language, you need to look at objects to understand what they are and how you can use them. The predefined objects in JavaScript are very useful; however, to use them effectively, it is a good idea to learn how objects work in general and how to create your own objects if you need them.

This chapter begins by defining what objects are and how objects can be useful to you in your scripts. You will then discover how to create and name your own objects that you can use in your code. Finally, this chapter introduces the properties and methods of the predefined navigator and history objects.

Defining Objects

To begin using JavaScript objects, you need to find out what they are and how they can be useful to you in your scripts. First take a look at what JavaScript objects are.

What Is an Object?

An object is a way of modeling something real, even though the object is an abstract entity. When you think of an object, you'll probably want to visualize something general, such as a car. When you see a car, you notice that it has certain features, or *properties*. You might see that the car has a radio with a CD player, leather seats, and a V-8 engine. All of these things are features of the car, or, in terms of objects, properties of the car object.

You could break this down further by making the radio have properties, or you could go the other way and make the car part of a larger object. For instance, you could say the CD radio has certain features, such as touch volume control, radio station presets, and a digital interface. If you go the other way, you could say that a car is part of an automobile object, which could include cars, vans, trucks, and various other motor vehicles as properties.

By doing this, you could create a visualization that could be followed down from the top. If you have an automobile that is a car, it would have properties of its own such as color, year, make, and model. It would also be made up of other objects such as tires, a radio, a steering wheel, and a dashboard, each of which could have properties and objects of its own.

If you follow the car down the path of the radio, you could suppose it has a CD radio with a digital interface, and you would see a pattern like the following:

```
Automobile -> Car -> CD Radio -> Digital Interface
```

You could instead have a truck, but leave the other features the same. Then you would have the following pattern:

```
Automobile -> Truck -> CD Radio -> Digital Interface
```

The preceding example works a little bit like a family tree, with the top level starting everything. Each level after the top level may have brothers and sisters (objects on the same level). Then the tree can continue expanding. The visualization can get confusing, but you shouldn't be confused when you work with the actual JavaScript objects. Many objects go just one level deep, so you probably won't need to worry about the "family tree" very much. The main thing you want to learn is that an object can hold a number of properties inside it that you can access from the outside to use in your scripts.

Why Objects Are Useful

Objects are useful because they give you another way to organize things within a script. Rather than having a bunch of similar variables that are out there on their own, you can group them together under an object.

If you take your car object and create variables to represent the features of the car, you can begin to see how this type of grouping works. You could create variables with the names seats, engine, and theradio. You will not create the car object until later in the chapter, so for now assume that the car object exists and that it has the properties of seats, engine, and theradio. Since these properties are variables, they can have values. The question is, how do you access these properties to get their values?

In JavaScript, you access object properties through the use of the dot operator, which is just a dot or period. For instance, if you wanted the value of the seats property of the car, you could access it with the following line:

```
var chtype= car.seats;
```

Don't let the assigning of the value of the seats property to a variable (chtype) be confusing. What you want to see here is the car.seats part of the code. The name of the object is written first, then the property you want to access is connected to it on the right using the dot operator.

The seats property doesn't currently have a value (since you haven't created the car object). You will see how to give it and other properties values when you begin creating objects in the next section.

Creating Objects

Now that you understand what objects are and their usefulness, you can begin creating your own JavaScript objects. To do this, you will learn about naming conventions, the structure of an object, and how to include methods in your objects.

Naming

As with variables and functions, there are certain rules you have to follow when naming your objects in JavaScript. They are essentially the same rules you follow for naming variables and functions, so I will just discuss them briefly here since you have been through this twice already.

Case Sensitivity

As with previous naming, object names are case sensitive. Thus, an object named car would be different from an object named Car, CAR, or caR. In order to access the right object, you have to be sure to use the proper case when you use it in the script; otherwise, you will receive an error such as "Car is not an object" when you try to run the script.

Avoiding Reserved Words/Objects

The other thing to remember when naming your own objects is that you cannot use a JavaScript reserved word (refer to the table of reserved words in the section "Avoiding Reserved Words" in Chapter 3); thus, trying to make an object named switch could give you problems because that word is used for the JavaScript switch statement.

Object Structure

There are two ways to create objects in JavaScript: by using a constructor function or by using an object initializer. First, you will learn how to use constructor functions to create objects. That is followed by a brief discussion of how to use the object initializers.

Constructor Functions

A constructor function allows you to build an object using the same basic syntax as a regular function. The only difference is the code you place inside of the function and how you access its contents.

For example, to create your car object, you would create a constructor function named car() and then add your properties within the function. The following example shows an outline of the car() function:

```
function car() {                           The constructor function is defined
   Properties go here.
}
                    The properties will be listed here for the object you are creating
```

To complete the preceding function, you need to add your properties to the function. Recall that you want to create an object named car with the properties of seats, engine, and theradio. The following code shows how this is done:

```
function car(seats,engine,theradio) {        The function takes in three parameters
   this.seats=seats;
   this.engine=engine;                       The parameter values are assigned
   this.theradio=theradio;                   to the properties of the object
}
```

In this code, on the first line, you see that the function takes three parameters, which is the number of properties you want the car object to have. The next thing you see is that the values of the parameters are assigned to the properties you want the car object to have; however, there is a new keyword named *this*. The keyword this in JavaScript is used to represent the current object being used, or "this object," so to speak.

Once you have the object's properties set with the constructor function, you need to create what is called an *instance* of the object in order to use it, because a constructor function creates only the structure of an object, not a usable instance of an object. To create an instance of an object, you use another JavaScript keyword: new.

The use of the new keyword to create an instance of your car object is shown in the following code:

```
var work_car= new car("cloth","V-6","Tape Deck");
```

The first thing you see is that you are creating a new variable named work_car. This variable will be a new instance of the car object due to the value you are assigning to it.

You next see that the work_car variable is assigned the result of the car constructor function, with a twist. In front of the call to the car function is the *new* keyword, which makes sure you are creating a new instance of the constructor function object.

Next, you see that the car function is called with values sent as parameters. These are the values you want to use for this instance of the car object. Given the order, you are saying that you want the seats to be cloth, the engine to be V-6, and the radio to be Tape Deck.

You can now access the work_car instance of the car object. If you want to know what type of engine the work_car has, you can access it with the dot operator:

```
var engine_type= work_car.engine;
```

This assigns the value of the engine property of the work_car instance of the car object to the variable engine_type. Since you sent V-6 as the engine parameter to the constructor function, the engine_type variable is assigned a value of V-6.

Putting the Pieces Together   To help you visualize this process, it's time to put all these parts together so that you can see how it works. The following code combines all the code of the previous examples to make things easier to see:

```
function car(seats,engine,theradio) {
  this.seats=seats;
  this.engine=engine;                          The constructor function
  this.theradio=theradio;
}
var work_car= new car("cloth","V-6","Tape Deck");    An instance of the object is
                                                      created, sending parameters
var engine_type= work_car.engine;                     to be used as property values
```

A property of the new instance of the object is assigned to an independent variable

Now you can see the constructor function, the creation of an instance of the car object, and the assignment of one of the properties of the object to a variable. When the work_car instance of the car object is set, it gets the values of cloth for the property work_car.seats, V-6 for the property work_car.engine, and Tape Deck for the property work_car.theradio.

In order to see how an instance of an object works, you need to add another instance of the car object to your code. The following code uses two instances of the car object, one named work_car and a new one named fun_car:

```
function car(seats,engine,theradio) {
   this.seats=seats;
   this.engine=engine;
   this.theradio=theradio;
}
var work_car= new car("cloth","V-6","Tape Deck");
var fun_car= new car("leather","V-8","CD Player");
var engine_type= work_car.engine;
var engine_type2= fun_car.engine;
```

The constructor function

Two object instances are created

One property value from each instance of the object gets assigned to two independent variables, which contain different values because they are from two different object instances

Notice how the new instance of the object uses the same constructor function, but with different values. You also have a new variable named engine_type2, which is given the value of the engine property of the fun_car instance of the car object.

By assigning the property values of the different instances of the car object to variables, you could now write out the features you would like to have in a custom car that combines features from each type of car. For example, take a look at the following code, which writes out the features you might like in a custom car:

The part of the script with the constructor function, instance creations, and variable assignments

```
function car(seats,engine,theradio) {
   this.seats=seats;
   this.engine=engine;
   this.theradio=theradio;
}
var work_car= new car("cloth","V-6","Tape Deck");
var fun_car= new car("leather","V-8","CD Player");
var engine_type= work_car.engine;
var seat_type= fun_car.seats;
var radio_type= fun_car.theradio;

document.write("I want a car with "+seat_type+" seats.<br />");
document.write("It also needs a "+engine_type+" engine.<br />");
document.write("Oh, and I would like a "+radio_type+" also.");
```

The document.write() commands are used in the body section so that they display in the browser

Using the variable values that grab what you want from each instance of the car object, you are able to print to the screen the description of the car you would like to have. Save this file as objects_01.js and create an HTML file with the following body code and save it as objects_01.html:

```
<body>
<script type="text/javascript" src="objects_01.js"></script>
</body>
```

Open the objects_01.html file in your Web browser. The results of this script are shown in Figure 8-1.

You could also achieve the result of the preceding example by creating a new instance of the car object with your choices and then printing those to the screen. If you create an instance named custom_car, you could use the following code:

A new instance of the object is created, sending the values of the properties of other object instances as parameters

```
function car(seats,engine,theradio) {
  this.seats=seats;
  this.engine=engine;
  this.theradio=theradio;
}
var work_car= new car("cloth","V-6","Tape Deck");
var fun_car= new car("leather","V-8","CD Player");
var custom_car= new car(fun_car.seats,work_car.engine,fun_car.theradio);

document.write("I want a car with "+custom_car.seats+" seats.<br />");
document.write("It also needs a "+custom_car.engine+" engine.<br />");
document.write("Oh, and I would like a "+custom_car.theradio+" also.");
```

The properties of the new instance of the object are used like variables in the document.write() statements

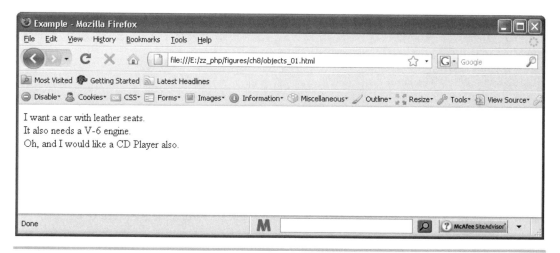

Figure 8-1   The features you like from each type of car are printed in the browser

Notice how the creation of the custom_car instance of the car object sends parameters that happen to be the properties of the other instances of the car object. You are able to use object properties like variables in many cases, so this cuts the amount of code you need to write. Also notice that the document.write() commands were changed to use the properties of the custom_car instead of the old variables. The output of the script is the same, as shown in Figure 8-2.

Property Values While this isn't real estate, you can alter your property values. In your scripts, you can change the value of an object property on-the-fly by assigning it a new value, just like a variable. For example, if you wanted to change the value of the work_car. engine property from the previous examples, you could just assign it a new value of your choice. The following example shows the assignment of a new value to the work_car.engine property:

```
work_car.engine= "V-4";
```

While perhaps not a good change, it could save you money on insurance (and gas)!

It is important to note that the preceding assignment will change the value of the work_car.engine property for any calls made to it after the change. Anything you do with its value before the change would not be affected. So, to have an effect on the outcome of your script, you would have to change the value of the work_car.engine property before you create your custom_car instance of the car object, which uses this property.

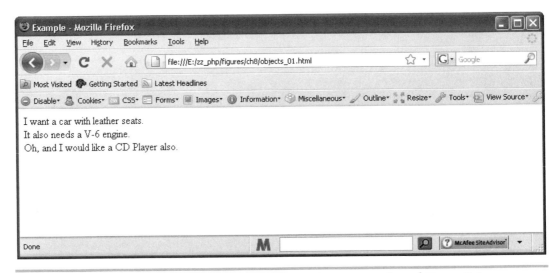

Figure 8-2 Although coded differently, the output is the same as that of Figure 8-1

The following code gives a new assignment to the property before the new instance of the object is created:

```
function car(seats,engine,theradio) {
  this.seats=seats;
  this.engine=engine;
  this.theradio=theradio;
}
var work_car= new car("cloth","V-6","Tape Deck");
var fun_car= new car("leather","V-8","CD Player");

work_car.engine="V-4";         ◄─────────── One of the properties of an object is changed, which
                                            alters that property for anything using it afterward

var custom_car= new car(fun_car.seats,work_car.engine,fun_car.theradio);

document.write("I want a car with "+custom_car.seats+" seats.<br />");
document.write("It also needs a "+custom_car.engine+" engine.<br />");
document.write("Oh, and I would like a "+custom_car.theradio+" also.");
```

The work_car.engine property is originally set to V-6, but it is changed to V-4 just before the custom_car instance of the car object is created. This means that when you use the work_car.engine property while creating your custom_car instance, it will use the changed value of V-4 because it is used after the change was made. Figure 8-3 shows the results of this changed code.

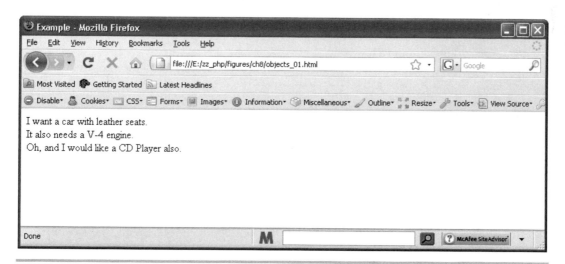

Figure 8-3 One of the property values is changed, changing the output of the script

To drive home the point, you could use the property both before and after it is changed to see how it affects the script. The following code shows this:

```
function car(seats,engine,theradio) {
  this.seats=seats;
  this.engine=engine;
  this.theradio=theradio;
}
var work_car= new car("cloth","V-6","Tape Deck");
var fun_car= new car("leather","V-8","CD Player");

var first_engine=work_car.engine;

work_car.engine="V-4";

var custom_car= new car(fun_car.seats,work_car.engine,fun_car.theradio);

document.write("At first, I wanted a "+first_engine+" engine.<br />");
document.write("But after thinking about it a bit:<br />");
document.write("I want a car with "+custom_car.seats+" seats.<br />");
document.write("It also needs a "+custom_car.engine+" engine.<br />");
document.write("Oh, and I would like a "+custom_car.theradio+" also.");
```

The original value of the property is assigned to an independent variable

The property is changed, changing the value of it when used afterward

Notice how the work_car.engine value is assigned to the first_engine variable. It is then changed before you create your custom_car instance of the car object. When you write the value of the first_engine variable to the browser, it has the old value of the work_car.engine property since it was assigned before the change was made.

When you write the values of your custom_car properties, you can see that the change was made sometime before you created the custom_car instance of the car object. Figure 8-4 shows the results of this script in a browser.

Now that you know how to use constructor functions, take a look at the object initializer method.

Object Initializers

An object initializer is a little bit shorter than a constructor function. The following is the syntax of an object initializer:

```
object_name={property:value}
```

In the preceding code, you would replace *object_name* with the name you want to give your object; replace *property* with the name you want to use for a property of the object; and replace *value* with the value of the property that precedes it. You can add more properties and values by separating each with a comma.

An object created with the initializer function is already an instance of the object, so you can just use the properties without the need to create a new instance of the object.

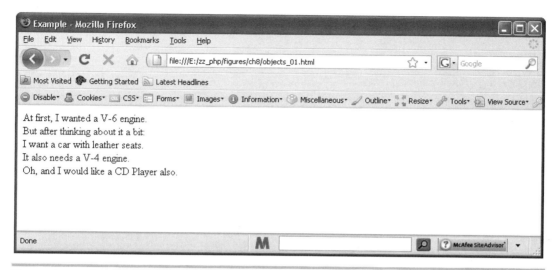

Figure 8-4 The change in the property value affects the statements that use it after the change, but not those that use it before the change

Next, you will create a work_car object by using the initializer method. You want the object name to be work_car, and you will have three sets of properties and values. The following code shows how to create the object by using the object initializer method:

```
work_car= {seats:"cloth",engine:"V-6",theradio:"Tape Deck"}
```

Since there is no need to create an instance of the object, you can use its properties just as you did before, and assign them to variables or write them to the page. For instance, the property of work_car.seats would be cloth.

If you want the fun_car object back as well, you can use another initializer, as shown in the following example code:

```
work_car= {seats:"cloth",engine:"V-6",theradio:"Tape Deck"}
fun_car= {seats:"leather",engine:"V-8",theradio:"CD Player"}
```

You can then write out what you want to have in a car using those properties, as shown in the following code:

Objects are created using object initializers

```
work_car= {seats:"cloth",engine:"V-6",theradio:"Tape Deck"}
fun_car= {seats:"leather",engine:"V-8",theradio:"CD Player"}

document.write("I want a car with "+fun_car.seats+" seats.<BR>");
document.write("It also needs a "+work_car.engine+" engine.<BR>");
document.write("Oh, and I would like a "+fun_car.theradio+" also.");
```

Properties of the objects are used in document.write() statements

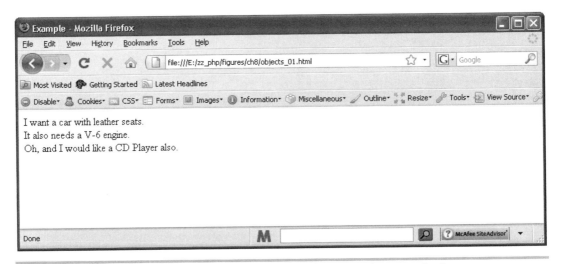

Figure 8-5 The properties you like from each type of car are shown in the browser

This prints what you like from each type of car to the browser screen. Figure 8-5 shows the results of this script in a browser.

This method can cut the coding a bit, at least if you only want to use one or two instances of the same type of object.

Adding Methods

A method is a function call that is part of an object. The function called can perform various tasks that you might want to execute with the properties of the object.

Consider the car object that you created with a constructor function earlier in the chapter. You might want to have functions for the car to stop, accelerate, or turn. You might also decide to make a calculation of some sort, like a payment. If you wanted to add a function for that object that would calculate the monthly payments on the various types (instances) of cars that you sent to it, you could create a function like the following:

Function to be used as a method is defined   The payment variable is created and given an initial value

```
function get_payment() {
   var the_payment=250;
   if(this.seats == "leather") {
     the_payment+=100;
   }
   else {
     the_payment+=50;
   }
```

An if/else statement decides how much to add to the payment variable based on the value of the seats property of an object

```
if(this.engine == "V-8") {
   the_payment+=150;
}
else {
   the_payment+=75;
}
```

An if/else statement decides how much to add to the payment variable based on the value of the engine property of an object

```
if(this.theradio == "CD Player") {
   the_payment+=35;
}
else {
  the_payment+=10;
}
```

An if/else statement decides how much to add to the payment variable based on the value of the theradio property of an object

```
return the_payment;
}
```

The value of the_payment is returned

Well, the previous function is really long. It can be shortened by using the conditional operator for each if/else statement here (for further information on the conditional operator, refer to Chapter 6):

The conditional operator is used in place of the if/else statements to make the code shorter

```
function get_payment() {
  var the_payment=250;
  the_payment += (this.seats == "leather") ? 100 : 50;
  the_payment += (this.engine == "V-8") ? 150 : 75;
  the_payment += (this.theradio == "CD Player") ? 35 : 10;
  return the_payment;
}
```

After you have defined the function, you need to assign it to your object within your object constructor function. Using your trusty car object constructor function, you would assign it as shown in the following code:

```
function car(seats,engine,theradio) {
  this.seats=seats;
  this.engine=engine;
  this.theradio=theradio;
  this.payment=get_payment;
}
```

The get_payment() function is assigned like a property, making it a method of the current object; notice that the parentheses are not used in the assignment

Notice that this example defines a method named payment that calls the get_payment() function from outside the constructor function. Also notice that when the function is called here, the parentheses are not used on the end of the function call. This is how your outside function becomes a method of the object (by assigning it the function rather than the result of the function).

In order to call the payment() method of the object, you need an instance of the car object. If you add the three instances you made earlier, you will be able to do some things with your new method. So, add those instances to the code you already have:

The function that is used as a method

```
function get_payment() {
  var the_payment=250;
  the_payment += (this.seats == "leather") ? 100 : 50;
  the_payment += (this.engine == "V-8") ? 150 : 75;
  the_payment += (this.theradio == "CD Player") ? 35 : 10;
  return the_payment;
}
function car(seats,engine,theradio) {
  this.seats=seats;
  this.engine=engine;
  this.theradio=theradio;
  this.payment=get_payment;
}
var work_car= new car("cloth","V-6","Tape Deck");
var fun_car= new car("leather","V-8","CD Player");
var custom_car= new car(fun_car.seats,work_car.engine,fun_car.theradio);
```

The constructor function, which makes the function a method function

Instances of the object are created and can use the method if needed

Now you have the function that is used to create the payment() method of the car object, the creation of the payment() method within the car object constructor function, and three instances of the car object.

To find the monthly payments for work_car, you would call the payment() method using the following syntax:

```
var work_car_payments= work_car.payment();
```

The value of the work_car_payments variable will be the value returned from the payment() method, which is what is returned from the get_payment() function when run with the values used for the work_car instance of the car object.

Since the seats are cloth, the_payment is increased by 50 (if they were leather it would have been 100). Since the engine is a V-6, the_payment is increased by 75. Finally, since the theradio property has a value of Tape Deck, the the_payment variable is increased by 10. This gives you a payment of 250 (initial value) + 50 (nonleather seats) + 75 (non-V-8 engine) +10 (radio without CD player), which turns out to be 385.

Using the payment() method, you could now write a script to display the payment amount for each type of car in the browser so the viewer can decide what type of car to buy. You would just expand on your previous code to include in the body of the page some document.write() commands that use the values returned from the payment() method. Save the JavaScript file as objects_02.js and create an HTML file with the following body code and save it as objects_02.html:

```
<body>
<script type="text/javascript" src="objects_02.js"></script>
</body>
```

The following JavaScript code for the objects_02.js file gives an example of the payment() method when used for each instance of the car object:

```javascript
function get_payment() {
  var the_payment=250;
  the_payment += (this.seats == "leather") ? 100 : 50;
  the_payment += (this.engine == "V-8") ? 150 : 75;
  the_payment += (this.theradio == "CD Player") ? 35 : 10;
  return the_payment;
}
function car(seats,engine,theradio) {
  this.seats=seats;
  this.engine=engine;
  this.theradio=theradio;
  this.payment=get_payment;
}


var work_car= new car("cloth","V-6","Tape Deck");
var fun_car= new car("leather","V-8","CD Player");
var custom_car= new car(fun_car.seats,work_car.engine,fun_car.theradio);

var work_car_payment= work_car.payment();
var fun_car_payment= fun_car.payment();
var custom_car_payment= custom_car.payment();

document.write("<h2>The information on the cars you requested:</h2>");
document.write("<strong>Work Car: </strong>");
document.write(work_car.seats+","+work_car.engine+","+work_car.theradio);
document.write("<br />");
document.write("<strong>Payments:</strong> $"+work_car_payment);
document.write("<p>");
document.write("<strong >Fun Car: </strong>");
document.write(fun_car.seats+","+fun_car.engine+","+fun_car.theradio);
document.write("<br />");
document.write("<strong>Payments:</strong> $"+fun_car_payment);
document.write("</p>");
document.write("<p>");
document.write("<strong>Custom Car: </strong>");
document.write(custom_car.seats+","+custom_car.engine+",");
document.write(custom_car.theradio);
document.write("<br />");
document.write("<strong>Payments:</strong> $"+custom_car_payment);
document.write("</p>");
```

The returned value of the method function for each of three instances of the object is assigned to three independent variables

Various object properties and variables are used in the document.write() statements to create a listing of the cars, their features, and the payment amounts

The script is quite long compared to most of the scripts you have done up to this point. The result of the preceding script is a listing of each type of car, its features, and the payment amount for the car.

Some of the document.write() statements in the previous code are being used to continue the statement preceding them, because of the limited space available to show the code. In your text editor, you don't have such space limitations, so you could put as much code in one document.write() command as you like. Figure 8-6 shows the results of the code when run in a browser. You are starting to make some scripts that are more useful!

Object Manipulation Statements

JavaScript allows you to use the for-in loop to help you manipulate objects and the with statement to access particular objects more easily.

The for-in Loop

The for-in loop allows you to cycle through the properties of an object to display them or to manipulate their values. The following code shows the structure of a for-in loop:

The loop begins by naming a variable to represent the property names in the object, along with the name of the object

```
for (var variable_name in object_name) {
  JavaScript statements
}
```

JavaScript statements go here

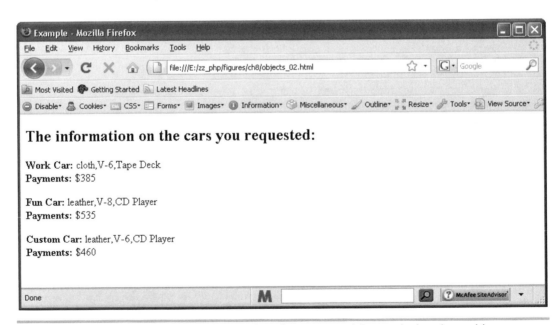

Figure 8-6 A listing of the types of cars, their features, and their calculated monthly payments

Suppose you wanted to cycle through the properties of a work_car instance of a car object in order to display the values of each property on the page. The for-in loop allows you to do this without the need to type each property name, as in this code:

```
                                     The object is created
function car(seats,engine,theradio) {
    this.seats=seats;
    this.engine=engine;                              An instance of the
    this.theradio=theradio;                          object is created
}
var work_car= new car("cloth","V-6","Tape Deck");
for (var prop_name in work_car) {                    The for-in loop begins
    document.write(work_car[prop_name]+"<br />");
}
                                     The value of each property of the work_car
                                     instance of the car object is written on the page
```

You will notice that the work_car[prop_name] part of the script is unfamiliar. The for-in loop uses an array to store the property values, which calls for this syntax. You will learn more about arrays in Chapter 11, so don't worry if this isn't clear yet. Once you have learned how to use arrays, the for-in loop will be a useful way to manipulate your objects. For now, you only need to know the function of the for-in loop.

The with Statement

The with statement allows you to access or manipulate the properties and methods of an object more easily if you plan to use a large number of statements that use the object. For instance, if you want to write a number of statements about an object named car on a Web page, you might grow weary of typing the object name (car), the dot operator, and then the property name.

The with statement allows you to leave off the object name and the dot operator for statements inside the with block, so that you only need to type the property names to access the properties you need. The following code shows the structure of a with statement:

```
with (object) {                The name of the object is placed inside the parentheses
    JavaScript statements
}
               JavaScript statements that use the object go here
```

Suppose you have an object named car with the properties seats, engine, and radio, and an instance of the object named work_car. You could use the with statement to avoid typing work_car and the dot operator repeatedly, as in the following example:

```
function car(seats,engine,theradio) {
    this.seats=seats;
    this.engine=engine;                      The object is created
    this.theradio=theradio;
}
var work_car= new car("cloth","V-6","Tape Deck");   An instance of the
with (work_car) {                                    object is created
               The with statement is used with the work_car instance of the object
```

```
document.write("Seats: "+seats+"<br />");
document.write("Engine: "+engine+"<br />");
document.write("Radio: "+theradio);
}
```

Now the properties of the work_car instance of the object can be accessed without the need to type work_car and the dot operator each time a property is used

This example writes the values of the properties of the work_car instance of the car object on the page. Notice that while inside the with block, the property names could be used without the need to type work_car and the dot operator in front of them.

Now that you have seen how to create objects, properties, and methods of your own, you can better understand how some of the predefined JavaScript objects work. A number of predefined JavaScript objects are discussed as you move through the rest of this chapter and through several of the chapters to follow.

Ask the Expert

Q: Do I really have to create an instance of an object every time I want one when I use a constructor function?

A: Yes. The constructor function only gives the browser the structure of an object. To use that structure, you need to create an instance of the object. You will see in Chapter 12 that you need to create instances with some of the predefined JavaScript objects as well.

Q: So what about object initializers? I don't have to create instances with them?

A: Object initializers create an object rather than just giving it a structure like a constructor function. So, the object created doesn't need to have instances created.

Q: Will I need to use self-written objects a lot?

A: Probably not, but it depends on your script and what you want to do. Many of the scripts in this book use predefined JavaScript objects; however, you may use a self-written object if it helps you with your scripts later.

Q: Can an object have more than one method?

A: You can include as many methods as you like in an object by repeating what you did with your method earlier in the chapter. For instance, you could have added another method to calculate the insurance costs of each type of car based on the properties you had for the car types.

Try This 8-1 Create a Computer Object

pr8_1.html
prjs8_1.js

In this project, you create objects on your own and develop the skills involved in object creation. The script will create a computer object and then use properties, methods, and instances of the object to create feature lists and price lists for the different types of computers.

Step by Step

1. Create an HTML page and save it as pr8_1.html. Add the necessary script tags to point to an external JavaScript file named prjs8_1.js.

2. Create an external JavaScript file and save it as prjs8_1.js. Use it for steps 3–12.

3. Create an object named computer that has three properties named speed, hdspace, and ram.

4. Create an instance of the computer object and name it work_computer. Send the string values of 2GHz for the speed parameter, 80GB for the hdspace parameter, and 1GB for the ram parameter.

5. Create an instance of the computer object and name it home_computer. Send the string values of 1.5GHz for the speed parameter, 40GB for the hdspace parameter, and 512MB for the ram parameter.

6. Create an instance of the computer object and name it laptop_computer. Send the string values of 1GHz for the speed parameter, 20GB for the hdspace parameter, and 256MB for the ram parameter.

7. Create a function named get_price() that will calculate the price of a computer. The base price of a computer is 500 and should be assigned to a variable named the_price. If the speed property of an object is equal to 2GHz, add 200 to the value of the_price; otherwise, add 100 to the_price. If the hdspace property of an object is 80GB, add 50 to the value of the_price; otherwise, add 25 to the_price. If the ram property of an object is 1GB, add 150 to the value of the_price; otherwise, add 75 to the_price. End the function with a return statement that returns the value of the variable the_price.

8. Add a call to the function created in step 6 to the computer object. Give the method the name price.

9. Assign the value returned by the price() method when used with the work_computer instance of the object to a variable named work_computer_price.

10. Assign the value returned by the price() method when used with the home_computer instance of the object to a variable named home_computer_price.

11. Assign the value returned by the price() method when used with the laptop_computer instance of the object to a variable named laptop_computer_price.

(continued)

12. Write the features and price for each type of computer to the browser screen in the same format you used in the car example earlier in the chapter.

13. Save the JavaScript file and view the HTML file in your browser. You should have a list of features and the price for each computer written on the screen.

Try This Summary

In this project, you were able to use your new knowledge of objects to create an object with properties and a method function. You were able to create a Web page that displays the prices of different computers in the browser.

Understanding Predefined JavaScript Objects

In JavaScript, there are many predefined objects you can use to gain access to certain properties or methods you may need. You can make your scripts even more interactive once you learn the various objects and what you can do with them.

This book will be covering a number of the major predefined objects. Some of them will be the basis for an entire chapter, while others are smaller and may only need a portion of a chapter. To get started, in this chapter, you are going to look at the navigator object and history objects, and what you can do with them.

The Navigator Object

The navigator object gives you access to various properties of the viewer's browser, such as its name, version number, and more. It got its name from the Netscape Navigator browser, which preceded Mozilla/Firefox.

The navigator object is part of the window object, which means you can access its properties and methods using window.navigator.*property_or_method_name*, but it can also be shortened to simply navigator.*property_or_method_name*. This is true even for direct properties or methods of the window object as well (for example, window.alert("Hi"); could be shortened to simply alert("Hi"); and it would still be valid). You'll commonly see such properties and methods of the window object shortened in this way to save extra typing or to help shorten the source code.

First, take a look at the properties of the navigator object.

Properties

The properties of the navigator object let you find out various things about the browser the viewer is using. The properties of the navigator object cannot be changed, because they are set as read-only. This is so you don't try to change the user's browser version from 6.0 to 7.0 or something similar. Instead, you can just find out what the value of the property is and use it to allow your scripts to do different things for different browsers.

Table 8-1 shows the properties of the navigator object and the values returned by each property. Also, if a property only works in one or two of the three major browsers mentioned in this book, there is a note in parentheses for that property.

Property	Value
appCodeName	The code name of the browser
appName	The name of the browser
appMinorVersion	A string representing the minor version of the browser (Internet Explorer only)
appVersion	The version of the browser and some other information
browserLanguage	The language of the browser being used (Internet Explorer and Opera)
buildID	The build identifier of the browser being used (Firefox only)
cookieEnabled	Specifies whether or not the browser has cookies enabled
cpuClass	A string representing the class of the CPU (Internet Explorer only)
language	The language of the browser being used (Firefox and Opera)
mimeTypes	An array of MIME types supported by the browser
onLine	Specifies whether or not the browser is in "global offline mode"
oscpu	A string representing the operating system of the computer (Firefox only)
platform	The machine type for which the browser was created
plugins	An array of the plugins the browser has installed on it
product	A string representing the product name of the browser being used (Firefox only)
productSub	The build number of the browser being used (Firefox only)
securityPolicy	An empty string—returned a value in Netscape 4.7 (Firefox only)
systemLanguage	The default language used by the operating system (Internet Explorer only)
userLanguage	The natural language of the operating system (Internet Explorer and Opera)
userAgent	The user agent header for the browser
vendor	An empty string—returned a string representing the vendor of the browser being used (Firefox only)
vendorSub	An empty string—returned the vendor version number of the browser being used (Firefox only)

Table 8-1 Properties of the Navigator Object

Now that you know the properties of the navigator object, you can begin to use them in your scripts. The following sections take a look at some of the more useful properties in more detail.

The appCodeName Property   This property holds the value of the application code name of the browser, which is often something like Mozilla. Other than writing it to the screen or sending an alert to the viewer, you don't have much use for it at this time. The following code shows how to send an alert to the viewer to tell him or her the appCodeName of the browser being used to view the page:

```
window.alert("You are using "+navigator.appCodeName);
```

Notice that you use the object name followed by the dot operator and then the property name, just like you did when you created your own objects. This is how you are able to access the properties of the navigator object.

Note that with this property, most every browser returns Mozilla, which was used as the code name for an early version of Netscape Navigator.

The appName Property This property allows you to find out which type of browser the viewer is using to browse the page. If the browser is Firefox, the value of this property will be Netscape. If the browser is Internet Explorer, then the value of this property will be Microsoft Internet Explorer. Other browsers will have corresponding values.

If you need to know the value for a particular browser, you can create a script to alert the value of this property, place the script inside script tags on a Web page, and then view the page in that browser. You will then be alerted to the value of the property for that browser. The following code shows how the alert can be coded:

```
window.alert("You have "+navigator.appName);
```

Since this enables you to find out the type of browser being used, you can create a simple browser-detection script.

Suppose you want to send the viewer an alert based on your opinion of the browser being used. You could use the navigator.appName property to create an if/else block and send the appropriate comment to the viewer based on the browser type.

The following code shows an example of how you could perform this task:

```
<body>
<script type="text/javascript">
switch (navigator.appName) {
  case "Netscape" : window.alert("Firefox/Netscape is cool."); break;
  case "Microsoft Internet Explorer" : window.alert("Internet Explorer is Cool.");
    break;
  case "Opera" : window.alert("Opera is cool."); break;
  default :  window.alert("What browser is this?");
}
</script>
Hi, and welcome!
</body>
```

A switch block is used to determine the value of the navigator.appName property and give the viewer the proper alert

As you can see, the viewer can now find out just what you think of the browser being used. Figure 8-7 shows the alert you would get if you were using Firefox to view the page.

The appVersion Property This property has a value of the version number of the browser and some additional information. For example, in Firefox 3 for Windows XP, you might see the following text as the value of this property:

```
5.0 (Windows; en-US)
```

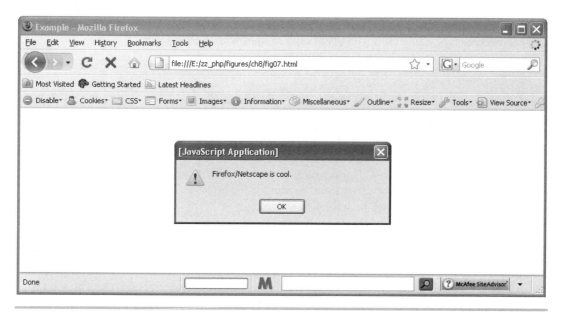

Figure 8-7 The alert you get when entering the page with Firefox

This can be beneficial when you use techniques that should only be executed in browser versions above a certain level. Note, though, that browsers return various results for this property, as the value returned for Internet Explorer 7 on Windows Vista shown here:

```
4.0 (compatible; MSIE 7.0; Windows NT 6.0; SLCC1; .NET CLR 2.0.50727;
 Media Center PC 5.0; .NET CLR 3.5.30729; .NET CLR 3.0.30618)
```

The first part of the string is 4.0, and later it describes itself as MSIE 7.0. Thus, you must use care when using this property as you will need to know what various browsers return to make the best use of the information.

The cookieEnabled Property   This property returns a Boolean value of true if cookies are enabled in the browser, and returns a Boolean value of false if cookies are not enabled in the browser. You will read about cookies in more detail in Chapter 16.

The onLine Property   This property returns a Boolean value of true if the viewer's system is not in global offline mode (see http://msdn.microsoft.com/en-us/library/aa768170(VS.85).aspx for details on this), and returns a Boolean value of false if the system is in global offline mode.

The platform Property   This property holds the value of the type of machine for which the browser was created. For example, on a Windows XP machine, the value would be Win32.

There are different values for various types of machines. If you want to let the viewer know the machine type being used, you could send an alert with this property:

```
window.alert("Your machine is a "+navigator.platform+" machine.");
```

While not very useful here, the property could be used to redirect viewers to an appropriate page based on their machine type.

The plugins Property   This array holds the values of all the plugins installed in the viewer's browser. You will find out more about arrays in Chapter 12.

The userAgent Property   This property gives you another long string of information about the browser. This string is the user agent header for the browser. For instance, in Firefox 3 for Windows XP, you might see the following string:

```
Mozilla/5.0 (Windows; U; Windows NT 5.1; en-US; rv:1.9.0.4)
Gecko/2008102920
  Firefox/3.0.4
```

It is pretty similar to the text you saw for the navigator.appVersion property, but with a little more information.

Now that you know about the properties of the navigator object, you are ready to look at the methods of the object.

Methods

The navigator object also has a number of methods you can use to perform various tasks. Table 8-2 shows the methods available in the navigator object.

The following section looks at the javaEnabled() method and how it can be used.

The javaEnabled() Method   This method returns a Boolean value of true if the viewer has Java enabled in the browser; otherwise, it returns false. The javaEnabled() method could be useful if you want to display a Java applet to the viewer, but only if the viewer has Java enabled in the browser.

Method	Purpose
javaEnabled()	Used to test whether or not Java is enabled in the browser
mozIsLocallyAvailable()	Checks to see if a file at a certain address is available locally (Firefox only)
preference()	Allows certain browser preferences to be set (requires signed script)
registerContentHandler()	Allows a Web site to set itself as a potential handler of a certain MIME type
registerProtocolHandler()	Allows a Web site to set itself as a potential handler of a certain protocol
taintEnabled()	Returns false— because the method is no longer being in use. It was used to specify whether or not data tainting was enabled in the browser

Table 8-2   Methods of the Navigator Object

For now, you will just see how to send the viewer an alert, as an example. This way you don't need to mess with any Java syntax yet. The following code sends one alert if the viewer has Java enabled and sends another if the viewer does not have Java enabled:

```
var hasJava= navigator.javaEnabled()
if (hasJava==true) {
  window.alert("Cool, you have Java!");
}
else {
  window.alert("Java disabled? You cannot see my Java Applet!");
}
```

This tests the value returned by the navigator.javaEnabled() method and gives the user the correct alert. Again, this is more useful if you have a Java applet that you want to use someplace on the page.

The History Object

The history object, which is also part of the window object, provides information on the browser history of the current window.

Property

The history object has only one property, named length (in Firefox, a few more are available, but they do not work with Web content). This property returns the number of pages in the session history of the browser for the current window, which includes the currently loaded page. It could be used in a manner similar to this:

```
<body>
<script type="text/javascript">
alert("Your current window has viewed "+history.length+" pages!")
</script>
</body>
```

This simply sends an alert to the viewer to say how many pages have been visited in the current browser window.

Methods

There are three methods of the history object, listed in Table 8-3.

Method	Purpose
Back()	Sends the browser window back one page in the history list
Forward()	Sends the browser one page forward in the history list
Go()	Sends the browser to a specified page in the history list using an integer value

Table 8-3   Methods of the History Object

The following sections discuss each of these methods in more detail.

The back() Method   The back() method sends the browser to the last page visited in the history list before the current page, which is like using the browser's "back" button. To use it, you simply call the method in your script where desired. Thus, if you wanted your own "back" button made from a form button, you could use something similar to the following code. First is the HTML body section code (save as history_01.html):

```
<body>
<form>
<input type="button" value="Back" id="back_button" />
</form>
<script type="text/javascript" src="history_01.js"></script>
</body>
```

Next is the external JavaScript code (save as history_01.js):

```
var bb = document.getElementById("back_button");
bb.onclick = function() {
  history.back();
};
```

Loading the HTML page will display the "back" button. When you click it, the browser will go to the last page visited before the current page. If the browser window has no previous history, clicking the button will do nothing.

The forward() Method   The forward() method sends the browser to the page visited in the history list after the current page, which is like using the browser's "forward" button. To use it, you simply call the method in your script where desired. Using this, you could update your previous script to add a "forward" button as well. The updated HTML and JavaScript code is shown next.
The HTML code:

```
<body>
<form>
<input type="button" value="Back" id="back_button" /><br />
<input type="button" value="Forward" id="forward_button" />
</form>
<script type="text/javascript" src="history_01.js"></script>
</body>
```

The updated external JavaScript code:

```
var bb = document.getElementById("back_button");
var fb = document.getElementById("forward_button");
bb.onclick = function() {
  history.back();
};
fb.onclick = function() {
  history.forward();
};
```

Loading the HTML page will now display both buttons. As with the back() method, the use of forward() without a forward page in the window's history list will do nothing.

The go() Method   The go() method takes in an integer as a parameter. The integer can be a negative number to go back in the history list or a positive number to move forward in the history list. For instance, the following code would go back two pages in the window's history:

```
history.go(-2);
```

The following code would go three pages forward in the history list:

```
history.go(3);
```

As with the other two methods, if the page the viewer is attempting to access does not exist (for example, something like history.go(15) may not exist in the window's history), then the method will simply do nothing.

The predefined JavaScript objects can be quite helpful. As you'll see in the next chapter, the document object gives you access to a number of additional properties and methods for working with the HTML document.

Try This 8-2 Practice with the Predefined Navigator Object

```
pr8_2.html
prjs8_2.js
```

This project allows you to practice using some of the properties and methods of the predefined navigator object. You will create a page that alerts the viewer to various types of information, based on the browser being used.

Step by Step

1. Create an HTML page and save it as pr8_2.html.

2. Create an external JavaScript file and save it as prjs8_2.js. Use it for steps 3–12.

3. Code an alert that pops up when the viewer enters the page. The alert should say "Hi! You are viewing my page with . . ." followed by the name of the browser being used by the viewer.

4. If the user has Java enabled, send a new alert to the viewer that says "You have Java enabled, that is cool!" If the viewer does not have Java enabled, send an alert that says "No Java? Well, no fun stuff here then."

5. Send a new alert that tells the viewer what type of machine is being used. The alert should say "You are using . . ." followed by the type of machine the viewer is using to view the page.

6. Save the files and open the HTML file in one or more browsers (or other computers if you can). See how the results vary based on what is being used while viewing the Web page.

(continued)

Try This Summary

In this project, you used your knowledge of the properties and methods of the predefined navigator object. You were able to create a Web page that sends different alerts to the viewer based on the browser, the machine type, and whether or not Java is enabled.

Chapter 8 Self Test

1. An object is a way of modeling something _____, even though the object is a(n) _____ entity.

2. When you think of an object, you'll probably want to visualize something _____.

3. Objects are useful because they give you another way to _____ things within a script.

4. In JavaScript, you access object properties through the use of the

   A addition operator

   B dot operator

   C multiplication operator

   D You can't access the properties of an object

5. The rules for naming objects are similar to those for naming _____ and _____.

6. You can create JavaScript objects using either a _____ function or an object _____.

7. A constructor function allows you to build an object using the same basic syntax as a regular function.

   A True

   B False

8. An object initializer is a little bit longer than a constructor function.

   A True

   B False

9. What could you say about the following code:

   ```
   var x=myhouse.kitchen;
   ```

   A It assigns the string myhouse.kitchen to the variable *x*.

   B It adds the values of myhouse and kitchen and assigns them to an object named *x*.

C Assuming the myhouse object exists, it assigns the value of the kitchen property of the myhouse object to the variable *x*.

D Assuming the kitchen object exists, it assigns the value of the myhouse property of the kitchen object to the variable *x*.

10. Which of the following lines correctly creates a method named cost from a function named get_cost(), if this line is within a constructor function?

   A this.cost=get_cost();

   B cost=get_cost;

   C get_cost=this.cost();

   D this.cost=get_cost;

11. Which of the following would send an alert to the viewer that tells the name of the browser being used?

   A window.alert("You are using "+navigator.appVersion);

   B window.alert("You are using "+navigator.appName);

   C window.alert("You are using "+navigator.javaEnabled());

   D window.alert("You are using navigator.appName");

12. What could you say about the following code?

   ```
   myhouse.kitchen="big";
   ```

   A Assuming the kitchen object exists, the myhouse property is assigned a new string value.

   B Assuming the myhouse object exists, the value of the variable kitchen is added to the string big.

   C Assuming the myhouse object exists, the kitchen property is assigned a new string value.

   D This wouldn't do anything.

13. In JavaScript, there are many _____ objects you can use to gain access to certain properties and methods you may need.

14. The _____ object gives you access to the various properties of the viewer's browser.

15. Which of the following is not a property of the navigator object?

   A appName

   B appCodeName

   C appType

   D appVersion

Chapter 9

The Document Object

Key Skills & Concepts

- Defining the Document Object

- Using the Document Object Model

- Using the Properties of the Document Object

- Using the Methods of the Document Object

- Creating Dynamic Scripts

Now that you know how objects work and how to use predefined JavaScript objects, it is time to look at some of the major predefined objects in JavaScript.

This chapter covers the document object, which helps you to gather information about the page that is being viewed in the browser. As you will find out in this chapter, some of the document object's properties and methods can be used to get information about the document or to change information about the document. You will also be introduced to the Document Object Model, and see how this can be used with style sheets to create dynamic scripts.

Defining the Document Object

The document object is an object that is created by the browser for each new HTML page (document) that is viewed. By doing this, JavaScript gives you access to a number of properties and methods that can affect the document in various ways.

You have been using the write() method of the document object for quite some time in this book. This method allows you to write a string of text into an HTML document.

To begin your journey through the document object, you will take a look at the Document Object Model (DOM) and the various properties you can access with this object. Many of these properties will turn out to be quite useful when writing scripts.

Using the Document Object Model

The Document Object Model (DOM) allows JavaScript (and other scripting languages) to access the structure of the document in the browser. Each document is made up of structured nodes (for example, the body tag would be a node, and any elements within the body element would be child nodes of the body element). With this structure in place, a scripting language can access the elements within the document in a number of ways, allowing for the modification of the elements within the document.

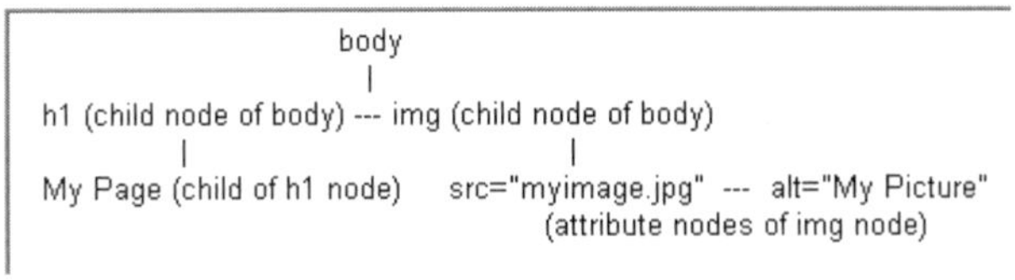

```
                              body
                               |
           h1 (child node of body) --- img (child node of body)
                   |                              |
           My Page (child of h1 node)    src="myimage.jpg" --- alt="My Picture"
                                              (attribute nodes of img node)
```

Figure 9-1 An example of part of a document's structure

If you had the following HTML code, you could use JavaScript to access its structure:

```html
<body>
  <h1>My Page</h1>
  <img src="myimage.jpg" alt="My Picture" />
</body>
```

Figure 9-1 shows how the body element is a node, and how it can have child nodes and attribute nodes.

The h1 and img elements are both child nodes of the body element. Each element also has its own nodes. The h1 element contains a text node as its child node (the text "My Page"), while the img element contains two attribute nodes (src="myimage.jpg" and alt="My Picture"). This type of structure is available throughout the document, so while this is a simple example, much more complex document structure trees could be drawn for most HTML pages.

You have already been accessing the DOM using the document.getElementById() method to access elements in the document by their id attribute values. You can also get groups of elements using such methods as getElementsByTagName() or getElementsByClassName().

Accessing the DOM with JavaScript allows you to create more dynamic scripts that can alter elements within the document in reaction to user events. You are also able to create elements and nodes using certain JavaScript methods of the document object (such as createElement() or createTextNode()). These types of scripts will be covered later in the chapter.

First, you will look at the properties and methods of the document object.

Using the Properties of the Document Object

Table 9-1 lists the properties of the document object with a short description of each. Following the table, some specific properties are discussed in more detail. Sample scripts are provided for several of the properties. Note that a number of the properties use arrays to hold information. If you would like to learn about arrays to better understand their use, see Chapter 11.

NOTE

Not all of these properties work cross-browser. Also, a number of them have been deprecated (alinkColor, bgColor, fgColor, linkColor, and vlinkColor). You can see more information on these properties by visiting http://developer.mozilla.org/en/DOM/document#Properties and http://msdn.microsoft.com/en-us/library/ms531073(VS.85).aspx.

Property	Description
activeElement	Returns a string holding the value of the active element in the document
alinkColor	Returns the hexadecimal value of the active link color of the document
anchors	An array of all the named anchors in the document
async	Used to tell the browser whether to load a document with an asynchronous request or a synchronous request
applets	An array of all the Java applets in a document
bgColor	Returns the hexadecimal value of the background color of the document
body	Returns the body or frameset element of the document
characterSet	Returns a string value that represents the character set used to encode the document
charset	Returns a string value that represents the character set used to encode the document
childNodes	An array of all of the child nodes of the document
compatMode	Returns the string "BackCompat" if the document is rendered in Quirks mode or the string "CSS1Compat" if the document is rendered in Strict mode
contentType	Returns a string for the Content-Type from the MIME header of the document
cookie	Used to set JavaScript cookies in a document
defaultCharset	Returns a string value that represents the default character set used to encode the document
defaultView	References the window object for the document
designMode	Returns a string value that provides information on whether or not the document can be edited
dir	Returns a string value that represents the reading direction of the document
doctype	Returns the doctype declaration associated with the document
documentElement	Returns a string representing the root node of the document
documentURIObject	Returns an object representing the URI of the document (only available to privileged JavaScript code)
domain	Returns the domain name of the server for the document
embeds	An array of all the embed tags in the document
expando	Returns a Boolean value based on whether or not arbitrary variables can be created within the document
fgColor	Returns the hexadecimal value of the default text color of the document
fileCreatedDate	Returns the date the document was created

Table 9-1 The Properties of the Document Object

Property	Description
fileModifiedDate	Returns the date the document was last modified
formName	Not a property itself, but creates a new property with each named form placed in the document
forms	An array of all the form tags in a document
frames	An array of all of the frames used in the document
height	Returns the height, in pixels, of the body element of the document
images	An array of all the image (img) tags in the document
implementation	Returns a string value representing the implementation object of the document
inputEncoding	Returns a string representing the document's encoding
lastModified	Returns the date of the last modification of the document
layers	An array of all the layer tags on the page (Netscape Navigator 4 only)
all	Allows access to all the objects on a page
linkColor	Returns the hexadecimal value of the default link color for the document
links	An array of all the link (<a>) tags in the document
location	Returns the URI of the document
namespaces	An array of all the namespaces in the document
parentWindow	Returns a reference to the parent window (the parent window's document object)
plugins	An array of all the plugins used in the document
protocol	Returns the protocol portion of the Web address (URL) of the document
readyState	Returns a string value that represents the current state of the document
referrer	Returns the URL of the document that referred the viewer to the current document
scripts	An array of all the script tags used in the document
styleSheets	An array of all the style sheets used in the document
tags	Sets the style of an HTML tag in the document
title	Returns the text used inside the title tags of the document
uniqueID	Returns a string value that represents a unique ID given to the document
URL	Returns the URL of the current document
URLUnencoded	Returns the URL of the document without any encoding
vlinkColor	Returns the hexadecimal value of the visited link color for the document
width	Returns the width, in pixels, of the body element of the document

Table 9-1   The Properties of the Document Object *(continued)*

The Color Properties

The alinkColor, bgColor, fgColor, linkColor, and vlinkColor properties were often used to obtain or change the color of various elements on the page. These properties are now recommended to be set with CSS or changed using style properties (discussed later in the chapter).

The anchors Property (Array)

The anchors property is actually an array that is set by the browser for all the named anchors in a document (such as <a name="top">). Since you haven't studied arrays yet, this won't be very helpful to you for now; however, you will find out more on how arrays like this one can be useful when you get to Chapter 11.

JavaScript gives you the length property to enable you to find out the number of named anchors on the page. You can use the length property to write to the browser window how many named anchors are on a page:

```
<body>

<h1>My Page</h1>

<a name="sec1"></a>          ←——————————— The first named anchor is
<h2>Section 1</h2>                               set with the anchor tag
This section is all about section 1 stuff...

<a name="sec2"></a>          ←——————————— The second named anchor
<h2>Section 2</h2>                               is set with the anchor tag
This section talks about all the section 2 issues and ...
<br />
<script type="text/javascript">
document.write("There are "+document.anchors.length+" named anchors"); ←┐
</script>
</body>                                  The number of named anchors
                                         is displayed on the page
```

This code creates two named anchors on the page and then writes the number of anchors on the page to the screen afterward. Figure 9-2 shows the result of this script in the browser window.

Again, this is more of an informational property for now. Once you learn arrays, you can make more use of the anchors property.

The cookie Property

The cookie property is used to set a JavaScript cookie to store information for the viewer. A cookie is a small text file saved to the viewer's computer for a particular amount of time (a set date or a browser session). Cookies can be helpful in allowing a site to remember and retrieve information for a viewer (such as the contents of a shopping cart, special settings, or session information).

Figure 9-2   The number of named anchors on the page is displayed in the browser window

To set a cookie, you set the value of the document.cookie property to a string that contains the information you want to store for the viewer. The following is the syntax:

```
document.cookie=string;
```

You would replace *string* with a text string that contains the information you want to use. Usually, this is in a format like the one shown in the following example setting of a cookie:

```
document.cookie="site=homepage";
```

You can see that there is one thing set by the cookie: the site is homepage. In between the two the equal sign is used to help separate the site and homepage when the cookie is read.

You will need to get a handle on more advanced string-handling techniques before you try to deal with cookies any further. You will see how to use the advanced string-handling techniques and how to set and read cookies in more detail in later chapters. For now, you just need to know that the document.cookie property is used to set cookies.

The dir Property

The dir property returns a string value that represents the reading direction of the document. This value can be either ltr (left to right) or rtl (right to left). This property is useful for displaying Web pages in languages that are read from right to left rather than left to right, by setting the value to rtl. For fun, you can change the way your page looks on-the-fly with this property, as in the following example code:

```
var the_button = document.getElementById("change_sides");
the_button.onclick = function() {
  document.dir = (document.dir!="ltr") ? "ltr" : "rtl";
}
```

The code checks for the values and changes them

Then, in your HTML file, you add a button to make the switch:

```
<body>
<form>
<input type="button" value="Change Sides" id="change_sides"
  onclick="switch_sides();" />
</form>
</body>
```

When the viewer clicks the button, the reading direction of the page will change. In this case, your button starts out on the left side of the page and moves to the right side when the button is clicked. Figure 9-3 shows the page before the button is clicked, and Figure 9-4 shows the page after the button is clicked.

The domain Property

The domain property holds the value of the domain name that served the page to the viewer. This value is whatever comes after http:// at the beginning of a Web address and before any forward slashes. So, if you were looking at a page from http://www.pageresource.com, the document.domain value would be www.pageresource.com.

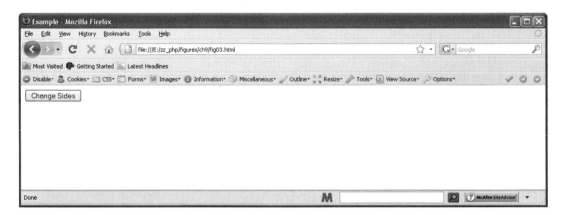

Figure 9-3 The Web page before the button is clicked

Figure 9-4 The Web page after the button is clicked

To use the domain property, you send an alert to the viewer that identifies the domain. Placing the following code in a document would pop up an alert with the value of the domain property:

```
<body>
<script type="text/javascript">
window.alert("You have reached the "+document.domain+" domain!");
</script>
</body>
```

If this code were placed on any page at http://javascriptcity.com, an alert saying "You have reached the javascriptcity.com domain!" would be sent to the viewer.

NOTE
When using this property locally without a Web server, the returned value may be an empty string rather than a domain name.

The formname Property

The formname property isn't actually a property itself. Any time you name a form, you create a formname property, but the property is actually the name of the form and not formname. To see the meaning of this, take a look at a page with a form on it. The following code will give you an HTML page that includes a form:

```
<body>                        The form is given a name to create a property
<form name="funform"> ◄───────────────────────┘
<input type= "button" name="funb" value="You can click me I suppose" />
</form>
</body>
```

This code creates a document.funform property from the name="funform" attribute in the opening <form> tag. While this doesn't do much on its own, it does allow you access to the form elements within the form.

The funform property actually has properties under it, which are named after the elements of the form. You could access the button you used in the form from its name="funb" attribute using document.funform.funb to get to it; however, even this doesn't let you do much by itself.

You need to dig down one more level. The value property allows you to set or change the value of the contents of a form element. These contents are usually set in the value attribute of the form element's tag. In the form here, you could change the value of the text on the button by accessing its value property using document.funform.funb.value and assigning it a new value.

The following example shows how you could use the onclick event handler to make the button text change when the button is clicked:

```
<body>
<form name="funform">
<input type="button" name="funb" value="You can click me I suppose"
 onclick="document.funform.funb.value='Thanks, you clicked me!';" />
</form>
</body>
```

The button text is changed by giving it a new value

Figure 9-5 shows how the page and the button will look before the button is clicked. Notice that the button shows the text that was set in the value attribute of its input tag. Now take a look at the button in Figure 9-6, after it has been clicked. The text on the button has been changed! The button lets you know that you clicked it, and it is displaying manners by saying "Thanks" to you for the click.

It should be noted that while this will work, modern browsers can simply access each form element and its value by assigning it an id and using the document.getElementById() method instead of going through the form's name first.

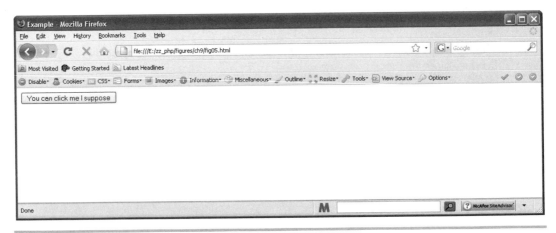

Figure 9-5 The browser display before the button is clicked

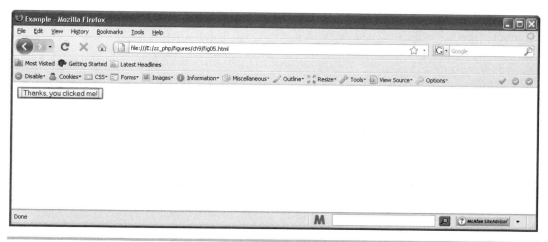

Figure 9-6   The browser display after the button is clicked

The forms Property (Array)

The forms property is an array that has an entry for each form on a Web page. The array gives you an alternative to using the formname property; however, you still need to study arrays in Chapter 11 before you can look into this array in more detail.

As with the other similar properties, you can use the length property in the form of document.forms.length to find out how many forms are on the page.

The images Property (Array)

The images property is another array. This array has an entry for each image on a Web page. As with the other similar properties, you can use the length property in the form of document. images.length to find out the number of images that are in an HTML document.

Another thing this property can be used for is to detect what browsers support the Image object in JavaScript. This is helpful if you wish to preload an image. Preloading an image is a good idea when using image rollover scripts (which you will create in Chapter 16) and can also be useful if you want to place in the viewer's cache file an image that will be used on another page within your Web site, to make that page load more quickly for the viewer.

To check whether a browser supports the Image object, you can place any code that needs the Image object within an if block. The if block will test for the existence of the document. images property, as shown in the following example code:

```
if (document.images) {
  JavaScript Statements              ◀————————  This is where you place the code that needs
}                                                the document.images property to work
```

Notice that all you need inside the parentheses is document.images. If this property exists, it returns true (since anything besides null would be treated as true—basically a short way of saying !=null), and the statements inside the block are executed. If the property does not exist, the block is ignored, and the older browsers are happy that they don't have to try any of that code.

To preload an image, you first need to create a new instance of the JavaScript Image object. The following code shows the syntax used for creating a new instance of the Image object:

```
var varname= new Image(width,height);
```

You replace *varname* with the name you want to give to this instance of the Image object. You replace *width* with the width, in pixels, of the image you wish to use, and replace *height* with the height, in pixels, of the image.

So, if you want to create an instance of the Image object named myimage, where the image would have a width of 100 pixels and a height of 75 pixels, you could use the following code:

```
var myimage= new Image(100,75);
```

The width and height parameters are optional. You can simply create the instance of the object without them as well:

```
var myimage= new Image();
```

Next, you need a way to define what image will be used (like the source [src] attribute in an image tag). The Image object comes with an src property that allows you to do this. You just have to set it by giving it a value. The following code shows how this is done:

```
var myimage= new Image();
myimage.src= "smile.gif";
```

Now the browser will try to load the image at the local address of smile.gif. You can also use a full URL if you need to do so. Since the image tries to load here without the need to be displayed, it is being preloaded.

TIP

Preloading is usually done in the head section of a document (or in an external script file that is called in the head section) so that the image starts loading as soon as possible.

To put all of this together, you need to place this code inside your if block so that it does not get run by browsers that don't support the Image object. The following code puts both pieces together and places the script inside the head section of a document. This will preload the image for later use.

```
<head>
<script language="javascript">
if (document.images) {
    var myimage= new Image();        A new instance of the Image object is created
    myimage.src= "smile.gif";
}
</script>                    The object is given a value for its
</head>                     src property, preloading the image
```

This does the job of preloading your image so you can use it later.

To preload more than one image, you need to create an instance of the Image object for each image you want to preload. So, if you want to preload three images, you could use the following code:

```
<head>
<script type="text/javascript">
if (document.images) {
   var myimage= new Image();
   myimage.src= "smile.gif";              The first image is preloaded
   var yourimage= new Image();
   yourimage.src= "friendly.gif";         The second image is preloaded
   var herimage= new Image();
   herimage.src= "happy.gif";             The third image is preloaded
}
</script>
</head>
```

This preloads three images for you. The new instance yourimage preloads an image with the filename friendly.gif. The instance herimage preloads an image with the filename happy.gif. You can add more images, using the same technique, if you'd like.

The lastModified Property

The lastModified property holds the value of the date and time the current document was last modified. This is used mostly for informational purposes, such as displaying the date the document was last modified so the viewer knows when you last updated your page. The value of this property depends on your browser, as different browsers have different results if you write the last modified date on the page.

Consider the following code, which writes the value of the document.lastModified property into a Web page to display the last modified date and time:

```
<body>
<h1>My Always Updated Web Page!</H1>
<script type="text/javascript">
   document.write("Last Updated: "+document.lastModified);
</script>
</body>
```

Figure 9-7 shows the result of this when viewed in Mozilla Firefox.

When writing the date of the last modification on the page, the differences only matter in terms of space on the page. Some layouts may need to have extra space arranged for the longer version of the property.

The layers Property (Array)

The layers property, yet another array, has an entry for each layer tag on the page, and you can use the length property in the form of document.layers.length to find the number of layers on a page. The layer tag was used in Netscape Navigator 4 as a way to create different sections

Figure 9-7 The last modified date when viewed in Mozilla Firefox

of a page (which could be layered) and access them for scripting. In modern browsers, it is no longer used, as each element can be accessed by other means (such as the document.getElementById() method).

Since this property is only available in version 4 of Netscape Navigator, you can use this property to see whether the browser being used is Netscape Navigator 4. You can test for the document.layers property in the same way you tested for the document.images property, which is nice and short:

```
if (document.layers) {
  window.alert("You have Netscape Navigator 4!");
}
```

This is useful if you need to make certain scripts are backward-compatible with Netscape Navigator 4.

The all Property

Whereas the layers property helps you to detect Netscape Navigator 4, the all property can help you to detect Internet Explorer 4 or higher. The all property was created to give JavaScript access to all the objects on a page. Again, this is better done in modern browsers using other methods such as the document.getElementById() method.

So, to see if the viewer is using Internet Explorer 4 or higher, you could use the following code:

```
if (document.all) {
  window.alert("You have Internet Explorer 4 or better!");
}
```

The links Property (Array)

The links property, another array, holds a value for each link (such as <a href="url">) and linked area of an image map (such as <area href="url">) on a page. You can find out how many links are on the page by using the document.links.length property.

The referrer Property

The referrer property is used for informational purposes and holds the value of the URL of the page that the viewer was on before arriving at your page (the referring page). While this can be useful, the viewer doesn't always come in with a referring URL (such as when using a bookmark or typing in the address), so the value could be nothing. Also, the value of this property isn't always correct, because different browsers may consider different types of things as referring the viewer to the new page, rather than just links.

To use this property, you could send an alert to the viewers of a page telling them where they were before they got to your page. Placing the code in the following example into the document would do the trick:

```
<body>
<script type="text/javascript">
  window.alert("You came from "+document.referrer+"!");
</script>
</body>
```

So, if the referring page were http://www.pageresource.com/webdes.htm, an alert saying "You came from http://www.pageresource.com/webdes.htm!" would be sent to the viewer.

The title Property

The title property holds the string value of the title of the HTML document. The title is set inside the <title> and </title> tags of a page.

You can use the title property to display the title of the page to the viewer someplace other than in the top bar of the window. The following code would allow you to do this:

```
<head>
<title>Lions, Tigers and Bears!</title>  ◀————— The title of the document is set here
</head>
<body>
<script type="text/javascript">
  document.write("<h1>" + document.title + "</h1>");  ◀——— The title is shown as a
</script>                                                       heading to the viewer
Lions and tigers and bears were what I saw when I went to ...
</body>
```

This displays your title as a heading on the page. Figure 9-8 shows the result of this when viewed in a browser.

Figure 9-8 The title of the document is shown as a heading on the page

The URL Property

The URL property holds the value of the full URL of the current document. This information can be useful if you print it at the bottom of your HTML page, because it will show the page URL for anyone who prints out your page.

While you could just type the URL at the bottom on your own, this could become tedious when it needs to be done on numerous pages. This is where this property can be handy, because you can cut and paste a little script to each page rather than type the various URL addresses each time. An example of writing the URL address on the page is shown in the following code:

```
<body>
<h1>Buy Something!</h1>
If you don't buy something I will be really upset so you had better...
<br/><br/>
<script type="text/javascript">
  document.write("You are at: "+document.URL);
</script>
</body>
```

Figure 9-9 shows the result of the preceding code in a browser. The last line of the page tells the viewer the current location. The figure shows a local file address, but it would show a regular URL if the page were online.

The URLUnencoded Property

The URLUnencoded property returns the URL of the document without any encoding. For instance, if there is a filename with a space in it, the property will return the space rather than a %20 in its place. For the URL http://www.pageresource.com/my script.html, the document.

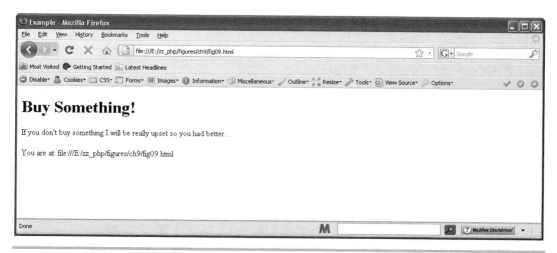

Figure 9-9   The URL of the document is shown at the end of the page contents

URL property would return http://www.pageresource.com/my%20script.html. The document. URLUnencoded property returns http://www.pageresource.com/my script.html, the URL without the encoding for the space. Note that at the time of this writing this property was only available in Microsoft Internet Explorer (of the three browsers mentioned in this book).

Ask the Expert

Q: So many of these properties were arrays that I couldn't really use yet. Will I ever use them for anything?

A: The reason the arrays weren't discussed in more detail is that you haven't yet learned how arrays work. When you do, you will be able to make better use of the properties that create arrays because you will know how to access the array and what you can do with the elements of the array when you access them.

Q: The referrer property is cool! Is there any way I can write that information to a file each time a visitor drops in so that I know where my visitors are coming from?

A: Unfortunately, client-side JavaScript cannot save information in a file (other than cookies, which are only useful to an individual viewer); thus, you can't use this property to track the URL addresses of referring pages in a personal file. To do this, you would need to use a server-side language to get the information and save it in a file on the server.

(continued)

Q: The creation of a formname property through naming a form was a little confusing. Then, trying to change the value of a form element by using its name and a value property made it more confusing. Can I see another example, perhaps with a text box or something other than a button?

A: This method of accessing form elements is not used as often with modern browsers. More often than not, a newer method such as getElementById() will be used, with which you are already familiar. If it is still confusing, do not fear. You have an entire chapter on the use of JavaScript with forms later in the book (Chapter 14).

Using the Methods of the Document Object

The methods of the document object allow you to do some new things that you haven't been able to do yet. Table 9-2 lists the methods with a short description of each. Because a number of these methods are browser-specific (as with the properties) at the time of this writing, only some specific methods are described in more detail following the table.

Method	Description
attachEvent()	Attaches a function to an event, so that the function runs when the event occurs (Internet Explorer only)
createAttribute()	Creates an attribute with a name that is sent to it as a parameter
createAttributeNS()	Creates a new attribute in a particular namespace
createCDATASection()	Creates a new CDATA section
createComment()	Creates a comment with the value that is sent to it as a parameter
createDocumentFragment()	Creates a new document fragment
createElement()	Creates an element of the type sent to it as a parameter
createElementNS()	Creates an element in a particular URI and a particular type sent to it as parameters
createEntityReference()	Creates a new entity reference
createEvent()	Creates an event
createEventObject()	Creates an event object for the purpose of passing event information
createNodeIterator()	Creates a node iterator object
createNSResolver()	Creates a namespace resolver
createProcessingInstruction()	Creates a processing instruction

Table 9-2 The Methods of the Document Object

Method	Description
createRange()	Creates a range object
createStyleSheet()	Creates a style sheet for the document to use (Internet Explorer only)
createTextNode()	Creates a text string from the value sent to it as a parameter
createTreeWalker()	Creates a treewalker object
detachEvent()	Detaches a function from an event (Internet Explorer only)
elementFromPoint()	Returns the element object that appears at the location that is sent to it in two parameter values (pixels from left and pixels from top)
evaluate()	Returns a result based on the parameters sent to it
execCommand()	Executes a command on the document when the document is in design mode
getElementById()	Returns a reference to the object with the ID attribute that is sent to it as a parameter
getElementsByClassName()	Returns references to the elements with the class name that is sent to it as a parameter
getElementsByName()	Returns references to the objects with the name attribute that is sent to it as a parameter
getElementsByTagName()	Returns references to the elements with the tag name that is sent to it as a parameter
getElementsByTagNameNS()	Returns references to the elements with the tag name and namespace sent to it as parameters
getSelection()	Returns the value of a string of selected text in the document
hasFocus()	Returns a Boolean value based on whether or not the document has focus
load()	Loads an XML document
mergeAttributes()	Copies attributes from an object
open()	Opens a new document that allows you to write its contents using write() or writeln() statements
close()	Closes a new document that has been opened with the open() method
queryCommandEnabled()	Returns a Boolean value based on whether or not a command sent to it as a parameter can be executed
queryCommandIndeterm()	Returns a Boolean value based on whether or not a command sent to it as a parameter is in the indeterminate state
queryCommandState()	Returns a Boolean value based on whether or not a command sent to it as a parameter has executed
queryCommandSupported()	Returns a Boolean value based on whether or not a command sent to it as a parameter is supported

Table 9-2   The Methods of the Document Object *(continued)*

Method	Description
queryCommandValue()	Returns the current value of the document for the command that is sent to it as a parameter
recalc()	Recalculates the dynamic properties in the document
releaseCapture()	Releases the mouse capture from the document
setActive()	Sets an object as active, but does not give it focus
write()	Allows you to write a string of text into an HTML document
writeln()	Allows you to write a string of text into an HTML document, but ends the line with a JavaScript newline character

Table 9-2 The Methods of the Document Object *(continued)*

NOTE

Not all of these properties work cross-browser. You can see more information on these properties by visiting http://developer.mozilla.org/en/DOM/document#Methods and http://msdn.microsoft.com/en-us/library/ms531073(VS.85).aspx.

The getElementById() Method

The getElementById() method is one that you have been using extensively in the book already. It allows you access to an element by the value of its id attribute. As you already know, if you have the following code, you can access the element with this method:

```
<div id="some_text">This is some text.</div>
```

Since the id attribute of the div element has the value of some_text, the document. getElementById() method can access the div element using that value as a string parameter:

```
var text_element = document.getElementById("some_text");
```

As you have done before, you could make use of an event that occurs on this element and script a reaction to the event.

The getElementsByClassName() Method

This method allows you to get an array filled with all the elements in the document that have the specified class name (from a CSS class) sent as a parameter. For example, to obtain all of the elements with a class name of number_one, you could use the following code:

```
var my_class = document.getElementsByClassName("number_one");
```

This can be a good way to access a particular group of elements on the page. Since it deals with arrays, this method will be discussed in more detail in Chapter 11.

The getElementsByTagName() Method

This method allows you to get an array filled with all the elements in the document that have the specified tag name sent as a parameter. For example, to obtain all of the image elements in the document, you could use the following code:

```
var all_images = document.getElementsByTagName("img");
```

Since it deals with arrays, this method will be discussed in more detail in Chapter 11.

The open() and close() Methods

The open() method allows you to open a new document and create its contents entirely with document.write() or document.writlen() statements. When the open() method is called, the browser looks for these statements so that it can write the new page. Once the write() and/or writeln() statements are completed, you need to use document.close() to finish the new page.

To get an example of the use of the open() method, suppose you want to write a new page based on the name of the viewer. To do this, you not only need to use the open() and close() methods, but also need to create a formName property to use so that you can grab the name entered by the viewer in a text box.

Start with the code for the body section of the initial page. You need a form with a text box and a way to invoke a function that will create the new document. The following code shows a way that you can do this (save the file as document_open.html):

```
<body>
<strong>Enter your name in the box below, then click
 the button to see a personalized page!</strong>
<br />
<form id="newp" onsubmit="newpage();">          ← The form is given an id
Name: <input type="text" id="yourname" size="25">  ←
<br/><br/>
<input type="submit" value="Submit">          ← The text box is given an id
</form>
<script type="text/javascript" src="document_open.js"></script>
</body>
```

This sets up your script, giving you a form with an id of newp and a text box with an id of yourname. It also has a button to submit the form. You now need to create the newpage() function in your external JavaScript file so that this form will work.

The newpage() function needs to grab the contents of the text box and assign it to a variable. It then needs to open your new customized page in the browser window. The following code shows how this can be done (save the file as document_open.js):

The value of the text box contents is assigned to a variable

```
function newpage() {
  var thename = document.getElementById("yourname").value;  ←
  document.open();          ←
```

A setup for a new document is opened

The new document uses these
statements to know what to display

```
document.write("<h1>Welcome!</h1>");
document.write("Hello, "+thename+", and welcome to my page!");
document.close();
}
```

The setup for the new document is
closed, allowing it to be displayed

The first thing the function does is to grab the contents of the text box. To get the contents of the text box, you need to use the value property, which you add to the end to get document. getElementById("yourname").value. This value is then assigned to the thename variable for easy use within your document.write() commands.

Once you have that value, you are ready to open the new page. To do this, you use the document.open() command, which allows you to use a series of document.write() statements until the document.close() command is used. You use the document.write() statements to write a greeting to the viewer on the page.

You can now try this out by opening the HTML page in your browser. Figure 9-10 shows the initial page with the form (the page before the form button is clicked). This is where the viewer can enter a name and click the button.

Figure 9-11 shows the result of entering the name "John" in the text box and clicking the button. The new page appears with a greeting!

TIP

The open() and close() methods can be useful to make pages on-the-fly based on variables like names, favorite foods, or other things for which you may want to customize a new page.

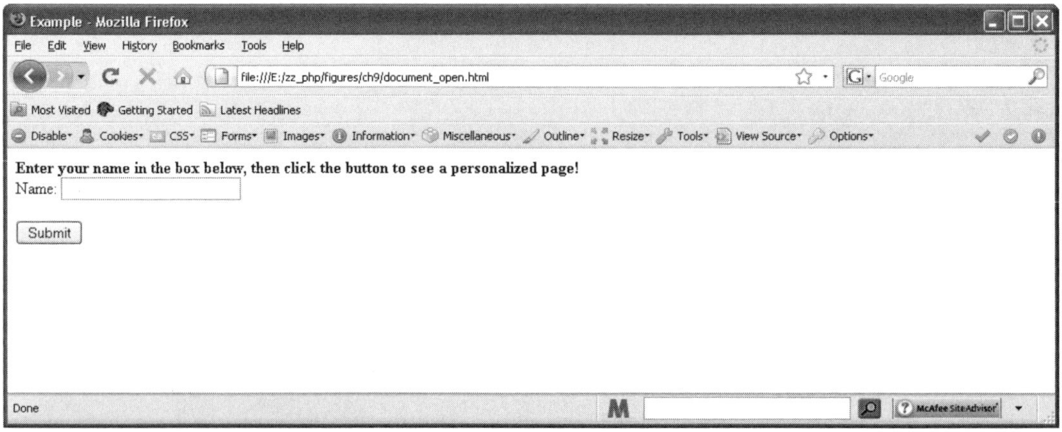

Figure 9-10 This is the page that allows the viewer to enter information

Figure 9-11 Once the button is clicked, the viewer will get a new page similar to this one

The write() Method

You started using the write() method early in the book, so you should know quite a bit about how it works already; but here's a brief description of this method, as a refresher.

The document.write() method is used to write a string value to the page. The following code would write "hi there" in the body of an HTML document:

```
<body>
<script type="text/javascript">
document.write("hi there");
</script>
</body>
```

The writeln() Method

The writeln() method works the same way as the document.write() method, but adds a JavaScript newline character (\n) at the end of the statement. Recall that Chapter 3 discussed how the JavaScript newline character works—it only places a new line in the page source code to make it easier to read.

TIP

While the newline character only affects the appearance of the source code when using document.write(), it can be used to create new lines in display elements created by JavaScript such as alert, prompt, and confirm boxes.

The appearance of the page itself is not affected by the JavaScript newline character. Recall the example from Chapter 3 that split the code into two different lines with the newline character:

```
<body>
<script type="text/javascript">
document.write("<strong>JavaScript Rules!</strong>\n This is fun.");
</script>
</body>
```

Since the document.writeln() method adds a newline character at the end of the statement, you could rewrite the preceding code using the following document.writeln() statements:

```
<body>
<script type="text/javascript">
document.writeln("<strong>JavaScript Rules!</strong>");
document.writeln(" This is fun.");
</script>
</body>
```

This would put the lines of code on two different lines in the page source, but would not affect the appearance of the page in the browser.

Creation Methods

There are also methods of the document object (such as createElement(), createAttribute(), and createTextNode()) that allow you to create various elements or nodes on the page using JavaScript. To make use of them, though, the new content must be appended as a child of an existing node in the DOM. This is where DOM node properties and methods are needed.

DOM Node Properties

The DOM node properties are listed in Table 9-3.

Property	Description
attributes	An array of all of the attributes in the specified node; the name and value properties of this property can be used to access the attribute name or attribute value for each member of the array
childNodes	An array of all the child nodes of the specified node
className	Returns the value of the class attribute of the specified node
clientHeight	Returns the height, in pixels, of the specified node
clientWidth	Returns the width, in pixels, of the specified node
dir	Returns the value of the direction of the text in the specified node (ltr or rtl)
firstChild	Returns the first child node of the specified node

Table 9-3 The DOM Node Properties

Property	Description
id	Returns the value of the id of the specified node
innerHTML	Returns the HTML code (text, image code, tags, etc.) within the specified node, such as all of the HTML code within a div element
lang	Returns the language value of the specified node
lastChild	Returns the last child node of the specified node
nextSibling	Returns the node following the specified node
nodeName	Returns the name of the specified node (such as div for a div element)
nodeType	Returns the type of the specified node
nodeValue	Returns the value of the specified node (such as the text within a div element or the value of an attribute)
offsetHeight	Returns the offset height of the specified node
offsetWidth	Returns the offset width of the specified node
ownerDocument	Returns the document object that contains the specified node
parentNode	Returns the parent node of the specified node
previousSibling	Returns the node before the specified node
scrollLeft	Returns the difference between the left edge and the left edge in view of the specified node
scrollTop	Returns the difference between the top edge and the top edge in view of the specified node
scrollHeight	Returns the entire height (including anything hidden and viewable via a scroll bar) of the specified node
scrollWidth	Returns the entire width (including anything hidden and viewable via a scroll bar) of the specified node
style	Returns the style object of the specified node
tabIndex	Returns the tab index of the specified node
tagName	Returns the tag name (in uppercase) of the specified node
title	Returns the value of the title attribute of the specified node

Table 9-3   The DOM Node Properties *(continued)*

When Table 9-3 mentions the specified node, a node works much like how you worked with elements in previous chapters. For instance, you might have the following HTML code:

```
<body>
<div id="div1" title="All about me!">
This page is about me, me, and... me!
</div>
</body>
```

If you wanted to obtain the value of the title attribute of the div element, you could use document.getElementById() to grab the div element by its id of div1. This would be the specified node for the DOM node title property. Then, you could access the title property of the element node, as in the following code:

```
                      Gets the element by its id and assigns it to a variable        Assigns the value of the
                                                                                    element's title property
var me_div = document.getElementById("div1");                                       to a variable
var me_title = me_div.title;
window.alert("The title of the div element is" + me_title);
                                                                                    Alerts the value to the viewer
```

This works just like object properties, as you learned in the previous chapter. The me_div.title property returns the string value "All about me!" which is the value of the div element node's title attribute.

Knowing this, you can use the DOM node methods in the same way.

DOM Node Methods

Table 9-4 lists the DOM node methods.

Method	Description
addEventListener()	Adds an event listener to the specified node to run a function on the event sent to it as a parameter
appendChild()	Appends a node as the last child of the specified node
attachEvent()	Attaches an event to the specified node to run a function on the event sent to it as a parameter
blur()	Removes focus from the specified node
click()	Executes the click event on the specified node
cloneNode()	Creates a clone of the specified node
detachEvent()	Detaches an event from the specified node
dispatchEvent()	Executes an event on the specified node
focus()	Gives focus to the specified node
getAttribute()	Returns the value of the attribute name sent to it as a parameter on the specified node
getAttributeNS()	Returns the value of the attribute name and namespace sent to it as a parameter on the specified node
getAttributeNode()	Returns the attribute node of the attribute name sent to it as a parameter for the specified node
getAttributeNodeNS()	Returns the attribute node of the attribute name and namespace sent to it as parameters for the specified node

Table 9-4 The DOM Node Methods

Method	Description
getElementsByTagName()	An array of all the child element nodes with the tag name sent to it as a parameter in the specified node
getElementsByTagNameNS()	An array of all the child element nodes with the tag name and namespace sent to it as parameters in the specified node
hasAttribute()	Returns true if the attribute name sent to it as a parameter exists on the specified node, or false if not
hasAttributeNS()	Returns true if the attribute name and namespace sent to it as parameters exist on the specified node, or false if not
hasAttributes()	Returns true if the specified node has any attribute nodes defined, or false if not
hasChildNodes()	Returns true if the specified node has any child nodes. or false if not
insertBefore()	Inserts a node sent to it as a parameter before the node sent to it as a second parameter inside the specified node
normalize()	Normalizes the specified node
removeAttribute()	Removes the attribute node for the attribute name sent to it as a parameter from the specified node
removeAttributeNode()	Removes the attribute node for the attribute node object reference sent to it as a parameter from the specified node
removeAttributeNS()	Removes the attribute node for the attribute name sent to it as a parameter with the namespace sent to it as a parameter from the specified node
removeChild()	Removes the child node sent to it as a parameter from the specified node
removeEventListener()	Removes an event listener from the specified node
replaceChild()	Replaces the child node sent to it as the second parameter with the child node sent to it as the first parameter in the specified node
scrollIntoView()	Scrolls the specified node into view in the browser window
setAttribute()	Sets an attribute node's name (first parameter) and value (second parameter) for the specified node
setAttributeNode()	Sets an attribute node as the attribute node object sent to it as a parameter for the specified node
setAttributeNodeNS()	Sets an attribute node as the attribute node object sent to it as a parameter with the namespace sent to it as a parameter for the specified node
setAttributeNS()	Sets an attribute node's namespace (first parameter), name (second parameter), and value (third parameter) for the specified node

Table 9-4   The DOM Node Methods (continued)

NOTE

When you see properties or methods listed that use namespaces, these are used mainly in XML documents and will not be referred to frequently in this book.

As mentioned earlier, to make the creation methods of the document object useful by adding the created node to the document, the DOM node method, such as appendChild() or insertBefore(), is needed to add the new node to the document.

For instance, you might have the HTML code used earlier, as follows:

```
<body>
<div id="div1" title="All about me!">
This page is about me, me, and... me!
</div>
</body>
```

This code has a div element node with a child text node (and attribute nodes). If you want to create another div element as the last child node of the div1 element node, you could use a combination of document.createElement(), document.createTextNode(), and the DOM node method appendChild().

First, go into the JavaScript code and grab the div1 element by its id:

```
var me_div = document.getElementById("div1");
```

Next, create the new element node using document.createElement():

```
var inner_div = document.createElement("div");
```

After that, create the text node for the inner_div node by using the document.createTextNode() method:

```
var inner_div_text = document.createTextNode("More about me...")
```

Next, use the DOM node method appendChild() to add the text node as a child of the new inner_div node:

```
inner_div.appendChild(inner_div_text);
```

Finally, use the DOM node method appendChild() to add the inner_div node to the document structure as the last child element of the me_div node:

```
me_div.appendChild(inner_div);
```

This adds your new div node at the end of the original div element (but before the original element is closed, since it will be a child node). Thus, the document structure for the HTML code would now be like this (though it won't show up using a "View Source" command):

```
<body>
<div id="div1" title="All about me!">
This page is about me, me, and... me!
```

```
<div>
More about me...
</div>
</div>
</body>
```

These properties and methods for the DOM nodes will be useful to you as you create more complex scripts. You will use the innerHTML and style properties quite often through the remainder of this book, as well as some of the other DOM node properties and methods.

Try This 9-1 Add a DOM Node to the Document

```
pr9_1.html
prjs9_1.js
```

This project allows you to practice using the new document and DOM node properties and methods you have learned in this chapter.

Step by Step

1. Create an HTML page with the following code for the body section and save it as pr9_1.html:

```
<body>
<div id="div1" title="Gosh!">
Whatever I feel like I want to write...
</div>
<script type="text/javascript" src="prjs9_1.js"></script>
</body>
```

2. Create an external JavaScript file and save it as prjs9_1.js. Use it for steps 3–5.

3. Get the value of the title attribute of the element with the id of "div1" and send that value as an alert to the viewer.

4. Create a new div element with the text "See you!" and add it to the document structure as a child of the div element with the id of "div1".

5. Save the JavaScript file and open the HTML file in your browser to view the results.

Try This Summary

In this project, you used your knowledge of the properties and methods of the document object and the DOM nodes to alert a DOM node property and to create a new div element in the document's structure.

Creating Dynamic Scripts

As you have seen, JavaScript gives you access to all of the elements in the document with the various methods such as document.getElementById() and document. getElementsByTagName(). Once you have access to the elements, you can also access their style attributes (typically initially set by a style sheet) to make changes to such things as their locations, colors, borders, sizes, or just about any other part of the element's style attributes using the style DOM node property.

Styles in JavaScript

When setting styles using Cascading Style Sheets (CSS), you may set up something like the following in your CSS code (save it as dyn_01.css):

```
#div1 { color:#000000; background-color:#FFFFFF; }
#div2 { border-style:solid; border-width:1px; border-color:#000000; }
```

This gives you style attributes for two ids, div1 and div2. Thus, if you had the following HTML code (save as dyn_01.html), the div elements would use the preceding styles in their presentation on the Web page:

The CSS file is linked to the document here

```
<head>
<link rel="stylesheet" type="text/css" href="dyn_01.css" />
</head>
<body>
<div id="div1">
I am in div1.  It seems like a nice place.          The div element with
</div>                                               an id of "div1"
<div id="div2">
I am in div2.  It's a little fancier here.          The div element with
</div>                                               an id of "div2"
<script type="text/javascript" src="dyn_01.js"></script>
</body>
```

The JavaScript file is called here

The HTML code is linked to the CSS code via the link tag. Thus, the div1 element is going to display as simple black text on a white background and the div2 element is going to have a plain, solid-black border around it.

As you can see, this page is using ids for each div element—so not only can you access those elements' ids with the CSS code, you can also access the elements via their ids in the JavaScript code. So, you can start out your JavaScript file (called in the preceding HTML code—save as dyn_01.js) with some code to grab both div elements by their ids by using the document.getElementById() method:

```
var d1 = document.getElementById("div1");
var d2 = document.getElementById("div2");
```

Now you have variables for both elements.

If you want to alter the styles that were set up in the CSS code via JavaScript, you'll need to make use of the style property that is a part of each element node. Then, JavaScript uses the same name as the CSS selector to access that particular property. For instance, if you wanted to change the color of the text in the div1 element to green, you would use the following code:

```
var d1 = document.getElementById("div1");
var d2 = document.getElementById("div2");
d1.style.color = "#00FF00";
```

In the CSS code, the selector color is used to alter the element's foreground color. In JavaScript, it is also the name of the property used to alter it after accessing the element's style property.

What if the CSS selector is not all one single word? For example, the background-color selector would not work in JavaScript if you used it the same way as in the CSS code. The following code attempts to change the background color to green:

```
var d1 = document.getElementById("div1");
var d2 = document.getElementById("div2");
d1.style.background-color = "#00FF00";
```

This wouldn't work, because JavaScript doesn't allow the hyphen (-) character as part of a property name. Instead, JavaScript puts both words together and capitalizes the first letter of any additional words after the first word. Thus, the CSS selector background-color becomes backgroundColor in JavaScript (also, something like border-right-color would become borderRightColor).

The JavaScript code could be rewritten as follows to make the change effective:

```
var d1 = document.getElementById("div1");
var d2 = document.getElementById("div2");
d1.style.backgroundColor = "#00FF00";
```

This will change the background color of the div1 element to green. The only issue now is that this will happen as soon as the script runs, which in this case is probably before the viewer ever notices there was another background color on the div1 element in the first place. To make this more useful, you can use this ability to access an element's style and combine it with your knowledge of handling events (covered in Chapter 7) to create a script that makes style changes in reaction to user events.

Coding a Dynamic Script

Now that you know how to alter an element's style properties, you can alter them in reaction to user events to create dynamic scripts. This offers you numerous possibilities to alter just about any style property in reaction to just about any event. Here, you will continue with the same CSS, HTML, and JavaScript files you have been using to create a dynamic, event-driven script.

With the current CSS and HTML code in place, you now can code the JavaScript to create the reactions to the events that will trigger your changes. Thus, if you want to alter the background color of the div1 element and also alter the border of the div2 element when the mouse moves over the div1 element, you could add the event handling code to the JavaScript to react to the event and make the style changes in the function handling the event:

```
var d1 = document.getElementById("div1");
var d2 = document.getElementById("div2");
d1.onmouseover = function() {
  d1.style.backgroundColor = "#00FF00";
  d2.style.borderWidth = "7px";
};
```

This will make the changes to the appearance of the div elements when the mouse moves over the div1 element.

To make the script more complete, you could also change the values back when the mouse moves off the div1 element:

```
var d1 = document.getElementById("div1");
var d2 = document.getElementById("div2");
d1.onmouseover = function() {
  d1.style.backgroundColor = "#00FF00";
  d2.style.borderWidth = "7px";
};
d1.onmouseout = function() {
  d1.style.backgroundColor = "#FFFFFF";
  d2.style.borderWidth = "1px";
};
```

Save the JavaScript file and open the HTML file in your browser. You should be able to move the mouse over the first div element to see the changes and to see the changes go back to the original look when the mouse moves off the first div element.

Of course, you can also alter the entirety of the HTML code within a given element using the DOM node innerHTML property.

The innerHTML Property

The innerHTML DOM node property allows you to change the HTML code that is inside of a given element. For instance, you could start out with the following HTML code:

```
<body>
<div id="div1">
What is 2+2?
</div>
<div id="div2">
<a href="answer.html" id="answer_link">Get the answer</a>
</div>
</body>
```

This code sets up a div element node with an id of div1, another div element node with an id of div2, and the link with an id of answer_link. Now, if you want to change the HTML code in the div1 element so that it displays the answer for the viewer when the link is clicked, you can use the click event on the link to start the script in motion and then change the innerHTML property on the div1 element node to change the contents of that element from the question to the answer:

```
var d1 = document.getElementById("div1");
var a_link = document.getElementById("answer_link");

answer_link.onclick = function() {
  d1.innerHTML = "That is easy, the answer is <strong>4</strong>!";
  return false;
};
```

Recall that in order to keep this link from being followed when clicked, you add the return false statement after performing the desired actions.

When run, this script changes the content inside the div1 element on the page, so that the HTML code would now be the following (though it will not be seen using the browser's "View Source" command):

```
<body>
<div id="div1">
That is easy, the answer is <strong>4</strong>!
</div>
<div id="div2">
<a href="answer.html" id="answer_link">Get the answer</a>
</div>
</body>
```

As you can see, this can be a handy way to make dynamic changes to the content of a Web page.

TIP

To make the script accessible to those without JavaScript, a default link destination (answer.html) is used. Including the answer text on the linked page allows users without JavaScript to still click the link and obtain the answer to the question.

Using what you have learned in this chapter to access the DOM and use the properties and methods of the document object and the DOM nodes, you can build scripts to make any number of alterations to the document's appearance or content.

Try This 9-2 Trying out Property Changes

pr9_2.html
prjs9_2.js

This project allows you to practice using the new style and innerHTML properties
you have learned in this chapter.

Step by Step

1. Create an HTML page with the following code for the body section and save it as pr9_2.html:

```
<body>
<div id="div1">
When will I update this page?
</div>
<div id="div2">
<a href="answer.html" id="c_link">Find out!</a>
</div>
<script type="text/javascript" src="prjs9_2.js"></script>
</body>
```

2. Create an external JavaScript file and save it as prjs9_1.js. Use it for steps 3–5.

3. Write some code so that when the link is clicked, the background color of the div element
   with the id of div1 changes to #CCCCCC and the content of the same element changes to
   the following:

```
<strong>Right now!</strong> Was that quick or what?
```

4. Make sure the same answer content is included in a separate HTML file named answer.html
   for those without JavaScript enabled.

5. Save the JavaScript file and open the HTML file in your browser to view the results.

Try This Summary

In this project, you used your knowledge of the style and innerHTML properties of DOM
nodes to make style and content changes to the Web page.

 ## Chapter 9 Self Test

1. The _____ object is an object that is created by the browser for each new HTML page
   that is viewed.

2. The _____ property of the document object returns the URL of the document that
   referred the viewer to the current document.

3. You can use the DOM node property style to alter the style sheet attributes of an element.

   A True

   B False

4. The _____ method of the document object allows you to get an element by the value of its id attribute.

   A getElementsByClassName()

   B createElement()

   C getSelection()

   D getElementById()

5. The appendChild() DOM node method allows you to add a child node as the first child node of a specified node.

   A True

   B False

6. Which of the following would be the value of the document.domain property if you were viewing a Web page at the URL http://www.pageresource.com/html/index.html?

   A pageresource.com

   B www.pageresource.com/html/index.html

   C www.pageresource.com

   D http://www.pageresource.com/html/index.html

7. The _____ property of the document object is an array that contains all of the anchor (<a>) tags on the page.

8. The _____ DOM node property allows you to change the HTML content of an element node.

9. The _____ property holds the value of the date and time the current document was last modified.

10. The Document Object Model (DOM) allows JavaScript (and other scripting languages) to access the structure of the document in the browser.

   A True

   B False

11. You can use the title property to display the title of a Web page someplace other than in the top bar of the browser window.

   A True

   B False

12. Which property returns the complete URL of the current document?

   A domain

   B referrer

   C URL

   D title

13. How does the writeln() method differ from the write() method?

   A It adds the equivalent of an HTML <br /> tag at the end of the line.

   B It adds the equivalent of an HTML <p> tag at the end of the line.

   C It adds a JavaScript newline character at the end of the line.

   D It is exactly the same as the write() method.

14. How is a formName type property created in JavaScript?

   A When a form is given a name, the name of the form becomes the property name.

   B When a form is given a name, the string formName is used as the property name.

   C The forms aren't given names; instead, formName is used as the property name.

   D When the form is given a name, an *f* is added to the beginning and is used as the property name.

15. What statements are most common between a document.open() and a document.close() statement?

   A HTML commands

   B document.write() and document.writeln() statements

   C Only document.writeln() statements

   D Only window.alert() statements

Chapter 10

Window Object

Key Skills & Concepts

● Using the Properties of the Window Object

● Using the Methods of the Window Object

The JavaScript window object gives you access to more properties and methods you can use in your scripts. By using the window object, you will be able to do a number of new things, such as prompt the user for information, open new windows, confirm an action by a viewer, and more.

An Introduction to the Window Object

The window object is created for each window that appears on the screen. A window can be the main window, a frame set or individual frame, or even a new window created with JavaScript. It differs from the document object in that the window object contains the document object (as well as many other objects, such as history, navigator, and so on). This object makes available for use in your scripts a number of new properties and methods that are directly under the window object.

In previous chapters, you have used the alert() method of the window object within your scripts. As you will recall, the alert() method enables you to pop up a message for the viewer. You will now see a number of new methods of this object that do things such as confirm a viewer's action or prompt the viewer for information, and this will enable you to add more interactivity to your scripts.

The first thing that you will look at are the properties of the window object. Then the next section will introduce and explain the methods that you can use with this object.

Using the Properties of the Window Object

To begin your study of the window object, take a look at its properties that you can use, which are listed and described in Table 10-1. Some of the properties are discussed in more detail following Table 10-1.

NOTE

As in previous chapters, some of the properties and methods listed in this chapter are not cross-browser or only work in modern browsers. For more information and more complete listings, see: https://developer.mozilla.org/en/DOM/window and http://msdn.microsoft.com/en-us/library/ms535873(VS.85).aspx.

Property	Description
closed	Holds the value based on whether or not a window has been closed
defaultStatus	Defines the default message displayed in the status bar
document	A reference to the document object of the window
frames	An array that represents all of the frames in a given window
history	Provides information on the browser history of the current window (discussed in Chapter 8)
innerHeight	Returns the height, in pixels, of the viewable area within the window
innerWidth	Returns the width, in pixels, of the viewable area within the window
length	Holds a value equal to the number of frames in a window
location	Holds the value of the current URL of the window
name	Enables a window to be named
opener	Refers to the window that opened another window
outerHeight	Returns the width, in pixels, of the entire browser window
outerWidth	Returns the width, in pixels, of the entire browser window
parent	Refers to the frame set that contains the current frame
screen.availWidth	Returns the available width of the browser window in pixels
screen.availHeight	Returns the available height of the browser window in pixels
screen.colorDepth	Returns the color depth of the screen in bits per pixel
screen.height	Returns the total height of the screen in pixels
screen.pixelDepth	Returns the bit depth of the screen in bits per pixel
screen.width	Returns the total width of the screen in pixels
self	Provides another way to reference the current window
status	Enables a message to be placed in the status bar; overrides defaultStatus
top	A reference to the top window containing a frame, frame set, or nested frame set
window	A reference to the current window

Table 10-1 Properties of the Window Object

The closed Property

The closed property is used to check whether or not a window has been closed by the viewer. The way it is normally used is with the name of a window, followed by the closed property, such as in the following example:

```
if (windowname.closed) {
  JavaScript Statements
}
```

You would replace the *windowname* part with the name of the window that you wish to check. This is often a new window that you opened with JavaScript; you will see how to name a new window later in the chapter in the section "The open() Method."

You can also use the closed property inside a new window to check whether the window that opened it has been closed. To do that, you would use closed after the opener property (discussed soon in "The opener Property" section), as in the following example:

```
if (window.opener.closed) {
  JavaScript Statements
}
```

This use of the closed property is really handy if you choose to create a new window that enables the viewer to navigate the main window through links in the new window.

The defaultStatus Property

The defaultStatus property sets the text string that is displayed by default in the status bar when nothing has been assigned to the window.status property. A change of the window.status property overrides this setting, because it is only shown as the default.

The defaultStatus property is often set in the load event. This is used mainly to display a custom message by default when the viewer is not performing an action that would change the text in the status bar. It can be set at any time, though, so you could set this using other events besides the load event.

CAUTION

Most modern browsers, by default, do not display status bar text altered by JavaScript, to keep unscrupulous Web sites from deceiving users with false link destinations and so forth in the status bar. Thus, the defaultStatus and status properties often do not work unless browser settings are altered by the viewer. Since it is a security risk to change browser settings to allow altered status bar text, using these properties in your scripts is not recommended.

The frames Property (Array)

The frames property is an array that holds a value for each frame within a frame set. It is often used to gain access to the properties of the various frames on a page. Since you have not studied arrays yet, you can't do much with the frames property now. You will be learning about arrays in Chapter 11, however.

You can find the number of frames in a window by using the window.frames.length property. This is handy if you decide to use the array later to perform tasks on the frames of a page in sequence.

The innerHeight and innerWidth Properties

The innerWidth and innerHeight properties hold values for width and height of the area of the window in view, which means that these values do not include scroll bars, menu bars, toolbars, or other browser features. These properties work in Mozilla Firefox and Opera, but (at the time of this writing) not in Internet Explorer. However, Internet Explorer offers alternatives to obtain these values (document.body.clientWidth and document.body.clientHeight).

So, if you wanted to obtain the width of the content area you have available to your script, you could use the following code:

```
var mywin_width = window.innerWidth;
```

Of course, if you want to use different HTML code for the browser depending on the available innerWidth of the window, you could use the following code:

> The value of the innerWidth property is assigned to the mywin_width variable

> The conditional operator is used for a quick if-else statement to determine how many pixels the width of the div element should be based on the available space

```
var mywin_width = window.innerWidth;◄┘
var div_width = (mywin_width >= 800) ? "750px" : "400px";◄┘
document.write('<div style="width:'+div_width+'; background-color:#CCC;">');◄
document.write('Some text for the new div element.');
document.write('</div>');
```

> The value obtained for the width of the div element is used on the div element that is written on the page

This will determine whether the viewer has 800 pixels of viewable width. If so, the width of the div element will be set to 750 pixels. Otherwise, the div element will have a safer width of 400 pixels. The background color should span the full width of the div element, allowing you to see the difference when the script is run with different browser widths.

To make this more cross-browser, you can grab the value for Internet Explorer users as well using the document.body.clientWidth property. You can also make sure a default value is set for the mywin_width variable for those using older browsers:

```
var mywin_width = 450; // Sets a low default value
if (window.innerWidth || document.body.clientWidth) {
  mywin_width = (window.innerWidth) ? window.innerWidth :
                document.body.clientWidth;
}
var div_width = (mywin_width >= 800) ? "750px" : "400px";
document.write('<div style="width:'+div_width+'; background-color:#CCC;">');
document.write('Some text for the new div element.');
document.write('</div>');
```

This time, a low default value is set for the mywin_width variable for those browsers that don't support either property (meaning those browsers will get a div element with the smaller width of 400 pixels). The script then checks to see whether either property exists in the browser being used. If so, the mywin_width variable is reassigned the value of the innerWidth property if it exists, or the document.body.clientWidth property otherwise. After that, the script works the same way as before, creating a div element with a width based on the available content area.

The length Property

The length property tells you how many frames are in a window, just like the window.frames .length property. This just shortens it to window.length (which is often more convenient when you are writing code).

The location Property

The location property holds the current URL of the window. It is also its own object with its own properties and methods. You have used this property already to create button links (back in Chapter 7).

You can also use the location property to cause instant redirection of the browser to a new page (if your page has moved to a new location, for instance). However, make sure that you don't use this technique on a page that is listed with search engines that do not allow quick redirection, because they may drop the page from their listings.

If a page has been moved and you want to redirect the viewer without any delay, you could just give the location property a new value with a script in the head section of the page, as shown in the following code:

```
<head>
<title>Page has moved</title>
<script type="text/javascript">
   window.location="page2.html";
</script>
</head>
<body>
Lacking JavaScript? Click the link below for the new page then!
<br />
<a href="page2.html">New Page</a>
</body>
```

This sends the viewer away instantly, since no action needs to take place to set this in motion

This would just take the viewer to the local URL page2.html. An option was included in the body section for browsers without JavaScript. Otherwise, the preceding code would load a blank page for those viewers and nothing would happen.

NOTE

Instant redirection is best suited for testing purposes on pages that are not indexed by a search engine, since the rules on redirection vary from one search engine to the next.

This property will become quite useful to you when you build scripts for navigation in Chapter 14.

The name Property

The name property holds the name of the current window and also enables you to give a window a name. If you want to give the main window a name, you could assign to this property the name you want to use. If you want to test to see that it worked, you could write the value of the property to the page in the body section.

The following code shows an example of assigning a name to a window and then writing the name into the body of the page:

```
<body>
<script type="text/javascript">
  window.name="cool_window";
  document.write("This window is named "+window.name);
</script>
</body>
```

The window is given its own name

The name of the window is written to the screen

The script gives the window a name, and then writes that name into the document. Figure 10-1 shows the result of this script in a browser. Notice how the name cool_window is written on the screen.

The opener Property

The opener property is used to reference the window that opened the current window. This is often used in new windows opened using the open() method, which you will see later in the chapter in the section "The open() Method." By using the opener property in a new window, you could detect whether the main window has been closed using the closed property you learned earlier. The following example shows how you could perform this test:

```
if (window.opener.closed)
```

This adds the closed property after the opener property to check whether the window that opened the current window has been closed. This is helpful if you want to perform an action in the main window through the new one, because you could check to see that it still exists before doing anything.

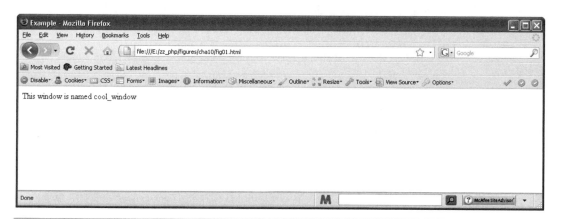

Figure 10-1   The name of the window is written on the screen

The parent Property

The parent property is only used when there are frames on a page. It enables you to access the parent frame set of the current frame. This is helpful when you wish to change a property in one frame from another frame. I will discuss this in more detail when I cover JavaScript and frames in Chapter 15.

The self Property

The self property is another way of saying "the current window" in JavaScript. It is used like the window object and can access the properties of the current window just like the window object. The self property is useful if you have a lot of windows with names and want to be sure you are using a property of the current window and not one in another named window.

The status Property

The status property contains the value of the text set in the status bar of the window. Changing this property overrides the content of the status bar set with the defaultStatus property.

CAUTION

Most modern browsers, by default, do not display status bar text altered by JavaScript, to keep unscrupulous Web sites from deceiving users with false link destinations and so forth in the status bar. Thus, the defaultStatus and status properties often do not work unless browser settings are altered by the viewer. Since it is a security risk to change browser settings to allow altered status bar text, using these properties in your scripts is not recommended.

The top Property

The top property is used to access the top window out of all the frame sets (which could be nested). This is a little different from the parent property, which only goes to the top of the frame set that contains the current frame. The top property instead goes all the way to the top window, even if the window contains nested frame sets.

You will see more on the use of this property when you get to Chapter 15 on JavaScript and frames.

Try This 10-1 Use the location and innerWidth Properties

```
pr10_1.html
prjs10_1.js
```

This project enables you to practice using the location and innerWidth properties of the window object. Also, you will help make the script more cross-browser compatible by adding the document.body.clientWidth property.

Step by Step

1. Create an HTML page, leaving the body section blank other than including a set of script tags to reference a JavaScript file named prjs10_1.js just before the closing </body> tag. Save the file as pr10_1.html.

2. Create a JavaScript file and save it as prjs10_1.js. Use this file for steps 3–6.

3. Set a default value for a variable named mywin_width.

4. Change the value of mywin_width to the value of the window.innerWidth property or the value of the document.body.clientWidth property, if one of these properties is available to use.

5. If the value of mywin_width is greater than or equal to 1000, send the viewer to the URL http://www.pageresource.com. Otherwise, send the viewer to the URL http://www .javascriptcity.com (use the window.location property).

6. Save the JavaScript file and open the HTML file in your Web browser. Try changing the width and then reopening the page with the new width to see which Web site it gives you.

Try This Summary

In this project, you were able to use your knowledge of the location and innerWidth properties of the window object to create a script that will redirect a viewer based on the available width of the viewing area in the viewer's browser.

Using the Methods of the Window Object

Now that you know how to use the properties of the window object, you can move on to using window methods. Table 10-2 lists a number of the methods of the window object with a description of each and particular methods are described in more detail next.

The alert() Method

You have used the alert() method extensively in earlier chapters in example scripts. This pops up a message to the viewer, and the viewer has to click an OK button to continue. Recall that the syntax is like the following alert:

```
window.alert("Hi there!");
```

This just gives the viewer the "Hi there!" message as an alert on the screen.

As noted when the alert() method was first introduced, this method is often shortened in scripts using syntax like the following:

```
alert("Hi there!");
```

Method	Description
alert()	Pops up an alert to the viewer, who must then click OK to proceed
back()	Takes the window back one item in its history list
blur()	Removes the focus from a window
clearInterval()	Cancels the action of a setInterval() method call
clearTimeout()	Cancels the action of a setTimeout() method call
close()	Closes a browser window
confirm()	Displays a confirmation dialog box to the viewer, who must then click OK or Cancel to proceed
escape()	Converts special characters in a string to hexadecimal characters
find()	Enables the viewer to launch the Find utility in the browser to find text on a page
focus()	Gives the focus to a window
forward()	Takes the window one item forward in its history list
home()	Sends the viewer to the home page the viewer has set in the Web browser settings
moveBy()	Moves a window by certain pixel values that are sent as parameters
moveTo()	Moves the top-left corner of the window to the coordinates sent as parameters
open()	Opens a new browser window
print()	Prints the contents of the window
prompt()	Pops up a prompt dialog box asking the viewer to input information
resizeBy()	Resizes a window by moving the bottom-right corner by certain pixel values that are sent as parameters
resizeTo()	Resizes an entire window to the height and width that are sent as parameters
scrollBy()	Scrolls the viewing area of a window by certain pixel values that are sent as parameters
scrollTo()	Scrolls the viewing area of the window to the specified coordinates that are sent as parameters
setInterval()	Calls a function each time a certain amount of time passes
setTimeout()	Calls a function once after a certain amount of time has passed
stop()	Stops the window from loading its content
unescape()	Converts an escaped string back to its normal characters

Table 10-2 Methods of the Window Object

How can you get away with that? Remember that JavaScript is fairly lenient, so you are allowed to take shortcuts like this in some instances. In this case, it is permissible because the window object is the default object in JavaScript. Since it is assumed to be there, you don't need to make the call to it. Instead, you can just call the method, and JavaScript will know it is a window method.

This type of shortcut will work for all the window properties and methods in most cases. In fact, the document object you studied in the last chapter is under the window object in the object hierarchy. You can leave the window part off the document object calls because the window is assumed to exist.

The cases in which you may need to be more specific are often with new windows and with the location property.

The confirm() Method

The confirm() method can be used to give the viewer a chance to confirm or cancel an action. This method returns a Boolean value of true or false, so its result is often assigned to a variable when it is used.

The following is the syntax for assigning the value to a variable:

```
var varname = window.confirm("Your Message");
```

You would replace *varname* with a variable name that you wish to use. You would then replace the "Your Message" text with the text you wish to have in the dialog box that pops up. So, if you wanted to assign the result to a variable named is_sure and ask the question "Are you sure?" you could use the following code:

```
var is_sure = window.confirm("Are you sure?");
```

Figure 10-2 shows a sample confirm dialog box that is displayed by the preceding code. Notice the two buttons the viewer can choose to click: OK and Cancel. Depending on the browser, this may look slightly different. If the viewer clicks OK, the method returns true. If the user clicks Cancel, the method returns false. The bad news is that you can't change the value of the text in the buttons. You are stuck with OK and Cancel, at least while using the confirm method.

As a real example of this method, suppose that you want to create a link to another page, but you want to be sure the viewer wants to leave before being sent away. You could use

Figure 10-2   An example of a confirm dialog box

the confirm dialog box to find out whether or not the viewer wishes to leave the page. The following code shows how you can get a confirmation from the viewer and react appropriately. First, the HTML code:

```
<body>
<a href="http://www.google.com" id="search_link">Go Searching</a>
</body>
```

Next, use JavaScript to confirm whether the user really wants to leave when the link is clicked:

```
var s_link = document.getElementById("search_link");

s_link.onclick = function() {
  var is_sure = window.confirm("Are you sure you want to leave?");
  if (!is_sure) {
    window.alert("OK. You can stay here.");
    return false;
  }
};
```

The function confirms whether or not the viewer wants to leave

Notice that if OK is clicked and the confirm() method returns true, the viewer is taken to the linked Web site. If cancel is clicked and the confirm() method returns false, an alert is sent to the viewer and the function returns false so that the link won't be followed by the browser (you can also simply omit the alert and just have nothing happen after Cancel is clicked, by using only the return false statement.)

Figure 10-3 shows the browser window after the link is clicked on the page. The confirm dialog box with your "Are you sure you want to leave?" message pops up on the screen.

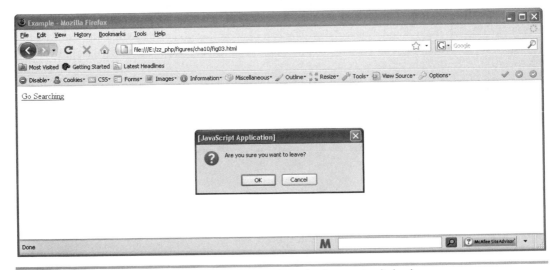

Figure 10-3 A confirm dialog box pops up when the button is clicked

The find() Method

You can use the find() method to let the viewer find a certain bit of text on your page. It tells the browser to use its built-in Find utility and enables the viewer to type in what to look for on the page.

For example, if you wanted to create a button for viewers to click when they want to find something on your page, you could use the following code:

```
<form>
<input type="button" value="Click to Find Text"
 onclick="window.find();" />
</form>
```

This pops up the Find dialog box in the browser and enables the viewer to search for text within the page. Figure 10-4 shows the result of this script when it is added to an HTML document.

This functionality is useful if you have a really long page and want the viewer to be able to find things more quickly by searching the page.

The home() Method

The home() method is used to send the viewer to the home page the viewer has set in the Web browser settings. For instance, you could use it to offer viewers a button that will take them to their selected home page when clicked, as in the following code (at the time of this writing this method worked in Mozilla Firefox and Opera but did not work in Microsoft Internet Explorer):

```
<form>
<input type="button" value="Go Home!" onclick="window.home();">
</form>
```

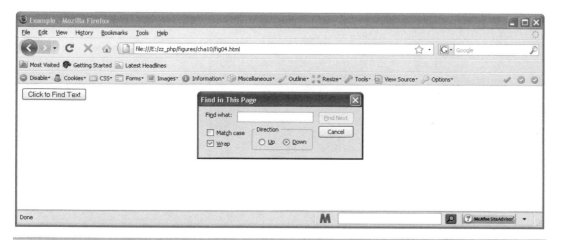

Figure 10-4   A Find dialog box pops up, enabling the viewer to search for text on the page

The print() Method

The print() method enables the viewer to print the current window. When this method is called, it should open the viewer's Print dialog box so that the viewer can set the printer settings to print the document.

To use it, you could create a button that enables the viewer to print the page they are viewing:

```
<form>
<input type="button" value="Click to Print Page"
 onclick="window.print();">
</form>
```

This code should open the user's Print dialog box when the user clicks the Click to Print Page button. Figure 10-5 shows the result of running this script in a browser. This dialog box may appear differently for different viewers, depending on the browser and printer being used.

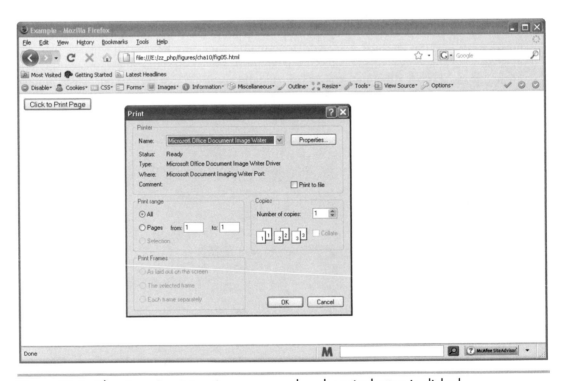

Figure 10-5 The viewer's print options pop up when the print button is clicked

The prompt() Method

The prompt() method is used to prompt the viewer to enter information. Using this method, you can do things based on what the viewer enters into the text box at the prompt.

First, you need to see the syntax for this method. As with the confirm() method, the result (what the viewer enters) is assigned to a variable for later use. The following is an example of the syntax:

```
var varname = window.prompt("Your Text","Default Entry");
```

You replace *varname* with a variable name, and replace "*Your Text*" with the message that you want to send to the viewer (usually a question). The second parameter, "Default Entry", enables you to enter a default entry for the viewer. Often this is left as " ", which is a blank entry. However, you could set it to something if you would like to have a default answer ready for the viewer to use.

You could use the prompt() method to get the viewer's name and send an alert while the page is loading. The following code prompts the viewer to enter their name and then includes the name in a message that is displayed to the viewer in an alert:

The viewer gets a prompt asking for a name here

```
var thename = window.prompt("What's your name?","");
if (thename.length < 1) {
    thename = "Anonymous Visitor";
}
window.alert("Hello "+thename+"!");
```

This tests to see whether the input box was left blank

The name input by the viewer is sent in an alert

Notice that the script checks to see if thename.length is less than 1. When using the length property on a string, it returns the number of characters in the string. So, if the length is less than one character, the prompt field was left blank by the viewer. If the viewer leaves the name field blank, the viewer will be named "Anonymous Visitor"; otherwise, the variable thename keeps the value entered by the viewer. Then, the viewer gets an alert with the value of the thename variable in a greeting. Figure 10-6 shows the result of this script when nothing is entered by the viewer in the prompt.

Instead of placing the name into an alert, you could write it on the page for the viewer instead. In this way, the viewer isn't bothered with an alert, and the name appears as though it is part of the page. First, start with the HTML code:

```
<body>
<div id="greeting">
<h1>Hello! Welcome!</h1>
</div>
<div id="content">
This page talks about what I think about...
</div>
</body>
```

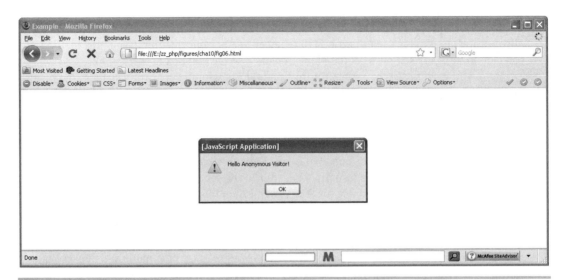

Figure 10-6 An alert greets the viewer

The HTML code uses two div elements, one for the greeting and one for the page content. Inside the greeting div element, a default greeting is provided for those without JavaScript. For those with JavaScript, you will use the prompt() method to offer them the opportunity for a more personal greeting. You could use the following JavaScript code:

```
var greet = document.getElementById("greeting");

var thename = window.prompt("What's your name?","");
if (thename.length < 1) {
  thename = "Anonymous Visitor";
}
greet.innerHTML = "<h1>Hello " + thename + "! Welcome!</h1>";
```

This script gets the greet element by its id (greeting), obtains the value of thename from the prompt, and then changes the value of the greet element's innerHTML property to a more personal greeting.

Figure 10-7 shows the result of this in the browser if the viewer enters the name John at the prompt.

The open() Method

The open() method is the method that enables you to open a new window with JavaScript. This method takes three parameters, the third of which sets a number of options that the window may need.

Figure 10-7   The viewer's name is written on the page after the viewer has entered it at a prompt

The general syntax for using the open() method is shown in the following example:

```
window.open("URL","name","attribute1=value,attribute2=value");
```

The first parameter, "URL", is replaced with the URL of the HTML document that is to be opened in the new window. The "name" parameter is replaced with the name you wish to give to the window. The last parameter enables you to add attributes for the new window. These attributes are set by using "yes", "no", or a numeric value on the right side of the equal sign. Notice that each time an attribute is set with a value, there is a comma before the next one and no spaces in between.

If you want to open a window with the features of the current window, you could do so by leaving off the last parameter with the attributes. The following example would open a new window with a local URL of newpage.htm and a name of my_window; it will have the same features as the window that opened it:

```
window.open("newpage.html","my_window");
```

Standard Attributes

If you want to include window features, you need to learn some of the attributes that you can use with the windows. Table 10-3 lists the standard attributes that you can use as part of the last parameter in the open() method.

If you begin to use the attribute parameter, you should note that once you place something in the attribute parameter, any attribute not defined will now default to "no" instead of copying the main window. So, if you want to open a basic new window with a width of 400 pixels and a height of 300 pixels, you could use the following code:

```
window.open("newpage.html","my_window","width=400,height=300");
```

Attribute Name	Possible Values	Function
width	number	Defines the width of the new window in pixels
height	number	Defines the height of the new window in pixels
directories	yes, no, 1, 0	Defines whether or not the new window has directory buttons (like the What's New or Link buttons near the top of the browser)
location	yes, no, 1, 0	Defines whether or not the new window has a location box to type in a new URL
menubar	yes, no, 1, 0	Defines whether or not the window has a menu bar (File menu, Edit menu, and so on)
resizable	yes, no, 1, 0	Defines whether or not the viewer is allowed to resize the new window
scrollbars	yes, no, 1, 0	Defines whether or not the new window has scroll bars if the contents of the window are larger than the window's size
status	yes, no, 1, 0	Defines whether or not the new window has a status bar at the bottom
toolbar	yes, no, 1, 0	Defines whether or not the new window has a toolbar (Forward and Back buttons, Stop button, and so on)

Table 10-3   Standard Attributes for a New Window

The only feature this window will have is a title bar that shows the title of the document and the buttons on the top right for the viewer to close or minimize it.

To set the other attributes (which are all Boolean), you can assign them a value of "yes" or "no" depending on whether or not you want each feature. You may also use 1 for yes and 0 for no if you prefer, as they will have the same effect. So, if you wanted to have a 300×200 pixel window with just a menu bar added (this adds the Forward, Back, Stop, and other similar buttons), you could use the following code:

```
window.open("newpage.html","cool","width=300,height=200,menubar=yes");
```

This gives you a new window with the contents of newpage.html, a name of "cool," dimensions of 300×200 pixels, and a menu bar.

You can add as many of the attributes as you want inside the quote marks of the third parameter by separating each one with a comma. Remember that you should include no spaces between anything and that the entire command should be on one line in your text editor.

NOTE

Due to space limitations, a new window command may occasionally be on more than one line in the code in this book. Be sure that when you use the code, you put everything from window.open to the ending semicolon (;) on one line to avoid JavaScript errors.

The following example opens a window with all the features mentioned in Table 10-3 (again, this takes up more than one line here, but when you enter it in your text editor, the code should go on a single line):

```
window.open("newpage.html","cool","width=300,height=200,directories=yes,
location=yes,menubar=yes,resizable=yes,scrollbars=yes,status=yes,
toolbar=yes");
```

This opens a 300×200 pixel window with all the standard features. If you want a viewable example, you need to make a page named newpage.html and create the code for the main page to include a window.open() command, as described next.

First, create the code for newpage.html (this is just a short page that has some text in it):

```
<body>
I am a new window! I am newer than that old window
 that opened me, so I am special. Ha, ha!
</body>
```

Now, create the main page (save as mainpage.html):

```
<body>
Click the link below to open an arrogant new window ...
<br />
<a href="newpage.html" id="nwin">New Page</a>         The link is
                                                      given an id
<script type="text/javascript" src="openwin.js"></script>
</body>
                                                      The external JavaScript is called
```

Finally, create the JavaScript code (save as openwin.js):

```
var nw_win =  document.getElementById("nwin");       The link element is
                                                      assigned to a variable
nw_win.onclick = function() {
   window.open("newpage.html","cool","width=400,height=300,status=yes");
   return false;
};
```

The anonymous function opens the new window and returns false

The anonymous function works when the link is clicked and launches the new window with the contents of your newpage.html document. This window is 400×300 pixels and has only a status bar at the bottom as an added feature. Note that the return false statement is added after opening the window, so that if the viewer has JavaScript, the newpage.html file will not also be opened in the main browser window when the link is clicked (if the viewer does not have JavaScript, the link will work normally and open the newpage.html file in the same window).

Figure 10-8 shows the result of opening the main page in the browser and clicking the link to open the new window.

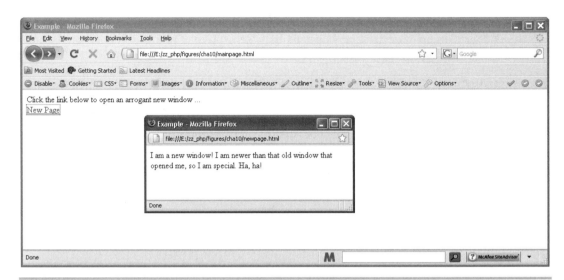

Figure 10-8 A new window is opened when a link is clicked

Just when you thought there could be no more features to digest…the following section describes additional options that newer browsers offer.

Extended Attributes

With newer browsers, you can use a number of new attributes for your new windows. The only trouble is that they may not work cross-browser, so you have to be careful to test the code to ensure that the attributes you use work in the browsers in which you need them to work. Table 10-4 lists a number of extended attributes for new windows.

The problem with the attributes in Table 10-4 is that they may not work cross-browser. For instance, to make the screen position work with Internet Explorer, Mozilla Firefox, and Opera,

Attribute	Possible Values	Function
fullscreen	yes, no, 1, 0	Defines whether or not the window should open in a full screen
left	number	Defines the distance from the left of the screen for the new window
personalbar	yes, no, 1, 0	Defines whether or not the new window has a personal toolbar
screenX	number	Defines the distance from the left of the screen for the new window
screenY	number	Defines the distance from the top of the screen for the new window
top	number	Defines the distance from the top of the screen for the new window

Table 10-4 Extended New Window Attributes

you need to add all four of the attributes to the last parameter of the open() method. Each browser will just ignore the attributes that it does not recognize. The following code (changing the open_win.js file from earlier) opens your newpage.html document in a new 300×200 pixel window in the top-left corner of the screen (0 pixels from the left, 0 pixels from the top) when the button is clicked:

```
var nw_win = document.getElementById("nwin");

nw_win.onclick = function() {
  window.open("newpage.html","cool","width=400,height=300,status=yes,
    screenX=0,left=0,screenY=0,top=0");
  return false;
};
```

The new window is given some standard attributes and then a position on the screen by using all four attributes (two for each browser)

In this version, you added the new attributes to set the new window at the coordinates (0,0) on the screen.

Figure 10-9 shows the result of this in a browser after the button is clicked. Notice how the new window now opens at the top left of the screen.

The other attributes are not as useful at this point; but as the browsers develop further, some of the attributes may begin to be supported in both browsers in one form or another.

Now back to examining the methods.

The close() Method

The close() method is used to close a window; however, unless your script has certain security rights, this can only be used to close a window that has been opened by you with JavaScript.

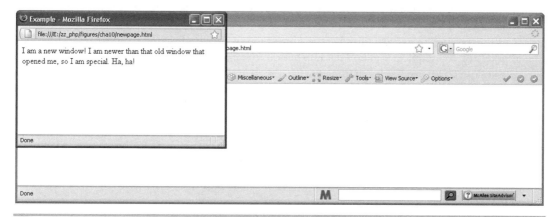

Figure 10-9   The new window opens where you want it to on the screen, at the top left

To use the close() method, you could modify your newpage.html code to provide a button at the end of the text that enables the viewer to close the window by clicking it. So, you could change the code of newpage.html to look like the following code:

```
<body>
I am a new window! I am newer than that old window
 that opened me, so I am special. Ha, ha!
<form>
<input type="button" value="Close Window" onclick="window.close();" />
</form> </body>
```

The window is closed when the button is clicked

When the button is clicked now, the window.close() method is invoked and closes the window just like the standard Close button at the top right of a window. If you want to try it out, use the main page you used in the previous section and click the button to open the new window. It should offer the new button with the option to close the window, and it should close the window if you click the button.

The moveBy() Method

The moveBy() method can be used to move a new window to a new location on the screen. This moves a window by the number of pixels given as parameters in the method call. The following is the syntax for using this method:

```
window.moveBy(x-pixels,y-pixels);
```

You replace *x-pixels* with the number of pixels you want to move the window from left to right. So, if you want the window to move to the right, you enter a positive number. If you want it to move to the left, you enter a negative number.

You replace *y-pixels* with the number of pixels you want to move the window from top to bottom, with positive numbers pushing the window down and negative numbers pulling the window up.

For example, if you want to give the viewer the option to move the window by the number of pixels of your choice, you could add a button to make it do so when the viewer clicks the button. You could use the following code:

The window will move 50 pixels to the right and 50 pixels down

```
<body>
I am a new window! I am newer than that old window
 that opened me, so I am special. Ha, ha!
<form>
<input type="button" value="Move Window" onclick="window.moveBy(50,50);" />
<br /><br />
<input type="button" value="Close Window" onclick="window.close();" />
</form> </body>
```

This moves the window 50 pixels to the right and 50 pixels down when the button is clicked. If you open this from the main window you coded earlier in the chapter, you can see this in

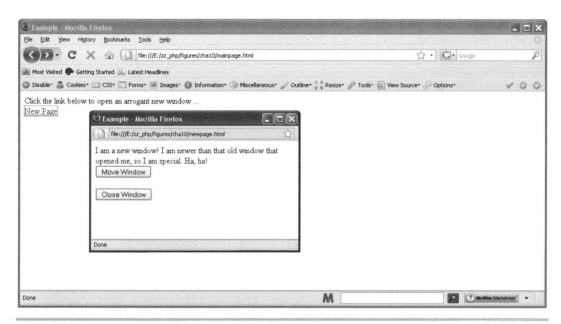

Figure 10-10 The new window in its initial position when it is opened

action. Figure 10-10 shows the initial position of the new window when it is opened from a button on the main page.

Figure 10-11 shows the window after the Move Window button is clicked in the new window. Notice it has moved to the right and down by 50 pixels in each direction.

The way this works, the viewer could continue clicking the button and moving the window by another 50 pixels in both directions as long as the button is viewable. The window just continues to move by the number of pixels it has been set to move by in the script. The next method discussed will move the window to a particular location, so that it will not continue to move on successive clicks like this one does.

The moveTo() Method

The moveTo() method is used to move a window to a specific destination on the screen based on the parameters given in the method call. The following is the general syntax for using this method:

```
window.moveTo(x-value,y-value);
```

Here, you replace *x-value* with the number of pixels from the left of the screen where you want the window to be moved. For example, if you input 300, the window is moved 300 pixels from the left of the screen. You then replace *y-value* with the number of pixels from the top of the screen that you want the window to be moved.

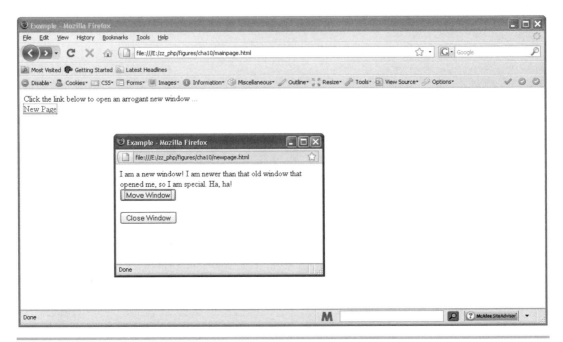

Figure 10-11 The window in its new position after being moved

As an example, you could recode your Move Window button in your newpage.html page to use moveTo() instead of moveBy(). The following is the example code:

```
<body>
I am a new window! I am newer than that old window
 that opened me, so I am special. Ha, ha!
<form>
<input type="button" value="Move Window" onclick="window.moveTo(50,50);" />
<br /><br />
<input type="button" value="Close Window" onclick="window.close();" />
</form> </body>
```

The window will move to the coordinates (50,50) on the screen, which is 50 pixels from the left and 50 pixels from the top

This time the window would be moved to the coordinates (50,50) on the screen when the button is clicked. By using your main page code, you can open the window again to test this out.

To see that this works differently than the moveBy() method, try clicking the button again. Rather than making another move, it stays in the same place because it has already made it to its destination.

The resizeBy() Method

The resizeBy() method is used to resize a window by the number of pixels given in the parameters sent in the method call. The syntax and usage are the same as for the moveBy() method; resizeBy() just performs a resize instead. To make the window larger, use positive numbers. To make it smaller, use negative numbers.

The resizeTo() Method

The resizeTo() method is used to resize a window to a specific dimension in pixels based on the parameters sent in the method call. The syntax and usage are the same as for the moveTo() method; resizeTo() just performs a resize instead. You input the new width and height in place of the coordinates used in the moveTo() method.

The scrollBy() Method

The scrollBy() method is used to scroll a window by the number of pixels given in the parameters sent in the method call. The syntax and usage are the same as for the moveBy() method; scrollBy() just performs a scroll instead. To make the window larger, use positive numbers. To make it smaller, use negative numbers.

The scrollTo() Method

The scrollTo() method is used to scroll a window to a specific destination in pixels based on the parameters sent in the method call. The syntax and usage are the same as for the moveTo() method; scrollTo() just performs a scroll to the specified point instead.

The setInterval() Method

The setInterval() method is used to execute a JavaScript function repeatedly at a set interval. The following is the general syntax for using this method:

```
window.setInterval("function()",time);
```

You replace *function()* with the name of the function you wish to repeat. You then replace *time* with the time (in milliseconds) you want to wait before each repetition of the function.

So, if you really wanted to annoy your viewers, you could use this method to pop up an alert every 10 seconds (10,000 milliseconds) once the page is viewed. You could do this by placing the following script inside the HTML of a document:

```
<body>
<script type="text/javascript">
function annoy_alert() {
  window.alert("Am I bothering you yet?");
}
window.setInterval("annoy_alert()",10000);
</script>
</body>
```

An interval is set; note the use of quote marks around the function call

Notice that this is a special case in which the function must be called inside quote marks. Normally, a function must be called outside quote marks. The reason for it here is to keep the function from executing immediately rather than at the set interval. The function name is being sent as a string parameter to the setInterval() method, where it is then called after the correct time lapse.

This, of course, could become quite annoying. The less time set in the interval, the more annoying it would become. Luckily, the ten-second interval gives you enough time to leave the page before another alert pops up.

The clearInterval() Method

To end the barrage of alerts from the previous script, you could use the clearInterval() method. The following is the general syntax for using this method:

```
window.clearInterval(name);
```

You must replace *name* with a variable name that has been assigned to the setInterval() method call you want to clear. The problem is, you didn't set your setInterval() call to a variable name in the previous example.

In order to clear it, you need to adjust your code. The following code is updated and assigns the setInterval() call to a variable name:

```
<body>
<script type="text/javascript">
function annoy_alert() {
  window.alert("Am I bothering you yet?");
}
var madness = window.setInterval("annoy_alert()",10000);
</script>
</body>
```

The method call is set to a variable for later reference

You now have a way to use the clearInterval() method, by calling it with the madness variable as the parameter. So, offer the visitor a button that enables them to stop the madness. As long as it is clicked between intervals, it will stop the interval from running any further. The following code gives you a full page with the button for the viewer to click:

```
<body>
<script type="text/javascript">
function annoy_alert() {
  window.alert("Am I bothering you yet?");
}
var madness = window.setInterval("annoy_alert()",10000);
</script>
Click the button below to end the endless barrage of alerts.<br />
<form>
<input type="button" value="Stop the Madness!"
  onclick="window.clearInterval(madness);" />
</form>
</body>
```

The method call is set to a variable for later reference

This method refers to the first method through the variable name to cancel its action

Now the viewer can stop the alerts by clicking the Stop the Madness button.

Of course, there are better uses for this method. You will see in later chapters that it can be handy for clocks and other things that need to be updated at regular intervals on the page.

The setTimeout() Method

The setTimeout() method enables you to execute a JavaScript function after a certain amount of time has passed. It differs from the setInterval() method because it is only executed once (unless it is put inside a loop of some sort). The general syntax is the same as that of the setInterval() method.

If you want to have only a single alert pop up after ten seconds and not repeat, you could use the following code:

```
<body>
<script type="text/javascript">
function annoy_alert() {                    The timeout is set, and also set to a variable
  window.alert("Sign my guest book NOW!");
}
var theguest = window.setTimeout("annoy_alert()",10000);
</script>
</body>
```

This would send the viewer an alert after ten seconds, demanding that the guest book be signed immediately.

The reason that you set the method to a variable is so that you could use the next method in line, the clearTimeout() method.

The clearTimeout() Method

The clearTimeout() method enables you to cancel a setTimeout() call if you call the clearTimeout() method before the time expires from the setTimeout() call. The general syntax is the same as that of the clearInterval() method: you use a variable name as a parameter so that it knows which setTimeout() call to cancel.

So, if you want to give viewers a chance to avoid getting an alert, you could add a button for them to click within ten seconds. If it is clicked in time, the setTimeout() call is canceled and no alert pops up. The following is the example code:

```
<body>
<script type="text/javascript">                The timeout is set, and set to
function annoy_alert() {                        a variable for later reference
  window.alert("Sign my guest book NOW!");
}
var theguest = window.setTimeout("annoy_alert()",10000);
</script>
Click the button below within 10 seconds to avoid an alert message.<br />
<form>
<input type="button" value="No Alert for Me!"
  onclick="window.clearTimeout(theguest);" />
</form>                              This method refers to the first method through
</body>                             the variable name to cancel its action
```

If the button is clicked in time, the viewer avoids receiving an alert about signing the guest book.

For now, you have finally finished with the window object methods. In the chapters that follow, you will use a number of these methods in various scripts.

Ask the Expert

Q: There are way too many properties and methods here! How am I ever going to remember all of these?

A: As you begin using them with more frequency, they will be easier to remember. I remember the ones I use more often better than those I don't use much. If you do a lot of coding, it is good to keep a reference handy, such as this book, in case you need to check the details of a property or method now and then. I keep a bunch of books and bookmarks to reference Web sites on hand.

Q: Aren't pop-up windows annoying to visitors? Should I use them frequently?

A: Pop-up windows are oftentimes used in a way that will annoy most viewers (such as opening several new windows at once, requiring pop-up windows to navigate a site, or opening every navigation link in a new window). Using pop-up windows without a particularly good reason is not recommended, since these can cause confusion when navigating a site or irritate viewers desiring to browse in one window or tab. (Note that if you receive revenue from advertising on your site, you may need to use pop-up ads to earn revenue. If you do have them, you will want to avoid opening your own pop-up windows in addition to the ads.)

Most browsers now offer the viewer the option of opening links in new tabs or new windows via the context menu, so it is best to let the viewer decide how the page should be opened.

Q: Will I be making window remote controls any time soon?

A: A new window that changes properties (like the location property) in the main window is a "remote control." Though remote controls are not discussed in this book, there are scripts for these at free script sites on the Web. For now, you want to be sure to master the coding that you need to create and manipulate a regular new window.

Q: Will I be using the timed methods like setTimeout() and setInterval() often?

A: They may not come up very often, but you will have a use for them when you need to build time-dependent scripts such as clocks, slide shows, or Dynamic HTML (DHTML) animations.

Try This 10-2 ## Use the setTimeout() and confirm() Methods

pr10_2.html
prjs10_2.js

This project enables you to practice using some of the window methods. You will have the browser wait a certain number of seconds and then ask the viewer to confirm whether or not to stay at the page or move on to an Internet search site.

Step by Step

1. Create an HTML page, with the following code in the body section, and save it as pr10_2.html:

```
<body>
<h1>Some Info. Here</h1>
<ul>
<li>An interesting point here...</li>
<li>A very interesting point here...</li>
<li>An incredibly interesting point here...</li>
</ul>
<script type="text/javascript" src="prjs10_2.js"></script>
</body>
```

2. Create a JavaScript file and save it as prjs10_2.js. Use it for steps 3–4.

3. After 20 seconds, have a confirm box display to the viewer asking them if they want to continue using this Web page. If so, do nothing. If not, send them to the URL http://www.google.com.

4. Save the JavaScript file and open the HTML file in a Web browser. After 20 seconds, you should see a confirm box.

Try This Summary

In this project, you were able to use your knowledge of the properties and methods of the window object to create a timed, interactive script. This allowed you to give the viewer a choice as to whether to stay at the current Web page or move on to an Internet search site.

Chapter 10 Self Test

1. A(n) _____ object is created for each window that appears on the screen.

2. The closed property is used to check whether or not a window has been closed by the viewer.

   A True

   B False

3. The _____ property holds the value of the number of frames within a window.

4. The location property can cause instant redirection of the browser to a new page.

   A True

   B False

5. The _____ property holds the name of the current window and also allows you to give the window a name.

6. The calls to properties and methods of the window object can often be shortened because

   A The window object is the default object in JavaScript.

   B The window properties and methods are assumed to be part of the navigator object.

   C There really is no window object.

   D The browser assumes the window object is part of the document object.

7. The _____ property is another way of saying "the current window" in JavaScript.

8. Why would this code not work:

```
onmouseover="window.status='Page 2'; return true;"
```

   A It should work without a problem.

   B The quote marks are not set correctly.

   C Newer browsers do not allow the window status to be changed by default, so the user would need to change security settings in order for it to work.

   D A change in the status property in an onMouseOver event must return false afterward.

9. What is the difference between the parent and top properties?

   A The parent property goes to the top of the current frame set, while the top property goes to the top window of all frame sets on the page.

   B The top property goes to the top of the current frame set, while the parent property goes to the top window of all frame sets on the page.

   C The parent property goes to the top of the current frame set, while the top property goes to the top of the current frame.

   D The parent property goes to the top of the outermost frame set, while the top property goes to the top window of all frame sets on the page.

10. The _____ method pops up a message to the viewer, and the viewer has to click an OK button to continue.

11. What value is returned by the confirm() method if the viewer clicks the OK button?

    A true

    B false

    C OK

    D 25

12. The _____ method enables the viewer to print the current window.

13. The prompt() method is used to _____ the viewer to enter information.

14. When setting the toolbar attribute as part of the third parameter in the open() method, what values may the attribute have?

    A yes and no only

    B 1 and 0 only

    C yes, no, true, and untrue

    D yes, no, 1, and 0

15. What is the difference between the setInterval() method and the setTimeout() method?

    A The setTimeout() method is used when the viewer needs to take a break from reading, while setInterval() is used when the viewer needs no breaks.

    B The setInterval() method is used to repeat a function at a set time interval, while setTimeout() executes a function only once after a set time delay.

    C The setInterval() method flashes an advertisement across the screen at a set interval by default, while setTimeout() is ad-free.

    D They both perform the same function.

Chapter 11

JavaScript Arrays

Key Skills & Concepts

- Defining and Accessing Arrays

- Understanding the Properties and Methods of the Array Object

- Using Arrays with Loops

- Using Associative Arrays

Previous chapters have discussed object properties for which, to use them, you need knowledge of arrays. In this chapter, you are going to learn about those JavaScript arrays and what they can do to help you improve your scripts.

You will begin with a basic overview of what arrays are and why they are useful to you. Then you will learn how to define and access arrays in JavaScript. After that, you will learn how to use loops to gain access to all the elements of an array during the course of a script. Finally, you will take a look at associative arrays and how to use them.

What Is an Array?

An array is a way of storing data of similar types for easy access later in a script. In JavaScript, an array is basically a user-defined object that is typically accessed in a different way than other objects are accessed. It uses a single variable name to store multiple values (for example, a list of favorite colors or favorite foods). In a regular array, access to an element is usually through the use of an index number. An associative array allows access using a string in place of the number. You will see how to use both of these later in the chapter.

To get an idea of how a regular array works, suppose you have a class full of students and, with a script, want to be able to quickly print out the name of every student. You could use regular variables to hold the name of each student, but typing each variable name into a document.write() statement would take a long time. Instead, you could store each student's name in an array, which will allow you to access it more easily with a few lines of code using a loop.

The array would allow you to put together a number and a name, such as in the following example:

- Student 0: Thomas

- Student 1: Roger

- Student 2: Amber

- Student 3: Jennifer

By storing it in a manner like this, you could use the numbers to get the name of each student. This is where arrays become useful as a way to store information and access it later.

NOTE

Notice that the first student in the array is Student 0 rather than Student 1. This is because arrays begin storing values with the number 0 rather than 1. This will be discussed in more detail as you move through this chapter.

Why Arrays Are Useful

Why would the use of numbers make it easier for you to access the stored information? Because, with the use of numbers, you are able to use a loop to cycle through the information, instead of manually typing each entry. If the list of students in the example becomes long, the loop would save you quite a bit of typing when you want to have all the names printed onto the browser screen.

For instance, if you assigned the name of each student in your example list to a variable and then wrote the names to the screen, you would need to rewrite each variable name in the document.write() statements. The following code shows an example of this:

```
var student0="Thomas";
var student1="Roger";
var student2="Amber";               The variables are given values
var student3="Jennifer";

document.write(student0+"<br />");
document.write(student1+"<br />");      Each variable value is individually
document.write(student2+"<br />");      written on the page
document.write(student3+"<br />");
```

If you were able to use a loop to repeat a single document.write() statement for each student, you could avoid writing four separate document.write() statements. An array is a handy way to store the values (student names), because you can cycle through the values with a loop instead of writing out each value with a separate document.write() statement—even if you don't know the number of students beforehand (by using the length property of the array).

An array is basically a quick way to create an object (since it already has a constructor function) with a list of properties. A regular object (like the objects you created in Chapter 8) can be accessed like an array; but it is often easier to create an array, rather than an object, since you do not need to deal with the constructor function.

Defining and Accessing Arrays

Now that you know what arrays are, you are ready to see how to name, define, and access arrays in JavaScript.

Naming an Array

You can name an array using the same rules you learned in Chapters 3, 4, and 8 on naming variables, functions, and objects. Basically, avoid numbers in the first character, avoid spaces, and avoid using reserved words.

Defining an Array

Defining an array is similar to creating an instance of an object. In fact, one method of defining an array looks and acts just like the method of creating an instance of an object. That's what you are actually doing—creating an instance of the JavaScript Array object.

Since the creation of an instance of an object is already familiar to you, that method is presented first. The following example shows the general syntax of an array definition in JavaScript:

```
var arrayname = new Array(element0,element1);
```

You replace *arrayname* with the name you wish to give to the array, and replace *element0* and *element1* with the values that each element will have. You can use as many elements as you like.

To see a real example, you are going to take the student names from the first section of this chapter and use them as array elements. This array will have four elements, and each one will be the value of a student's name. The following example shows the definition of the array, with the names as string values:

```
var s_list = new Array("Thomas","Roger","Amber","Jennifer");
```

Now you have the values stored inside a four-element array named s_list. Because the values are strings, quote marks are used (as with a regular object). The question is, how do you begin to access the values now that they are in an array?

Accessing an Array's Elements

To access the elements of an array, you use what is often called an "index number" that allows you access to each element of the array by its position in the array. For instance, the syntax to assign the first element of an array to a variable is shown in the following example:

```
var varname = arrayname[0];
```

You would replace *varname* with a variable name and *arrayname* with the name of the array you wish to access. The 0 in brackets after *arrayname* is the index number for the first element of the array. The index number is 0 because arrays begin counting at 0 instead of 1; thus, you need to be careful that you do not get confused about the index number of an element in an array. The first element has an index number of 0, the second has an index number of 1, the third has an index number of 2, and so on.

Inside the square brackets immediately following the array name is where you place the index number of the element you wish to access in the array. To see this in action, consider again the example of the four students. The array for the name of each student was defined as in the following code:

```
var s_list = new Array("Thomas","Roger","Amber","Jennifer");
```

Now, suppose you want to assign the value of the first element in the array (Thomas, in this case, since that is the first element in the list) to a variable named tall_student.

Remember that the first element has an index number of 0; so, to get the value of the first element assigned to the variable, you would use the following code:

```
var tall_student = s_list[0];
```

To see that the value of the tall_student variable comes out as you planned, you could write a short script to write it on the page. The following example writes the value on the page as part of a sentence:

```
<body>
<script type="text/javascript">
var s_list = new Array("Thomas","Roger","Amber","Jennifer");
var tall_student = s_list[0];
document.write("The tallest student in class is "+tall_student);
</script>
</body>
```

The array is defined with four elements

The value of the first array element is assigned to a variable

The value of the variable is printed on the page

You don't really need to assign the array element to a variable in this case (it just makes you type more). You could just write the array element into the document.write() statement to save the extra line of code:

```
<body>
<script type="text/javascript">
var s_list = new Array("Thomas","Roger","Amber","Jennifer");
document.write("The tallest student in class is "+s_list[0]);
</script>
</body>
```

The array is defined with four elements

The value of the first array element is written on the page

Now you are accessing the array element directly, and you save a little typing in the process.

Other Ways to Define Arrays

You have seen one way to define an array, but there are other methods of doing so that will come in handy later in the chapter. The following methods of defining arrays will allow you to use the method best suited for various situations.

Space Now, Assign Later

One method of defining an array is to assign a certain amount of space (elements) to an array, and then allow the values to be assigned later in the script. This is done using a single number inside the parentheses when defining the array:

```
var s_list = new Array(4);
```

This creates an array named s_list, which will initially have four elements (you can add elements to an array later if you wish). Keep in mind the index numbers will be 0, 1, 2, and 3, rather than 1, 2, 3, and 4. In this case, you will give the four elements of the array values later in the script.

To give an element a value, you just assign a value to it using the array name and the index number to which you want the value assigned. So, if you want to assign a value of "Amber" to the third position in the array (index number 2), you would use the following code:

```
s_list[2] = "Amber";
```

You can use a line such as this anywhere after the array has been defined. The technique used in the preceding code also allows you to add elements to an array if you decide you need more elements later in the script. You can also use a loop to assign all the elements of the array, but that will be discussed later in the chapter when you work with arrays and loops.

So, suppose you would like to add a fifth element to your s_list array. By assigning it a value (index number 4), you can add a new name to the array in the fifth position:

```
s_list[4] = "Pat";
```

This adds a fifth element to your s_list array with a value of Pat.

Space Now, Assign Numerically Now

Another way you can define an array is very similar to the one just covered. The only difference is that some or all of the elements of the array are assigned right after the new array is created.

To see an example, consider the s_list array again. The following code shows how you can assign the elements of an array right after the line that creates the array space:

```
var s_list = new Array(4);
s_list[0]="Thomas";
s_list[1]="Roger";
s_list[2]="Amber";
s_list[3]="Jennifer";
```

This time all four elements are assigned as the array is created. This method is advantageous if you want to assign each element but do not wish to use one long list of parameters on the same line. It is also easier to look back and see what value is assigned to which element more quickly, as there isn't a need to count across. This can be quite advantageous in a long list of elements.

As with the other methods, you can still add more elements later in the script by using the next index number in the sequence.

Array Name, No Parameters

Another option for defining an array is to define it with no parameters. This creates an array with no elements, but you can add elements later, as with the other options for defining arrays.

To create an array with no elements, you create an array with no parameters:

```
var s_list = new Array();
```

This creates an array named s_list with no elements. You can still add more elements later in the script by using the next index number in the sequence. So, if you decide later that you want the array to contain one element, you could use the following code:

```
var s_list= new Array();   ←—— The array is defined
var x = 17;
var y = x+2;                        This just fills space and shows that you
var my_message = "Hi!";            can assign values later in the script
s_list[0]="Thomas";   ←—— An assignment is made for the first
                                    (and, so far, only) element of the array
```

If you assign a value to an element that has a higher index number, the array expands to have a slot for any elements that come before it. For instance, take a look at the following code:

```
var s_list = new Array();  ←—— The array is defined
var x = 17;
var y = x+2;                       Space-filling code
var my_message = "Hi!";
s_list[29]="Thomas";  ←—— This creates the 30th element in the array and
                                   also causes the array to have 30 elements
```

The last line of this code assigns the string "Thomas" to the 30th element (index number 29) in the array. This means that the array went from having 0 elements to having 30. By assigning a value to this element, the array expands to have enough slots to compensate, and values for those slots can be assigned later if you wish.

Now that you know how to define arrays in various ways, you need to look at some of the properties and methods of an Array object in JavaScript.

Understanding the Properties and Methods of the Array Object

As with other objects, an instance of the JavaScript Array object is able to use various properties and methods of the Array object. As you will see as you read through the descriptions of the individual properties and methods of the Array object, you access the properties by using the array name followed by the property or method name you wish to use.

Properties

Table 11-1 lists the properties of the Array object and provides a short description of each. Each property is discussed in more detail in the sections that follow.

The constructor Property

The constructor property contains the value of the function code that constructed an array:

```
function Array() { [native code] }
```

Property	Description
constructor	Refers to the constructor function used to create an instance of an object
index	Used when an array is created by a regular expression match
input	Used when an array is created by a regular expression match
length	Contains a numeric value equal to the number of elements in an array
prototype	Allows the addition of properties and methods to objects such as the JavaScript Array object

Table 11-1 Properties of the Array Object

The constructor property is mainly useful for informational purposes or for comparisons. To access the property, you use the array name followed by the dot operator and the constructor keyword. The following is the general syntax for using an Array object property:

```
arrayname.property
```

You replace *arrayname* with the name of the array you need to have use the property, and you replace *property* with the property you wish to use.

So, to use the constructor property, you need to create an array so that you have an instance of the Array object to use. Instead of creating a new array, the s_list array from earlier is used here, allowing you to use the following code:

```
var s_list = new Array(4);
window.alert(s_list.constructor);
```

This would send an alert with the text function Array() { [native code] } (the constructor function of the array).

The index and input Properties

To understand the index and input properties, you first need to understand regular expressions (which are used to match text strings), which requires a lengthy explanation, as provided in Chapter 13. Discussion of the index and input properties will be saved for this chapter.

The length Property

The length property returns a number that tells you how many elements are in an array.

NOTE

The length property is useful later when you begin using loops to cycle through arrays. You may need to know the length of the array (in case you add elements after the array is defined) to make the loop go through each element of the array.

To use the length property, you use the name of the array and then add the length property afterward. The following code shows an example of the length property being used to tell the viewer how many elements are in an array:

```
var s_list = new Array(4)
s_list[0]="Thomas";
s_list[1]="Roger";
s_list[2]="Amber";
s_list[3]="Jennifer";
window.alert("The array has "+s_list.length+" elements");
```

This will send an alert that says "The array has 4 elements" to the viewer.

The prototype Property

The prototype property allows you to add properties and methods to an object that already exists, such as the Array object. By using this property, you can add properties to the object from outside the constructor function. Keep in mind, however, that a change made with the prototype property affects each instance of an object that uses the same constructor function.

For example, if you decide that the Array object needs another property for one of your pages, you could use the prototype property to assign a new property using the following syntax:

```
Array.prototype.new_property=default_value;
```

You would replace *new_property* with the name you wish to use for your new property and then replace *default_value* with a default value for that property.

So, if you want to add a new property named attitude to the Array constructor function on your page and give it a default value of "cool", you could use code such as the following:

A new property is given to the Array object for this page   A new array is created that
                                                                   will have the new property

```
Array.prototype.attitude = "cool";
var s_list = new Array();
window.alert("This place is "+s_list.attitude);
```

The value of the property
is sent in an alert

This will cause an alert to the viewer of the value of the new property. In this case, the default value is used because you didn't change it (more on that soon).

You need to remember that the addition of a property like this affects every array in the document afterward. So, by adding the property in this way, every array on the page (or every page that uses the script if it is external) now has this new property that you can access.

The following code shows the use of the prototype property with two arrays on the page. The first array alerts the default value of your new property, while the second array alerts the new value. The following example shows how you can use the prototype property using the new attitude property:

The new property is added

```
Array.prototype.attitude = "cool";
var s_list = new Array();
window.alert("This place is "+s_list.attitude);
```

The first array has the new property

The value of the property for
this array is sent in an alert

```
var fish = new Array();
fish.attitude = "wide-eyed";
window.alert("Fish are "+fish.attitude);
```

The second array also has the new property

The value of the property for the second array is changed

The new value of the property for this array is sent in an alert

The first array and alert are the same as in the previous example. The second array is named fish. The second array also has the new attitude property; but, rather than keep the default value, it is changed by using the array name followed by the property and the new value.

The value of the changed property is then alerted to the viewer; thus, the viewer gets an alert saying "Fish are wide-eyed" after clicking the OK button on the first alert.

Methods

Now that you know the properties of the Array object, this section presents the methods that you can use to do different things with your arrays. Table 11-2 lists the methods and provides a description of what each method does. Following the table, each method is described in more detail.

Method	Description
concat()	Combines the elements of two or more arrays into one new array
join()	Combines the elements of an array into a single string with a separator character
pop()	Removes the last element from an array and then returns the removed element if needed
push()	Adds elements to the end of an array and then returns the numeric value of the new length of the array if needed
reverse()	Reverses the direction of the elements in an array: the first element is moved to the last slot and the last element is moved to the first slot, and so on
shift()	Removes the first element from an array and then returns that element if needed
unshift()	Adds elements to the beginning of an array and returns the numeric value of the length of the new array if needed
slice()	Pulls out a specified section of an array and returns the section as a new array
splice()	Removes elements from an array or replaces elements in an array
sort()	Sorts the elements of an array into alphabetical order based on the string values of the elements
toString()	Combines the elements of an array into a single string with a comma as a separator character

Table 11-2 Methods of the Array Object

The concat() Method

The concat() method is used to combine (or concatenate) the elements of two or more arrays and return a new array containing all of the elements. You use array names as parameters, and set them in the order in which you want the array elements to be combined.

The first example combines the elements of two arrays. To do this, only one parameter needs to be used—the name of the array to add to the end of the array used to call the method:

```
var fruits = new Array("oranges","apples");
var veggies = new Array("corn","peas");
var fruits_n_veggies = fruits.concat(veggies);
```

This code creates an array named fruits with two elements, and an array named veggies with two elements. Next, it defines a new array, fruits_n_veggies, based on the combination of the previous two arrays. The value returned by the concat() method is assigned to this array name, creating the new combined array.

The reason you use the fruits array to call the concat() method and send the veggies array name as a parameter is so that you get the elements of the fruits array at the beginning of the new array and the elements of the veggies array added to the end of the new array. The previous code creates the new array fruits_n_veggies with the following elements:

```
oranges, apples, corn, peas
```

If you wanted to have the elements of the veggies array listed first, you would call the method using the veggies array name and send the fruits array name as the parameter:

```
var fruits = new Array("oranges","apples");
var veggies = new Array("corn","peas");
var fruits_n_veggies = veggies.concat(fruits);
```

Now the elements of the veggies array are listed first, and the new fruits_n_veggies array has the following elements:

```
corn, peas, oranges, apples
```

When using this method, you want to be sure to set the order the way you want it by using the techniques just described.

If you combine three arrays, the elements of the array with which you call the concat() method will come first, and then the elements of each array name sent as a parameter will be added in the order in which they are sent:

```
var fruits = new Array("oranges","apples");
var veggies = new Array("corn","peas");
var meats = new Array("fish","chicken");
var three_groups = fruits.concat(veggies,meats);
```

Now you are combining three arrays, and the following are the elements of the new three_groups array:

```
oranges, apples, corn, peas, fish, chicken
```

If you code it in the following way instead, you will get an array with the same elements, but in a new order:

```
var fruits = new Array("oranges","apples");
var veggies = new Array("corn","peas");
var meats = new Array("fish","chicken");
var three_groups = meats.concat(veggies,fruits);
```

The following is the order of the elements in the new three_groups array when using this code:

```
fish, chicken, corn, peas, oranges, apples
```

The join() Method

The join() method is used to combine the elements of an array into a single string, with each element separated by a character sent as a parameter to the method. If no parameter is sent, a comma is used as the default separator character when the method is called.

To see how this method works, take a look at a bit of code. The following example defines an array and then calls the join() method using the array name:

```
var fruits = new Array("oranges","apples","pears");
var fruit_string = fruits.join();
```

This code assigns to the variable fruit_string the result of the join() method when called with the fruits array. Since a parameter was not sent, the elements of the array will be separated by commas in the new string. The fruit_string variable will have the following string value:

```
oranges,apples,pears
```

You can see this result by writing the string variable into a Web page. The following code will do this for you:

```
<body>
<script type="text/javascript">
var fruits = new Array("oranges","apples","pears");
var fruit_string = fruits.join();
document.write("The new string is "+fruit_string);
</script>
</body>
```

The array is created with three elements

The elements of the array are joined into a single string with commas separating the elements

The string is printed to the screen

Now you can see the string that is returned from the join() method. Figure 11-1 shows what this code produces when run in a browser.

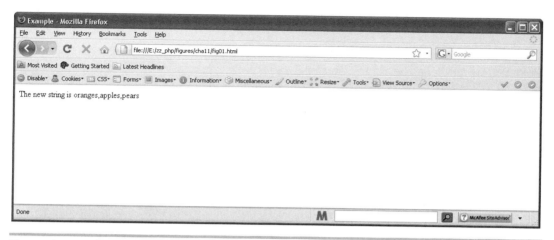

Figure 11-1   The new string is written on the page

If you want to separate the elements in the new string with something other than a comma, you can send the character you want to use as a parameter. The following code sends a colon as a string parameter to the join() method:

```
<body>
<script type="text/javascript">
var fruits = new Array("oranges","apples","pears");
var fruit_string = fruits.join(":");
document.write("The new string is "+fruit_string);
</script>
</body>
```

The array is created with three elements

The elements of the array are joined into a single string with colons separating the elements

The string is printed to the screen

This time the string will be a little different from the previous one, because it has colons in place of the commas in the previous example. Figure 11-2 shows how this string would print in the browser window.

The pop() Method

The pop() method is used to remove the last element from an array. If you assign the result of the method to a variable, the popped element will be returned and assigned to the variable.

To use the pop() method, take a look at some code that creates an array and then removes the last element from the array using the pop() method:

```
var fruits = new Array("oranges","apples","pears");
fruits.pop();
```

This creates an array named fruits with three elements (oranges, apples, pears). Then, the last element is removed using the pop() method, shortening the array to have only the first two elements (oranges, apples).

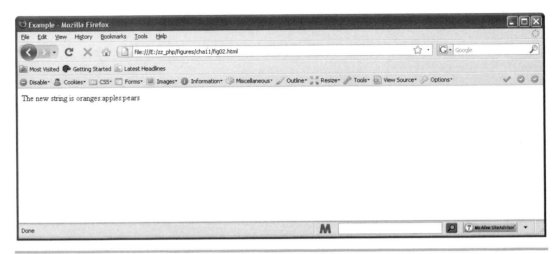

Figure 11-2 The new string is written on the page with colons as separators

If you want to remove an element but still use it in some way later, you can assign the result of the method to a variable. The variable will be assigned the value of the element that was removed. The following example removes the last element of an array and then sends the removed element as an alert to the viewer:

```
var fruits = new Array("oranges","apples","pears");
var picked_fruit = fruits.pop();
window.alert("You picked my "+picked_fruit);
```

This will pop up an alert that says "You picked my pears" to the viewer.

The push() Method

The push() method is used to add elements to the end of an array. The parameters sent to the method are the new element or elements you wish to add to the array.

CAUTION

The value returned by the push() method in older browsers is the last element that has been added to the array. In modern browsers that use newer versions of JavaScript (1.3 or later), it returns the numeric value of the new length of the array.

As an example, look at some code that adds one element to the end of an array:

```
var fruits = new Array("oranges","apples");
fruits.push("pears");
```

This code creates an array named fruits with two elements (oranges, apples) and then uses the push() method to add a third element, pears. The array now contains three elements (oranges, apples, pears), with pears being the last element in the array.

You can add more than one element by sending more than one parameter. The elements will be added in the order in which they are sent in the parameter list. The following code adds two elements to the fruits array:

```
var fruits = new Array("oranges","apples");
fruits.push("pears","grapes");
```

This code takes an array with two elements (oranges, apples) and adds two more elements to it. In the end, the array contains four elements (oranges, apples, pears, grapes).

If you want the value that is returned by the method, you can assign the result to a variable. The following code does this and then alerts the viewer to the returned value:

```
var fruits = new Array("oranges","apples");
var who_knows = fruits.push("pears","grapes");
window.alert("The method returned "+who_knows);
```

The value of the who_knows variable will be different depending on your browser. In older browsers, the value should be the string grapes (the last element added to the array). If the browser has JavaScript 1.3 or better, the value of the variable should be the numeric value of 4 (the new length of the array).

NOTE
For those who have programmed in other languages, push() and pop() treat an array like a stack (last in, first out). The shift() and unshift() methods also do this, and mixing the two sets treats an array like a queue.

The reverse() Method
The reverse() method is used to reverse the order of the elements in an array. Since that is all it does, there is no need to send any parameters or return a value.

To demonstrate how to use this method, the following code creates an array and then reverses the order of the elements in the array:

```
var fruits = new Array("oranges","apples","pears");
fruits.reverse();
```

The initial order of the array is oranges, apples, pears. When the reverse() method is called for this array, the order of the elements is reversed, and the array now is in the order pears, apples, oranges.

The shift() Method
The shift () method is used to remove the first element of an array. It returns the value of the element that was removed in case you need to use it later in the script.

So, if you want to remove the first element in an array, you could use something similar to the following code:

```
var fruits = new Array("oranges","apples","pears");
fruits.shift();
```

This code creates an array with three elements (oranges, apples, pears) and removes the first element with the shift() method. This causes the array to have only two elements remaining (apples, pears).

To use the value of the element that was removed, you can assign the result of the method to a variable. The following code assigns the removed element to a variable and then alerts the viewer about what was removed:

```
var fruits = new Array("oranges","apples","pears");
var picked_fruit=fruits.shift();
window.alert("You picked my "+picked_fruit);
```

This code displays the alert "You picked my oranges" in the browser window.

The unshift() Method

The unshift() method is used to add elements to the beginning of an array. The elements you wish to add to the array are sent as parameters to the method. The value returned by the method is the numeric value of the new length of the array.

The following example adds one new element to the beginning of an array:

```
var fruits = new Array("apples","pears");
fruits.unshift("oranges");
```

This creates an array named fruits with two elements (apples, pears) and then adds an element to the beginning of the array using the unshift() method. The array then contains three elements (oranges, apples, pears).

If you want to add more than one element at a time, you send them all as parameters in the order in which you wish to add them. The following example adds two elements to the beginning of the array:

```
var fruits = new Array("apples","pears");
fruits.unshift("oranges","grapes");
```

This takes the initial array of two elements (apples, pears) and adds two elements to the beginning of the array. The array ends up containing four elements (oranges, grapes, apples, pears) after the unshift() method is called.

The slice() Method

The slice() method is used to slice a specified section of an array and then to create a new array using the elements from the sliced section of the old array.

The following is the general syntax for using this method:

```
arrayname.slice(start,stop)
```

You would replace *arrayname* with the name of the array from which you want to remove a certain set of elements for a new array. You would replace *start* with the index number from which to start the slice. You would replace *stop* with the index number that comes after the last element you wish to slice.

For an example, the following code slices two elements from an array and creates a new array with those elements:

```
var fruits = new Array("oranges","apples","pears","grapes");
var somefruits = fruits.slice(1,3);
```

This slices the second element (index number 1) through the third element (index number 2) of the array. It does not pull out the fourth element (index number 3) because 3 is the index number after 2, which is the index number of the last element designated to be removed. The new array named somefruits contains the sliced elements (apples, pears).

The splice() Method

The splice() method allows you to remove or replace elements within an array. The parameters that can be sent include the index number at which to begin the splice, the number of elements to remove, and the option to add new elements to the array.

If you want to remove a single element from an array, you could use code such as the following:

```
var fruits = new Array("oranges","apples","pears","grapes");
var somefruits = fruits.splice(2,1);
```

This begins removing elements at index number 2. The next parameter is 1, so only one element will be removed; thus, only the element at index number 2 is removed here, which is pears. The array after the splice contains only three elements (oranges, apples, grapes).

To remove more than one element, you increase the value of the second parameter. The following code removes two elements, starting at index number 2:

```
var fruits = new Array("oranges","apples","pears","grapes");
var somefruits = fruits.splice(2,2);
```

This time the array is cut down to two elements (oranges, apples), as the last two elements are removed by the splice() method.

You can also use the splice() method to replace spliced elements in an array or to add elements to an array. The following code replaces the spliced element at index number 2 with a new element by sending an additional parameter:

```
var fruits = new Array("oranges","apples","pears","grapes");
var somefruits = fruits.splice(2,1,"watermelons");
```

This time, the element at index number 2 is removed. Since the second parameter is 1, only one element is removed. The next parameter tells the browser to add this value at the index number specified in the first parameter (index number 2). This value replaces the value that was removed (pears). The array will still have four elements, just different elements (oranges, apples, watermelons, grapes).

If you want to use the splice() method to add one or more elements to an array but not remove anything, you can set the second parameter to 0 (thus removing zero elements).

You set the first parameter to the index number at which you wish to begin adding elements. For example, take a look at the following code:

```
var fruits = new Array("oranges","apples","pears","grapes");
var somefruits = fruits.splice(2,0,"watermelons","plums");
```

This time the addition of elements begins at index number 2, as specified in the first parameter, and nothing is removed, as specified in the second parameter. Two elements are added, after which the array will have six elements (oranges, apples, watermelons, plums, pears, grapes).

The sort() Method

The sort() method sorts an array in alphabetical order (like a directory listing). This is not in numerical order, however. As an example, consider the fruit array once again. If you want to change the order of the elements so that they are in alphabetical order, you could use the following code:

```
var fruits = new Array("oranges","apples","pears","grapes");
fruits.sort();
```

Ask the Expert

Q: Among all the properties, are there any that are specifically useful for arrays?

A: The length property will come in handy in a number of cases. The other properties are useful in certain situations (such as when needing to reverse the order of the array elements). You will likely find them useful in your own scripts as you progress.

Q: Is there an easy way to remember all of these methods?

A: As with other lists, how well you remember them depends on how often you use the methods. One helpful thing is to look for the pairs that complement each other, like pop() and push(), or shift() and unshift().

Q: So, the reverse() method just turns everything around backward? Why would I want to do that?

A: You probably won't want to do it that often, but it can be helpful after using the sort() method to place a list of strings in reverse alphabetical order. It can be helpful in a few other ways as well; it just depends on the data in the array.

Q: So, the sort() method sorts the data in alphabetical order, but why does 70 come before 9 when this is sorted?

A: When the sort() method is used, it sorts using alphabetical order by default, meaning it converts all values to string values and then compares them. In that case, anything that begins with 7 comes before anything that begins with 9, even if the numeric value of the former is higher.

This will reorder the array so that the elements will be in alphabetical order, changed from oranges, apples, pears, grapes to apples, grapes, oranges, pears.

You may find this useful when you want to display the contents of an array on a page. You will see later in this chapter how to use loops to make the display of array contents easy.

The toString Method

The toString() method combines the elements of an array into a single string with a comma as a separator character. For example, you could use the following code:

```
var fruits = new Array("oranges","apples","pears","grapes");
var fruit_list = fruits.toString();
document.write(fruit_list);
```

This will write the string below to the document:

```
Oranges,apples,pears,grapes
```

Extended Array Methods

With JavaScript 1.6 or higher, there are some additional methods you can use. Since (at the time of this writing) these are not currently cross-browser, these will only be listed and described in Table 11-3. For more information on these methods, see https://developer.mozilla.org/En/Core_JavaScript_1.5_Reference:Global_Objects:Array (clicking one of the methods will give a more detailed description, often with code you can implement in order to use the same functionality in browsers that do not directly support the method).

Method	Description
filter()	Returns a new array containing elements from an array that returned true based on the function used to filter it
forEach()	Calls a specified function for each element in the array
every()	Returns true if all elements in the array return true for the specified function used to test them
indexOf()	Returns the lowest index number for an element that has a value equal to the specified value sent as a parameter
lastIndexOf()	Returns the highest index number for an element that has a value equal to the specified value sent as a parameter
map()	Returns a new array that results from calling a specified function on every element in the array
reduce()	Runs a function on two values in the array at a time, from left to right, until only a single value is left
reduceRight()	Runs a function on two values in the array at a time, from right to left, until only a single value is left
some()	Returns true if one or more elements return true for the specified function used to test them

Table 11-3 Extended Array Object Methods

Using Arrays with Loops

Loops allow you to move through array elements without the need to deal with each element one at a time with new lines of code. Instead, you can use a loop to cycle through each element of an array and cut down the number of lines you would need to write for a large array.

To begin, take a look at how you can create the elements of an array using a loop instead of a straight assignment of values.

Creating Array Elements

A loop can be useful in the creation of the elements of an array. This is especially useful if you need the viewer to enter the contents of the array for some reason, or if you wish to perform a similar calculation in creating each element.

Suppose you want the viewer to be able to input the names of the four students from the s_list array of student names introduced earlier in the chapter. Using a for loop, you could use the following code to allow the viewer to enter each name:

A new array with four elements is created

```
var s_list = new Array(4);
for(var count=0;count<4;count++) {        The loop cycles through from 0 to 3
  s_list[count] = window.prompt("Enter a name","");
}
```

A prompt is given to the viewer each time through the loop, and the text the viewer types in is assigned to the element

This code creates a new array with four elements. It then uses a for loop to assign each value. The loop begins by setting the loop's count variable to 0 and will run until the expression count<4 is no longer true.

Since 1 is added to the value of count each time through (count++), this means that the count variable will have the value of 0 the first time through, 1 the second time, 2 the third time, and 3 the fourth time. It doesn't go through another time because count would be equal to 4, which is no longer less than 4.

NOTE

The advantage of starting the count variable at 0 is that you are less likely to become confused when you use the loop. The count variable will represent the index number of each array element, so you won't need to subtract 1 from its value as you would if you had started count at 1 instead.

Inside the loop, a value is assigned to the element at the index number represented by the count variable each time through. The value assigned is the result of what the viewer types in when prompted for a name. The viewer will get four prompts in this case and will assign all four of the elements' values.

Another use for assigning element values with a loop would be to perform a similar calculation that would affect each element. For instance, if you wanted an array of ten even numbers, you could use the following code:

An array with ten elements is defined

```
var even_nums = new Array(10);
var a_count = 0;
for (var count=0;count<20;count+=2) {
even_nums[a_count] = count+2;
a_count ++;
}
```

A new variable to hold a count incremented by 1 is declared

The loop increments by 2, from 0 to 18

The a_count variable is incremented

The elements are assigned here based on the value of the count variable

By increasing count by 2 each time through, you ensure that an even number is used for your calculation. You then assign the value of the count value plus 2 to each array element while going through the loop. The use of the a_count variable allows you to keep the array from missing elements based on your count variable being incremented by 2. The a_count variable is incremented by 1 to keep the array index numbers increasing by only 1 (instead of assigning even_nums[0] and then even_nums[2], and skipping over even_nums[1]—which is what would have happened if you had used the count variable for the index number slot, rather than a_count, which increases by only 1 each time).

The first time through, count is 0, so even_nums[0] is assigned a value of 0+2, or 2. The next time through, count is equal to 2, so even_nums[1] is given a value of 2+2, or 4. This happens until you have ten array elements (index numbers 0–9) that are all even numbers.

Moving Through Arrays

You can also cycle through an array that has been created to change it, gain information from it, or list its contents in a way you like. This is quite useful and can save you some time with larger arrays.

If you go back to the old s_list array listing the names of students in a class, you can see that a loop would save you a little typing when you decide to print the list of students on the screen. You can also set the loop so that it will adjust itself if you decide to add to the array later. First, take a look at how to print the list of names to the browser screen using a loop. The HTML code would look like this (save it as s_names.html):

```
<body>
<h1>Student Names</h1>
<script type="text/javascript" src="s_names.js"></script>
</body>
```

Next, you can use the following JavaScript code (save the JavaScript file as s_names.js):

```
var s_list = new Array(4);
s_list[0]="Thomas";
s_list[1]="Roger";
s_list[2]="Amber";
s_list[3]="Jennifer";
for(var count=0;count<4;count++) {
    document.write(s_list[count]+ "<br />");
}
```

An array is created and its elements are assigned values

The elements of the array are printed on the page using a loop to cycle through the array elements

You are basically using the same method in the loop as you did while creating an array. This time, however, you use the loop to print the contents of the array to the screen. Figure 11-3 shows how this script looks when run in a browser.

Now, if you want to be sure the loop adjusts itself to show every element just in case you add or take away students, you need to have the loop use the length of the array rather than a plain number to find out when to stop itself. Recall that JavaScript can use the length property to find out how many elements are in an array. So, instead of using the number 4 in your loop for the comparison, use the length property of the array:

```
for(var count=0;count<s_list.length;count++)
```

The array can have any number of elements, and the loop will cycle through until the full array is used (until count<s_list.length is no longer true). The last element will have an index number that is one less than the length of the array, which is what you want since arrays begin counting at 0 instead of 1.

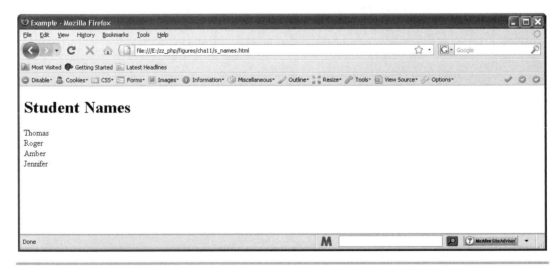

Figure 11-3 The names from the array are written on the page

To put this all together, you can make a few changes to your array and then print the array elements in the browser window. The following changes to the JavaScript code allow you to make adjustments to the array later while still allowing the script to display all the names:

```
var s_list = new Array();
s_list[0]="Thomas";
s_list[1]="Roger";
s_list[2]="Amber";
s_list[3]="Jennifer";
s_list[4]="Pat";
s_list[5]="Kelly";
s_list[6]="Jerry";
for(var count=0;count<s_list.length;count++) {
    document.write(s_list[count]+ "<br />");
}
```

An array is created and its elements are assigned values

The elements of the array are printed on the page using a loop to cycle through the array elements, and using the length property to know when to stop the loop

You have now adjusted the array so that it initially has no direct number of elements, but you define them as you go by assigning values to each element. This array has added three names to the list, giving you an array with seven elements (index numbers 0–6). The list is then written to the page. Figure 11-4 shows the result of this script when run in a browser. Notice that the list now has all the new names.

You could take this one step further and use the sort() method to put the names of the students in alphabetical order. To do this, you only need to add a single line calling the sort() method for the s_list array before you print the elements to the screen. The order of

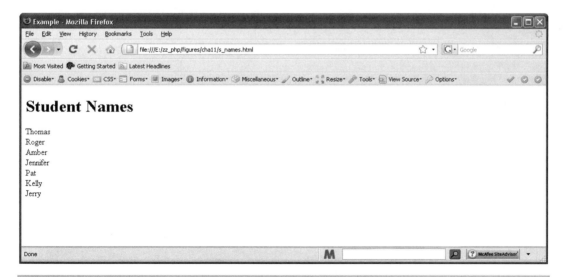

Figure 11-4   All the names are listed on the page

the elements is adjusted, and the alphabetized list is printed. The following is the code for alphabetizing:

```
var s_list = new Array();
s_list[0]="Thomas";
s_list[1]="Roger";
s_list[2]="Amber";
s_list[3]="Jennifer";
s_list[4]="Pat";
s_list[5]="Kelly";
s_list[6]="Jerry";
s_list.sort();
for(count=0;count<s_list.length;count++) {
   document.write(s_list[count]+ "<br />");
}
```

An array is created and its elements are assigned values

The array is sorted into alphabetical order

The sorted elements of the array are printed on the page using a loop to cycle through the array elements, and using the length property to know when to stop the loop

Notice the addition of the s_list.sort() call. This sorts the array to give you alphabetized output. Figure 11-5 shows the result of this script when it is run in a browser.

The for each in Loop

With later versions of JavaScript (1.6 and up), you can use the for each in loop to run through the list of array elements. It allows you to use a variable for the value of the array element each time through the loop (rather than using something like s_list[count], you could simply use

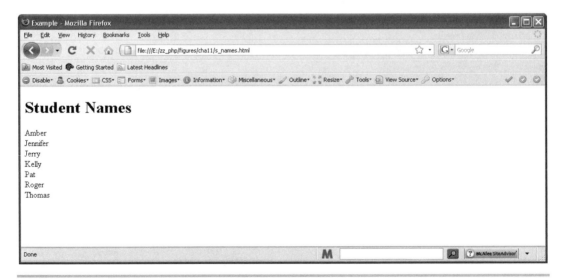

Figure 11-5 The names are listed in alphabetical order

a name such as student). The following code shows an example using the s_list array you have been using in this chapter:

```
var s_list = new Array();
s_list[0]="Thomas";
s_list[1]="Roger";
s_list[2]="Amber";
s_list[3]="Jennifer";
for each (student in s_list) {
   document.write(student + "<br />");
}
```

Notice that for and each are two separate reserved words, followed by the opening parenthesis, followed by the variable name you want to use (student in this case), followed by the reserved word in, followed by the array name, and ending with the closing parenthesis. Then, the opening curly bracket allows you to write the loop code as usual, except you will use the variable name (student in this case) instead of keeping a count variable and using s_list[count].

Since this does not yet (at the time of this writing) work cross-browser, it is best for now to continue using a traditional for loop (which is backward-compatible) or to use a for in loop as in the following code:

```
var s_list = new Array();
s_list[0]="Thomas";
s_list[1]="Roger";
s_list[2]="Amber";
s_list[3]="Jennifer";
for (student in s_list) {
   document.write(s_list[student] + "<br />");
}
```

You can begin to use loops that become much more involved with the arrays, and use more of the properties and methods as well. For now, this will get you started and build a foundation from which you can build the more complex loops for your JavaScript arrays.

Try This 11-1   Use Loops with Arrays

pr11_1.html
prjs11_1.js

This project allows you to practice using loops with arrays and to practice using some of the properties of arrays. You will create a list of computer parts that you want to print to the screen.

Step by Step

1. Create an HTML page with a heading with the text "Computer Parts Needed". Add script tags that include an external JavaScript file named prjs11_1.js. Save the HTML file as pr11_1.html.

2. Create an external JavaScript file and save it as prjs11_1.js. Use it for steps 3–10.

(continued)

3. Create a new array and assign the following list of parts as values for the elements in the array:

monitor
motherboard
chip
hard drive

4. Print out each computer part on its own line in the browser window (use a loop).

5. Save the JavaScript file and load the HTML file in a browser to view the results.

6. Reopen the JavaScript file in your text editor, and make the changes described in the next three steps.

7. If you didn't before, use the length property in the comparison instead of a number.

8. Add some elements to the array by coding them into the script. Add the following items after the first four you already have:

CD-RW drive
power supply

9. Have the array sort itself so that it is in alphabetical order.

10. Save the JavaScript file and view the HTML file in your browser. The new elements should show up in an alphabetical listing of the array elements.

Try This Summary

In this project, you used your knowledge of loops, arrays, and Array object properties to create two different results. One result lists the elements of an array, while the other adds some elements to the array and lists the elements in alphabetical order.

Using Associative Arrays

Associative arrays (also referred to as hash tables) allow you to use strings in place of index numbers. Using an associative array is quite similar to using a property name with a regular object; you just do it in an array format. Since numbers are not used, the use of associative arrays is more limited, but they can still be useful to store information and make the elements easier to remember when you want to access them. To begin, take a look at how to define an associative array.

CAUTION

JavaScript does not use true associative arrays (what you see here to mimic them is really a creation of property/value pairs within that Array object rather than being true associative arrays). Also, certain properties such as length won't work as expected with this type of array. Thus, use caution, because this can at times cause unexpected values to occur within your scripts. More often than not, it is better to simply use a numbered array or to create a new object, depending on what you need the script to do.

Defining Associative Arrays

You can define an associative array in much the same way as you define a normal array, but you will want to use the methods that allow you to assign each element individually. Here, you will create a blank array and give it values by assigning values to elements.

To assign a value to an element, you need to give the element a string in place of its index number. The value you would use for the string would be something you could associate with the value you are going to assign to the element. For instance, if you wanted to change the old s_list array into an associative array based on a trait of each student, you could use the following code:

```
var s_list= new Array();
s_list["tall"]="Thomas";
s_list["cool"]="Roger";
s_list["clever"]="Amber";
s_list["attentive"]="Jennifer";
```

The assignments here give an index string of a trait, and then a student's name is assigned to the element that has his or her trait.

This will make it easier to remember when you want to access an element of the array later, since you can remember a trait instead of a number when you need an element. This makes array declarations semantically richer, which can also be useful if you wish to query or otherwise reference a certain element.

Accessing Associative Arrays

Accessing an associative array is done in the same way that you access a normal array, except that you use an index string rather than an index number.

If you wanted to access the element that had the name of the tall student, for instance, you could access it using the following syntax:

```
s_list["tall"]
```

Thus, you could print out a listing of the students by their traits by using the following example code:

```
<body>
<h1>Student Names</h1>
<script type="text/javascript">
var s_list= new Array();
s_list["tall"]="Thomas";
s_list["cool"]="Roger";
s_list["clever"]="Amber";
s_list["attentive"]="Jennifer";
document.write("The tall one is " +s_list["tall"]+ "<br />");
document.write("The cool one is " +s_list["cool"]+ "<br />");
document.write("The clever one is " +s_list["clever"]+ "<br />");
document.write("The attentive one is " +s_list["attentive"]+ "<br />");
</script>
</body>
```

An array is created and its elements are assigned values

The elements of the array are printed on the page

This will print out the list based on the traits. Figure 11-6 shows the results of this script when run in a browser.

You will be using arrays in the next chapter to help you create scripts that use random numbers.

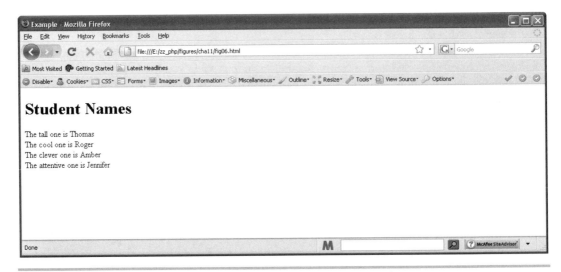

Figure 11-6 The names are listed based on the traits of each student

Try This 11-2 Use Associative Arrays

`pr11_2.html`
`prjs11_2.js`

This project allows you to practice using associative arrays. You will create an array of elements based on the qualities of various cars.

Step by Step

1. Create an HTML page with a heading with the text "List of Cars". Add script tags to include an external JavaScript file named prjs11_2.js. Save the HTML file as pr11_2.html.

2. Create an external JavaScript file and save it as prjs11_2.js. Use it for steps 3–6.

3. Create an associative array with the following index strings:

    cool
    small
    long

4. Assign a value of "Mustang" to the element with the index string of "cool". Assign a value of "Bug" to the element with the index string of "small". Assign a value of "Station Wagon" to the element with the index string of "long".

5. Print the value of each element to the browser window.

6. Save the JavaScript file and view the HTML file in your browser. You should see the list of cars.

Try This Summary

In this project, you used your knowledge of associative arrays to create a page that displays the elements of an associative array.

Chapter 11 Self Test

1. An array is a way of _____ data of similar types for easy access later in a script.

2. In JavaScript, an array is basically a user-defined _____.

3. In a regular array, access to an element is usually through the use of a(n) _____.

    A string

    B index number

    C random number

    D random string

4. A(n) _____ array allows access using a string in place of the number.

5. Which of the following is a valid name for an array?

   A my array

   B 1stArray

   C for

   D soap

6. Which of the following does not correctly create an array?

   A var myarray= new Array();

   B var myarray= new Array(5);

   C var myarray= new Array("hello","hi","greetings");

   D var if= new Array[10];

7. Which of the following will correctly access the fifth element of an array named "cool"?

   A cool[5];

   B cool(5);

   C cool[4];

   D cool.array[4];

8. What does the following code do?

```
var s_list= new Array()
```

   A Creates an empty array named s_list

   B Creates an array named s_list with the default number of elements, 10

   C Creates an empty array named list

   D Creates an array that can never have any elements added to it

9. What property of the Array object will return the numeric value of the length of an array?

   A The length property

   B The getlength property

   C The constructor property

   D The lengthOf property

10. The _____ property allows you to add properties and methods to an object that already exists.

11. The _____ method is used to combine the elements of two or more arrays and return a new array containing all of the elements.

12. The join() method is used to combine the elements of an array into a single _____, with each element separated by a specified character.

13. The _____ method is used to remove the last element from an array.

14. By default, how does the sort() method sort the contents of an array?

    A It reverses the contents of the array.

    B It sorts the contents numerically.

    C It sorts the contents alphabetically.

    D It removes the last element from an array.

15. What is used in place of an index number in an associative array?

    A A floating-point value

    B A Boolean value

    C A negative number

    D A string value

Chapter 12

Math, Number, and Date Objects

Key Skills & Concepts

- Using the Math Object

- Understanding the Number Object

- Using the Date Object

The previous chapter presented JavaScript arrays and the Array object, including an overview of the Array object's various properties and methods. In this chapter, you will learn about the JavaScript Math, Number, and Date objects, in that order. For each object, a short introduction is provided along with a description of why the object can be useful to you. Following that is a look at the various properties and methods that you can use for that object.

Using the Math Object

The Math object can be useful when you need to perform various calculations in your scripts. To begin, take a look at what the Math object is.

What Is the Math Object?

The Math object is a predefined JavaScript object. Like the other predefined objects you have studied in this book, the Math object gives you properties and methods to use. The Math object is used for mathematical purposes to give you the values of certain mathematical constants or to perform certain operations when you use a method function.

How the Math Object Is Useful

As mentioned, the Math object is useful when you need to make mathematical calculations in your scripts. For instance, if you need the value of pi for a calculation, the Math object gives you a property to use so you can get that value.

Also, if you need to find the square root of a number, a method of the Math object enables you to do this. Another thing this object provides is a way to generate random numbers in JavaScript, which you will find useful in certain scripts.

Properties

The Math object gives you a number of properties that can help you if you need to perform certain mathematical calculations. Table 12-1 lists the properties of the Math object, with the values of each.

As you can see in Table 12-1, all of the properties simply hold numeric values that can be useful in mathematical calculations. Because these are irrational numbers, the values listed are nonterminating and are thus approximations.

Property	Value
E	Value of Euler's constant (E), which is about 2.71828…
LN10	Value of the natural logarithm of 10, which is about 2.302585…
LN2	Value of the natural logarithm of 2, which is about 0.693147…
LOG10E	Value of the base 10 logarithm of E, which is about 0.43429…
LOG2E	Value of the base 2 logarithm of E, which is about 1.442695…
PI	Value of pi, often used with circles, which is about 3.14159…
SQRT2	Value of the square root of 2, which is about 1.4142…
SQRT1_2	Value of the square root of one half, which is about 0.7071…

Table 12-1   Properties of the Math Object

Using the Properties

The properties contain read-only values, which tend to be useful in particular types of calculations. For instance, if you want to find the area of a circle, you use the formula Area = $pi*r^2$. Knowing that, you could write an application to determine the area of a circle based on the radius input by a viewer. You could use the following code, starting with the HTML code:

```
<form>
To find the area of a circle, input a radius:<br />
<input type="text" id="radius" />
<input type="button" value="Get the Area!" id="getarea" />
</form>
```

Next, the JavaScript code:

The input button element is retrieved by its id (getarea)

```
var area_button = document.getElementById("getarea");
```

```
area_button.onclick = function() {
```

The value of the text box (with an id of radius) is retrieved using its value property

```
  var rad = document.getElementById("radius").value;
```

```
  if (rad.length < 1) {
    window.alert("Please enter a radius!");
    return false;
  }
```
Checks to see if data is entered

```
  else if (rad != (rad*1)) {
    window.alert("Radius must be numeric!");
    return false;
  }
```
Checks to see if the data entered is not numeric

```
else {
  var the_area = Math.PI * (rad * rad);
  window.alert("The area is " + the_area + " square units. ");
  return false;
}
};
```

Performs the calculation and displays the answer

This code first grabs the input button element by its id (getarea) and assigns it to a variable named get_area. When this element is clicked, an anonymous function is executed. It grabs the value input in the text field for the radius using the value property of that element and assigns it to a variable named rad.

Next, the code performs two checks. It checks that the length property of rad is not less than 1, to ensure that the viewer entered data into the field. If it is less than 1, the code gives an alert asking the viewer to enter the information. After that, it checks to see if the value of rad is not numeric. This is done by testing whether or not the value can be multiplied by 1 and returning a number equal to what was entered. (This check can also be done in other ways, such as with regular expressions, which will be covered in Chapter 13.) If the data entered contains a string, the calculation will return NaN (Not a Number), which will give the viewer an alert saying that the radius must be numeric.

Finally, if the data entered passes those tests, the calculation of the area of the circle is performed and assigned to a variable named the_area. Notice that for now you multiply the radius by itself to get the radius squared. When you get to the math methods in the next section, you will see that the method pow() may be used instead.

Once the calculation is complete and assigned to the variable, an alert is displayed to the viewer with the area in generic "square units." The script could of course be altered to suit your needs or to offer options (centimeters, inches, or other units of measure).

NOTE
The script can be made more accessible by using the submit event rather than the click event and providing a server-side backup. This will be discussed more in Chapter 14.

Figure 12-1 shows the result of running this script in a browser and entering 2 into the text field.

Methods
The methods of the Math object enable you to perform certain calculations that can be helpful in your scripts. Table 12-2 lists various methods of the Math object and briefly describes the purpose of each. Each method is discussed in more detail in the following sections.

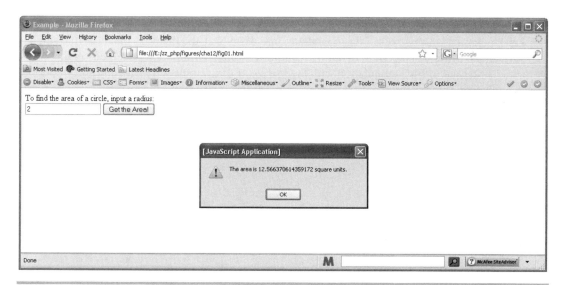

Figure 12-1   The area of the circle is displayed for the viewer

Method	Purpose
abs()	Returns the absolute value of the number sent as a parameter
acos()	Returns the arccosine of the number sent as a parameter, in radians
asin()	Returns the arcsine of the number sent as a parameter, in radians
atan()	Returns the arctangent of the number sent as a parameter, in radians
atan2()	Returns the arctangent of the quotient of two numbers sent as parameters, in radians
ceil()	Returns the smallest integer greater than or equal to the number sent as a parameter
cos()	Returns the cosine of the number sent as a parameter, in radians
exp()	Returns the value of E to the power of the number sent to the method as a parameter
floor()	Returns the largest integer less than or equal to the number sent as a parameter
log()	Returns the natural logarithm of the number sent as a parameter
max()	Returns the larger of the two numbers that are sent as parameters
min()	Returns the smaller of the two numbers that are sent as parameters
pow()	Returns the numeric value of the first parameter raised to the power of the second parameter
random()	Returns a random number between 0 and 1; does not require a parameter
round()	Returns the value of the number sent as a parameter rounded to the nearest integer
sin()	Returns the sine of the number sent as a parameter, in radians
sqrt()	Returns the square root of the number sent as a parameter
tan()	Returns the tangent of the number sent as a parameter, in radians

Table 12-2   Methods of the Math Object

The Basic Methods

For the purpose of this book, "basic methods" are defined as the methods that take in a single number, do a simple calculation with it, and return a value. Grouping the methods in this way avoids the need to list each method with the same sort of example—it is not any sort of official organization of the methods, just a way to expedite this discussion.

The following basic methods are the ones that work in generally the same way:

- abs()
- acos()
- asin()
- atan()
- cos()
- exp()
- log()
- sin()
- sqrt()
- tan()

Each of these basic methods takes in a numeric value and sends back another value. Since the general usage is the same, this discussion uses sqrt() as an example of how the rest could be used to get their various values. If you need to know what type of value is returned from a different method, refer to Table 12-2 to see what each method does.

The easiest way to use the sqrt() method is to input a positive number as the parameter to the method, as shown in the following example:

```
window.alert(Math.sqrt(4));
```

This alerts the value of the positive square root of 4, which is 2.

Instead of calculating a static number, you could get the user to input a number, and then send an alert to the user with the square root of the number input by the user. You could do this using the following code, starting with the HTML code:

```
<body>
<form>
Enter a (positive) number or zero: <br />
<input type="text" id="sr_num" />
<input type="button" value="Get a Square Root" id="getroot" />
</form>
</body>
```

Next, the JavaScript code:

If the number entered is negative, the viewer has to try again

The value of the text box (with an id of sr_num) is retrieved

The anonymous function to perform the task begins

```javascript
var root_button = document.getElementById("getroot");
root_button.onclick = function() {
  var thenum = document.getElementById("sr_num").value
  if (thenum < 0) {
    window.alert("Hey! I said to enter a positive number! Try again.");
    return false;
  }
  else if (thenum != (thenum*1)) {
    window.alert("Input must be numeric!");
    return false;
  }
  else {
    var theroot = Math.sqrt(thenum);
    window.alert("The square root of "+thenum+" is "+theroot);
    return false;
  }
};
```

Checks to see if the
input is not numeric

If the value is not negative, the square root is
calculated and the alert shows the square root

The preceding code uses an anonymous function, which is called when the viewer clicks the button in the HTML code. The function begins by assigning the value input into the text box to the thenum variable.

Next, the function checks to see if the viewer entered a negative number. If so, an alert appears, telling the viewer to try again. It then checks to see if the data entered was not numeric (which gives another alert). Otherwise, the Math.sqrt() method is called using the number entered by the viewer (thenum) as a parameter. This returns the number's square root, which is then assigned to the variable named theroot. Finally, an alert appears telling the user the square root information.

NOTE

The script can be made more accessible using the submit event rather than the click event and providing a server-side backup. This will be discussed more in Chapter 14.

The result of this script when the viewer enters the number 4 is shown in Figure 12-2.

The other methods in this section work in much the same way; they just return different results such as absolute values, tangents, or logarithms.

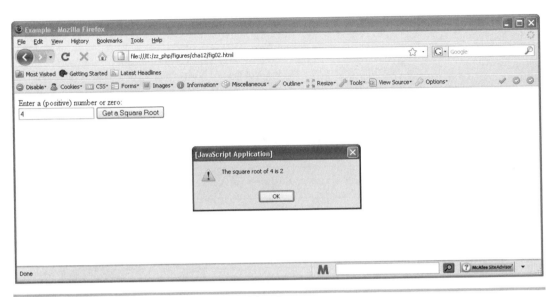

Figure 12-2 The square root is displayed for the viewer

The Two-Parameter Methods

This section discusses the methods that take in two parameters instead of just one. These methods include the following:

- atan2()
- max()
- min()
- pow()

The max() and min() methods are very similar, while the pow() method does something a bit different.

The max() and min() Methods The max() method takes two numbers and returns the larger number. The min() method also takes two parameters, but returns the smaller number. You could use these methods in a script that enables the viewer to enter two numbers and then alerts the user which number is larger.

The following example code uses both of these methods and gives the viewer the results in an alert. First, the HTML code:

```
<body>
<form>
<input type="button" value="Which Number is Bigger?" id="getmax" />
</form>
</body>
```

Next, the JavaScript code:

```
var max_button = document.getElementById("getmax");          The prompts get two
max_button.onclick = function() {                            numbers from the viewer
  var num1 = window.prompt("Enter a number.","");
  var num2 = window.prompt("Enter another number","");
  var largenum = Math.max(num1,num2);        The results of the maximum and
  var smallnum = Math.min(num1,num2);        minimum are assigned to variables
  if (largenum == smallnum) {
    window.alert("Those two numbers are equal!");      A check in case the
  }                                                    numbers are equal
  else {
    window.alert(largenum+" is larger than "+smallnum);
  }
};
                                   The alert to display if the numbers are not equal
```

This script prompts the viewer for two numbers and assigns them to variables. It then takes the maximum and minimum from both numbers and assigns the values returned to variables. Those variables are then used to check whether they are equal. If so, an alert comes up saying they are; otherwise, an alert pops up with the results.

The following illustration shows the results of this script in a browser if the viewer enters 2 as the first number and 54 as the second number.

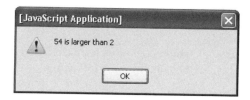

The pow() Method   The pow() method takes two parameters and calculates the value of the first parameter to the power of the second parameter. For instance, the following code would return the value of 2 to the 3rd power:

```
Math.pow(2,3);
```

Other than its difference in calculations, you can use it in the same general way that you used the other two-parameter methods by assigning the result to a variable and then using the variable in a script. As an example, you could use the following script, starting with the HTML code:

```
<body>
<form>
<input type="button" value="Find a Power" id="getpow" />
</form>
</body>
```

Next, the JavaScript code:

```
var pow_button = document.getElementById("getpow");
pow_button.onclick = function() {
  var num1 = window.prompt("Enter a base number.","");
  var num2 = window.prompt("What power should we set it to (a
number)?","");
  var theresult = Math.pow(num1,num2);
  window.alert(num1+" to the power of "+num2+" is "+theresult);
};
```

Using this code, if the viewer enters 2 as the first number and 3 when asked for a power, the script will compute the result of 2 to the 3rd power. The viewer then is given an alert showing the answer. Clicking the button in the HTML code is how the viewer starts the function. The result of this script when the numbers 2 and 3 are input is shown here:

Now that you know about the two-parameter methods, take a look at some other methods that haven't been covered yet.

The Other Methods

These methods take in a single parameter, but what each does with that parameter warrants a closer look. The individual methods include the following:

- ceil()
- floor()
- round()

The ceil() Method   The ceil() method stands for *ceiling* and returns the smallest integer that is greater than or equal to the number sent as the parameter. This method is used mainly when there are likely to be numbers after the decimal point in a number. It rounds the number up to the next highest integer, unless the number is an integer already. In that case, the same number is returned (because it can be equal). For instance, Math.ceil(12.23); would return 13, but Math.ceil(12); would return 12.

The following script shows an example of how the ceil() method can be used to return different values, starting with the HTML code:

```
<body>
<form>
```

```
<input type="button" value="Find a Ceiling" id="getceiling" />
</form>
</body>
```

Next, the JavaScript code:

```
var ceil_button = document.getElementById("getceiling");
ceil_button.onclick = function() {
  var num1= window.prompt("Enter a number.","");
  var theceil= Math.ceil(num1);
  window.alert("The ceiling of "+num1+ " is "+theceil);
};
```

This script displays an alert that states the ceiling of the number entered by the viewer. The following illustration shows the result of this in the browser when the viewer enters 4.55 at the prompt:

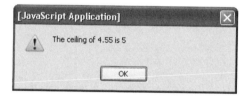

The floor() Method   The floor() method is like the ceil() method, but it goes the opposite way. The floor() method returns the largest integer less than or equal to the parameter sent to the method. This rounds down to the next lowest integer, unless the parameter is an integer already. In that case, it returns the same integer since it is already equal to an integer. Basically, this method just removes the decimal part of a number and leaves the integer as the result.

For instance, Math.floor(12.23); will return 12 and Math.floor(12); will also return 12. You can use the floor() method in the same way the ceil() method was used in the preceding section—by assigning the result to a variable.

The round() Method   The round() method works like the previous two methods, but instead rounds the number entered as the parameter to the nearest integer whether it is greater or less than the number. Any number having the decimal portion's value at .5 or greater will be rounded up, while any decimal portion with a value less than .5 is rounded down.

The .5 cutoff is strict, so Math.round(12.49999999); would return 12 even though your tendency may be to round it up.

The random() Method   The random() method is very useful for creating scripts that require random integers. It returns a random number between 0 and 1. This means that you get a number with a decimal that can be quite long and not useful on its own. For instance, it might return something like 0.36511165498095293.

To get a random integer that you can use, you need to do some things to get the type of value that you want to use.

Random Integers   To get a random integer, the first thing you will want to do is to make the result have a greater range of values so that you are not stuck between 0 and 1. To get a greater range of values, you can multiply the result of the random() method by an integer to create a larger range. Like an array, the range would begin counting from 0; so, to get a range of five possible integers, you would multiply the result by 5. The following code shows how you can do this:

```
var rand_num= Math.random()*5;
```

This gets the result between 0 and 4, but does not give you an integer yet. The number could still come out as a long decimal number.

To get an integer between 0 and 4, you need to find a way to make all of these decimal numbers convert to integers. Recall that earlier you ran through three methods, floor(), ceil(), and round(), that converted numbers to integers in various ways. The floor() method is the one you will choose here because it simply removes the decimal places after the integer and gives you the integer portion of the number.

To use the floor() method, you could write the following code:

```
var rand_num = Math.random()*5;
var rand_int = Math.floor(rand_num);
```

The floor() method takes in the value of the rand_num variable as a parameter and then gives you an integer from it.

If you want to save a line of code, you could get a little fancy. You could just insert the random() method and calculation as the parameter to the floor() method. You can do this because the result of the calculation, Math.random*5, is a number, and the floor() method can take a number as a parameter. The following code shows how you can code this on a single line:

```
var rand_int = Math.floor(Math.random()*5);
```

Now the variable rand_int will have the value of a random integer between 0 and 4. As you might have noticed, this sort of number range could be quite useful with arrays. This is how you can begin to code some fun scripts with random numbers.

Random Numbers for Scripts   Now you can have a little fun with the Math object by using the random() method. By setting up some arrays, you can create a script that provides random quotes or shows a random image each time the page is loaded.

Random Quotes for Fun   If you have thought about adding a quote to your page but don't want to deal with changing the quote all the time to have something different, a random-quotes script could be just the thing for you.

To make such a script, you first need some quotes to use. Suppose you want to set up ten different quotes that will be displayed in random order each time the page is loaded. Since you have a number of values that are similar (and so that you can use them with the random integer later), you should use an array so that you can store all of these values and retrieve them easily.

So, you need to set up an array with ten elements similar to the following example, in which each element is a random (and perhaps peculiar) quote that I have thrown into the mix for you:

```
var quotes= new Array(10);
quotes[0]="Look in the mirror. Are you looking at me?";
quotes[1]="It is time for a rhyme, I guess.";
quotes[2]="Where is my JavaScript book?";
quotes[3]="If I had a buck for every dollar I spent--Oops, never mind.";
quotes[4]="I suppose you were expecting a real quote here.";
quotes[5]="Quotes are great, but don't quote me on that.";
quotes[6]="What should I write here?";
quotes[7]="Wut hapns iff eye miss spel ohn purpas?";
quotes[8]="Mark my words, I will mark my words.";
quotes[9]="This spot reserved for a better quote.";
```

Now that you have this odd list of quotes in an array, you can use them by generating a random integer.

You need a random integer between 0 and 9 (ten numbers), so you can use the following code to assign a random integer between 0 and 9 to a variable:

```
var rand_int = Math.floor(Math.random()*10);
```

Now the value of the variable rand_int will be a random integer between 0 and 9. You can use it to access the element of the array whose index number matches the random integer in the rand_int variable. You just need to access the array element using the variable as the index number, as in the following example:

```
quotes[rand_int]
```

You can write this value in the body of the page in a document.write() statement, or you can reassign the innerHTML property of an element. An example using innerHTML is provided next. The HTML document is saved as random_quotes.html and the JavaScript file is saved as random_quotes.js. The HTML code:

```
<body>
<h1>My Random Quote for You:</h1>
<div id="my_quote">
Look in the mirror. Are you looking at me?
</div>
<script type="text/javascript" src="random_quotes.js"></script>
</body>
```

The JavaScript code:

```
var quotes= new Array(10);
quotes[0]="Look in the mirror. Are you looking at me?";
quotes[1]="It is time for a rhyme, I guess.";
```

```
quotes[2]="Where is my JavaScript book?";
quotes[3]="If I had a buck for every dollar I spent--Oops, never
mind.";
quotes[4]="I suppose you were expecting a real quote here.";
quotes[5]="Quotes are great, but don't quote me on that.";
quotes[6]="What should I write here?";
quotes[7]="Wut hapns iff eye miss spel ohn purpas?";
quotes[8]="Mark my words, I will mark my words.";
quotes[9]="This spot reserved for a better quote.";

var q_div = document.getElementById("my_quote");
var rand_int = Math.floor(Math.random()*10);
q_div.innerHTML = quotes[rand_int];
```

The code writes one of the random quotes on the page based on the random integer value in the rand_int variable. A default quote (the first one in the array data) is provided for those without JavaScript, which is then overwritten with the random quote if JavaScript is available. Reloading the page enables the random number to be reset and will probably (though not necessarily, because it is random) show a different quote.

Figure 12-3 shows one of the possible results of this script when run in a browser.

Figure 12-4 shows another one of the possible results of this script when run in a browser. You can keep getting different (or sometimes the same) results by refreshing the page.

Now that you can write random quotes into a page, how about displaying a random image? It is very similar to the last script; you just need to make some small adjustments.

Random Images for the Updated Look   A random-image script can give your page the feel of being updated without requiring you to change an image all the time. Of course, the images all need to fit the content where you decide to place the randomly chosen image. A random-image script could be useful, for example, for an art gallery to display its collection.

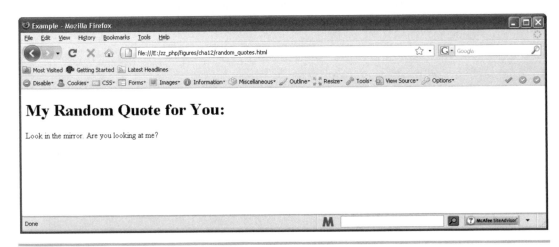

Figure 12-3   A possible result of using the random-quote script

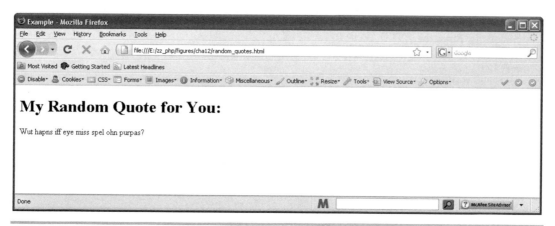

Figure 12-4   Another possible result of using the random-quote script

The first thing you need is an array of image Universal Resource Locator (URL) addresses (which can be local or absolute—local addresses are used here). The array used for this script is shown in the following example code:

```
var r_image= new Array(10);
r_image[0]="image0.gif";
r_image[1]="image1.gif";
r_image[2]="image2.gif";
r_image[3]="image3.gif";
r_image[4]="image4.gif";
r_image[5]="image5.gif";
r_image[6]="image6.gif";
r_image[7]="image7.gif";
r_image[8]="image8.gif";
r_image[9]="image9.gif";
```

This array sets up the addresses of images that can be displayed at random each time the page is loaded.

Next, you need a way to get a random integer between 0 and 9. This is the same as in the previous random-quote script:

```
var rand_int= Math.floor(Math.random()*10);
```

The next step is to access the array in the body section of the document to show a random image from the array when the page is loaded in the browser.

The following code enables you to display the random image using the innerHTML property of a div element to write the img tag for a random image if JavaScript is available.

The HTML file is saved as random_images.html and the JavaScript file is saved as random_images.js. First, the HTML code:

```
<body>
<h1>My Random Image for You:</h1>
<div id="my_image">
<img src="image0.gif" alt="Random Image" />
</div>
<script type="text/javascript" src="random_images.js"></script>
</body>
```

Next, the JavaScript code:

```
var r_image= new Array(10);
r_image[0]="image0.gif";
r_image[1]="image1.gif";
r_image[2]="image2.gif";
r_image[3]="image3.gif";
r_image[4]="image4.gif";
r_image[5]="image5.gif";
r_image[6]="image6.gif";
r_image[7]="image7.gif";
r_image[8]="image8.gif";
r_image[9]="image9.gif";

var i_div = document.getElementById("my_image");
var rand_int = Math.floor(Math.random()*10);
i_div.innerHTML = '<img src="'+r_image[rand_int]+'" alt="Random Image"
/>';
```

As you can see, this is quite similar to the random-quote script. You just needed to change the contents of the array and the statement to replace the contents of the innerHTML property to make the script display an image rather than a quote.

NOTE
For this example, the images are saved as image0.gif, image1.gif, and so on; however, you could save your image files under any name you like.

This discussion of the random() method could go on for some time because there are numerous things that you could randomize. However, you now know the basics of how this feature works, so it's time to move on.

Ask the Expert

Q: Will I ever have any use for any of the properties of the Math object? They are all numbers that I don't even use!

A: This depends on how often you perform different types of calculations. It would be unlikely for you to use any of them as a beginner, but there are some scripts out there that use them for various advanced purposes, such as JavaScript calculators.

Q: I have no interest in writing a calculator. Do I really have to bother memorizing all the properties of the Math object?

A: Well, probably not, since a situation to use them probably won't come up all that often. It is good to have a reference on hand just in case, though, and to know generally what they are since they appear in scripts on the Web from time to time.

Q: Some of these properties and methods could be handy if I don't have a calculator around. I could write a little script to calculate some things for myself, couldn't I?

A: Of course! Just be sure to double-check the numbers with something you know the answer to first to be sure that there are no mistakes in your code.

Q: The random() method is fun so far, but I can't think of anything else I could use it for. Could you give me some ideas for using it to do other things?

A: There are a number of other things you could use it for. You can randomize pretty much anything that can be displayed with an HTML tag or plain text, so try out some ideas and see if they work for you. Here are some thoughts off the top of my head for you, though: random links, random linked images, random tasks for a JavaScript game of some sort (like rolling dice or drawing a card), random page greetings, random alerts...and I'm sure there are plenty more.

Try This 12-1　Display a Random Link on a Page

`pr12_1.html`
`prjs12_1.js`

This script enables you to work with the random() method a little more by enabling you to create a script to display a random link on a page.

Step by Step

1. Create an HTML page with script tags that point to an external JavaScript file named prjs12_1.js. Add a heading that says "Random Link" and add a div element with an id of random_link. Inside the div element, insert a default link for those without JavaScript. Save the HTML file as pr12_1.html.

(continued)

2. Create an external JavaScript file and save it as prjs12_1.js. Use it for steps 3–6.

3. Create a set of five Web addresses in an array. Use the following addresses or some of your own choosing:

http://www.pageresource.com
http://www.javascriptcity.com
http://www.mydemos.com
http://www.yahoo.com
http://www.google.com

4. Use the random() method to create a random integer you can use to access the array with the integer as an index number.

5. Display a random link on the page in the format shown next by changing the innerHTML property of the div element with the id of random_link:

```
<a href="random address here">Random Site!</a>
```

6. Save the JavaScript file and open the HTML file in your Web browser. Try reloading a few times to see how the random addresses show up for the link.

Try This Summary

In this project, you were able to use your knowledge of the Math object. Using the random() method, you created a Web page that displays a link that goes to a random Web address.

Understanding the Number Object

The Number object is another predefined JavaScript object that offers several useful properties and methods for use with numbers. Its most common use is to access some of its helpful properties that represent certain values that can aid you when creating scripts.

Properties

Table 12-3 lists the properties of the Number object and briefly describes the purpose of each. Each property is described in more detail in this section.

The constructor Property

The constructor property holds the value of the constructor function of the object, much like the use of this property in the Array object (refer to Chapter 11). The property returns a value similar to what you get with the Array object: the name of the constructor function and any public code in the function. Since the function code is private, you get the [native code] text in place of the actual function code.

Property	Purpose
constructor	Holds the value of the constructor function that created the object
MAX_VALUE	Holds a constant number value, representing the largest value before JavaScript interprets a number as infinity
MIN_VALUE	Holds a constant number value, representing the smallest value before JavaScript interprets a number as negative infinity
NaN	Represents the value of "Not a Number"
NEGATIVE_INFINITY	Represents the value of negative infinity
POSITIVE_INFINITY	Represents the value of infinity
prototype	Enables you to add properties to the object if you wish

Table 12-3 Properties of the Number Object

The MAX_VALUE Property

The MAX_VALUE property is a constant number value, approximately 1.79E+308. The reason this property is helpful is that any number greater than its value is represented as infinity in JavaScript. Thus, using it in a comparison could provide a way to avoid calculations that are too large to display a numerical value. The following code is an example of how this works:

```
var big_num = num1*num2*num3;
if (big_num > Number.MAX_VALUE) {
  window.alert("The number is too large, try smaller numbers.");
}
else {
  window.alert(big_num);
}
```

Assuming num1, num2, and num3 were entered by the viewer, the alert, instead of displaying the word "infinity" as the answer, informs the viewer to try entering smaller numbers for the calculation if the value of big_num is greater than the value of the MAX_VALUE property.

The MIN_VALUE Property

The MIN_VALUE property is a constant number value, approximately 5e –324. The reason this property is helpful is that any number less than its value is represented as negative infinity in JavaScript. Thus, using it in a comparison could provide a way to avoid calculations that are too small to display a numerical value. The following code is an example of how this works:

```
var small_num = num1*num2*num3;
if (small_num < Number.MIN_VALUE) {
  window.alert("The number is too small, try larger numbers.");
}
else {
  window.alert(small_num);
}
```

Assuming num1, num2, and num3 were entered by the viewer, the alert informs the viewer to try entering larger numbers for the calculation if the result of the calculation is less than the value of the MIN_VALUE property.

The NaN Property

The NaN property is a value that represents "Not a Number." It is displayed by the browser as a string value of NaN and is not equal to any number or another instance of NaN.

The NEGATIVE_INFINITY Property

The NEGATIVE_INFINITY property is a constant value that represents negative infinity. It can be used in a similar fashion to the way MIN_NUMBER and MAX_NUMBER are used.

The POSITIVE_INFINITY Property

The POSITIVE_INFINITY property is a constant value that represents positive infinity. It can be used in a similar fashion to the way MIN_NUMBER and MAX_NUMBER are used.

The prototype Property

The prototype property enables you to add a property or method to the Number object, much like you did with the Array object in Chapter 11.

Methods

Table 12-4 lists the methods of the Number object and briefly describes the purpose of each. The following sections discuss each method in more detail.

The toExponential(), toFixed(), toPrecision(), and toString() Methods

These methods return a string value representing what the Number object would look like formatted in a particular way. Note that these methods cannot be used with a number itself (a numeric value), as in the following code:

```
document.write(10.toExponential());
```

Method	Purpose
toExponential()	Returns a string value that represents the number in exponential notation
toFixed()	Returns a string value that represents the number rounded to the specified number of digits after the decimal
toPrecision()	Returns a string value that represents the number rounded to the specified number of significant digits
toSource()	Returns a string value that represents the source code of the object
toString()	Returns a string value for a Number object
valueOf()	Used by JavaScript internally most often

Table 12-4 Methods of the Number Object

This will cause a JavaScript error because it expects a Number object. To avoid this, use the methods by assigning numeric values to variables (which will make them Number objects), as in the following code:

```
var the_num = 10;
document.write(the_num.toExponential());
```

NOTE
You could also use the syntax of var the_num = new Number(10); (which you may be used to from previous objects) and it would also be valid.

The toExponential() Method
The toExponential() method returns a string representing a Number object in the form of exponential notation. Thus, the following code would write the result of 1.0e+1 (or a similar notation, depending on your browser) on the screen:

```
var the_num = 10;
document.write(the_num.toExponential());
```

The toFixed() Method
The toFixed() method returns a string representing a Number object rounded to the specified number of places after the decimal. For instance, if you need to format the results of calculations to appear as monetary values, you could use this method to get the result of your calculation rounded at the second digit after the decimal and displayed in your currency format. For example, this code uses dollars and cents:

```
var mymoney = 2000;
var mykids = 7;
var one_share = mymoney/mykids;
document.write("One share of my money is $"+ one_share.toFixed(2));
```

The result of the calculation for one share is 285.7142857142857, but since it is displayed using the toFixed() method on it with 2 as the parameter, the sentence displays as follows:

```
One share of my money is $285.71
```

The toPrecision() Method
The toPrecision() method returns a string representing a Number object rounded to the specified number of significant digits. This is for all digits before and after the decimal. Thus, if you wanted a number like 45.57689349 rounded to five significant digits, you could use the following code:

```
var the_num = 45.57689349;
document.write(the_num.toPrecision(5));
```

The browser will display the string 45.577, which is the number rounded to five significant digits (two before and three after the decimal place in this case).

The toString() Method

The toString() method returns the string value of a Number object (or a numerical variable value). This can be useful if you want to convert a numerical value to its corresponding string value (for example, change 10 to "10").

The toSource() Method

The toSource() method returns a string value that represents the source code of the object. With the predefined Number object, this method returns the value of the constructor property. This method is most often called by JavaScript internally and is less likely to be used in code.

The valueOf() Method

This is another method that is mainly used by JavaScript internally. For now, you just need to know that it is a valid method of the Number object.

Using the Date Object

The Date object is another predefined JavaScript object. It enables you to set certain time values and to get certain time values that you can use in your scripts. To use this object, you need to create an instance of the object to which you can refer.

To create an instance of the Date object, you use the new keyword (as you have with a number of other objects), as shown in the following example:

```
var instance_name = new Date();
```

You would replace *instance_name* with a name that you want to use for the instance of the Date object. So, if you wanted an instance named rightnow, you could use the following code:

```
var rightnow = new Date();
```

Now you have an instance of the object named rightnow.

Once you have an instance of the object, you can use the properties and methods of the Date object to perform various tasks (such as create JavaScript clocks). These properties and methods are described in the following sections.

Properties

The Date object has only two properties. Table 12-5 lists the properties and their purposes (these may look familiar, because the Array and Number objects have these same properties). Each property is described in more detail in the following sections.

Property	Purpose
constructor	Holds the value of the constructor function that created the object
prototype	Enables you to add properties to the object if you wish

Table 12-5 Properties of the Date Object

The constructor Property

The constructor property holds the value of the constructor function of the object, much like the use of this property in the Array and Number objects. To see what the value is, you could write it to the page, as shown in the following code:

```
<body>
<script type="text/javascript">
var rightnow= new Date();
document.write(rightnow.constructor);
</script>
</body>
```

If you run the code, you will probably see something similar to the following line written on the page:

```
function Date() { [native code] }
```

This is pretty much what you get using this property with the Array object: the name of the constructor function and any public code in the function. Since the function code is private, you get the [native code] text in place of the actual function code.

The prototype Property

The prototype property enables you to add a property or method to the Date object, much like you did with the Array object in Chapter 11. For instance, if you want to add a new property named attitude for each instance of the Date object, you could use the following code:

```
Date.prototype.morning="a.m.";
var rightnow= new Date();
window.alert("This date is "+rightnow.morning);
```

This code creates the new property, creates an instance of the Date object, and then alerts the value of the new property to the screen.

Now that you know the properties of the Date object, take a look at the methods you can use.

Methods

The Date object doesn't give you many properties, but it does have quite a large number of methods you can use. Table 12-6 lists various methods of the Date object and the purpose of each method. Each method is discussed in more detail in the sections that follow.

Now that you have the long list of methods, take a look at them in a little more detail, beginning with the methods used to get date values in an instance of the Date object.

Method	Purpose
getDate()	Returns the day of the month based on the viewer's local time
getDay()	Returns the number of days into the week based on the viewer's local time (0–6)
getHours()	Returns the number of hours into the day based on the viewer's local time (0–23)
getMilliseconds()	Returns the number of milliseconds into the second based on the viewer's local time (0-999)
getMinutes()	Returns the number of minutes into the hour based on the viewer's local time (0–59)
getMonth()	Returns the number of months into the year based on the viewer's local time (0–11)
getSeconds()	Returns the seconds into the minute based on the viewer's local time (0–59)
getTime()	Returns the number of milliseconds since 1/1/1970 for the Date object
getTimezoneOffset()	Returns the time-zone offset (from Greenwich Mean Time) in minutes based on the viewer's local time zone
getYear()	Returns the year based on the viewer's local time (two digits)
getFullYear()	Returns the full year based on the viewer's local time (four digits)
getUTCDate()	Returns the day of the month in Coordinated Universal Time
getUTCDay()	Returns the number of days into the week in Coordinated Universal Time (0-6)
getUTCFullYear()	Returns the full year in Coordinated Universal Time (four digits)
getUTCHours()	Returns the number of hours into the day in Coordinated Universal Time (0–23)
getUTCMilliseconds()	Returns the number of milliseconds into the current second in Coordinated Universal Time (0-999)
getUTCMinutes()	Returns the number of minutes into the hours in Coordinated Universal Time (0–59)
getUTCMonth()	Returns the number of months into the current year in Coordinated Universal Time (0–11)
getUTCSeconds()	Returns the number of seconds into the current minute in Coordinated Universal Time (0-59)
parse()	Returns the number of milliseconds since 1/1/1970 of a date sent as a parameter based on the viewer's local time
setDate()	Sets the day of the month for an instance of the Date object
setHours()	Sets the hours for an instance of the Date object
setMilliseconds()	Sets the milliseconds for an instance of the Date object
setMinutes()	Sets the minutes for an instance of the Date object
setMonth()	Sets the month for an instance of the Date object

Table 12-6 Methods of the Date Object

Method	Purpose
setSeconds()	Sets the seconds for an instance of the Date object
setTime()	Sets the time (in milliseconds since January 1, 1970, at midnight) for an instance of the Date object
setYear()	Sets the year for an instance of the Date object (two digits)
setFullYear()	Sets the full year for an instance of the Date object (four digits)
setUTCDate()	Sets the day of the month in Coordinated Universal Time
setUTCFullYear()	Sets the full year in Coordinated Universal Time (four digits)
setUTCHours()	Sets the number of hours into the day in Coordinated Universal Time (0–23)
setUTCMilliseconds()	Sets the number of milliseconds into the current second in Coordinated Universal Time (0-999)
setUTCMinutes()	Sets the number of minutes into the hours in Coordinated Universal Time (0–59)
setUTCMonth()	Sets the number of months into the current year in Coordinated Universal Time (0–11)
setUTCSeconds()	Sets the number of seconds into the current minute in Coordinated Universal Time (0-59)
toDateString()	Returns the date portion of the Date object as a string in American English
toGMTString()	Returns a string that is the date in Greenwich Mean Time (GMT) format (toUTCString() is now used instead)
toLocaleString()	Returns a string that is the date in a format based on the locale
toLocaleDateString()	Returns the date portion of the Date object as a string based on the locale
toLocaleTimeString()	Returns the time portion of the Date object as a string based on the locale
toString()	Returns a string that is the date in American English
toTimeString()	Returns the time portion of the Date object as a string in American English

Table 12-6 Methods of the Date Object *(continued)*

Methods That Get Values

Methods that get values enable you to get various time and date values that you can use in your scripts. The methods that enable you to get values for an instance of the Date object include the following:

- getDate()
- getDay()
- getHours()
- getMilliseconds()

- getMinutes()
- getMonth()
- getSeconds()
- getTime()
- getTimezoneOffset()
- getYear()
- getFullYear()
- getUTCDate()
- getUTCDay()
- getUTCFullYear()
- getUTCHours()
- getUTCMilliseconds()
- getUTCMinutes()
- getUTCMonth()
- getUTCSeconds()

To use these methods, you need an instance of the Date object. Once you have that, you can call any of the methods by using the instance name. The following is the syntax for doing this:

```
instance_name.method();
```

You would replace *instance_name* with the name of your instance of the Date object, and you would replace *method* with the method function you wish to use.

So, if you wanted to use the getDate() method with an instance of the Date object named rightnow, you would use the following code:

```
var rightnow= new Date();
var theday= rightnow.getDate();
```

This assigns the value returned from the getDate() method to a variable named theday.

Because the values returned from the Date methods are often numeric, the methods need to be explained a bit further; thus, the following sections take a look at these methods more closely.

The getDate() Method

The getDate() method enables you to get the day of the month for use in a script. The value returned is a number that represents the day of the month. So, if it is the 5th of the month, the getDate() method would return 5. If it is the 22nd, the getDate() method would return 22. This method is nice because it is fairly straightforward.

The getDay() Method

The getDay() method enables you to get the day of the week; however, rather than returning a name such as Monday or Friday, it returns a number. The number represents the number of days *into* the week (0–6) rather than the day *of* the week you would commonly have in mind (1–7). So, if it is Sunday, the method returns 0; and if it is Wednesday, the method returns 3. You have to remember that it counts from 0 when you begin using it in your scripts. Many of the methods that follow will count beginning at 0.

The getHours() Method

The getHours() method enables you to get the number of hours into the day (0–23). The count begins at 0. So, when it is midnight, the method returns 0; and when it is 2:00 P.M., it returns 14.

The getMilliseconds() Method

The getMilliseconds() method enables you to get the number of milliseconds stored in the instance of the Date object (0–999).

The getMinutes() Method

The getMinutes() method enables you to get the number of minutes stored in the instance of the Date object (0–59). Again, the counting begins at 0. So, if it is 2:00 (either A.M. or P.M., or any hour) on the dot, the method returns 0; and if it is 2:23, the method returns 23.

The getMonth() Method

The getMonth() method enables you to get the number of months stored in the instance of the Date object (0–11). This method also begins counting at 0, which makes the result a little tricky. For instance, if it is January (the month people tend to think of as 1), the method returns 0; and if it is October (the month people tend to think of as 10), the method returns 9. This is one you have to watch a little more closely when you use it in scripts, because you will need to remember to make an adjustment if you want to use numeric dates (like 10/24/2000).

The getSeconds() Method

The getSeconds() method enables you to get the number of seconds stored in the instance of the Date object (0–59). So, if the time is 2:42:23, the method returns 23; and if the time is 2:23:00, the method returns 0.

The getTime() Method

The getTime() method gets the time (in milliseconds since January 1, 1970, at midnight) for an instance of the Date object. So, if you wanted to know the number of milliseconds since that date at your current time, you could use the following code:

```
var rightnow= new Date();
var theday= rightnow.getTime();
```

This assigns the result of the method to a variable so that you can use it later if you need it in your script.

The getTimezoneOffset() Method

The getTimezoneOffset() method gives you the number of minutes that separate the local time from GMT. So, if you are 6 hours apart from GMT, the method would return 360 (6 × 60); and if you are only 1 hour apart, the method returns 60.

The getYear() Method

This method returns the last two digits of the year (at least if the year is between 1900 and 1999). For instance, if the year is 1988, the method returns 88. After the year 2000, some browsers will return a three-digit year and others will return a four-digit year. To avoid this, you can use the getFullYear() method, which is supported by the newer browsers and returns a four-digit year.

The getFullYear() Method

The getFullYear() method is very similar to the getYear() method, except it returns a four-digit year consistently to avoid the year 2000 problem.

The getFullYear() method works like the getYear() method, but you do not need to run any extra checks to be sure the year is correct:

```
var rightnow= new Date();
var theyear= rightnow.getFullYear();
```

This assigns the value returned by the method to the theyear variable. This time, the value is already four digits and won't need any adjusting.

The UTC Methods

These methods work the same as their counterparts (for example, getDate() and getUTCDate() work the same), but return the information in terms of Universal Time rather than the viewer's local time.

Now that you have seen the methods that get values, take a look at the methods that enable you to set values for an instance of the Date object.

Methods That Set Values

The methods that set values work with the same types of values as the methods that get values. The methods that enable you to set values for an instance of the Date object include the following:

- setDate()
- setHours()
- setMilliseconds
- setMinutes()
- setMonth()
- setSeconds()

- setTime()
- setYear()
- setFullYear()
- setUTCDate()
- setUTCFullYear()
- setUTCHours()
- setUTCMilliseconds()
- setUTCMinutes()
- setUTCMonth()
- setUTCSeconds()

To set these, you send them a numeric parameter based on the time or date you want to use. For instance, if you wanted to set the day of the month for an instance of the Date object, you could use the following code:

```
var rightnow= new Date();
rightnow.setDate(22);
```

This would set the day of the month to the 22nd for the rightnow instance of the Date object.

The other methods work in the same way. In order to know what value needs to be sent to one of these methods, take a look at what type of value is returned by its counterpart in the methods that get values. The parameter the method will expect will be a value like the one returned by the method.

Other Methods

The remaining methods perform various tasks that the other methods don't cover in some way.

The parse() Method

The parse() method is used to find out the number of milliseconds since January 1, 1970, at midnight for a date string (such as Dec 12, 1999) input as a parameter. This is often used with the setTime() method since it needs a parameter in milliseconds to set the time. You could use the parse() method to find the number of milliseconds since January 1, 1970, for the date Dec 12, 1999 at midnight (the rightnow instance of the Date object will use this as the date that all of the methods will use to return values), as shown in the following code:

```
var rightnow= new Date();
var thenum= Date.parse("Dec 12, 1999")◄                This method can be used
rightnow.setTime(thenum);                              directly from the Date object
```

This code parses the date into a number of milliseconds, and then sends it to the setTime() method used with the rightnow instance of the Date object.

The toString(), toDateString(), toTimeString(), toLocaleDateString, and toLocaleTimeString() Methods

These methods return a string representing the date and time, or a portion thereof. For instance, the toString() method returns a date in string format. You can use it to get a formatted date for an instance of the Date object, as shown in the following code:

```
var rightnow= new Date();
var thedate= rightnow.toString();
```

This will assign a date string value to the variable thedate. The value of the string depends on what browser the viewer is using to view the page. It can then be written to the page or used with other methods of the Date object in a script.

The toGMTString() Method

The toGMTString() method returns a date string in GMT format. You can use it to get the GMT format for an instance of the Date object, as shown in the following code:

```
var rightnow= new Date();
var thedate= rightnow.toGMTString();
```

This will assign a value, such as Wed, 21 Dec 2003 11:12:44 GMT, to the variable thedate. It can then be written to the page or used with other methods of the Date object in a script.

The toLocaleString() Method

The toLocaleString() method returns a date string in the format of the viewer's locale. You can use it to get the locale format for an instance of the Date object, as shown in the following code:

```
var rightnow= new Date();
var thedate= rightnow.toLocaleString();
```

This will assign a date string value to the variable thedate. The value of the string depends on what browser the viewer is using to view the page. It can then be written to the page or used with other methods of the Date object in a script.

Now that you have the methods down, see if you can have a little fun with the Date object.

How About Some Date Scripts?

With the technical overview out of the way, you are ready to create some scripts that use the methods of the Date object. First you will write a script to display the date on the page, and then you will create a script for a simple status bar clock.

Write the Date on the Page

To write the date on the page, you need to use some of the Date object methods to get the values you need. Suppose you want to write a date with the format of Tuesday, M/D/Y (month, day, year). To do this, you need to find out the day of the week, the month, the day of the month, and the year. You can do this using the getDay(), getMonth(), getDate(), and getFullYear() methods.

The following script will write the date to the page. First, the HTML code (save as write_date.html):

```
<body>
<h1>Today's Date</h1>
<div id="write_date">
<!-- call to a server-side script for backup could go here -->
</div>
<script type="text/javascript" src="write_date.js"></script>
</body>
```

Note the comment within the div element. If you want to make this accessible to browsers that do not support JavaScript, you can place a call to a PHP (or other server-side technology) script here for those lacking JavaScript. For example, if you had the page set up to parse PHP, you could use the following to display the date much like the JavaScript code will:

```
<body>
<h1>Today's Date</h1>
<div id="write_date">
<?PHP
$the_date = date(l, n/j/Y);
echo "$date";
?>
</div>
<script type="text/javascript" src="write_date.js"></script>
</body>
```

You will see that the PHP script is much shorter than the JavaScript script due to its built-in date-formatting capability. The date displayed may differ from the viewer's date as it displays the date on the Web server. An in-depth discussion of server-side technology is beyond the scope of this book, but this serves as an example of a way to provide the same basic feature for those without JavaScript.

Next, the JavaScript code (save as write_date.js):

```
var rightnow = new Date();                    A new instance of the
                                              Date object is created
var weekday = rightnow.getDay();
var themonth = rightnow.getMonth();
var thedate = rightnow.getDate();             The methods of the Date object are
var theyear = rightnow.getFullYear();         used to obtain the needed values

// Set the Days of the Week
var someday= new Array(7);
someday[0]="Sunday";
someday[1]="Monday";
someday[2]="Tuesday";                         An array is created to hold the name of each day
someday[3]="Wednesday";                       of the week, with the index values corresponding to
someday[4]="Thursday";                        what will be returned by the getDay() method
someday[5]="Friday";
someday[6]="Saturday";
```

```
//Set the Month Numbers to Be Recognizable
themonth++;
```

The month value is incremented in order to look like its standard numerical month value

```
var date_div = document.getElementById("write_date");
date_div.innerHTML = someday[weekday]+ ", "+themonth+"/"+thedate+"/"+theyear;
```

The div element is obtained by its id and has its innerHTML property changed to display the formatted date

This script sets the results of the methods to variables. It then creates an array to hold the days of the week, which are later accessed using the number returned from the getDay() method as the index number. The script then makes an adjustment, adding 1 to the number returned by the getMonth() method, so that the month will show up the way you would expect it (recall that it counts months starting at 0 instead of 1, so this ensures that January is represented by the number 1 rather than 0, for example).

The formatted output is written onto the page for the viewer to see. The result of this script when run in a browser is shown in Figure 12-5.

Create a Simple Clock

To create a simple clock, you need the hours, minutes, and seconds of the current time. To get these, you can use the getHours(), getMinutes(), and getSeconds() methods.

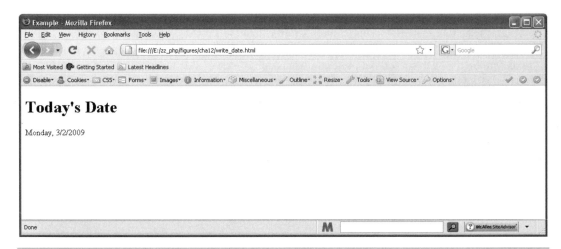

Figure 12-5 The date is shown on the page

The following code will create a clock that is displayed on the page. First, the HTML code (save as clock.html):

```
<body>
<h1>Current Time:</h1>
<div id="my_clock">
<!-- call to a server-side script for backup could go here -->
</div>
<script type="text/javascript" src="clock.js"></script>
</body>
```

CAUTION

If you use a server-side script as a backup to the JavaScript clock, you almost surely do not want it to update every second because this could put undue strain on the Web server. In such a case, it is often best to simply display the time without updating it.

Next, the JavaScript code (save as clock.js):

```
function startclock() {

    var thetime = new Date();
    var hours = thetime.getHours();
    var mins = thetime.getMinutes();
    var secn = thetime.getSeconds();
    var ap = (hours >= 12) ? "p.m." : "a.m.";

    if (hours >= 13) {
        hours -= 12;
    }
    if (hours < 1) {
        hours = 12;
    }
    if (mins < 10) {
        mins = "0" + mins;
    }
    if (secn < 10) {
        secn = "0" + secn;
    }

    var clock_div = document.getElementById("my_clock");
    clock_div.innerHTML = hours + ":" + mins + ":" + secn + " " + ap;
    setTimeout("startclock()", 1000);
}
startclock();
```

The methods of the Date object are used to obtain the hours, minutes, and seconds

A variable is set so that a.m. or p.m. may be displayed after the time

The hours, minutes, and seconds are adjusted so that they will display like a typical 12-hour digital clock

The div element is obtained so that the innerHTML property can be adjusted to display the clock

The script is called every second using the setTimeout() method

The hours, minutes, seconds, and ap variables are combined and displayed as the new innerHTML for the div element

Calling the function here starts the process

Figure 12-6 A clock is displayed on the page

The script creates a function that sets the results of the methods to variables. It takes the hours variable and sets the ap variable to p.m. if hours is greater than or equal to 12 and sets it to a.m. if hours is less than 12 (at this point the hours variable still holds 13 for 1 p.m., 14 for 2 p.m., and so on). Once this is done, the hours variable is adjusted so that it will display the expected value for a 12-hour clock.

The script then adjusts the values of the variables that show the minutes and seconds by adding a leading 0 when the number is less than 10. This way the clock will show 12:02:34 for 12:02:34, instead of leaving out the 0 and displaying 12:2:34 (this can also be done for the hours variable if you would like it to have a leading zero).

At the end, the function displays the output on the page. The function is initially called right after it is defined. The function is repeated at intervals of 1000 milliseconds, or 1 second. This enables the clock to stay current. The results of this script when run in a browser are shown in Figure 12-6.

Try This 12-2 Create a JavaScript Clock

pr12_2.html
prjs12_2.js

This project enables you to work more with the methods of the Date object, as well as learn how to adjust the values that are returned so they can be used in various ways. This creates a JavaScript clock with a few more options than your simple clock in the previous section.

Step by Step

1. Create an HTML page with script tags that point to an external JavaScript file named prjs12_2.js. Add a heading that says "Current Time" and add a div element with an id of my_clock. Save the HTML file as pr12_1.html.

2. Create an external JavaScript file and save it as prjs12_2.js. Use it for steps 3–6.

3. Write some code that will display a clock. In this clock, include the following information:

The time with hours, minutes, and seconds
Whether it is A.M. or P.M.
The date in the form mm/dd/yyyy

4. This will be a 12-hour clock, so be sure to adjust the value of the hours so that they stay between 1 and 12. Also, note the format of the date and adjust the month and day values accordingly.

5. Begin the clock, and have it update every second.

6. Save the JavaScript file and open the HTML file in your browser. The time and date should appear on the page.

Try This Summary

In this project, you used your knowledge of the Date object. Using the methods of the Date object, you created a clock that appears on the Web page.

Chapter 12 Self Test

1. What do the properties and methods of the Math object enable you to do?

   A Take the square roots and other such values of strings and return a number

   B Perform mathematical calculations

   C Go to math class to learn new theorems

   D Nothing, they are useless

2. The _____ property holds the value of Euler's constant.

3. The LN10 property holds the value of the natural _____ of 10.

4. The LOG10E property holds the value of the logarithm of 10*E.

   A True

   B False

5. Which of the following would correctly write the value of pi on a Web page?

   A document.write(Math.Pi);

   B document.write(Math.pi);

   C document.write(Math.PI);

   D document.write(Date.PI);

6. The _____ property holds the value of the square root of 2.

7. The abs() method returns the _____ value of a number sent to it as a parameter.

   A absent

   B absurd

   C absolute

   D absolute square root

8. The _____ method returns the arcsine of a number sent to it as a parameter.

9. The pow() method returns the numeric value of the _____ parameter raised to the power of the _____ parameter.

10. Which of the following would correctly generate a random number between 0 and 7?

   A var rand_int= Math.floor(Math.random()*7);

   B var rand_int= Math.floor(Math.random()*6);

   C var rand_int= Math.floor(Math.random()*8);

   D var rand_int= Math.sqrt(Math.random());

11. The _____ method returns the square root of a number sent to it as a parameter.

12. What must be created in most cases before the Date object's properties and methods can be used?

   A Nights string

   B A number for reference to the date

   C A time for the date to be set

   D An instance of the Date object

13. The _____ method returns the number of days into the week.

14. The getMonth() method returns the same number as the number that represents the current month (for example, returns 1 if the current month is January).

   A True

   B False

15. Which of the following correctly assigns the day of the week for an instance of the Date object named rightnow to a variable named weekday?

   A var weekday= rightnow.getDate();

   B var weekday= rightnow.getDay();

   C var weekday= right now.getDay();

   D var weekly= rightlater.getMinutes();

Chapter 13

Handling Strings

Key Skills & Concepts

- Using the Properties of the String Object

- Using the Methods of the String Object

- Using Regular Expressions

To work with strings in JavaScript, you need to learn about the various methods that handle them. The methods come from the JavaScript String object.

This chapter first explains what the String object is and how to create strings that use its properties and methods. Then, the String object's properties and methods are discussed in more detail so you can see how they work. Finally, you'll code a script that uses some of the properties and methods you've learned.

Introduction to the String Object

The String object provides properties and methods to get information about strings or to modify strings. A String object is created in either of two ways: a programmer creates one by using the new keyword with the constructor function, or JavaScript creates one temporarily when one of the methods is called from a string literal. What makes a String object and what makes a string literal? To find out, take a look at how to create a String object in JavaScript.

The String Object

As just explained, one way to create a String object is to use the new keyword, as you've done with other objects previously. The syntax is shown here:

```
var instance_name = new String("string value here");
```

You replace *instance_name* with the name you want to use for the instance of the String object. You then replace *string value here* with the string of characters to use as the new String object.

So, if you want to create an instance of the String object named guitar_string, you could use the following code:

```
var guitar_string = new String("G");
```

This script creates an instance of the String object for the string "G".

Although creating a String object with the new keyword can be useful for things such as comparing String objects, string literals are used more often.

The String Literal

You can create a string literal just by assigning a string value to a variable. This technique is a bit shorter than creating a String object using the new keyword and still allows you to use all the methods of the String object (as well as one of the properties).

A string literal is created in the code that follows. Notice that the code assigns a string value to a variable.

```
var guitar_string = "G";
```

This makes the string "G" a string literal, which you know as a regular text string. With text strings, you're also allowed to use the properties and methods of the String object.

What's the Difference?

The difference between a String object and a string literal is that a regular text string has the value of the string itself, and it can be compared against another string easily, as in the following code:

```
var guitar_string1 = "E";              Both variables have the same string value
var guitar_string2 = "E";
if (guitar_string1 == guitar_string2) {
   window.alert("The strings are the same!");
}
                                       The strings are compared
else {
   window.alert("The strings are not the same!");
}
```

Because this code uses regular string literals, the result is what you'd expect. An alert says that the strings are the same.

However, if you used String objects to run through the same if block, you would see something unexpected. The code that follows uses String objects instead:

```
var guitar_string1 = new String("E");   The String objects are given
var guitar_string2 = new String("E");   the same string values
if (guitar_string1 == guitar_string2) {
   window.alert("The strings are the same!");
}                                        The values are compared,
else {                                   but an unexpected
   window.alert("The strings are not the same!");   answer is the result
}
```

This time the alert would tell you that the strings are not the same, even though the string values are both "E"—because a String object is an object value and not a literal value. Objects aren't going to be equal to one another in the same way regular text strings would be. To find out if two objects are equal, you would have to write extra code to determine that. For most purposes, you wouldn't want to go to all that trouble. Instead, you would probably use string literals and let them use the String object's methods.

A regular text string is able to use the String object's methods because JavaScript takes the string literal and turns it into a temporary String object. Once the method's execution is complete, it returns a string literal. This allows you to use the String object's methods without having to create String objects.

Using the Properties of the String Object

The String object has only three properties, so this section is relatively short. Table 13-1 provides a brief description of these properties, each of which is discussed in turn in the sections that follow.

The constructor Property

This property performs the same task as it does in the other objects that have it (like the Date and Array objects). It sends back the value of the constructor function. To use the constructor property, you have to use a String object rather than a literal.

NOTE

You can use a string literal for the length property and all of the methods of the String object, but the constructor and prototype properties require String objects.

The following code writes the value of the constructor property onto a Web page:

```
<body>
<script type="text/javascript">
var guitar_string = new String("G");  ◀———— A new String object is created
document.write(guitar_string.constructor);  ◀———— The value of the constructor
</script>                                            property is printed on the page
</body>
```

This code produces text similar to the following:

```
function String() { [native code] }
```

The length Property

This property returns the length of the string, which is the number of characters contained in the string. You can use it with both String objects and string literals. You've seen this property

Property	Purpose
constructor	Holds the value of the constructor function for an instance of the object
length	Holds the numeric value of the length of the string (its number of characters)
prototype	Allows you to add properties to the object

Table 13-1 Properties of the String Object

with other objects as well, such as the Array object. (In that case, the value was the number of elements in an array.)

The following code uses a regular text string. It writes the length of the string variable onto the page.

```
<body>
<script type="text/javascript">
var myname="John";  ───────────── A string literal is created
document.write("The name has "+myname.length+" characters.");
</script>
</body>
                              The length of the name in characters
                              is written on the page
```

Notice how the name of the variable is used like an object name here. This is how to get JavaScript to create a temporary String object to use the property. The script writes the result to the page. Because the name has four characters, the length property has a value of 4 here.

The length property will be quite useful when you want to break strings apart to get information or make changes to them, especially if the viewer enters the string and you don't know its length beforehand.

The prototype Property

As with the other objects that have the prototype property, you can use it to add properties or methods to String objects on the page. The following code shows an example:

```
                              The prototype value adds a
                              property to the String object

String.prototype.attitude="cool";  ──┘
var rightnow= new String("Joe");  ←─────────────  A new instance of the
                                                  String object is created
window.alert("This string is "+rightnow.attitude);  ←──┐
                              The new property is used with the
                              instance of the String object
```

Now the String object "Joe" has an attitude property of "cool"!

Using the Methods of the String Object

The String object has a lot of methods, as shown in Table 13-2.

Yes, this list is quite long! The following sections take a look at the methods of the String object.

Methods That Add HTML Tags

Many of the methods in Table 13-2 are used to create HTML tags around a string (or create HTML tags with attribute values sent to them as parameters). Many of these effects can be done using the more up-to-date method of accessing an element's style and/or innerHTML properties; however, these methods may be helpful to know in different situations.

Method	Purpose
anchor()	Creates an HTML anchor tag with a target on a page
big()	Adds <big> and </big> tags around a string value
blink()	Adds <blink> and </blink> tags around a string value
bold()	Adds <b> and </b> tags around a string value
charAt()	Finds out which character is at a given position in a string
charCodeAt()	Finds the character code of a character at a given position in a string
concat()	Adds two or more strings together and returns the new combined string value
fixed()	Adds <tt> and </tt> tags around a string value
fontcolor()	Adds <font color="*color*"> and </font> tags around a string value, which change the color of the string to a specified color
fontsize()	Adds <font size="*number*"> and </font> tags around a string value, which change the size of the string to a specified size given as a number
fromCharCode()	Uses character codes sent as parameters to create a new string
indexOf()	Searches for a character sent as a parameter in a string: if it's found, the position of the first instance of the character is returned; otherwise, it returns −1
italics()	Adds <i> and </i> tags around a string value
lastIndexOf()	Searches for a character sent as a parameter in a string: if it's found, the position of the last instance of the character is returned; otherwise, it returns −1
link()	Creates HTML links using the string as the link text and linking to the URL sent as a parameter
match()	Compares a regular expression and a string to see if they match
replace()	Finds out if a regular expression matches a string and then replaces a matched string with a new string
search()	Executes the search for a match between a regular expression and a specified string
slice()	Pulls out a specified section of a string value and returns a new string
small()	Adds <small> and </small> tags around a string value
split()	Separates a string into an array of strings based on a character sent as a parameter to the method
strike()	Adds <strike> and </strike> tags around a string value
sub()	Adds _{and} tags around a string value
substr()	Allows a portion of the string specified with a starting position and ending after a certain number of characters to be returned
substring()	Allows a portion of the string specified with a starting position and an ending position to be returned
sup()	Adds ^{and} tags around a string value
toString()	Returns the string literal value of a String object
toLowerCase()	Converts a string to all lowercase letters and returns the result
toUpperCase()	Converts a string to all uppercase letters and returns the result

Table 13-2   Methods of the String Object

The basic methods (big(), blink(), bold(), fixed(), italics(), small(), strike(), sub(), and sup()) simply add the basic HTML tags around the string. For example, to create some small text, you could use the small() method:

```
var little_bit = "I only want a little bit of cake.";
var tagged_phrase = little_bit.small();
document.write(tagged_phrase);
```

This code would then write the following into the HTML code:

```
<small>I only want a little bit of cake.</small>
```

When viewed in the browser, this text would appear smaller than it would normally have appeared without the <small> and </small> tags.

NOTE

The HTML tags may be created in lowercase or uppercase, depending on the browser. Since tags built with JavaScript after the page has loaded aren't typically a problem with page validation, the case of the tags likely won't cause any issues with your HTML code. However, the case of a tag is helpful to know if you decide to use that element later in the script, as its tag name could, for example, be small or SMALL.

The remaining HTML tag methods (anchor(), fontcolor(), fontsize(), and link()) take in parameters and build the tags based on the string value and the parameter(s) sent to them. These are discussed in more detail in the following sections.

The anchor() method

This method places a text string as the text for a named anchor. The anchor() method takes a parameter that will be the name attribute for the named anchor. Basically, it creates an HTML tag set with the following syntax:

```
<a name="parameter_string">text_string</a>
```

The *parameter_string* is a string you send as a parameter in the method call. The *text_string* is the value of the string from which you call the method.

For example, take a look at this code:

A string literal is created

```
var anchor_text = "Part 1";
var full_anchor = anchor_text.anchor("part1");
document.write(full_anchor);
```

The result of the anchor() method is assigned to a variable

The value of the variable is written on the page

Here, you assign a string literal to the variable anchor_text. You then call the anchor() method with a parameter of "part1" from the string literal. The result is assigned to the full_anchor variable. The value of the full_anchor variable is then written on the page. The code writes the following link into the code for the page:

```
<a name="part1">Part 1</a>
```

Figure 13-1 shows what this code looks like when viewed in the browser. Notice that the viewer sees only the anchor text for the section.

The fontcolor() Method

The fontcolor() method adds font color to the text string that is used to call it. It takes in a string parameter that indicates what color the text should be. The color can be sent using either the color name or its red-green-blue (RGB) value.

This method formats some code around the text much like the example syntax:

```
<font color="color_value">text_string</font>
```

Here, *color_value* would be replaced with the color name or RGB value sent as a parameter to the method. The *text_string* part would be replaced with the text string used to call the method.

For an example, this code creates some red text on the page:

```
<body>
<script type="text/javascript">
var the_text = "I am so mad I am red!";
document.write(the_text.fontcolor("red"));
</script>
</body>
```

The text is given a font color based on the color name sent as the parameter

This script places the following code into the page source:

```
<font color="red">I am so mad I am red!</font>
```

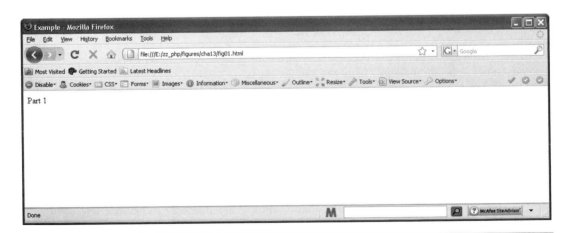

Figure 13-1 A named anchor is placed on the page

You can also use the RGB value in place of the color name. In this code, the RGB value is used instead:

```
<body>
<script type="text/javascript">
var the_text = "I am so mad I am red!";
document.write(the_text.fontcolor("#FF0000"));
</font>
```

The text is given a font color based on the RGB code sent as the parameter

This time, the code produced would be changed to include the RGB value in place of the color name in the previous example, as shown here:

```
<font color= "#FF0000">I am so mad I am red!</font>
```

The fontsize() Method

The fontsize() method adjusts the font size of the text string that calls the method. It takes in a numeric value to represent the size of the text (between 1 and 7).

The method formats the code so that it uses a syntax like the example here:

```
<font size="number">text_string</font>
```

The *number* gets replaced with the number sent as the parameter in the method call, and *text_string* gets replaced by the text string that is used to call the method.

The example that follows shows this method in action:

```
<body>
<script type="text/javascript">
var the_text = "I am pretty small!";
document.write(the_text.fontsize(2));
</script>
</body>
```

The text is given a font size based on the number sent as the parameter

This script provides the code that follows in the page source:

```
<font size="2">I am pretty small!</font>
```

The link() Method

The link() method works like the anchor() method, but instead it creates a typical hyperlink on the page. It takes in a string parameter that is the value of the URL for the link, while the text for the link will be the text string that called the method.

The method creates a link with the general syntax as shown here:

```
<a href="url">text_string</a>
```

The *url* is replaced with the URL sent as the parameter in the method call, while *text_string* is replaced with the text string that made the call.

Look at this example that uses the link() method:

```
<body>
<script type="text/javascript">
var link_text = "A Web Site";
var full_link = link_text.link("http://www.pageresource.com");
document.write(full_link);
</script>
</body>
```

The link is created based on the URL sent as the parameter and the string

This code creates the link shown here in the page source code:

```
<a href="http://www.pageresource.com">A Web Site</a>
```

The technique in the preceding code example could also be used as the other side of the anchor() method to create a link to the named anchor on the page. For example, take a look at this code:

```
<body>
<p>
<script type="text/javascript">
var anchor_text = "Part 1";
var full_anchor = anchor_text.anchor("part1");
document.write(full_anchor);
</script>
</p>
<p>
Part 1 is about this, that and the other thing.<br />
<br /><br /><br /><br />
This is irrelevant text in this case used for filler.
</p>
<p>
<script type="text/javascript">
var link_text="Back to Beginning of Part 1";
var full_link= link_text.link("#part1");
document.write(full_link);
</script>
</p>
</body>
```

An anchor is created

A link to the anchor is created

This code creates an anchor that can be referenced elsewhere on the page to get to the Part 1 text by clicking a link. You can substitute some text for whatever might be under the Part 1 section of the page. After that, a link is created that points back to the named anchor, offering the viewer a chance to go back to the beginning of the Part 1 section of the page.

Figure 13-2 shows the result of this script when run in a browser. You get the named anchor, the extra text, and the link back to the anchor.

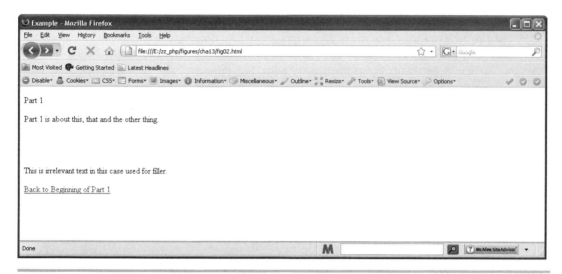

Figure 13-2   A named anchor and a link back to the location of the named anchor

The Other Methods

The remaining methods of the String object—charAt(), charCodeAt(), concat(), fromCharCode(), indexOf(), lastIndexOf(), match(), replace(), search(), slice(), split(), substr(), substring(), toString(), toLowerCase(), and toUpperCase()—allow you to obtain information about or alter a string. All of these are quite useful when working with strings and are discussed in more detail in the following sections.

The charAt() Method

This method determines which character resides at a particular position in a string. You can find out what the first or last character is, or you can find any character in between. The charAt() method takes in a number representing the position where you want to know the character.

Finding a Character   When you want to find a character, remember that the position count begins at 0 (as with arrays) rather than 1, so the first character is at position 0. The following code shows how to get the first character in a string by using the charAt() method:

```
var the_text = "Character";                    The charAt() method finds the character at
var first_char = the_text.charAt(0);◄────── position 0 (the first character) in the string
window.alert("The first character is "+first_char);
```

This code assigns the result of the charAt() method call to a variable named first_char, which is then used in an alert. The alert will tell the viewer the first character in the text string that called the method. In this case, the alert would say "The first character is C".

Finding the Last Character with the length Property   If you want to find the last character, either you need to know how many characters are in the string before you use the method, or you can use the length property to determine the number of characters in the string. When using the length property, remember that it returns the number of characters, not the position of the last character.

The length property begins counting at 1, while you must begin counting at 0 using the charAt() method. Thus, the last character in a string will be at a position one less than the number of characters it contains. In other words, if the string has 10 characters (1–10), the last position (0–9) is at 9. If the string has 23 characters (1–23), the last position (0–22) is at 23–1=22.

Look at an example of this to see how it works. The code finds the last character in a string:

Subtract 1 from the length property to find the last position available in the string

```
var the_text = "Character";
var position = the_text.length-1;
var last_char = the_text.charAt(position);
window.alert("The last character is "+last_char);
```

The charAt() method uses that value to find out which character is in the last position in the string

This code assigns the value of the length of the string minus1 to a variable named position. The position variable now holds the position of the last character in the string. The result of calling the charAt() method with the value of position sent as the parameter is assigned to a variable named last_char. Finally, an alert provides the last character in the string, which is *r*. Thus, the viewer gets an alert saying "The last character is r".

The charCodeAt() Method

The charCodeAt() method works the same way as the charAt() method, but it returns the character code for the character at the positions sent as the parameter.

The character code is a numeric code that can be substituted for characters in HTML. In HTML, you can write an angle bracket (<) to show code on a Web page—without the angle bracket converting to HTML itself—by using a special character code. In place of a regular angle bracket, for example, you could use &#60. The charCodeAt() method returns the numeric part of that code, the 60.

The charCodeAt() method can be useful if you want to find out the character code for a certain character. This script allows you to do this:

The charCodeAt() method finds the character code for the character at position 0 (the first character) in the string

```
var the_text = "Hello";
var char_code = the_text.charCodeAt(0);
window.alert("The character code is &#"+char_code+";");
```

An alert would then tell you the character code at position 0 in the string (the letter *H*), which is 72. The alert will add the string "&#" on the front and the string ";" to the back end of the character code for you and say "The character code is H".

The concat() Method

This method works much like the Array object's concat() method. It combines the text string that calls the method with any number of other text strings sent as parameters and returns the combined value. The text string calling the method comes first in the order, while the strings sent as parameters are added in order after it.

The following code shows an example that combines three strings using the concat() method:

```
var string1 = "I went to the store ";
var string2 = "then ";
var string3 = "I played a video game";          The three strings are combined
window.alert(string1.concat(string2,string3));  ◄——  in order from left to right
```

This code combines the strings in the order string1, string2, and then string3. The result is an alert that says "I went to the store then I played a video game".

If you want it in a different order, you can adjust which string calls the method and the order of the parameters, as this code shows:

```
var string1 = "I went to the store ";
var string2 = " then ";
var string3 = "I played a video game";          The three strings are combined in
window.alert(string3.concat(string2,string1)); ◄—— order from left to right (again)
```

This time, string3 calls the method, so it comes first in the new string. The values of string2 and string3 are added in order after that. The result in this case is an alert that says "I played a video game then I went to the store".

The fromCharCode() Method

The fromCharCode() method creates a string from a series of character codes sent as parameters to the method. The charCodeAt() method returns a numeric code for the character at a given position. This is the type of value you must send to the fromCharCode() method. Also, fromCharCode() is called directly from the String object rather than from an existing string, because it is piecing together a string on-the-fly and doesn't require one to run. Instead, it uses the parameters sent to it to return a string.

So, if you want to alert the text string "HI" to the viewer, you could use the example code shown here:

```
window.alert(String.fromCharCode(72,73));
```

This code takes in the first parameter (the character code 72) and converts it to an *H*. It then takes in the second parameter (the character code 73) and converts it to an *I*. The two are combined in the order they were sent to form the string "HI", which is sent as an alert to the viewer.

The indexOf() Method

The indexOf() method finds out where a certain character or string begins in a string. It returns the position of only the first occurrence of the character or string that is sent as the parameter. If the character or string isn't found in the string value, a value of –1 is returned.

The following code looks for the letter *C* in the string "Cool":

```
var the_text = "Cool";
var position = the_text.indexOf("C");
window.alert("Your character is at position "+position);
```

Remember that the position count begins at 0, so when it finds *C* as the first character in the string, it returns 0. Thus, the alert will say "Your character is at position 0".

Note that the method is case sensitive, so *C* and *c* are two different characters to JavaScript in this case. Thus, the code that follows returns –1 (telling you the character isn't in the string), even though an uppercase *C* is in the string.

```
var the_text = "Cool";
var position = the_text.indexOf("c");
window.alert("Your character is at position "+position);
```

The alert would now say "Your character is at position –1".

If you want to check for that –1 to keep from getting it as a position, you could use this code to send a different alert in case the character you want to find isn't in the string:

```
var the_text = "Cool";
var position = the_text.indexOf("c");
if (position == -1) {
  window.alert("Your character is not in the string!");
}
else {
  window.alert("Your character is at position "+position);
}
```

This time, the if statement checks to see whether the method returns –1 to the position variable. If so, the alert says "Your character is not in the string!" Otherwise, the regular alert will tell you the position. In the previous code, the lowercase *c* isn't in the string, so the "Your character is not in the string!" alert appears.

The indexOf() method returns the position number only for the first occurrence of the character you send as the parameter. So, if you use the code that follows, you will be alerted that your character is at position 1, even though it's also at position 2:

```
var the_text = "Cool";
var position = the_text.indexOf("o");
if (position == -1) {
  window.alert("Your character is not in the string!");
}
else {
  window.alert("Your character is at position "+position);
}
```

The lowercase *o* is in the string twice, but indexOf() locates only the first occurrence of the character. To locate the next occurrence, you would need to have the method look for "oo" instead of "o" (which will tell you the position of the first "o" but give you the knowledge that the next position also contains an "o") or you could have the method start looking from a different starting point using a second parameter.

If you add an integer as the second parameter to the indexOf() method, the search for your character or string will begin at that position rather than from the 0 position. Thus, one way to find that second "o" would be to skip past the first one at position 1 and start looking at position 2.

```
var the_text = "Cool";
var position = the_text.indexOf("o",2);
if (position == -1) {
  window.alert("Your character is not in the string!");
}
else {
  window.alert("Your character is at position "+position);
}
```

This time, the method returns 2 as the result, since it finds it right at the specified starting position.

Oftentimes, this method is used to ensure that a particular character or string either is or is not present within a string. For instance, if you want a string to contain "fruit" somewhere in it, and do not want it to contain "candy", you could write the following code:

```
var the_text = "I like fruit!";
if ((the_text.indexOf("fruit") != -1) && (the_text.indexOf("candy") ==
-1)) {
  window.alert("Yes, fruit is good for you!");
}
else {
  window.alert("Please consider fruit rather than candy.");
}
```

This requires the string to contain "fruit" but not contain "candy". If it passes the test, an alert is sent praising fruit. If not, an alert is sent that offers fruit as an alternative to candy.

The lastIndexOf() Method

The lastIndexOf() method finds out where the last instance of a certain character or string is located in the string. It returns the position of only the last occurrence of the character or string that is sent as the parameter. If the character or string isn't found in the string value, a value of −1 is returned.

The following code looks for the letter *C* in the string "Cool Cruising Car":

```
var the_text = "Cool Cruising Car";
var position = the_text.indexOf("C");
window.alert("Your character is at position "+position);
```

This code will display an alert that tells the viewer "Your character is at position 14." This method can be a handy way to find the last instance of a character or string within a string value.

The match() Method

The match() method compares a regular expression and a string to see whether they match. Because it deals with regular expressions, I won't go into detail about this method now, but regular expressions will be covered later in this chapter in the section "Using Regular Expressions."

The replace() Method

The replace() method finds out if a regular expression matches a string and then replaces a matched string with a new string. Because it deals with regular expressions, I won't go into detail about this method until later in this chapter.

The search() Method

The search() method executes the search for a match between a regular expression and a specified string. Because it deals with regular expressions, I won't go into detail about this method until later in this chapter.

The slice() Method

This method pulls out a portion of a string and returns a new string, which is the text string that was sliced. The slice() method takes in two numeric parameters to tell it where to begin and end the portion of the string to be pulled.

This method works much like the slice() method of an array. The first parameter tells it the position at which to start slicing, while the second parameter is one greater than the position where it will stop. For instance, take a look at the code that follows:

```
var the_text = "Do not cut this short!";
var shorter_string = the_text.slice(0,7);
window.alert(shorter_string);
```

This code slices the string from position 0 through position 6. Position 7 is where the *c* is in "cut"; but it isn't sliced because the parameter to end is not included as a position to slice, but is one greater. Thus, the alert will say "Do not ".

The split() Method

The split() method creates an array of string elements based on the string it splits (the opposite of the join() method). The string is split based on a character sent as a parameter that acts as a separator.

For instance, the code that follows has a string with a bunch of colons in it:

```
var the_text = "orange:apple:pear:grape";
var split_text = the_text.split(":");
var end_count = split_text.length;
for (var count=0; count<end_count; count++) {
  document.write(split_text[count]+"<br />");
}
```

The string assigned to the the_text variable has a bunch of fruits separated by colons. The next line creates an array named split_text by using the split() method on the text string the_text. The parameter sent is a colon, which is what is used to separate the string into array elements. In this case, the array ends up with four elements.

NOTE

The separator character that is sent as a parameter won't end up in the array: it serves only as a divider between the text so that the method knows where to begin and end each element.

The next line gets the length of the split_text array and places that value in the variable end_count. This information is then used to loop through the new array and print the elements on the page.

Figure 13-3 shows the result of this script in a browser, which is a listing of fruit names.

The substr() Method

This method pulls out a portion of a string and returns the portion that is removed as a new string. It takes two numeric parameters. The first parameter specifies the beginning of the removal, and the second parameter specifies how many characters to remove.

For instance, the following code removes a portion of a string beginning at position 0 and continues until seven characters are removed:

```
var the_text = "Do not cut this short!";
var shorter_string = the_text.substr(0,7);
window.alert(shorter_string);
```

This code removes everything up to the beginning of the word cut in the string. The string returned is the portion of the string that has been removed. Thus, the alert will say "Do not ". Notice that the space character after "not" is included because it was the seventh character removed.

The substring() Method

This method works much like the substr() method, but it allows you to send parameters for the beginning position and the ending position of the portion of the string you want to remove. It then returns the removed portion as a new string.

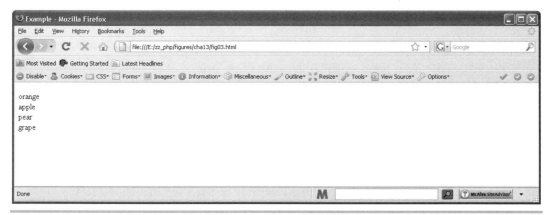

Figure 13-3 The array elements created using the split() method are printed on the page

For example, take a look at the code that follows. Rather than specifying the number of characters to remove, you give an ending position. The characters are removed beginning at the starting position and ending at one less than the ending position. (Remember the slice() method.)

```
var the_text = "Do not cut this short!";
var shorter_string = the_text.substring(3,7);
window.alert(shorter_string);
```

You remove everything between the beginning of the string and the beginning of the word "cut". The alert will say "not ".

The toString() Method

The toString() method returns a string literal value for a String object that calls it. Here's an example of how you can use this method:

```
var string_obj = new String("Cool");
var string_lit = string_obj.toString();
```

This code takes the String object and uses the toString() method to get its string literal value. It then assigns that value to the string_lit variable.

The toLowerCase() Method

This method returns in lowercase letters the value of the string that called it. Take a look at this code:

```
<body>
<script type="text/javascript">
var the_text = "I FEEL CALM, REALLY.";
document.write(the_text.toLowerCase());
</script>
</body>
```

This code writes the string in all lowercase letters on the page, like this sample text:

```
i feel calm, really.
```

The toUpperCase() Method

This method returns in uppercase letters the value of the string that called it. Here's an example:

```
<body>
<script type="text/javascript">
var the_text = "I am yelling!";
document.write(the_text.toUpperCase());
</script>
</body>
```

This code writes the string in all uppercase letters on the page, like this sample text:

```
I AM YELLING!
```

That's the last of the methods! Now you are ready to test what you've learned.

Ask the Expert

Q: So the length property returns the number of characters in the string, but the string methods start counting at 0. This is a little confusing, just like it is with arrays. Is there an easy way to remember this?

A: The easiest way is probably to remember that the length property begins counting at 1, while the methods count positions beginning at 0. Thus, the length property ends up one greater than the last position in a string. So, if the string has a length of 5, that means the last position in the string is position 4.

Q: Yes, but it's also confusing because the second parameter in the slice() and substring() methods is a position higher than the point where the methods stop removing characters. Why is this?

A: It is confusing in the beginning. You just have to get used to how each method works. The slice() and substring() methods are a bit confusing. But if you use them often enough, you'll remember which numbers to use in which situations.

Q: Why do I need the split() method? Couldn't I just make my own array and be done with it?

A: Yes. However, once you learn about JavaScript cookies, the split() method will be useful because you'll be able to split up the information stored in the cookie to make use of it. Cookies store information in long text strings, usually with some character as a separator. This is just one example of when the split() method can be useful to you.

Q: A lot of those methods just add tags around a text string. Couldn't I just write out the HTML for that? It seems easier.

A: You could, if you feel more comfortable using HTML, although with a String object, these methods might be more useful.

Try This 13-1 Use charAt() to Find a First Letter

```
pr13_1.html
prjs13_1.js
```

In this project, you practice using the charAt() method by creating a script that will determine whether the first character in a viewer's entry is valid.

Step by Step

1. Create an HTML page that includes a "Welcome" heading and calls a JavaScript file named prjs13_1.js. Save the HTML file as pr13_1.html.

(continued)

2. Create an external JavaScript file and save it as prjs13_1.js. Use it for steps 3–6.

3. Write code that gets the result of a prompt that asks for a name, and assign the result of the prompt to a variable named the_name.

4. Use the charAt() method to find out what is entered as the first character of the name in the prompt, and assign the result to a variable named first_char.

5. Set it up so that the page will display the name the viewer entered, but only if it started with an uppercase *S*. Otherwise, display a message saying the viewer needs a name that starts with an uppercase *S* to have it displayed.

6. Save the JavaScript file and open the HTML file in your browser to see what it does.

Try This Summary

In this project, you used your knowledge of the charAt() method to create a script that determines whether the first character in a viewer's entry is a valid character. If the entry starts with an uppercase *S*, then the viewer's entry is displayed on the page. Otherwise, a message is displayed to the viewer.

Putting Methods Together

Now that you know how to use the script object's properties and methods individually, you are ready to create a script that uses several of them to see how they can work together. You'll do this by creating a script that will mess with the viewer's name (in good humor, of course).

You want the script to get the viewer's first and last name, change the first letter of each name, and then alert the result to the viewer. The following script does this:

The prompt allows the viewer to input a name

This line tests to see if there is a space in the entry by the viewer

If there is no space, the alert tells the viewer to try again

```
<body>
<h1>Welcome!</h1>
<script type="text/javascript">
function getname() {
  var the_text=window.prompt("Enter your first and last name","");
  if (the_text.indexOf(" ") == -1) {
    window.alert("Put a space between your first and last name. Try again.");
    getname();
  }
  var split_text= the_text.split(" ");
  if ((split_text[0].charAt(0) != "Z") || (split_text[0].charAt(0) != "z")) {
    var shorter_fn_string = split_text[0].substring(1,split_text[0].length);
    new_fn_name = "Z"+shorter_fn_string;
  }
```

The function starts over if the viewer has to try again

The entry by the viewer is split on the space character

This is a test to see whether the first name started with a *Z* or a *z* and if not, the first letter is replaced with a *Z*

If the first name starts with a *Z* or *z*, the first
letter is taken out and replaced with W

```
    else {
       var shorter_fn_string = split_text[0].substring(1,split_text[0].length);
       new_fn_name = "W"+shorter_fn_string;
    }
    if ((split_text[1].charAt(0) != "Z") || (split_text[1].charAt(0) != "z")) {
       var shorter_ln_string= split_text[1].substring(1,split_text[1].length);
       new_ln_name="Z"+shorter_ln_string;
    }
    else {
       var shorter_ln_string= split_text[1].substring(1,split_text[1].length);
       new_ln_name="W"+shorter_ln_string;
    }
    window.alert("Now your name is "+new_fn_name+" "+new_ln_name+"!");
}
getname();
</script>
</body>
```

The function is called to begin the
process while the page is loading

The result of the name change
is alerted to the viewer

The same tests and tasks are
executed on the last name

Notice that a function named getname() is what gets things going. The first task the function performs is to prompt the viewer for a first and last name. The idea is that the viewer will enter a first name, a space, and a last name (although other entries are certainly possible and can be better dealt with using regular expressions).

Once the name has been obtained, the script uses the indexOf() method to see if the entry has a space in it. If no space exists, there will be only a single name, and that isn't what you want. Thus, if there is no space, the script alerts the viewer to try again and then restarts the function from the beginning. If there is a space, then the script proceeds to the next line after the if block.

The script then uses the split() method to create an array of any data separated by spaces. In theory, a single space should be between the first and last names. If the viewer uses more than one space, then only the first two elements of the resulting array will be used. (They are specifically called later in the script.) So, if the viewer enters John Doe, the elements of the resulting array are John and Doe. However, if the viewer enters John J Doe, the first two elements are John and J, and the Doe won't be used. (With more advanced validation, this problem could alert the viewer to try again.)

Once the string is split into an array, the script uses charAt() to test the first letter of the first element in the array (the first name). If it isn't *Z* or *z*, then the code in the if block is executed. The if block uses the substring() method to get all the letters in the name except the first one, and then assigns that value to the shorter_fn_string variable. Thus, if the first name is John, the variable would have a value of "John." Once that's accomplished, a string value of *Z* is added to the front of that variable and the result is assigned to a variable name new_fn_name. This basically replaces the first letter in the original name with *Z*. Thus, John would become Zohn and Mary would become Zary.

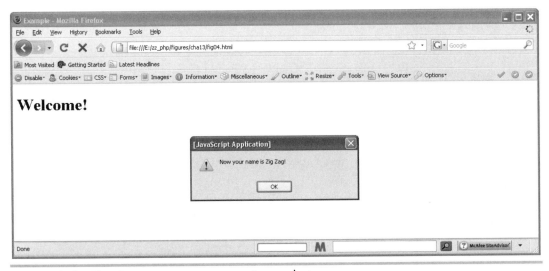

Figure 13-4 The viewer gets a new name in an alert

If the original name did start with Z or z, the else block is executed instead. Rather than replacing the first letter with Z, it is replaced with W. The next if/else segment performs the same tasks on the second entry in the array, which, if entered correctly, will be the last name. The viewer is then alerted to the result, telling the user the new name. Figure 13-4 shows the result of this script in a browser when the viewer enters Big Mag.

Try This 13-2 Use indexOf() to Test an Address

pr13_2.html
prjs13_2.js

In this project, you practice using the indexOf() method by creating a script that performs a very basic test on an e-mail address that the viewer enters.

Step by Step

1. Create an HTML page that points to a JavaScript file named prjs13_2.js. Create a button the viewer can click with an id of "email". Label it "Click to enter an e-mail address." Save the HTML file as pr13_2.js.

2. Create an external JavaScript file and save it as prjs13_2.js. Use it for steps 3–7.

3. Create a function named get_add(). In it, assign the results of a prompt asking for an e-mail address to a variable named email_add.

4. Also in the function, use indexOf() to see if the address has an at (@) character in it.

5. Also in the function, use indexOf() to see if the address has a dot (.) character in it.

6. Also in the function, if the address has both an at (@) character and a dot (.) character, send an alert thanking the viewer. If not, send an alert to the viewer saying that he or she needs these characters and to try again.

7. Save the JavaScript file and open the HTML file in your browser to see what you can do with it.

Try This Summary

In this project, you used your knowledge of the indexOf() method to test an e-mail address entered by the viewer for certain characters. If one of the characters is missing, an error alert is sent to the viewer. Otherwise, an alert is sent thanking the viewer.

Using Regular Expressions

Regular expressions give you much more power to handle strings in a script. They allow you to form patterns that can be matched against strings, rather than trying to use the String object's methods, which may make it more difficult to be precise.

For example, you may want to know whether the value entered in a text box for an e-mail address included at least one character at the beginning, followed by an at (@) symbol, followed by at least one character, followed by a dot (.), followed by at least two more characters (matching a traditional e-mail address like jon@jon.com or the shortest type of email address j@j.jj). Section 13-2 Try This provides a similar but simpler test for you to try out.

The String object's methods don't provide a neat and clean way to perform this task (although with enough tinkering, it may be possible). However, a regular expression can shorten the task or even turn a match that seemed impossible with the String object's methods into one that can be completed.

Creating Regular Expressions

To create regular expressions, you must create an instance of the JavaScript RegExp object. You can do this almost the same way as you would create a string literal. To create a RegExp literal, you just assign the regular expression to a variable. Instead of using quotation marks to surround the expression, you use forward (/) slashes, as shown here:

```
var varname = /your_pattern/flags;
```

You replace *varname* with the name you want to use for a variable and replace *your_pattern* with the regular expression pattern of your choice. You can follow the last slash with one or more flags (which are discussed in the upcoming section "Adding Flags").

NOTE

JavaScript uses forward slashes to let the browser know that a regular expression is between them, the same way quote marks are used to set off strings. Thus, if a forward slash is used within the regular expression, it must be escaped with a backslash in order to work properly. For instance, instead of writing /02/03/2009/, you would need to write /02\/03\/2009/.

The easiest regular expression pattern to create is one that looks for an exact match of characters. For instance, if you wanted to see if the sequence *our* is present in a string, you could create the following regular expression pattern:

```
var tomatch = /our/;
```

The preceding code creates a RegExp literal named tomatch. Now you need a string against which to test the pattern. If you test the word *our* against the expression, it's a match.

If you test *your*, *sour*, *pour*, or *pouring* against it, then it's a match. If you test *cool*, *Our*, *oUR*, *OUR*, or *souR*, then it won't be a match. So how do you perform this test?

Testing Strings Against Regular Expressions

To test a regular expression against a string, you can use the test() method of the RegExp object. The basic syntax is as follows:

```
regex_name.test(string_to_test);
```

This syntax is similar to using a string method. You replace *regex_name* with the name of the regular expression and replace *string_to_test* with a string or a string variable name. For instance, look at the following example:

```
var tomatch = /our/;
tomatch.test("pour");
```

This code will test the "pour" string against the regular expression named "tomatch." It doesn't use the result, though.

The test() method returns a Boolean value of true or false. It returns true when any portion of the string matches the regular expression pattern. Using the test() method, you can already write a short script, as shown here:

The prompt gets a name from the viewer

A regular expression is set up to see if the name entered will match it

```
var thename = window.prompt("Enter your name","");
var tomatch = /John/;
var is_a_match = tomatch.test(thename);
if (is_a_match) {
   window.alert("Wow, we have the same name!");
}
else {
   window.alert("Not my name, but it will work!");
}
```

A variable is used to hold the result of the test() method

If the result is true, this alert appears

If the result is not true, this alert appears

The prompt gathers a name and holds the value in a variable. The pattern to match is John, and it is case sensitive. Thus, only an entry containing John with a capital *J* followed by lowercase *o*, *h*, and *n* will create a match and return true when it is tested (though it could contain more than just John, so entries such as Johnny or John Doe would also return true—if you want only a specific set of characters, you need to use some additional special characters, which will be discussed later in this section).

The result of the test() method is assigned to a variable named is_a_match. The variable is then used as the condition for the if statement. If the variable holds a value of true, then the viewer gets the "Wow, we have the same name!" alert. If it holds a value of false, the viewer gets the "Not my name, but it will work!" alert instead.

If you want to shorten the script, you can just make the result of the test() method the condition for the if statement (rather than create another variable), as in the following code:

```
var thename = window.prompt("Enter your name","");
var tomatch = /John/;
if (tomatch.test(thename)) {            The result of the test() method
  window.alert("Wow, we have the same name!");    is used as the condition
}
else {
  window.alert("Not my name, but it will work!");
}
```

Because the method returns true or false, it can be placed as the condition for the if statement on its own. (You could make it (tomatch.test(thename)==true) if you wanted to, though.)

Adding Flags

Flags allow you to make the match case insensitive or to look for every match in the string rather than just the first one (a global test). To add a flag, place it after the last slash in the regular expression. You can use three options, as shown in Table 13-3.

If you wanted to adjust the name script used previously to be case insensitive, you could add an i flag to the regular expression, as shown in the following code:

```
var thename= window.prompt("Enter your name","");
var tomatch=/John/i;            The i flag makes this regular
if (tomatch.test(thename)) {     expression case insensitive
  window.alert("Wow, we have the same name!");
}
else {
  window.alert("Not my name, but it will work!");
}
```

Flag(s)	Purpose
i	Makes the match case insensitive
g	Makes the match global
m	Makes the match work in multiline mode

Table 13-3   Regular Expression Flags

The test() method will now return true as long as the pattern of John is in the string. It can be in any case, so now John, JOHN, john, and even JoHn are all matches and will cause the test() method to return true.

You can also use more than one flag or all three flags at once. For example, if you want to have the match be both case insensitive and global (where it grabs each match in the entire string), you could use the following:

```
var tomatch=/John/ig;
```

Creating Powerful Patterns

Although it's nice to be able to create such an exact pattern, you won't always be looking for a match that is so precise. In many cases, you will be looking to match a more general pattern, such as an entry that needs to have at least three characters or that needs to have two characters of any type followed by a special character.

By using special characters in your expressions, you can create the type of patterns you need to match a given sequence you want. JavaScript regular expressions use the syntax of Perl regular expressions as a model. Thus, if you've used regular expressions in Perl, much of this material will be familiar. Table 13-4 lists a number of the characters to help you create your patterns.

As you can see, extensive options exist for creating the pattern you need. Now you could easily verify strings according to the standards you decide to set.

Now, if you want to make sure a text field contains one or more digits, you could use the /d and + characters from Table 13-4 with the following HTML and JavaScript code, starting with the HTML code:

```
<body>
<form>
Enter some text: <input type="text" id="has_digits" />
<input type="button" id="t_btn" value="Test" />
</form>
</body>
```

Next, the JavaScript code:

```
var t_button = document.getElementById("t_btn");
t_button.onclick = function() {
  var has_num = document.getElementById("has_digits").value;
  var tomatch = /\d+/;
  if (tomatch.test(has_num)) {
    window.alert("Your entry contained one or more numbers!");
  }
  else {
    window.alert("Your entry did not contain any numbers!");
  }
}
```

Character	Purpose	Example
^	Matches only from the beginning of a line	/^c/ matches *c* in *corn* /^c/ does not match *c* in *acorn*
$	Matches only at the end of the line	/r$/ matches *r* in *Car* /r$/ does not match *t* in *Cat*
*	Matches the character preceding it if the character occurs zero or more times	/co*/ matches *co* or *c* /co*/ does not match *pi*
+	Matches the character preceding it if it occurs one or more times	/co+/ matches *co* or *cooooo* /co+/ does not match *ca*
?	Matches the character preceding it if it occurs zero or one time	/o?l/ matches *style* or *column* /co?l/ does not match *cool*
.	Matches any individual character, excluding the newline character	/.l/ matches *al* or *@l* /.l/ does not match \nl or *l*
(x)	By replacing *x* with characters, matches that sequence and keeps it in memory to be used later; used for grouping of expressions	/(a)/ matches *a* /(cool)/ matches *cool* /(cool)/ does not match *coal*
|	Used as a logical OR symbol to allow a match of what is on the left of the symbol OR what is on its right	/cool|bad/ matches *cool* /cool|bad/ matches *bad* /cool|bad/ does not match *car*
{x}	Using a number to replace *x*, matches when there are exactly *x* occurrences of the character preceding it	/n{1}/ matches *n* /nn{2}/ matches *nnn* /nn{1}/ does not match *nnn*
{x,}	Using a number to replace *x*, matches when there are *x* or more occurrences of the character preceding it	/n{1,}/ matches *n* /n{1,}/ matches *nnnnn* /n{3,}/ does not match *nn*
{x,y}	Using numbers to replace *x* and *y*, matches when there are at least *x* occurrences of the character preceding it but no more than *y* occurrences of it	/n{1,2}/ matches *n* /n{1,2}/ matches *nn* /n{2,3}/ does not match *n* /n{4,7}/ does not match *nnn*
[]	Matches a character set of your choice; will match when any one of the characters in the brackets (such as [abc]) or any one of a range of characters (such as [a-k]) is present	/[abc]/ matches *a* /[abc]/ matches *b* /[abc]/ matches *c* /[a-k]/ matches *j* /[a-k]/ does not match *n*
[^]	Matches when the characters in your character set are *not* present; may be a set (such as [abc]) or a range (such as [a-k])	/[^abc]/ matches *d* /[^abc]/ does not match *b* /[^a-k]/ matches *n* /[^a-k]/ does not match *j*

Table 13-4 Regular Expression Codes *(continued)*

Character	Purpose	Example
\	Used to escape special characters or to make a normal character special	\@ escapes the @ character \n represents a newline character
[\b]	Matches a BACKSPACE keystroke	/[\b]/ matches a backspace
\b	Matches when the character before or after it is located at a word boundary, such as before or after a space character; to match the beginning of a word, place the character to the right of the symbol (\bc); to match the end of a word, place the character to the left (c\b)	/\bc/ matches c in *my car* /\bm/ matches m in *my car* /\bc/ does not match c in *ace* /\bm/ does not match m in *Sam* /m\b/ matches m in *Sam* /c\b/ matches c in *Mac W* /m\b/ does not match m in *emu* /c\b/ does not match c in *my car*
\B	Matches a character that is not located at a word boundary	/\Ba/ matches a in *car* /\Bc/ does not match c in *car*
\cX	Using a letter character to replace X, matches when the user presses the CTRL key followed by typing the letter X	/\cX/ matches CTRL-X /\cV/ matches CTRL-V /\cS/ does not match CTRL-Z
\d	Matches if the character is a single numeric character	/\d/ matches 4 /\d/ does not match s
\D	Matches a single character if it is *not* a numeric character	/\D/ matches s /\D/ does not match 4
\f	Matches if there is a form feed	/\f/ matches a form feed
\n	Matches if there is a new line	/\n/ matches a new line
\r	Matches if there is a carriage return	/\r/ matches a carriage return
\s	Matches a single character if it represents white space (such as a space or a new line)	/\s/ matches the space in *b c* /\s/ matches the tab in *b c* /\s/ does not match *bc*
\S	Matches a single character if it does *not* represent white space	/\S/ matches d /\S/ does not match a blank space
\t	Matches if there is a tab	/\t/ matches the tab in *b c*
\v	Matches if there is a vertical tab	/\v/ matches a vertical tab
\w	Matches any single character that is a letter, number, or underscore	/\w/ matches 4 /\w/ does not match @
\W	Matches any single character that is *not* a letter, number, or underscore	/\W/ matches @ /\W/ does not match g

Table 13-4 Regular Expression Codes *(continued)*

This code simply checks to see whether any digits are in the string. If you want to ensure that the viewer typed in *only* digits without any other types of characters, you need to be sure the regular expression is written to test from the beginning to the end of the string. Using the ^ and $ symbols from Table 13-4, you can ensure that the string is tested for the match starting at the beginning of the string and ending at the end of the string. Thus, the following patterns would allow only digits:

```
var tomatch = /^\d+$/;
```

Since the only valid characters from the beginning to the end of the string are digits, this will return true only for entries containing digits without other characters present in the string. This is especially helpful for validating forms and other types of user input to ensure that it is the type of input you expect.

NOTE
Regular expressions can be quite powerful for validation because they allow less erroneous information to be accepted.

Client-side validation of form submissions with data such as e-mail addresses or phone numbers can save unnecessary trips to the server. However, users may disable JavaScript support and make form submissions directly. Therefore, client-side validation should support server-side validation (by a CGI script or a Java servlet, for example), but should never replace it (it could cause a great security risk to store or display data from a viewer that has not been validated).

Grouping Expressions

You will notice in Table 13-4 that an expression surrounded by parentheses indicates a group that can be stored for later use in the expression (or using a method such as the match() method where it will store each match of a group along with the overall match in an array).

For example, you might decide to use a particular sequence of numbers and to have that sequence repeat a particular number of times. To match the number of times something is repeated, you can use curly brackets ({}) along with a number or number range. For instance, if you want to match five instances of the number 3, you could use the following expression:

```
/3{5}/
```

If you wanted this to be a match if the number 3 occurs at least five times but no more than ten times, you could use the following expression:

```
/3{5,10}/
```

Now, suppose you wanted the match to start with a 3 and have any digit as the next character, and wanted to match that entire sequence five times (thus, something like 3234353637 would be a match). You might write the following:

```
/3\d{5}/
```

The trouble with this is that it gets the 3 correct, but matches five digits afterward without the need to repeat the 3. Thus, a number like 387643 would match even though you wanted to have five sets of two numbers with each set beginning with a 3. To fix this, you can group the 3 and the \d together with parentheses, and follow that with the number of times it should repeat:

```
/(3\d){5}/
```

This time, the 3 and the second digit are grouped together, and that sequence must be repeated five times.

Grouping is a helpful way to get more out of your use of regular expressions, and you will see more of this when you get to form validation in the next chapter.

The replace(), match(), and search() Methods

These methods of the String object were mentioned earlier in the chapter, and will make more sense now that regular expressions have been introduced.

The replace() Method

To replace information in a string, you can use regular expressions and the replace() method of the String object. The syntax for using the replace() method is as follows:

```
varname= stringname.replace(regex,newstring);
```

You replace *varname* with the name of the variable that will hold the new string value once the information has been replaced. You replace *stringname* with the name of the string variable that will undergo the replacement. You replace *regex* with the name of the regular expression to be used to match against the string. Finally, you replace *newstring* with the string or string variable to replace any matched values in the string.

As an example, the following code replaces the first instance of "car" in mystring with "skunk":

A string literal is created

```
var mystring= "I like the way a new car smells, and cars are fun.";⏎
var toreplace=/car/;◄─────── The pattern to replace is set as a regular expression
var newstring= mystring.replace(toreplace,"skunk");◄─┐
window.alert(newstring);◄─┐
```

The alert shows the updated string

The first instance of a match is replaced in the string, and the result is assigned to a variable

The preceding code replaces only the first instance of car, giving the alert "I like the way a new skunk smells, and cars are fun." If you want to change every instance of "car" instead, the g flag is helpful at the end of the regular expression, as shown in the following code:

```
var mystring= "I like the way a new car smells, and cars are fun.";
var toreplace=/car/g;◄──────────────────────── Adding the g flag causes all
var newstring= mystring.replace(toreplace,"skunk");    matches of the pattern to be
window.alert(newstring);                               replaced when the replace()
                                                       method is run
```

The g flag will match every instance of the regular expression it finds in the string. Thus, when the replace() method is run, all instances of "car" will be replaced with "skunk." The viewer will see this alert: "I like the way a new skunk smells, and skunks are fun."

You could also use the replace() method to make a name-changing script that is shorter and somewhat less complex than the one earlier in this chapter. By using the replace() method with a regular expression, the first letter of the first and last name can be changed more easily. The following code shows how:

```
function getname() {
 var tomatch=/^[A-Za-z]+\s[A-Za-z]+$/;
 var toreplace=/\b[A-Za-z]/gi;
 var thename=window.prompt("Enter your first and last name","");
  if (tomatch.test(thename)) {
   newname=thename.replace(toreplace,"Z");
   window.alert("Now your name is "+newname);
  }
  else {
   window.alert("Name invalid. Please Try Again");
   getname();
  }
}
getname();
```

Regular expressions are used to validate and change the viewer's entry

This script changes the first letter of the first and last name to *Z* regardless of what it was before. The regular expression for the replacement simply looks for a letter at the beginning of a word using the word boundary (\b) code. Each time a letter is at the beginning of a word, it is replaced.

The validation of the input keeps the script from getting more than two names and one space, and it also ensures that at least one letter is in each name, with no numbers or special characters. The illustration shows the result of the script if the viewer enters Debra Loo at the prompt: the viewer's name is changed.

The match() Method

The match() method compares a regular expression and a string to see whether they match. It returns an array containing one or more matches, depending on how it is used. If no match is found, it returns –1.

The basic use of the match() method is as follows:

```
string.match(regex);
```

The *string* will be your string literal, and *regex* will be your regular expression literal. Note the difference in the order between this method and the test() method. You could use it in this way:

```
var mystring = "I am Ironman!";
var tomatch = /Iron/;
if (mystring.match(tomatch)) {
  window.alert("Your string contains Iron!");
}
else {
  window.alert("Sorry, no Iron in your string.");
}
```

If this is used with the g flag or with grouping using (), it will remember each match made (including matches on groups or nested groups) and return each match as an array element.

The search() Method

The search() method executes the search for a match between a regular expression and a specified string. If a match is found, it returns the position in the string where the beginning of the match was found. Otherwise, it returns −1. Here is an example of this method in action:

```
var mystring = "I am Ironman!";
var tomatch = /Iron/;
if (mystring.search(tomatch)) {
  window.alert("Iron found at position "+mystring.search(tomatch)+"!");
}
else {
  window.alert("Sorry, no Iron in your string.");
}
```

As you can see, the syntax is much like that of the match() method.

More Information

For more information on regular expressions and how to create more complex patterns, you can look at the following online resources:

- www.regular-expressions.info/

- www.regular-expressions.info/javascript.html (includes specifics on the JavaScript engine)

- https://developer.mozilla.org/en/Core_JavaScript_1.5_Guide/Regular_Expressions

With these techniques down, you are ready to move on to working with forms in JavaScript and working on the validation of form contents.

Chapter 13 Self Test

1. The _____ object provides properties and methods to get information about strings or to modify strings.

2. What are the two ways in which you created String objects?

   A Creating an instance of the String object and creating a string literal

   B Creating an instance of the Array object and creating a string literal

   C Creating a numeric variable and creating a numeric object

   D Creating a string and adding numbers

3. You can create a string _____ by assigning a string value to a variable.

4. A regular text string is able to use the String object's methods because:

   A It is already a String object

   B It can use other methods as well, so it can use the methods of the String object

   C JavaScript takes the string literal and turns it into a temporary String object

   D The String object uses the string literal as-is

5. Which property of the String object can you use with both String objects and string literals?

   A prototype

   B constructor

   C length

   D color

6. The _____ property returns the length of a string.

7. Which of the following correctly creates a string literal?

   A var the_text= "Look at me!;

   B var the_text= "Look at me!";

   C var the_text= Look at me!;

   D var the_text= new String("Look at me!");

8. Which method of the String object can you use to find which character is at a given position in a string?

   A indexOf()

   B charAt()

    C charIsAt()

    D indexOfThePosition()

9. The _____ method adds <big> and </big> tags around a string value.

10. The concat() method _____ two or more strings together and returns the new combined string value.

11. Which one of the following statements is true?

    A The charAt() method returns a numeric value that is the position of a character sent as a parameter.

    B The split() method creates a new string by removing a portion of the string and returning the string minus the portion removed.

    C The length property allows you to add longer properties and methods to the String object.

    D The indexOf() method returns a numeric value that is the position of a character sent as a parameter, but only the position of the first occurrence of that character.

12. The _____ method adds <i> and </i> tags around a string value.

13. The _____ method returns the string literal value of a String object.

14. To replace information in a string, you can use regular expressions and the method of the String object.

15. The _____ method compares a regular expression and a string to see whether they match.

Chapter 14

JavaScript and Forms

Key Skills & Concepts

- Accessing Forms

- Using the Properties and Methods of the Form Object

- Ensuring the Accessibility of Forms

- Validating Forms

- Using Forms for Navigation

When you use JavaScript to access forms, you can create new scripts for your Web pages. This chapter begins by explaining how to access a form with JavaScript. Then you'll learn about the various properties and methods to use with forms and form elements. You'll also learn about forms and accessibility, how to validate form elements, and how to use <select></select> elements as navigational tools.

Accessing Forms

Each time you add a set of <form> and </form> tags to an HTML document, a form object is created. To access one of the forms using JavaScript, you can use any one of the following options:

- Use the forms array of the document object

- Name the form in the opening form tag and use that name to access the form

- Give the form an id in the opening form tag and access it using the document.getElementById() method

Using the forms Array

The forms array allows you to access a form using an index number in the array. Each set of <form> and </form> tags on the page will create an additional element in the forms array, in the order in which they appear in the document. Thus, you can reference the first form in a document like this:

```
document.forms[0]
```

As you will recall, arrays begin counting at 0, so the previous example will access the first form in the document. If you want to access the second form, you could use the following:

```
document.forms[1]
```

This will work for the rest of the forms on the page in the same way. Just remember to begin counting at 0 rather than 1 to access the correct form.

Accessing the form doesn't do anything on its own. The form that you access is an object. To use it, you need a property or method of the object. The properties and methods of the form object are listed in a later section, "Using the Properties and Methods of the Form Object," but for now, take a look at the length property to see what it does.

A Property Value

The examples in this section use the form object's length property. This property allows you to find out how many elements exist (such as input boxes, select boxes, radio buttons, and others) in an HTML form. For example, take a look at this code:

```
<body>                          The first element is this text box
<form>
Name: <input type="text" />◄─────┐
E-mail: <input type="text" />◄──────────────── The second element is this text box
<input type="submit" value="Submit" />◄────┐
</form>
</body>                         The third element is this submit button
```

The code creates a short form that contains three elements: two text boxes and the submit button. Because it's the only form on the page, it will be the first form, allowing you to access it using document.forms[0]. To use the length property, add it to the end like this:

```
document.forms[0].length
```

Using the preceding code, you can create a short script to tell the viewer how many elements are in the form. (You wouldn't typically use the length property this way, but it's good for an example.) The code that follows will write the information on the page after the form:

```
<body>
<form>
Name: <input type="text" /> <br /> ─────────┐
E-mail: <input type="text" /> <br />        ├──── The elements of the form are here
<input type="submit" value="Submit" /> ─────┘
</form>
<p>
<script type="text/javascript">
document.write("The form has "+document.forms[0].length+" elements.");◄─┐
</script>
</p>                                    The number of elements in the
</body>                                 form is printed on the page
```

This code informs the viewer that the form has three elements. Figure 14-1 shows this script's results when run in a browser.

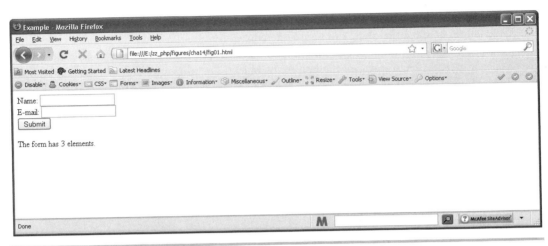

Figure 14-1 The number of elements in the form is displayed to the viewer

Covering Two Length Properties

If you want to try to show the number of elements in the forms on a page when there is more than one form, you can use a more complex script that prints a message for each form on the page. Recall that because forms are an array, you can find the length of the array.

The length of the array is the number of forms on the page (much like the length property of a particular form is the number of elements in the form). To find the number of forms on the page rather than the length of a form, remember not to specify a form by leaving off the brackets and the index number, as in the following example:

```
document.forms.length
```

This syntax finds the number of forms on the page. Thus, you must remember this:

- document.forms.length finds the number of forms on the page.

- document.forms[*x*].length finds the number of elements in a specific form on the page, where *x* is the index number of the form to be accessed.

This syntax might look a bit confusing, but just remember that one length property is for the array in general, while the other length property is used on a specific form.

CAUTION

Remember the difference between document.forms.length and document.forms[*x*] .length. The former finds the number of forms on the page, while the latter finds the number of elements in a specific form (by replacing *x* with a number).

The following script uses both of the length properties and a loop to cycle through each form. The code displays the number of elements in each form on the page. First, the HTML code (save as lengths.html):

```
<body>
<h1>Form Lengths</h1>

<h2>Form 1</h2>
<form>
Name: <input type="text" /><br />
E-mail: <input type="text" /><br />
<input type="submit" value="Submit" />
</form>
```

The elements of the first form

```
<h2>Form 2</h2>
<form>
Favorite Color: <input type="text" /><br />
Favorite Food: <input type="text" /><br />
<input type="reset" value="Reset" /> 
<input type="submit" value="Submit" />
</form>
```

The elements of the second form

```
<h2>Results</h2>
<script type="text/javascript" src="lengths.js"></script>

</body>
```

Next, the JavaScript code (save as lengths.js):

A variable is created to hold the form number (one more than its index number)

The loop to cycle through all the forms on the page begins

```
for(var count=0;count<document.forms.length;count++) {
  var formnum = count+1;
  document.write("Form "+formnum+" has "+document.forms[count].length);
  document.write(" elements.<br />");
}
```

The results are written on the page

The code creates two forms in the HTML document. The script then opens a loop beginning at 0 (where arrays begin counting) and ending before it gets to the value of document.forms.length, which is the number of forms on the page. Because there are two forms (which will make 2 the value of document.forms.length), the count runs from 0 to 1 and then stops. The count allows you to access the forms array at positions 0 and 1, which will turn out to be Form 1 and Form 2 in the HTML code.

The formnum variable has the value of the position number in the array plus one, which is the number of the form as seen in the HTML code. The script then writes the number of elements in each form on the page using the document.write() statements.

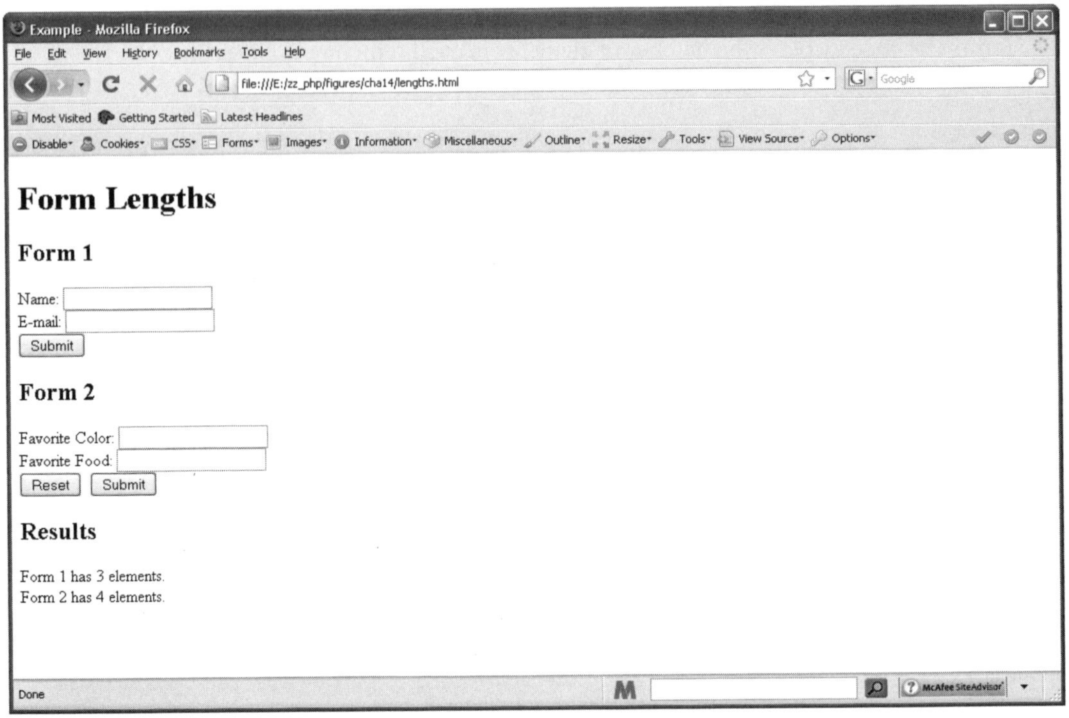

Figure 14-2 The number of elements in each form is displayed

The forms array is used with the value of the count variable as the index number, which finds the number of elements in the specified form each time through the loop. Figure 14-2 shows the results of this code when run in a browser.

Using Form Names

Using form names allows you to name the forms on the page that you want to access later. This option can help eliminate any confusion between document.forms.length and document .forms[*x*].length because you won't need to use the latter unless you're trying to loop through each element in each form on the page.

To use a form name, you must add a name="*yourname*" attribute to the opening form tag on the form you want to access. Replace *yourname* with a name you want to use for the form, as in the following code:

```
<form name="info_form">
Name: <input type="text" /><br />
<input type="submit" />
</form>
```

The name of the form is now info_form, and you can use this name to access the form in your script.

The name of the form allows it to become an instance of the form object that you can access through its name. To use JavaScript to access a form that uses a form name, you can use the syntax shown here:

```
document.yourname
```

Replace *yourname* with the name given to the form in the name="*yourname*" attribute in its opening form tag. Thus, if you wanted to write a script to find the number of elements in a named form, you could use the following code:

```
<body>
<form name="info_form">  ◄──────────── The form is given a name
Name: <input type="text" /><br />
<input type="submit" />
</form>                                    The number of elements in the
<p>                                        named form is written on the page
<script type="text/javascript">
  document.write("The form has "+document.info_form.length+" elements.");◄─┘
</script>
</p>
</body>
```

Notice how the form is accessed in the document.write() statement. Instead of the forms array, the name of the form is in its place. It can now access the properties of the form object and does so by accessing the length property.

Using an ID

The third way to access a form is to use an id attribute and to then use document.getElementById() to access the form element. This is often the clearest way to access a form and its elements, because you can access each element by using its individual id, whereas the previous two access methods require you to know which array index the form is at or the form name and the element's name.

If you wanted to write the script from the previous section using the id method, you could use the following code:

```
<body>
<form id="info_form">  ◄──────────── The form is given an id
Name: <input type="text" /><br />
<input type="submit" />
</form>
<p>
<script type="text/javascript">
  var f_length = document.getElementById("info_form").length;
  document.write("The form has "+f_length+" elements.");◄──┐
</script>                                                     │
</p>                                    The number of elements in the
</body>                                 named form is written on the page
```

Since you are familiar with using document.getElementById() from previous chapters, this should be a straightforward method for you.

The method you use to access a form and its elements will depend on the types of scripts you are writing. If you are using multiple forms on a page, then the forms array can be a handy way to cycle through each form. If you are trying to get as much backward compatibility with older browsers as possible, using the name method may be the way to go. On the other hand, trying to validate in XHTML 1.0 strict will require you to use an id to name each form element, so using the id method would be more appropriate in that case.

Using the Properties and Methods of the Form Object

The JavaScript form object will help you when you need to access certain elements or attributes of the form in a script. The form object has only a few properties and methods. The properties are described first.

Properties

The form object's properties provide information you might need when working with forms in your scripts. Table 14-1 lists the properties of the form object and their values.

Most of these properties just hold values corresponding to the various attributes in an HTML form tag. A few of them have different types of values, though, as explained next.

The action Property

This property allows you to access the value of the action=*"url"* attribute in the opening form tag. This attribute is used to send the form to a server-side script for processing (such

Property	Value
action	The value of the action attribute in the HTML form tag
elements	An array that includes an array element for each form element in an HTML form
encoding	The value of the enctype attribute, which varies with different browsers
length	The value of the total number of elements in an HTML form
method	The value of the method attribute in an HTML form tag
name	The value of the name attribute in an HTML form tag
target	The value of the target attribute in an HTML form tag

Table 14-1 Properties of the Form Object

as a Perl or PHP script). The following example shows how to access the property with a named form:

An action attribute is defined

```
<body>
<form name="info_form" action="http://someplace.com/php/form.php">
Name: <input type="text" /><br />
<input type="submit" />
</form>
<p>
<script type="text/javascript">
  document.write("The form goes to "+document.info_form.action);
</script>
</p>
</body>
```

The value of the action property is written on the page

This script writes the URL on the page given in the action attribute. Figure 14-3 shows the result of this script when run in a browser.

The elements Property (Array)

The elements property is an array that allows you to access each element within a specific form in the same order it appears in the code, starting from 0. It works much like the forms array but has an entry for each element in a given form.

To use the elements array to access an element in a form, use the index number for the element you want to access. For instance, the following form has two elements:

```
<form name="info_form">
Name: <input type="text" /><br />
<input type="submit" />
</form>
```

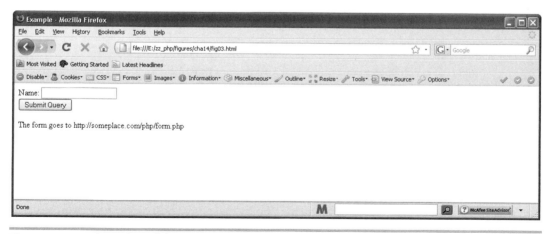

Figure 14-3 The value of the action attribute in the form is printed on the page

To access the first element (the text box), you can use the syntax shown here:

```
document.info_form.elements[0]
```

Alternatively, if you want to use the forms array (assume this is the first form on the page), you could use this syntax:

```
document.forms[0].elements[0]
```

Yet another option to access the text box is to name it (like with the form) and access it using its name. You can do this with each element, as well as the form itself; you can choose which method is best for accessing a form and its elements in each situation.

The following code gives the form and the text box a name, and allows you to access them using those names:

```
<form name="info_form">
Name: <input type="text" name="yourname"><br />
<input type="submit">
</form>
```

In this case, you could access the text box using the form name and the text box name, as in the syntax shown here:

```
document.info_form.yourname
```

Also, you can of course use the id method:

```
<form>
Name: <input type="text" id="yourname"><br />
<input type="submit">
</form>
```

Then, you can access the input element using document.getElementById():

```
document.getElementByID("yourname");
```

To create scripts that use the elements of a form, you must be able to access a property for a form element. Each form element is an instance of an object with its own properties and methods, as shown in Table 14-2.

The form elements all have their own selection of properties and methods, but many of them are used with most or all of the form elements. The following sections look in more detail at the properties and methods listed in Table 14-2 and how they are used with the form elements.

The checked Property

This property is used with check boxes and radio buttons. It has a Boolean value, which is true if the box or button is checked and false if it isn't. For instance, use the following code to try it out with a check box:

```
<body>
<form>                                          The check box is given an id
Check box to say Yes: <input type="checkbox" id="yes_no">
<br /><br />
<input type="button" value= "See the Answer" onclick="is_it_checked();" />
</form>
<script type="text/javascript">               The button starts the function to
  function is_it_checked() {                   check the state of the check box
    var y_n = document.getElementById("yes_no");
    if (y_n.checked) {
      window.alert("Yes! The box is checked!");
    }                                          The condition of the check box is
    else {                                     checked using the checked property
      window.alert("No, the box is not checked!");
    }
  }
}
</script>
</body>
```

The HTML body has the form with a check box with the id of yes_no. A button will call the function is_it_checked() when it is clicked. The function then checks whether the check box is currently checked using an if/else statement. The if condition uses a shortcut that allows you to shorten it from

```
if (y_n.checked==true)
```

to this:

```
if (y_n.checked)
```

Element Type	Object Name	Properties	Methods
Button	button	form, name, type, value	blur(), click(), focus()
Check box	checkbox	checked, defaultChecked, form, name, type, value	blur(), click(), focus()
Hidden field	hidden	form, name, type, value	None
Radio button	radio	checked, defaultChecked, form, name, type, value	blur(), click(), focus()
Reset button	reset	form, name, type, value	blur(), click(), focus()
Select box	select	form, name, options, selectedIndex, type	blur(), focus()
Submit button	submit	form, name, type, value	blur(), click(), focus()
Text box	text	defaultValue, form, name, type, value	blur(), focus(), select()
Text area	textarea	defaultValue, form, name, type, value	blur(), focus(), select()

Table 14-2   Form Elements with Their Objects and Methods

The checked property will return true or false without needing to test the value of the checked property against anything. The checked property already has a value, so the value doesn't need to be compared to anything (unless you prefer to do it that way, which is also okay).

The defaultChecked Property

This property is also a Boolean value of true or false. The value depends on whether the check box or radio button has the checked attribute in its HTML (which sets the element to be checked by default on the page). If the element has the checked attribute, the value is true. If not, the value is false.

For instance, the following HTML code uses the checked attribute:

```
<form>
Do you want us to send you e-mail updates and offers?<br />
Yes <input type="checkbox" id="yes" checked="checked" />
No <input type="checkbox" id="no" />
</form>
```

Because the first check box has the checked attribute set to checked, the checked property for that element would return true. For the second check box element, the property would return false.

The defaultValue Property

You use this property with text boxes and text areas. It holds the value of the default value set in the value attribute of the element's tag. This capability can be useful if you set a default value in a text box, the user deletes it, and then the user decides it would be nice to have the default value back. You could code a button to return that value if clicked by the viewer, as shown in the following code:

```
<body>
<form>                                          The text box is assigned a default value
Favorite URL:<br />
<input type="text" id="favurl" value="http://www.yahoo.com">
<br /><br />
<input type="button" value="Reset Default" onclick="back_to_default();">
</form>                                          The button calls the function
<script type="text/javascript">                 that resets the default value
  function back_to_default() {
    var url_box = document.getElementById("favurl");
    url_box.value = url_box.defaultValue;
  }
</script>                     The current value of the check box is
</body>                      changed back to the default value
```

In the HTML code, the value attribute in the input tag for the text box is set to http://www .yahoo.com. This gives it a default value. When the function is called, it assigns this default value back to the text box by changing its current value (url_box.value) to the default value (url_box.defaultValue).

NOTE

This technique is useful if you desire to switch specific values back to their defaults. If you want to change *everything* back to default values, you can simply use a reset button in your HTML code (that is, <input type="reset" value="Reset" />).

The form Property

This property is often used with the keyword "this" to refer to the form that contains the element that uses it. For instance, if you want to change the value of a text box by clicking a button, you could refer to the form by using this.form rather than needing the name or id of the form:

```
<form>
Favorite URL:<br />
<input type="text" name="favurl" value=http://www.yahoo.com />
<br /><br />
<input type="button" value="Change"
 onclick="this.form.favurl.value='http://www.lycos.com';" />
</form>
```

This code changes the current value of the text box to http://www.lycos.com when the button is clicked. Using this.form.favurl.value allows you to access the same form from an element within it without having to go back and use a form name or id, which is a bit longer.

The name Property

This property holds the value of the name attribute of an element. For instance, the following code prints the value of the name of the first element (the text box) on the page:

```
<body>
<form name="info_form">
Name: <input type="text" name="yourname" /><br />
<input type="submit" value="Submit" />
</form>
<p>
<script type="text/javascript">
  document.write("The first element is "+document.info_form.
elements[0].name);
</script>
</p>
</body>
```

This is a handy way to find an element name without having to search the code for it.

The options Property (Array)

The options property is an array that contains an element for each option listed in a select box in a form. The index numbers count from 0, and each option is placed in the array in the order in which it is written in the HTML code. The following code shows how you can access the value of an option (this is the value in the value attribute of the option tag, not the content of the tag) and write it on the page:

```
<body>
<form>
Fruits:                                              The first option
<select id="optlist">
<option selected="selected" value="orange">Orange</option>
<option value="apple">Apple</option>      The second option
<option value="pear">Pear</option>
</select>
</form>                              The third option
<p>
<script type="text/javascript">
  var fbox = document.getElementById("optlist");
  document.write("The second option is ");        The value of the second
  document.write(fbox.options[1].value);          option is written on the page
</script>
</body>
```

Figure 14-4 shows the results of this script when run in a browser. Notice that the value printed is the value contained in the value attribute of the option tag (all lowercase) rather than the content of the tag (first letter capitalized).

The selectedIndex Property   This property holds the value of the index number of the option (in the options array just discussed) that the viewer has selected. If the first option is selected, the value is 0. If the second option is selected, the value is 1. This property is discussed in more detail when it is used for a navigation script later in this chapter.

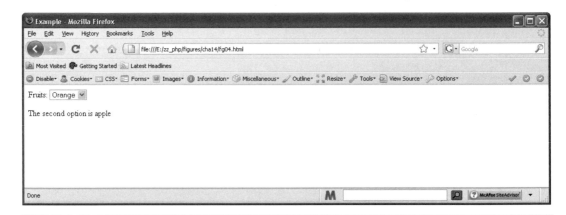

Figure 14-4   The value of the second option is written on the page

The type Property

This property holds the value of the type property for a form element, such as type="text" or type="button". The value of the type attribute for these is text and button, respectively.

The value Property

This property holds the current value of an element. For instance, a text box may have no default value; but when the viewer inputs information into the box, the text box has a current value. If nothing is in the box, the current value would be an empty string. (You used this property for some scripts in previous chapters.)

You will use this property frequently for information, validation, and navigation with forms. You'll see it used a lot more throughout this chapter.

The blur() Method

This method allows you to create a blur event on an element in your code. For example, if you want to keep your default value in a text box from being adjusted by the viewer, you could use the blur() method to remove focus from an element if it receives focus from the viewer. An example of this is shown in the following code:

```
<body>
<form>
Your Favorite Food
<input type="text" name="fav_food" value="Pizza"
 onfocus="this.form.fav_food.blur();" />
</form>
</body>
```

Clicking the text box gives it focus, but the onfocus event handler catches the focus on the text box and then uses the blur() method on the element to remove focus from it. Of course, you could also use this script with no default value to create a text box that can't be filled out because it can't receive focus. In either case, this script is overridden if the viewer turns off JavaScript in the browser and thus is not recommended as a protection from the user filling in something in a field. Such things can be handled via input validation on the client side and server side.

The click() Method

This method allows you to create a click event on a button in your code. However, a click created this way doesn't activate the onclick event handler if it is used in the button. Thus, the click() method is most useful for activating buttons such as submit and reset buttons, which don't need an onclick event handler to be able to work.

For instance, a reset button will reset a form when clicked. If you want to reset a form when a field loses focus (and really irritate the viewer), you could use the following code:

```
<body>
<form>
Your Favorite Food
<input type="text" name="fav_food" onblur="this.form.annoy.click();"
```

```
/><br />
Drink <input type="text" />
<br /><br />
<input type="reset" name="annoy" value="Reset Form">
</form>
</body>
```

This code uses the onblur() event to cause the button named "annoy" (the reset button) to be called to action when the viewer removes focus from the first text box.

The focus() Method

The focus() method lets you create a focus event in your code so that you can bring a certain form element into focus for the viewer.

For example, you might want to give focus to the first form element on a page (usually a text box) as soon as the page loads so that the viewer doesn't have to click the element to bring it into focus and begin typing. The following code shows how you can do this:

```
<body>
<form>
Your Favorite Food
<input type="text" id="fav_food" /><br />
Drink <input type="text" />
</form>
<script type="text/javascript">
  var f_box = document.getElementById("fav_food");
  f_box.focus();
</script>
</body>
```

The script is loaded after the form and its elements exist. It then uses the focus() method to give focus to the first text box for the viewer.

The select() Method

This method allows you to automatically select (highlight) the contents of a text box or a text area for the viewer. This is useful if you have set a default value for the element and would like the viewer to be able to quickly delete the value to type a new one, or if you want to make it easy for the viewer to copy and paste the contents of the element.

The following code selects the text in a text area when the viewer gives it focus, making it possible for the viewer to quickly delete the text or to easily copy it to the clipboard:

```
<body>
<form>
<textarea name="sometext" onfocus="this.form.sometext.select();">
This text is the default text for the text
 area and is selected when the text area is given focus by the viewer.
</textarea>
</form>
</body>
```

The onfocus event handler causes the call to the method to be executed when the viewer clicks inside the text area. All of the default text within the <textarea> and </textarea> tags is selected.

That's the end of the properties and methods of the form elements. It's time to return to the properties of the form object.

The encoding Property

This property often holds the value of the enctype attribute of a form tag. However, the results can be different for each browser.

The length Property

The length property holds the number of elements in a given form on a page. This chapter has already covered this property pretty extensively, so there's no need to discuss it again here.

The method Property

This property holds the value contained in the method attribute of a form tag. Thus, if you're sending the form to the server to be processed, you might use something similar to the following code:

```
<form name="f1" method="post" action= "http://site.com/cgi-bin/form.cgi">
<!-- form contents here -->
</form>
```

The value of the method property for this form would be post because it's within the method attribute of the form.

The name Property

This property holds the value of the form's name, which is given to it in the name attribute of the form tag. You might have some code like this:

```
<form name="cool_form">
<!-- form contents here -->
</form>
```

Here, the value of the name property is cool_form, because it's the value inside the name attribute of the form.

The target Property

This property holds the value given in the target property in a form tag. For instance, you might have the following code:

```
<form name="cool_form" target="place" action="program.cgi">
<!-- form contents here -->
</form>
```

Here, the value of the target property is place, because it's the value inside the target attribute of the form.

Methods

Now take a look at the form object's methods. The form object has only two methods, reset() and submit(), which are described next.

The reset() Method

This method enables you to reset a form using your script, allowing you to reset the form on any event you like. So, if you want to reset a form after the viewer removes focus from an element, you could use the following:

```
<body>
<form
Your Favorite Food
<input type="text" name="fav_food" onblur="this.form.reset();" /><br />
Drink <input type="text" />
<br /><br />
<input type="reset" value="Reset Form" />
<input type="submit" value="Submit Form" />
</form>
</body>
```

The form is reset if this field loses focus

The submit() Method

This method allows you to submit a form without the viewer clicking the submit button. The following code shows how to do this when the viewer removes focus from an element (much the same way as with the reset() method):

```
<body>
<form action="http://site.com/php/form.php">
Your Favorite Food
<input type="text" name="fav_food" onblur="this.form.submit();" /><br />
Drink <input type="text" />
<br /><br />
<input type="submit" value="Submit Form" />
</form>
</body>
```

The form is submitted if this field loses focus

Ensuring the Accessibility of Forms

Ensuring that your forms are accessible to viewers can be somewhat challenging because your preferred layout might not be interpreted properly by an assistive technology (such as Jaws or Homepage Reader). There are several things you can do to help ensure that most of your viewers can access and use your forms. You can place elements and their labels in the expected order, use <label></label> tags, use <fieldset></fieldset> tags, and be sure not to assume the user has client-side scripting (such as JavaScript) enabled.

Using Proper Element and Label Order

In your HTML code, the order of your label text and form elements can help assistive technology in reading the form. For instance, consider the following input fields:

```
<input type="text" name="yourname" id="yourname" /> Name<br />
<input type="text" name="zip_code" id="zip_code" /> Zip Code<br />
```

Here, an assistive technology looks for label text to appear before the form element. Since the first input element does not have any label text before it, the viewer is simply prompted for input, with no indication of what information to enter. Afterward, the label text "Name" is associated with the zip_code text box, which can cause the viewer to enter unexpected input.

To correct this, you can simply move the label text and place it before the form element, as in the following code:

```
Name <input type="text" name="yourname" id="yourname" /><br />
Zip Code <input type="text" name="zip_code" id="zip_code" /><br />
```

Now, the assistive technology likely will pick up the form label and allow the user to enter the expected information. Using both the name and id attributes also helps, because various assistive technologies will pick these up as well.

This works for text boxes, text areas, and select boxes as well. However, when dealing with check boxes and radio buttons, many assistive technologies expect the element first, followed by the descriptive label. Thus, these should be switched around when being used.

When dealing with buttons (such as submit, reset, or created buttons), be sure to use the value attribute to describe what the button does, as that is what assistive technologies will likely expect.

Using <label></label> Tags

Using label tags helps you to further specify which label text belongs with which form element. Here is an example:

```
<label for="yourname">Name</label>
<input type="text" name="yourname" id="yourname" /><br />
```

Here, you assign the for attribute of the opening label tag the value of the id attribute for the form element that will use the label text contained within the <label> and </label> tags. In the preceding example, the for attribute contains yourname, which links the text to the element with the id of yourname in the HTML code.

Using <fieldset></fieldset> Tags

Using a fieldset can be helpful when dealing with radio buttons and check boxes in order to group them together into a logical set. Using a legend tag to label the options to choose from allows the user to know what is expected to be selected. The following code uses a fieldset to group together a group of radio buttons used to select a type of fruit:

```
<fieldset>
<legend>Select a Fruit:</legend>
<input type="radio" name="fruits" id="fruits1" value="Orange" />
<label for="fruits1">Orange</label>
<input type="radio" name="fruits" id="fruits2" value="Banana" />
<label for="fruits2">Banana</label>
<input type="radio" name="fruits" id="fruits3" value="Apple" />
<label for="fruits3">Apple</label>
</fieldset>
```

Here, you group all of the radio buttons within the <fieldset> and </fieldset> tags and use a legend tag after the opening fieldset tag to give the group a label. Then, each element is labeled normally within the fieldset (also using the label tags).

Not Assuming Client-Side Scripting

When initially coding a form, it's best not to assume JavaScript or another client-side technology will be available. If JavaScript is required to make the form usable, then a number of users will not be able to use it because they will have JavaScript disabled for any number of reasons, such as security.

The best practice is to allow the form to be sent to the server side (which will handle the form and provide the most important validation routines) even if JavaScript is unavailable. Code like the following wouldn't be usable for those without JavaScript:

```
<input type="button" onclick="this.form.submit();" value="Submit Form" />
```

In this case, a JavaScript event handler and method are required to submit the form. It would be better to use the traditional submit element to create a submit button.

If you are using some JavaScript validation, you could use code such as the following:

```
<form method="post" action="form.php" onsubmit="return check_form();">
<!-- form contents here -->
<input type="submit" name="submit" id="submit" value="Submit Form" />
</form>
```

This allows you to run the JavaScript function check_form() if JavaScript is available. Otherwise, the onsubmit event handler will be ignored and the form will be submitted to the server-side script for validation and handling. If JavaScript is available, that validation routine can save a trip to the server side. If not, the server-side script will need do the work, but the user will still be able to use the form as expected.

Validation

Validating JavaScript forms is extremely useful. For example, you can validate input before it is submitted, to help reduce the number of forms with incomplete or inaccurate information. Validation of form data prior to submission to, say, a Common Gateway Interface (CGI) script, PHP script, or a Java servlet can save time and reduce load on the server. To begin with validation, you will look at how to use the onsubmit event handler with the return statement as well as learn some validation techniques.

onsubmit and the return Statement

To validate the contents of one or more elements in a form, you need to know when the viewer tries to submit the form. When the viewer clicks the submit button, a submit event occurs, which can be captured with the onsubmit event handler in the opening form tag.

Thus, the following form would be able to do something when the submit button is clicked, before acting on its action attribute:

```
<form method="post" action="form.php" onsubmit="script">
<label for="yourname">Name:</label>
<input type="text" name="yourname" id="yourname" />
<br /><br />
<input type="submit" name="submit" id="submit" value="Submit">
</form>
```

You would replace *script* here with some JavaScript to be executed when the submit button is clicked. This is often a call to the function that will be run to test one or more of the form fields.

For the function to do its work, however, you must be sure the submit button is not able to perform its default action if the viewer's input doesn't pass the validation. This means that you need a return statement in the onsubmit event handler. You want this statement to return true if the validation passes and to return false if the validation fails. Thus, you want an end result to be either

```
onsubmit="return true;"
```

which allows the submission to continue normally, or

```
onsubmit="return false;"
```

which makes the submission void and thus does nothing.

For the technique in the preceding code to work with a function, the return statement in the onsubmit event handler must call a function that returns a value of true or false. Thus, you would get a statement like this:

```
onsubmit="return yourfunction();"
```

You would replace *yourfunction* with a real function name.

The key here is that the function must return a value of true or false so that the previous statement will evaluate to what you need (return true; or return false;). The function itself can do anything else, but it needs to have a return statement that sends back a value of true or false to the event handler.

So, you could perform a validation on a form to be sure a text box is not left completely blank. The following code shows how to do this using a function with the onsubmit event handler. First, the HTML code (save as val_form.html):

```
<body>
<form method="post" action="form.php" onsubmit="return check_it()">
<label for="yourname">Name:</label>
<input type="text" name="yourname" id="yourname" />
<br /><br />
<input type="submit" name="submit" id="submit" value="Submit">
</form><script type="text/javascript" src="val_form.js"></script>
</body>
```

Next, the JavaScript code (save as val_form.js):

```
function check_it() {
  var thename = document.getElementById("yourname").value;
  if (thename.length < 1)  {
    window.alert("Name field is blank, please try again.");
    return false;
  }
  else {
    return true;
  }
}
```

The function uses an if statement to check whether the text field has been left blank (using the value of the text element's length property). If so, an alert tells the viewer to try again and the function returns false. Otherwise, the function will return true. If it returns true, the submission continues. Otherwise, the form is not submitted and the viewer can try again by entering the necessary information and clicking the submit button again. Keep in mind that the check_it() function invalidates only a totally empty form field. You would need to make the function more complex to eliminate submission of names such as a space, a pound (#) symbol, and so on (which could be handled using regular expressions).

Techniques

For the most part, validation can be as simple or as complex as you need it to be for your purposes. All you need to do is create your own custom functions to validate the form fields of your choice based on the information needed.

For instance, the example in the preceding section checked for an empty text box in a name field. However, for a Zip code, you could check whether the field contains five digits by using a regular expression. If it does not, then you can send an alert telling the viewer the Zip code is invalid and asking for it to be reentered. The following code shows a way to do this:

```
<body>
<form method="post" action="form.php" onsubmit="return check_it()">
<label for="zip_code">Zip Code:</label>
<input type="text" name="zip_code" id="zip_code" />
<br /><br />
<input type="submit" name="submit" id="submit" value="Submit">
</form>
<script type="text/javascript">
  function check_it() {
    var zip = document.getElementById("zip_code").value;
    var tomatch = /^\d{5}$/;
    if (tomatch.test(zip)) {
      return true;
    }
    else {
      window.alert("An invalid zip code was entered");
      return false;
    }
  }
</script>
</body>
```

The code uses the regular expression to check for five digits. If anything other than five digits is entered, then the function will return false. You can, of course, expand this to allow for the extra four digits that are sometimes used to designate more precisely a specific area within a Zip code. To do so, add another input field and require that it have four digits if a value is entered in that second field.

You can make the validation as strict or as loose as you need it in your JavaScript. Keep in mind, though, that at the application layer (your server-side script or program) you will need to take extra care with your validation routines to ensure that bad and/or malicious data cannot be submitted to your application.

TIP

One way to find validation scripts is to try checking some JavaScript sites on the Web. A number of them have special functions that are made to validate different types of data. This can save you some work if you can find a function to suit your purposes.

Ask the Expert

Q: All of the elements like text areas and select boxes have too many properties and methods to remember. Any suggestions?

A: A number of these properties and methods are used with all of the element types, while only a few are more specific. As you continue to write scripts, you will start to know which elements have which properties and methods, so it won't be as confusing. If you notice which properties and methods are used with each element, it will be easier to see when there is one that is specific to a certain type of element.

Q: What types of input can I validate?

A: For the most part, you can validate anything you like in the manner you see fit. You can validate dates, names, times, addresses, e-mail addresses, phone numbers, or anything else you might need.

Q: Can I validate the selections in a select box or the text in a text area, or maybe some of the other input types?

A: In some of these cases, you will already have your own values built into the elements. However, if you can, you should still validate those values against other information to be sure the information you receive matches your needs. You just need to adjust your function to perform the needed tasks based on the different types of input devices (text areas, radio buttons, and so on). For instance, the next section covers select boxes as they relate to navigation. However, some of the information (such as the selectedIndex property) is useful for validation as well.

Q: I don't use server-side scripts, but I use JavaScript for fun and want to validate the information. Do I really need to add a server-side script?

A: The need for a server-side script depends on your purposes. If you have a form that needs to have information saved, sent by e-mail, or sent to a database, then you need a server-side application.

Try This 14-1　Request a Number

```
pr14_1.html
prjs14_1.js
```

In this project, you create a script for basic validation of a phone number entered by the viewer, such as 222-222-2222.

Step by Step

1. Create an HTML page with a form and a text box with the label text "Phone Number (XXX-XXX-XXXX):". Make sure the form has a submit button and calls the JavaScript function check_it() to validate the input. Insert the necessary script tags after the form to call an external JavaScript file named prjs14_1.js. Save the HTML file as pr14_1.html.

2. Create an external JavaScript file and save it as prjs14_1.js. Use it for step 3.

3. Use a regular expression to ensure that the number entered into the text box is in the format XXX-XXX-XXXX. If it is, send an alert saying "Phone number validated." Otherwise, send an alert saying "Invalid phone number entered. Valid format is XXX-XXX-XXXX."

4. Save the JavaScript file and open the HTML file in your browser. See if it works by typing various values into the text box and submitting the form.

Try This Summary

In this project, you used your knowledge of JavaScript and forms to create a script to validate a form. The script validates a time entry by the viewer to see if it is a valid phone number by a particular set of standards.

Using Forms for Navigation

By using JavaScript with forms, you can create some alternatives to the regular text link and image link navigation if you wish. This section discusses how to create navigation for your site using select boxes.

This type of navigation allows the viewer to choose a destination from a list in a select box and then go to the new location either by clicking a button or by changing the value. To get started, you will create a navigation select box that uses the viewer's click of a button to go to the new location.

Clicking a Button

Creating a select box is pretty straightforward. First, you set up the code for the select box like this (save the HTML as select.html):

```
<form>
<label for="s1">Select Page:</label>
<select name="s1" id="s1">
<option selected="selected" value="page1.html">Page 1</option>
<option value="page2.html">Page 2</option>
<option value="page3.html">Page 3</option>
</select>
</form>
```

Note that the select box is given an id of s1. Also, notice the value attributes are given URL values (local URLs here). These are the destinations you want the viewer to go to when he or she chooses the specified option from the list and clicks the button. Finally, the text to be shown for each option is added inside the <option> and </option> tags.

Next, code the script that will set this in motion when a button is clicked. The button needs to perform the action of transferring the viewer to the new destination. To do this, the script must be able to access the option that has been selected in the select box and get its value (the URL). Then, the browser needs to take the viewer to the new URL.

To access the option that has been selected, you must work your way down to the options array for the select box. Recall that the select box was given an id of s1, so you can set up a variable to hold the select box element:

```
var s = document.getElementById("s1");
```

Then, to get to the options array for this select box, you can use the following syntax:

```
s.options[]
```

The question is, which option do you want to get from the array? You don't want to guess by just inserting an index number of choice; you want the index number of the option that has been selected by the viewer. This is where the selectedIndex property of a select box becomes useful. Recall that this holds the value of the index number of the option that has been selected by the viewer. By using the value of this property as the index number in the options array, you can access the correct option when the viewer makes a selection. The following is the syntax to use:

```
s.options[s.selectedIndex]
```

You now have the correct option from the list. Next, you must get its value so that the URL in the value attribute is retrieved. To do this, you just need to add the value property on the end of the long line, like this:

```
s.options[s.selectedIndex].value
```

This is now the value you want, which is the URL of the selection made by the viewer.

Next, you must get this syntax into a working form. This value is the URL where you want the browser to go when a button is clicked. Thus, you need to add a submit button and then use the onsubmit event handler to change the window.location property to this value when it is clicked. The following code creates a button to do this:

```
<body>
<form onsubmit="return go_there();">
<label for="s1">Select Page:</label>
```

```
<select name="s1" id="s1">
<option selected="selected" value="page1.html">Page 1</option>
<option value="page2.html">Page 2</option>
<option value="page3.html">Page 3</option>
</select>
<input type="submit" name="go" id="go" value="Go!" />
</form>
<script type="text/javascript" src="select.js"></script>
</body>
```

This now tells the browser to run a JavaScript function named go_there() when this form is submitted (by clicking the Go! button). It also calls an external JavaScript file named select.js, which is where you will place the code that makes the change to the new URL:

```
function go_there() {
  s = document.getElementById("s1");
  window.location = s.options[s.selectedIndex].value;
  return false;
}
```

Notice how the selected value is used to change the window.location property to the new URL. Returning false prevents the form from being submitted to the server so that the client-side script can handle it. The viewer should be able to navigate by making a selection from the box and clicking the Go! button. Figure 14-5 shows the initial drop-down box when viewed in a browser.

Figure 14-6 shows the result of selecting the option for Page 2 and clicking the Go! button. A new page is shown in the browser as a result.

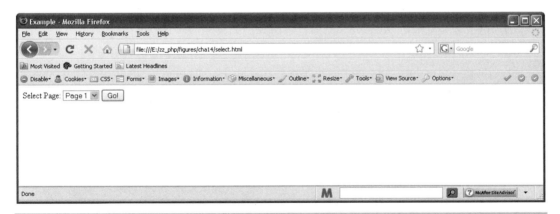

Figure 14-5   The drop-down box before a selection is made and the button is clicked

Figure 14-6 The page displayed after the selection is made and the button is clicked

If you want to make this script more accessible, you can use a server-side script to back up the JavaScript. You would write the code for the server-side script, add the method attribute, and add the action attribute to the HTML code:

```
<body>
<form method="post" action="/php/select.php" onsubmit="return go_there();">
<label for="s1">Select Page:</label>
<select name="s1" id="s1">
<option selected="selected" value="page1.html">Page 1</option>
<option value="page2.html">Page 2</option>
<option value="page3.html">Page 3</option>
</select>
<input type="submit" name="go" id="go" value="Go!" />
</form>
<script type="text/javascript" src="select.js"></script>
</body>
```

Now, if the viewer does not have JavaScript available, the onsubmit attribute will be ignored, but the action attribute will be used to handle the form. This will go to a script named select.php in the php directory on the server (these are simply example file and directory names). The server-side script can then do the work of sending the viewer to the new URL, allowing the script to work even for those without JavaScript.

One more thing that should be noted is that this script will only work if the viewer's browser can handle the document.getElementById() method. If you anticipate that some of your users might have older browsers, it may be a good idea to ensure that they use the server-side script in this case (or you can add options for this to work using the forms array or using a form name and select box name). To keep older browsers from running the JavaScript code, you could do the following:

```
function go_there() {
  if (document.getElementById && document.createTextNode) {
    s = document.getElementById("s1");
```

```
        window.location = s.options[s.selectedIndex].value;
        return false;
    }
    return true;
}
```

Now, the code will work only for those browsers that support getElementById() and createTextNode() (this is added for browsers that support only getElementById() but don't support it quite the way one would expect). Otherwise, the script will return true and the server-side script will be called.

No Button

To create a select box for navigation without a button, you would use the onchange event handler. However, for accessibility reasons, this type of navigation is not recommended because it not only makes it very difficult for those using assistive technology to select the desired option, but also can be confusing in general as the viewer is taken immediately to the selected destination once it is selected.

If you are using the script for leisure and do not need the script to be accessible, you can find numerous versions of this type of navigation script on the Web.

Try This 14-2   Build a Select Box Navigation Script

`pr14_2.html`
`prjs14_2.js`

In this project, you build a navigational select box that will have five destinations for the viewer to choose.

Step by Step

1. Create an HTML document and add script tags so that the HTML file will call an external JavaScript file named prjs14_2.js. Save the HTML file as pr14_2.html.

2. Create a select box with a button for navigation. You can choose whichever destination sites and descriptions you like. Name the select box s1. Save the HTML file.

3. Create a JavaScript file and save it as prjs14_2.js. Use it for step 4.

4. Add the code in this file so that the browser will open the selected URL when the button is clicked.

5. Save the JavaScript file and open the HTML file in your browser. Check to see whether the navigation system works.

Try This Summary

In this project, you used your knowledge of JavaScript and forms to create a navigational system.

✓ Chapter 14 Self Test

1. Each time you add a set of <form> and </form> tags to an HTML document, a(n) _____ object is created.

2. The forms _____ allows you to access a form using an index number.

3. Which of the following would access the fourth form on a page?

   A document.forms[4]

   B document.forms[3]

   C document.forms(4)

   D document.forms(3)

4. Which of the following would find the number of elements in the third form on a page?

   A document.forms[2].length

   B document.forms[3].length

   C document.forms.length

   D document.forms(3).length

5. Which of the following holds the value of the number of forms in a document?

   A document.forms[0].length

   B document.form.length

   C document.forms.length

   D document.forms[1].length

6. Using form _____ allows you to name the forms on the page that you want to access later.

7. Which of the following accesses the value of an element named e1 in a form named f1?

   A document.f1.e1.value

   B document.e1.f1.value

   C document.f1.e2.value

   D document.forms1.e1.value

8. The _____ property allows you to access the value of the action="*url*" attribute in the opening form tag.

9. The _____ property is an array that allows you to access each element in a specific form.

10. The options property is an array that contains an element for each _____ listed in a select box in a form.

11. The _____ method allows you to reset a form using your script.

12. Which type of value should a function return when it is used to validate a form?

    A yes or no

    B true or false

    C maybe so

    D a floating-point number

13. When the viewer clicks the submit button on a form, a submit event occurs and can be captured with the _____ event handler.

14. The _____ method allows you to submit a form without the viewer clicking the submit button.

15. What do you use to get the currently selected option in a select box?

    A The length property

    B The reset() method

    C The getSelected() method

    D The selectedIndex property

Chapter 15

JavaScript and Frames

Key Skills & Concepts

- An Introduction to Frames

- Accessing Frames

- Changing Frames

- Frame Navigation

Although using frames to create Web sites typically isn't recommended, because of usability and accessibility issues, occasionally they (especially inline frames) are the right choice to achieve particular purposes. You can perform some helpful tasks with frames in JavaScript. This chapter provides a basic overview of frames and then explains how you can access frames from other frames. You'll also learn how to change one frame from another frame, and then you'll use some fun frame navigation tricks. Finally, you'll learn how to use variables across frames to store and retrieve information.

An Introduction to Frames

The decision of whether or not to use frames on your Web site is up to you. It depends on your navigational requirements and other Web site issues you might have. If you don't know anything about frames, learning some basic information will help you determine whether they would be useful to you.

If you're already comfortable using frames, you can skim this section or skip it entirely. However, if you have little or no experience with frames, you should read this introduction to frames thoroughly. Frames can get quite messy, especially when you add JavaScript to the picture.

Purpose of Frames

Frames divide a window into two or more separate areas (a *frameset*), each containing different content. This differs from tables in that the divisions in a frameset each contain a separate Hypertext Markup Language (HTML) document, and you can change one of the sections without affecting the other sections.

NOTE

Each frame shown on a Web page is actually a separate HTML document.

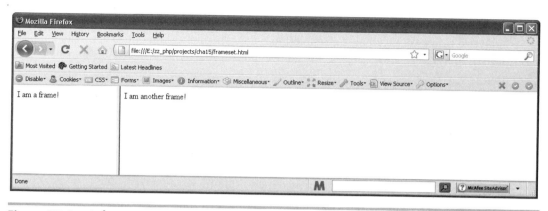

Figure 15-1   A frameset containing two frames

For example, Figure 15-1 shows a Web page with two frames. Each frame is actually a separate HTML document. The HTML document that creates the frames uses a set of <frameset> and </frameset> tags to create a frameset.

Frames have several applications. For instance, you can use them to create a site-wide navigation system, or you can create a reference system where the table of contents is in one frame and the corresponding content appears in another.

The Code Behind the Frames
The following code contains the frameset element. It puts together the number and structure of the frames that will be shown when the document is opened.

The frameset begins, setting up
two frames from left to right

The first frame and
its URL are set

The second frame
and its URL are set

```
<html>
<frameset cols="20%,80%">
<frame src="frame1.html"></frame>
<frame src="frame2.html"></frame>
</frameset>
<noframes>
Sorry, your browser does not support frames. Use the link
 below to go to the frameless version of the site.<br />
<a href="noframes.html">Frameless Site</a>
</noframes>
</html>
```

The frameset ends

This code creates a basic frameset that produces a smaller frame on the left side of the window and a larger frame on the right. Here's how it works:

1. The opening frameset tag tells the browser that a frameset is to begin. Notice that it replaces the body tag used in a regular window.

2. The cols attribute of the opening frameset tag tells the browser the window will be divided into two columns (which move from left to right). The first column (left) is to take up 20 percent of the screen space, while the second column (right) is to take up 80 percent of the screen space.

3. The first frame tag creates the first frame on the page. The browser displays the frames from left to right, top to bottom, in the order that they appear in the source code. Thus, this frame is in the top-left portion of the page—which, in this case, is just the left side of the page.

4. The src attribute tells the browser the URL of the HTML document to display as the contents of the frame, which is actually what the viewer sees on the left side of the window. In this case, the document is a file named frame1.html.

5. The second frame tag does the same thing as the first, but the frame is the next one in order from left to right and top to bottom. Again, because there are only two columns, this frame is just on the right side of the window. The src attribute points to the URL of the HTML document to be displayed in this frame. In this case, the document is a file named frame2.html.

6. The </frameset> tag ends the frameset.

7. The content between the <noframes> and </noframes> tags is displayed in browsers that don't support frames so that the viewer has something displayed on the screen. You can place a link to a version of the site with no frames, or you can use any other HTML code you wish. I used the text and the link to keep the section short for the example.

The document created from the previous code is the page you want to open in the browser to display the frames. Save this document as frameset.html so you can use it once you add some code for the documents used in the frames.

Once the frameset is created, you must create the documents that will fill in the frames. First, create a document to be used for the left frame (frame1.html):

```
<html>
<body>
I am frame1.html, and I am on the left side!
</body>
</html>
```

This simple code tells you which document is being shown in which frame. (You can make the code as complex as you wish.) Save this as frame1.html in the same directory as frameset.html.

Next, you must supply code for the other frame (frame2.html):

```
<html>
<body>
I am frame2.html, and I am on the right side!
</body>
</html>
```

Save this as frame2.html in the same directory as frameset.html and frame1.html.

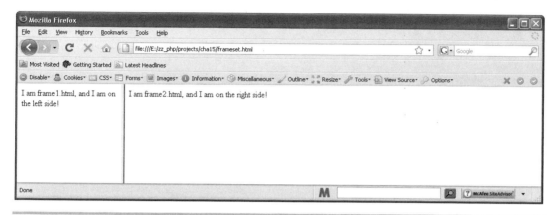

Figure 15-2   A frameset with two frames, one in each column created by the frameset

Now, when you open frameset.html in your browser, it should display the window with two frames, each containing the appropriate HTML document, as shown in Figure 15-2.

Frame Options

As you have seen, the opening frameset tag can take on the cols attribute to divide the window into columns. In the same way, it can instead use the rows attribute to divide the page into rows from top to bottom. Here is an example of code that creates a frameset with two rows:

```
<html>
<frameset rows="20%,80%">          This time the frames go from top to
<frame src="frame1.html"></frame>  bottom, since the rows attribute is used
<frame src="frame2.html"></frame>
</frameset>
<noframes>
Use the link below to go to the frameless version of the site.<br  />
<a href="noframes.html">Frameless Site</a>
</noframes>
</html>
```

This time, the page is divided into two frames, one on top and the other. An example of what this might look like if both frame1.html and frame2.html exist is shown in Figure 15-3.

Rows or Columns

If you prefer, the numbers used in the rows or cols attribute can be in pixels rather than percentages. Also, you can use an asterisk (*) if you want a certain frame to take all of the space remaining after other frames have been set. For example, look at this code:

```
<html>
<frameset rows="150,*">            The asterisk tells the second frame to take any
<frame src="frame1.html"></frame>  remaining space not used by the first frame
```

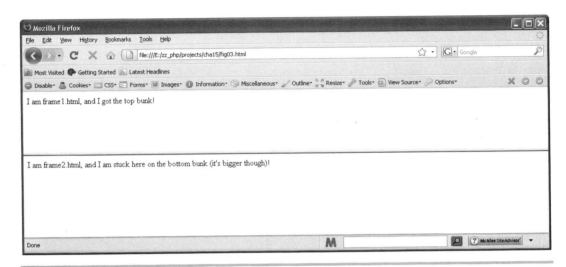

Figure 15-3 A frameset based on rows instead of columns

```
<frame src="frame2.html"></frame>
</frameset>
<noframes>
Use the link below to go to the frameless version of the site.<br  />
<a href="noframes.html">Frameless Site</a>
</noframes>
</html>
```

This time, the first row (top) takes up 150 pixels, while the second row (bottom) takes the rest of the remaining space in the window.

More Than Two Rows or Columns

Of course, you aren't limited to only two rows or two columns. You can have as many rows or columns as you like. For instance, if you want a frameset with three columns, you could use this code:

```
<html>
<frameset cols="150,*,150">
<frame src="frame1.html"></frame>
<frame src="frame2.html"></frame>
<frame src="frame3.html"></frame>
</frameset>
```

The asterisk tells the middle frame to use any remaining space not taken by the other frames

```
<noframes>
Use the link below to go to the frameless version of the site.<br  />
<a href="noframes.html">Frameless Site</a>
</noframes>
</html>
```

Here, the left and right columns have a width of 150 pixels each. The column in the center takes all of the remaining space in the window.

Nesting to Allow Both Rows and Columns

Finally, if you want to have a more complex frameset that includes both rows and columns, you must nest one frameset within another. For instance, you may want a row that spans the top portion of the page that is 100 pixels in height. Then, you might want to have two columns below it: one on the left taking up 150 pixels and one on the right taking the remaining area.

To do this, you need to have a frameset that represents the rows (because the top row must span the entire top portion of the page). Inside the bottom row, you need another frameset that uses columns to divide the lower row into the two areas. The following code shows how this nesting can be done:

```
<frameset rows="100,*">◄——————————————— The main frameset begins
  <frame src="frame1.html"></frame>
    <frameset cols="150,*">◄——————————  The frameset nested in the
      <frame src="frame2.html"></frame>        bottom frame begins
      <frame src="frame3.html"></frame>
    </frameset> ◄————————————————————— The nested frameset ends
</frameset> ◄——————————— The main frameset ends
<noframes>
Use the link below to go to the frameless version of the site.<br  />
<a href="noframes.html">Frameless Site</a>
</noframes>
```

Notice that in place of another frame tag for the frame in the second (bottom) row, a new frameset is used, dividing the bottom row into two more frames. These frames run in columns and go from left to right.

TIP

Be sure to close each <frameset> tag with a </frameset> tag. As with tables, forgetting one of these can cause the frames to be displayed improperly or not at all.

Figure 15-4 shows an example of how this nested frameset appears in a browser (assuming all the documents and files exist).

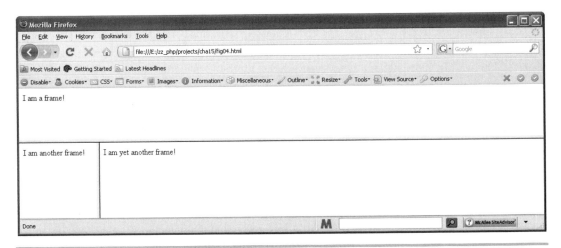

Figure 15-4 A nested frameset allows both rows and columns to be used in a window

Accessing Frames

How do you access a frame in JavaScript? You can either use the frames array or name the frame and use the frame name instead. To begin, take a look at how to access a frame using the frames array.

The frames Array

You use the frames array to access frames based on their order in the source code. You will access one frame from within another frame, so you must be able to find the frame you want to access.

Recall that the frames array comes from the window object. Frames carry most of the same properties and methods as regular windows, but you access them differently. For instance, take a look at this code, which creates a frameset with two frames. Name it frameset1.html. (This replaces the previous example.)

```
<html>
<frameset cols="60%,40%">
<frame src="frame1.html"></frame>
<frame src="frame2.html"></frame>
</frameset>
<noframes>
Use the link below to go to the frameless version of the site.<br />
<a href="noframes.html">Frameless Site</a>
</noframes>
</html>
```

If you're coding some script inside the first frame (frame1.html) and want to know the value of the location property in the second frame (frame2.html) to display it for the viewer, you must figure out how to access the second frame. Remember, you're working inside a frameset. You are working in the code for one of the documents that will be the content for the first frame within the frameset. Thus, to access the other frame, you need to find a way to get back to the main window and reference the frame. Recall from Chapter 10 that the window object's top property allows you to access the topmost window in a frameset (the main window).

You can now use the frames array because you have access to that main window, which contains the code for the frameset. The frames array contains an entry for each frame tag in the code. The count starts at 0 and continues in the order that each frame tag appears in the source code. Thus, to access the first frame in a frameset, you could use the following syntax:

```
top.frames[0]
```

Using the top property allows you to access the main window and the frameset code. Then, frames[0] is used to access the first frame in the source code. So, if you're coding within the second frame and want to access the first frame, you would use this syntax:

```
top.frames[0]
```

Now, you can make the code in the second frame access the needed information in the first frame for the viewer. The following code is for the first frame (frame1.html):

```
<body>
I am frame 1 and the other frame took information from me! How rude!
</body>
```

To complete this script, you could use the following code for frame2.html:

```
<body>
The first frame is from: <br  />
<script type="text/javascript">
  document.write(top.frames[0].location);
</script>
</body>
```

The value of the location of the second frame is printed on the page using the frames array to access the information in the frame

Now you can see the result by opening the main window (frameset1.html). The right frame should tell you the location of the document used for the left frame. Figure 15-5 shows how this may appear in a browser. (Your location value will probably be different from the filename.)

The frames array is a good way to access unnamed frames or to access frames if you need to loop through them. If you recall from Chapter 10, the length property of the frames array provides the number of frames in a document. Thus, you could loop through the frames array to print the location of each of the frames in one frame for your viewer to see. First, you will need the document containing the frameset to be used.

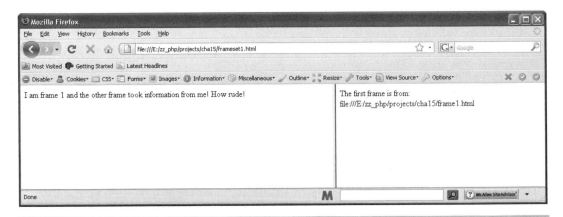

Figure 15-5 The second frame shows information taken from the first frame

For this example, save this main window as frameset2.html. The code for this document is shown here:

```
<html>
<frameset cols="20%,80%">
<frame src="frame1.html"></frame>
<frame src="frame2.html"></frame>
</frameset>
<noframes>
Use the link below to go to the frameless version of the site.<br  />
<a href="noframes.html">Frameless Site</a>
</noframes>
</html>
```

This time, frame1.html will just have a brief statement:

```
<html>
<body>
I am frame 1!
</body>
</html>
```

Now, frame2.html is where the script and results will appear, and could be coded as shown here:

```
<body>
<script type="text/javascript">
  for (var count=0; count<top.frames.length; count+=1) {
    var framenum = count+1;
    document.write("Frame "+framenum+" is from "+top.frames[count].location);
    document.write("<br  />");
  }
</script>
</body>
```

The loop begins, using the length property to know when to quit

A new variable is created to number the frames

The results are printed on the page using the frames array for access

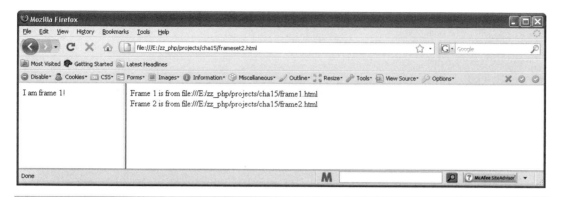

Figure 15-6   The location value for each frame is printed in one of the frames

As you've seen in previous scripts, the length property determines when the loop should end. The framenum variable prints out the frame number beginning at 1 rather than its index number in the array (which begins at 0). The frames array is then used in the document.write() statement to print the value of the location property for each frame.

Figure 15-6 shows the results of this script when run in a browser (when frameset1.html is opened). Again, your location values will probably differ from the filenames.

Using a Frame Name

Another way to access one frame from another is to use the name of the frame (much like the way you used form names in the previous chapter). For example, this code gives each frame a name by adding the name attribute to the frame tag (call this frameset3.html):

```
<html>
<frameset cols="50%,50%">
<frame src="frame1.html" name="left_side"></frame>
<frame src="frame2.html" name="right_side"></frame>
</frameset>
<noframes>
Use the link below to go to the frameless version of the site.<br  />
<a href="noframes.html">Frameless Site</a>
</noframes>
</html>
```

You can now access one of the frames from the other using the frame name rather than the frames array. Thus, if you want to access the second frame (right_side) from the first one, you could use this syntax:

```
top.right_side
```

In the same way, you could access the first frame from within the second frame with this syntax:

```
top.left_side
```

Now you can make each frame tell the viewer the location of the other frame by coding the frames with a short document.write() statement in each. The document for the first frame (frame1.html) could be coded like this:

```
<body>
The second (right) frame is from: <br  />
<script type="text/javascript">
  document.write(top.right_side.location);
</script>
</body>
```

The name of the right frame is used to print information from it in the left frame

After that, frame2.html could be coded as follows:

```
<body>
The first (left) frame is from: <br  />
<script type="text/javascript">
  document.write(top.left_side.location);
</script>
</body>
```

The name of the left frame is used to print information from it in the right frame

Each frame now gives out information about the other one.

Changing Frames

To change the content of one frame from another frame, you can use the target attribute in HTML for a single change. However, by using the location property in JavaScript, you can change more than one frame at a time. The following sections cover both possibilities.

Change a Single Frame

In HTML, if you want to change one frame from within another, use the target attribute within your link tag and give it the value of the name of the frame. For instance, if you want to change the contents of a frame named right_side from another frame in the frameset, you could create a link like this:

```
<a href= "nextpage.html" target="right_side">Next Page</a>
```

This would open nextpage.html in the frame right_side rather than in the current frame (which is the default for a link).

TIP

Be sure the target matches the frame name exactly. If it doesn't match a frame name or a predefined target, the page to be displayed will open in a new browser window instead of in the frame or window you intended.

To perform the same task with JavaScript, you can use the frame name along with the location property to make it work, as in the following syntax:

```
top.right_side.location="nextpage.html";
```

Here, right_side is the name of the frame to have its contents changed, and nextpage.html is the page that appears in place of the original document. To code this into a link, you could use the return false technique used in previous chapters:

```
<a href="n" onclick= "top.right_side.location='newpage.html'; return false;">
New Page</a>
```

On the other hand, you could also use a method that allows you to point the href attribute of a link tag to perform JavaScript statements, as shown here:

```
<a href="javascript:top.right_side.location='newpage.html'">
New Page</a>
```

Notice the addition of the word "javascript" in lowercase followed by a colon. After that, you can use JavaScript statements as you would use them in an event handler.

The technique in the preceding code also eliminates the need to add the return false statement to the code. Either method works (aside from the accessibility issues involved with both of them since the links don't work without JavaScript enabled… you could change this to link to the file and use scripting to override it when JavaScript is available, but when changing multiple frames you couldn't make the single link change both frames without JavaScript).

Change Multiple Frames

To change more than one frame at a time, you can use JavaScript. Grab the basic frameset again and save it as frameset4.html. Here's the code:

```
<html>
<frameset cols="20%,80%">
<frame src="frame1.html" name="left_side"></frame>
<frame src="frame2.html" name="right_side"></frame>
</frameset>
<noframes>
Use the link below to go to the frameless version of the site.<br  />
<a href="noframes.html">Frameless Site</a>
</noframes>
</html>
```

To change the contents of both frames, you need two additional HTML files so that the two documents in the two frames can be changed to two new documents. Thus, you need a document list similar to the following:

- frameset4.html (the main window code)
- frame1.html (document initially shown in the left frame)

- frame2.html (document initially shown in the right frame)

- frame3.html (new document to appear in the left frame)

- frame4.html (new document to appear in the right frame)

You already have the code for frameset4.html, so you just need the code for the four remaining documents. The fun occurs in the example in frame1.html, so that's where you'll start.

Frame 1, the Action Frame

This frame contains the link that makes both frames show a new HTML document. To do this, you can use a function and then call the function from the link. Here's the code for frame1.html:

```
<body>
<script type="text/javascript">            The right frame is changed
  function twoframes() {
    top.right_side.location="frame4.html";  ◄──────┐
    self.location="frame3.html";  ◄─── The current frame    The link calls the function
  }                                     is changed           to change both frames
</script>
<a href="javascript:twoframes();">Change Both Frames</a>  ◄──────┘
</body>
```

The link tag calls the twoframes() function. The function first changes the contents of the right frame by referring to its name (right_side). It then changes the location of its own frame (recall that "self" is a way to refer to the current window or frame, which makes what is being changed in the code a little less ambiguous). When the link is clicked, both documents will change to the new documents.

NOTE

You will notice that the frame you are not currently in is changed first and the self.location is changed last. This is because if you change the self.location before you change any other frame locations, the browser will move on and the script will not finish executing.

The Other Frames: Basic Code

In the remaining frames, you can just add some simple code to make the frame identify itself. Here is some code for frame2.html:

```
<body>
I am frame 2!
</body>
```

Here is some code for frame3.html:

```
<body>
I am frame 3!
</body>
```

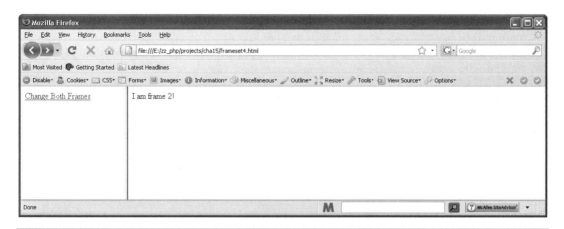

Figure 15-7   The view of the frameset before the link is clicked

Finally, here is some code for frame4.html:

```
<body>
I am frame 4!
</body>
```

Once these are all set up, open frameset4.html to see the link change both frames. Figure 15-7 shows the initial view of frameset4.html before the link is clicked.

Figure 15-8 shows the page after the link has been clicked and the content of both frames has been changed.

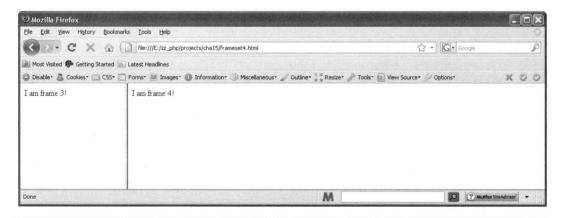

Figure 15-8   After the link is clicked, two new documents appear in the frames

You could certainly use more detailed code if you wanted to. You could set it up with more frames and then change as many of them as you like. You could also code one of the new frames to have a link that takes the viewer back to the original two frames. In addition, you could use the URLs or filenames as parameters to the function.

Try This 15-1 Change Frames

```
pr15_1.html
pr15_1_frame1.html
pr15_1_frame2.html
pr15_1_frame3.html
pr15_1_frame4.html
pr15_1_frame5.html
```

In this project, you create framesets and change more than one frame at once. You also create a frameset that will use one frame to change the contents of two other frames in the document.

Step by Step

1. Create an HTML document to serve as the frameset. Create a frameset that contains three frames from top to bottom (rows). The top and bottom frames should each use 33 percent of the available window space, while the middle frame should use the remaining space.

2. Use the following filenames for each frame:

    Top frame: pr15_1_frame1.html
    Middle frame: pr15_1_frame2.html
    Bottom frame: pr15_1_frame3.html

3. Use these names for each frame:

    Top frame: t_frame
    Middle frame: m_frame
    Bottom frame: b_frame

4. Save the file as pr15_1.html.

5. In the code for the top frame (pr15_1_frame1.html), provide a link that causes the two lower frames to receive new content. Use these filenames for the two new frames: pr15_1_frame4.html and pr15_1_frame5.html.

6. Save the file (pr15_1_frame1.html).

7. Add any content you like to the remaining frame files (pr15_1_frame2.html, pr15_1_frame3.html, pr15_1_frame4.html, pr15_1_frame5.html).

8. Open pr15_1.html in your browser and try out the link. It should change the lower two frames in the frameset while the top frame remains the same.

Try This Summary

In this project, you used your knowledge of JavaScript and frames to code a frameset. When opened in a browser, the viewer can change multiple frames by clicking a link.

Frame Navigation

JavaScript also provides handy frame navigational techniques. For instance, you could adjust the select box navigation created in Chapter 14 to work from one frame to another. Or, you could create code to allow your viewers to break out of frames. You also could create code that sends viewers to your frames if they accidentally enter on a page that should be in a frameset.

Using the Select Box with Frames

If you want the select box in one frame to open a document in another frame, you must alter select box navigation slightly. To do this, you need to change only one part of the code in the select box.

Let's use the filename frameset5.html to see how the frames will be shown. The code is shown here:

```
<html>
<frameset rows="120,*">
<frame src="frame1.html" name="t_frame"></frame>
<frame src="frame2.html" name="b_frame"></frame>
</frameset>
<noframes>
Use the link below to go to the frameless version of the site.<br  />
<a href="noframes.html">Frameless Site</a>
</noframes>
</html>
```

In this case, the frames are going from top to bottom using rows. The top frame (t_frame) spans 120 pixels from the top, and the bottom frame (b_frame) takes up the remaining space on the page.

In the preceding example, a select box changes when the viewer makes a choice (no button). The select box is placed in the top frame to allow the viewer to change the document shown in the bottom frame. Thus, you need to see the code in frame1.html, as shown here:

```
<body>
<form onsubmit="return go_there();">
<label for="s1">Change the lower frame:</label>
<select id="s1">
<option selected="selected" value="#">Choose Destination</option>
<option value="frame3.html">Frame 3</option>
<option value="frame4.html">Frame 4</option>
<option value="frame2.html">Back to Frame 2</option>
</select>
<input type="submit" id="submit" value="Go!" />
</form>
<script type="text/javascript">
function go_there() {
  s = document.getElementById("s1");
```

```
    top.b_frame.location = s.options[s.selectedIndex].value;
    return false;
}
</script>
</body>
```

Notice that the only major difference in the code for the select box is the second line of the code in the go_there() function. Instead of using window.location (which changes the same frame), it uses the name of the bottom frame so that its location is changed (top.b_frame .location).

The three available choices are to go to Frame 3 (frame3.html), Frame 4 (frame4.html), or back to the frame that was there initially (frame2.html). Choosing one changes the bottom frame to the new page.

The only other task is to add some code to the other frame files (frame2.html, frame3.html, and frame4.html) so there is something to view in the bottom frame. Figure 15-9 shows how frameset5.html might look initially, before a choice is made (depending on the code you add to frame2.html).

Figure 15-10 shows an example of how the window might appear if Frame 3 is chosen from the drop-down box (depending on the code you add to frame3.html).

Breaking Out of Frames

Sometimes another Web site will code links that don't break the user out of the site's frames before arriving at your site. Your site is then left in a smaller portion of the viewer's window with the navigation from the other site still showing in other frames. When this happens, you

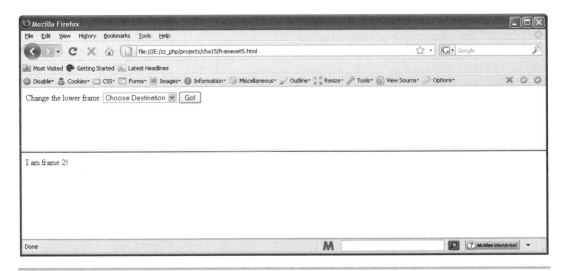

Figure 15-9 A possible initial appearance of the frameset

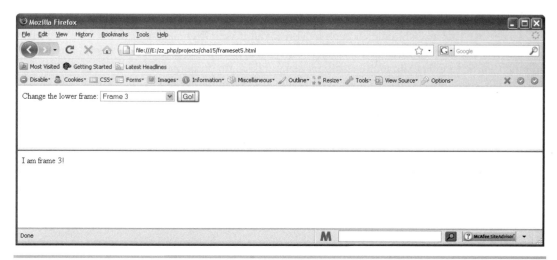

Figure 15-10   A possible appearance once the Frame 3 option is chosen

may want to offer your viewers a way to break out of the other site's frames, or you may want to do it automatically.

Using an Optional Link

You can place a link on your page for viewers to click to break out of frames. You need to add a special target in the <a> tag, as shown here:

```
<a href="http://yoursite.com" target= "_top">Break Out of Frames</a>
```

The target of _top tells the browser to use the full window when opening the URL in the link, rather than opening the link inside a frame. You just need to replace the URL in the tag with your own.

NOTE

Using a target of _top in an anchor (<a>) tag tells the browser to use the full window when opening the URL in the link, rather than opening the link inside a frame.

If you use frames on your site and want to be sure viewers aren't stuck in your frames when going to a new site, you can use this same target to be sure the new URL is opened in the full window rather than in the frame. The following code shows an example of this:

```
<a href="http://www.pageresource.com" target= "_top">Another Site</a>
```

This technique doesn't even require JavaScript (you could do it with JavaScript if you really felt like it), but the next technique does.

Automatically Removing Frames

To remove frames automatically, you must find out if your Web page is inside a frameset when it loads. If your page doesn't use frames, then you can determine whether or not it is stuck in frames from another site pretty easily by using the length property.

If your page is inside a frameset, the value of the length property will be greater than 0 for the frames array in the main window. Thus, you can check for a value greater than 1 in the length property and reload your page in the full window if there are frames. Try this code:

```
<head>
<script type="text/javascript">
  function check_frames() {
    if (top.frames.length > 0) {
      top.location="http://yoursite.com";
    }
  }
</script>
</head>
<body onload="check_frames();">
<h1>Welcome to my Page</h1>
</body>
```

The number of frames in the main window is checked

The main window is reset to show in the entire window if frames are present

The function is called

The check_frames() function is called as the page loads. The function checks whether any frames are in the main window. If so, then the location of the top window is changed to the URL of your page, making your page open in the main window instead of within a frame. You would replace the URL shown in the code with your own URL.

Sending Viewers to Frames

When you use frames, a visitor might enter your site on one of your pages meant to be inside your frameset rather than in the full window. This can happen when a search engine is used, which may index the document and list it. The viewer sees it but may not be able to navigate through the rest of the site because the frames aren't there.

The following code checks whether the page is loaded without frames and redirects the viewer to the main page of the site if the frames have not been loaded:

```
<head>
<script type="text/javascript">
  function check_frames() {
    if (top.frames.length == 0) {
      top.location="http://www.yoursite.com";
    }
  }
</script>
</head>
<body onload="check_frames();">
<h1>Some Inner Page</h1>
I should be inside a frameset; the script that is run
 when this page loads will check to see if I am.
</body>
```

This time the check is to see whether the main window is lacking the necessary frames

Ask the Expert

Q: Why do I need to nest framesets to get rows inside columns or columns inside rows? Why can't I just use both the rows and cols attributes on one frameset instead?

A: You must nest framesets so that the browser knows where to place all of the rows and columns. If you just tell the browser you want three rows and two columns, it won't necessarily know where to place all of them. For instance, does one of the columns hold the three rows, or does one of the rows hold both of the columns? When the framesets are nested, the browser knows where you want things to appear.

Q: What is that "self" thing again?

A: Flip back to Chapter 10 for a short explanation of this concept. Basically, it's another way to write "window." Instead of window.location, you can write self.location. (You can do this with any of the window properties or methods.) It is just a way to help make the code clearer, because with frames, in some cases, it's easier to determine what the code means if you use "self" rather than "window."

Q: Why would I ever want to change more than one frame at a time?

A: Some Web sites have so much information that, for navigational purposes, changing more than one frame at a time can be helpful. Also, if you have more than two frames, sometimes it's helpful to be able to change all but one of the frames, leaving the lone frame the same for navigation.

Q: I don't like frames and don't plan to use them. Do I really need to read this stuff about them?

A: Although you may not use them yourself, learning about frames can help you if you need to code them for someone else, or debug someone's code, break out of frames from other Web sites, or even if you just want to understand what a Web site is doing while you're surfing.

The check_frames() function checks whether the length property is 0. If so, your frameset hasn't been loaded. In that case, the viewer is taken to your main page, where your frameset can be loaded. You would replace the URL in the code with the URL for the document containing your frameset (usually your main page).

Using Variables Across Frames

Another advantage of using frames is that you can use variables stored in one frame in another frame. You could store form information in one frame and use it again in another frame after that frame has loaded a new document, for instance.

The script you'll create takes information a viewer entered in a form and stores it in the other frame when the viewer clicks the button to send the information. The information can then be used on the page to which the viewer is sent.

First, you need a frameset. You can use a simple two-frame system for this, like the following code:

```html
<html>
<frameset cols="150,*">
<frame src="frame1.html" name="left_side"></frame>
<frame src="frame2.html" name="right_side"></frame>
</frameset>
<noframes>
Use the link below to go to the frameless version of the site.<br  />
<a href="noframes.html">Frameless Site</a>
</noframes>
</html>
```

Save this as frameset6.html. You should have a frame on the left (left_side) that spans 150 pixels and a frame on the right (right_side) that takes the remaining window space.

In the left frame, you want a document that contains some variables. This is the frame that won't be changed, so it can keep track of the variable values while the contents in the other frame are changed. For this script, you want to have a variable named thename and a variable named thefood to hold information the viewer will enter into a form in the other frame. Here is some code for frame1.html:

```html
<head>
<script type="text/javascript">
   var thename="";————————     Two variables are declared to hold values
   var thefood="";————————     that will be taken from the other frame
</script>
</head>
<body>
This is frame1.html; it holds the variable values.
 You can put any content you like here.
</body>
```

The variables are initially given a value of an empty string. The values will be changed when the viewer sends the information from the other frame.

The document shown initially in the right frame contains a form that allows the viewer to enter a name. This name is then stored in the thename variable in the left frame. The code for frame2.html is shown here:

```
<body>
I'd like to get your name. Please enter it below.
<br />
<form onsubmit="return store_info();">
<label for="yourname">Your Name:</label>
<input type="text" id="yourname" size="25" />
<br /><br />
<input type="submit" value="Continue" />
</form>
<script type="text/javascript">
  function store_info() {
    var yn = document.getElementById("yourname").value;
    top.left_side.thename= yn;
    self.location="frame3.html";
    return false;
  }
</script>
</body>
```

The variable in the left frame is given a value from the form in the current frame

The document in the frame is changed

The store_info() function is called when the viewer clicks the button to continue. Notice the use of top.left_side to access the left frame. Then the variable name is added (top.left_side .thename) to access the thename variable in the other frame. The value that has been entered into the text box in the form is then assigned to the thename variable in the left frame. After that, the document in the frame is changed to frame3.html, which will be able to get the information back from the left frame.

In the frame3.html document, the viewer's name is written in a greeting. It is also filled into a field in a new form to keep the viewer from writing it over again. (This just shows a use for the stored variable value; you don't really need the name in the form again in this case.) The form also asks for the viewer's favorite food, which the viewer must enter. The code for this page is shown here:

The value of the variable in the left frame is used to write a greeting

```
<body>
<script type="text/javascript">
  document.write("Hi, "+top.left_side.thename+"!<br />");
</script>
Now I'd like to get your favorite food. Please enter it below:
<br />
<form onsubmit="return more_info();">
<label for="yourname">Your Name:</label>
<input type="text" id="yourname" size="25" />
<br />
<label for="yourfood">Favorite Food:</label>
<input type="text" id="yourfood" size="25" />
<br /><br />
<input type="submit" value="Continue" />
</form>
<script type="text/javascript">
  var tn = document.getElementById("yourname");
  tn.value = top.left_side.thename;
```

The value of the first text box is set using information stored in a variable in the left frame

```
   function more_info() {
     var fd = document.getElementById("yourfood");
     top.left_side.thefood= fd.value;          The value from the Food field in the form
     self.location="frame4.html";              is stored in the variable in the left frame
     return false;
   }
</script>
</body>
                                    The document in the frame is changed
```

Here, the form field for the name is given the value from the left frame when the page loads. The name is also printed in a greeting on the page. After the viewer fills in a food and clicks the button, the value is stored in the thefood variable in the left frame and the document in the frame is changed to frame4.html.

In frame4.html, the values of both of the variables stored in the left frame will just be used to print a special message for the viewer on the page, as shown in the following code:

```
<body>
<script type="text/javascript">
  function print_info() {
    document.write("Thank you, "+top.left_side.thename+"!");
    document.write("<br /><br />");
    document.write("You must really like "+top.left_side.thefood+"!");
  }
print_info();          The function is called here        The information stored in variables in
</script>                                                 the left frame is printed for the viewer
</body>
```

The information is just printed out in a message to the viewer in the preceding code. The printed information marks the end of the line for this script because there are no more forms or variables to use. (You could add more forms and variables if you wanted to, though.) Figure 15-11 shows how frameset6.html looks initially, before anything is changed.

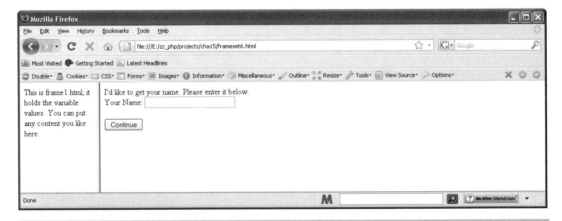

Figure 15-11 The initial appearance of the frameset

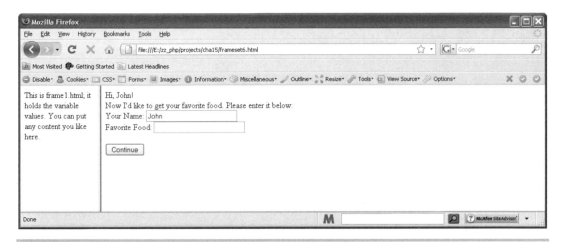

Figure 15-12   The result of entering John into the first form and clicking the button

Figure 15-12 shows how the page looks if the viewer enters John as the name in the first form and clicks the button.

Figure 15-13 shows how the page looks if the viewer enters sandpaper as the food in the second form and clicks the button. This doesn't sound very tasty.

Remember that even though frames are useful in various contexts, you shouldn't go overboard. Frames require minimal screen real estate and may not be suitable for devices with small screens. If you do want to use them, just remember to add the tag set <noframes> and </noframes> and to offer a frameless version for viewers with smaller screens or screen resolutions (or better yet give all viewers an option not to use frames).

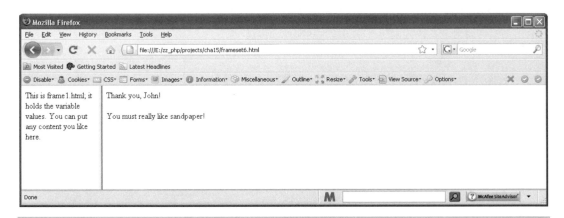

Figure 15-13   Eating sandpaper is not recommended!

Try This 15-2 Use Variables

```
pr15_2.html
pr15_2_frame1.html
pr15_2_frame2.html
pr15_2_frame3.html
```

In this project, you practice storing variable values in a static frame and using them in another frame. You'll create a form that first lets the viewer fill in some information and then uses that information when the document in the frame is changed.

Step by Step

1. Create a frameset with two frames, one on the left taking up 150 pixels and one on the right that uses the remainder of the window space. Name the left frame left_side and the right frame right_side. The filename for the first frame should be pr15_2_frame1.html, and the filename for the second frame should be pr15_2_frame2.html. Save the frameset file as pr15_2.html.

2. In pr15_2_frame1.html, create three variables and assign empty strings as their initial values. Use these variable names:

   thename
   thecolor
   thecar

3. In pr15_2_frame2.html, create a form that asks the viewer for a name, a favorite color, and a favorite car. When a button is clicked, the information should be stored in the variables in the left frame and the document should be changed to pr15_2_frame3.html.

4. In pr15_2_frame3.html, the following greeting should be printed on the page for the viewer, using the values stored in the variables in the left frame:

   Hello, *<viewer's name>*! I bet you would really love to have a *<favorite color> <favorite car>*! Too bad I can't give you one!

5. Open pr15_2.html in your browser and try it out.

Try This Summary

In this project, you used your knowledge of JavaScript and frames to create a frameset that uses variables across frames. The viewer is able to enter information in one frame and see the results in another frame.

Chapter 15 Self Test

1. _____ divide a window into two or more separate areas, each containing different content.

2. Frames differ from tables because the divisions in a frameset contain separate _____ documents.

3. The _____ tags are used to create a frameset.

4. A single frame is created with the _____ tags.

5. The _____ attribute divides a frameset into columns.

6. If you want to have a more complex frameset that includes both rows and columns, you can _____ one frameset within another.

7. What are two methods that can be used to access frames?

   A The frames array or a frame name

   B The frame array or a frame name

   C The frames array or a special code

   D There is only one way to do it

8. Using JavaScript, you can change the content of more than one frame at a time.

   A True

   B False

9. What is the value of the length property of the frames array?

   A The length of a specific frame based on its width or height

   B The number of framesets on a page

   C The number of frames in a window

   D The number of arrays in a frame

10. What does an asterisk (*) mean when used in the rows or cols attribute of a frameset?

   A There's no room for another frame.

   B The frame should take up any remaining space in the window.

   C The frame never ends.

   D The frame is shown in a pop-up window.

11. What is used to access the main window so that you can access another frame?

    A top

    B self

    C window

    D this

12. Which of these would correctly change the document in a frame named right_side to frame3.html from another frame?

    A self.location="frame3.html";

    B top.right_side.location="frame3.html";

    C self.location="frame3.htm";

    D top.location="frame03.html";

13. Using a target of _____ tells the browser to use the full window when opening a URL rather than opening the URL in a frame.

14. You can use variables stored in one frame in another frame.

    A True

    B False

15. The _____ attribute divides a frameset into rows.

Chapter 16

An Introduction to Advanced Techniques

Key Skills & Concepts

- Debugging Scripts

- JavaScript and Accessibility

- Using Cookies

- Working with Images

- JavaScript Security

- Introduction to AJAX

- JavaScript Libraries

This chapter introduces a number of advanced techniques that you may wish to pursue further once you have finished this book. You'll learn about debugging troublesome scripts (which is helpful when things go wrong), JavaScript and accessibility (which helps users access your information when JavaScript is disabled), using cookies (which allows you to store and retrieve small bits of information for the user), working with images (which allows you to preload and change images), JavaScript security (which helps you protect your users), AJAX (which enhances the user experience), and JavaScript libraries (which can be helpful to keep you from rewriting code). In addition to what is covered in this book, further information on these topics can be found in links provided at the end of the chapter.

Debugging Scripts

Even though JavaScript is fun, sometimes it can also be quite frustrating. One error in the code can cause an entire script to run incorrectly or not run at all. Debugging a script can be a time-consuming and arduous process, but there are a few techniques you can use that may help save some time while looking over the code. The first step in debugging a script is to figure out what type of error is likely to be causing the problem.

Types of Errors

The two main types of errors are syntax errors and logical errors. A syntax error occurs when the coder forgets to add a semicolon, forgets a quotation mark, misspells a word, and so on. A logical error occurs when the code is implemented incorrectly.

For example, a while loop could go on infinitely if the condition for executing the loop never becomes false. While it may be coded with the correct syntax, the results won't be what the programmer expected.

Find the Syntax Errors

A syntax error could be as simple as leaving out a necessary semicolon. For example, the following code is missing a semicolon between statements:

```
<input type="button" value="Click" onclick="analert() analert2()" />
```

In this case, the semicolon is very important because the two statements (function calls) are on the same line. To fix this, you just need to add the needed semicolon, as shown here:

```
<input type="button" value="Click" onclick="analert();analert2()" />
```

Syntax errors often cause the browser to display an error message so that you can debug the script. For example, you might see a message like the one in Figure 16-1.

These messages can help you figure out what's causing the problem. The line number shown in the error message often tells you where the error is. For instance, if the message says the error is on line 15, you would start at the 15th line from the top of your document and see what's there. The rest of the message might tell you what's missing or what has been placed improperly.

However, sometimes the line stated in the message is not the line where the actual problem is located. It could be on the preceding line, a few lines away, or even somewhere else entirely. You will need to do a little searching to figure out where the problem started. (The upcoming section "Scanning the Script" covers this in more detail.)

Use the Error Message If you get an error message, it can either make the problem easier to find or give you a bigger headache. Some messages are just better than others. First, go to the line given in the error message. If the text in the message makes any sense (such as "Expected ';'"), then look to see if the message is leading you in the right direction.

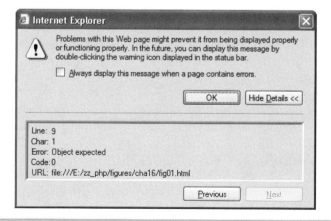

Figure 16-1 A JavaScript error message

For example, if it tells you it was expecting a semicolon, then look to see if a semicolon is missing on that line or on a line near it.

If you don't see a problem in the near vicinity, you'll have to search for it. If the line in question is calling a function or using a variable from another part of the script, take a look at where the function or variable was defined. Go to the function or variable to see if the name is the same as what you used to call it. If so, see if all the syntax is correct (such as the curly brackets, quotation marks, and parentheses). For instance, look at the following code:

```
<body>

<form>
<input type="button" value="Click" onclick="cool();"></input>
</form>

<script type="text/javascript">
  function cool()          ◄─────────────  Notice that the opening
    window.alert("Cool!");                  bracket is missing
  }
</script>

</body>
```

When you click the Click button, the code will produce an error message that says "Object Expected" (this will differ depending on the browser used) and points to the line in the code where the button is placed on the page (line 4, in this case). If you look at that line, nothing appears to be wrong. However, if you go further in the code (line 8) to the function cool() that is called on that line, you will notice that the opening curly bracket is missing. The missing bracket is the problem, and adding it will fix the code.

Scanning the Script   If the error message doesn't help you locate the problem, try scanning the script for errors on your own. This solution can be more tedious, but it may help you find the problem if the error message isn't helpful. Table 16-1 shows some items you should try to find.

Item	Appearance
Missing semicolon	;
Missing curly or square brackets	{ } [ ]
Missing parenthesis	( )
Missing single or double quote	' "
Misspelling	*coool* instead of *cool*, for example

Table 16-1   Items to Look for When Scanning a Script for Errors

The following code is riddled with errors; see how many of them you can find.

```
<script type="text/javascript">
var mycar="Mustang";
function send_alert()
 window.alery("You like+mynar+"!");
 window.alert("Cool";
}
var somearray= neq Array(2)
somearray[0]="Me";
somearray1]="Me2";
for var count=0;count<somearray.length;count+=1) {
  document.write(somearray[0+"and"+somearray[1]);
</script>
```

The code is missing a number of necessary items. Following is the list of items you should have found:

● Between lines 3 and 4: The function is missing its opening curly bracket.

● Line 4: The word *alert* is misspelled as *alery*; the double quote mark is missing after the word *like*; the mycar variable is misspelled as *mynar*.

● Line 5: The alert method is missing a closing parenthesis.

● Line 7: The word *new* is misspelled as *neq*.

● Line 9: The array index number is missing its opening square bracket.

● Line 10: The opening parenthesis for the loop is missing.

● Line 11: The index number for somearray[0] is missing its closing square bracket.

● Between lines 11 and 12: The closing curly bracket to end the loop is missing.

You probably won't make that many errors, but the example provides a nice way to see how to catch them while scanning a script. After you become more experienced with locating these small errors, you'll be able to find them quickly when you have a problem in a script.

Find the Logical Errors

Logical errors are often tougher to find because the syntax of the code is correct. You will be trying to find a mistake in how the code was implemented. For example, look at the following code (but do not run it!):

```
<script type="text/javascript">
x=1;
y=2;
while (x<=y) {          ←——————  Problem: x is never
  window.alert("Hi");              greater than y!
}
</script>
```

The code has no syntax errors. All the semicolons and quote marks are where they should be. The problem here is that the variable *x* is never greater than the variable *y*. This situation would cause an infinite loop, possibly crashing the browser.

You can fix the code by adding a line inside the loop to increase the value of *x*, decrease the value of *y*, or both increase *x* and decrease *y*. The important point is that something must be done to make the condition false. The following code shows a possible fix for this problem:

```
<script type="text/javascript">
x=1;
y=2;
while (x<=y) {
   window.alert("Hi");
   x++;
}
</script>
```

Increasing *x* within the loop will allow
x to become greater than *y* over time

The techniques described in the following sections can help you find logical errors.

Alert Technique for Problem Variables   One way to find the problem in the previous example is to go back and rerun it with an alert to test the value of one or both variables each time through the loop (assuming it didn't crash the browser). An alert can be an excellent way to find out what is happening, and it can give you an idea of how to fix the problem.

For example, the following code takes the previous example (before the fix) and adds an alert that shows the values of *x* and *y* each time the loop is run:

```
<script type="text/javascript">
x=1;
y=2;
while (x<=y) {
   window.alert("x is: "+x+" and y is "+y);
   window.alert("Hi");
}
</script>
```

The alert gives you the value of both
variables to help you find the problem

Provided the script doesn't crash the browser, you will be able to see what the problem is. Each time the alert shows up, it will say the same thing: "x is 1 and y is 2." Therefore, you'll know you need to make an adjustment in the loop to fix it.

This technique is quite helpful when you have a variable that goes through numerous reassignments and calculations in a script. By using a well-placed alert, you can find out where the problem starts. For example, take a look at this code:

```
<script type="text/javascript">
   var item1="10";
   var item2=20;
   var total=item1+item2;
   upcharge=5;
   total+=upcharge;
   window.alert("The total is $"+total);
</script>
```

This alert does not display
the expected result

Ask the Expert

Q: The error message I get says something I don't understand. What should I do?

A: Error messages don't always make sense and don't always point to the right line in the code. You may need to trace any variables or functions you have called on the line that the message gave you or check the lines near it for errors. Once you've seen an error message a few times, its meaning becomes easier to figure out.

Q: Something in my code crashed the browser when I tried to run it, and I can't try adding alerts to help find the problem because it crashes every time! What should I do?

A: If the script crashes the browser, look closely at your variables, loops, objects, and functions. As a last resort, write some new code from scratch.

Q: An error in my code crashed not only the browser, but also the computer! What do I do?

A: Restart the computer but *do not* run the code again. Check it very carefully to see if you can find the problem.

Q: Can any other strategies help me debug my scripts?

A: Some text editors use color coding to mark HTML tags, JavaScript code, or other types of code. Color coding helps you see the code more clearly and makes it easier to detect an error. (Try the Vim or NoteTab text editor.)

The variable total is assigned on the fourth line and then reassigned by adding another variable to it on line six. The alert with the total after all the calculations gives a funny result of 10205. Do you see the problem? If not, you could place an alert after the first assignment to see if the calculation of item1+item2 works correctly:

```
<script type="text/javascript">
  var item1="10";
  var item2=20;
  var total=item1+item2;
  window.alert(total);          The alert allows you to see whether the
  upcharge=5;                   first calculation is working correctly
  total+=upcharge;
  window.alert("The total is $"+total);
</script>
```

When you run the script again, the first alert gives a result of 1020. Now the problem becomes a bit clearer. For some reason, the script is adding item1 and item2 as strings and not as numbers, causing the two numbers to be combined instead of adding them mathematically.

Looking back at the assignment for item1, notice that it was assigned as a string accidentally. Removing the quotation marks around the 10 fixes the script and gives you the expected final result of 35.

The Hard Way: Trace Everything or Make Changes   If all the shortcuts fail, then the final option is to try to run through the entire script piece by piece again to see if you can detect an error. If not, see if you can find another way to code the task. For example, try using a different type of loop. Hopefully, a new strategy will help you clear up the problem and complete the script.

JavaScript and Accessibility

One topic you have seen many times in this book is how a script or HTML code for the script relates to accessibility. In some cases, such as Web sites of government agencies, a state or federal law (such as the Americans with Disabilities Act) might require that the Web site be accessible to viewers with disabilities. Even if it is not a legal issue for your Web site, it is still a usability issue: you will want as many visitors as possible to be able to use your site and access the information you have for them.

The general theme for accessibility is that content needs to be made accessible to all browsers and other software that may access a Web site. This means that your content should be readable not only by various Web browsers, but also by assistive technologies like screen reading software (for example, JAWS from Freedom Scientific), or Web browsing software on portable devices like cellular phones.

Separate Content from Presentation

The first step in making your Web site content accessible typically is to build the accessibility into your HTML/XHTML code, but you'll also need to tweak your JavaScript code. As you may already know, when coding your HTML you can use Cascading Style Sheets (CSS) for presentation of the content (how many columns are displayed, the font style, the width of various divisions, and so forth) while using HTML to simply mark up the content itself (such as dividing it into sections with <div></div> tags or inserting objects like images). This takes care of issues dealing with plain HTML content because the use of a style sheet rather than HTML markup for presentation ensures that you can offer different CSS styles for different types of browsers, or that those not using browsers with CSS capabilities will still get the structural markup of the plain text (for example, there won't be columns or font colors, etc.), which allows them to still view the content of the page.

With JavaScript, making the content accessible often means making sure that the content you use in your script is already displayed on the page or is available through a link or other means. One thing that may help is to move all JavaScript code (or as much as possible) into external JavaScript files while leaving as little JavaScript code in the HTML code as possible.

For example, you might have a Web page that uses the following code:

```
<body>
<script type="text/javascript">
function send_alert() {
  window.alert("Hi, there is a sale today! 20% off everything!");
  return false;
}
</script>
<a href="#" onclick="send_alert();">Hi</a>
</body>
```

This code will function just fine for those with JavaScript. However, having the script in the HTML code makes for a lot of extra scrolling through the file when you need to update the HTML code (especially if you have a long script). Thus, the first move you may want to make is to move the script to an external file, as shown in the following code samples. First the new HTML code:

```
<body>
<a href="#" onclick="send_alert();">Hi</a>
<script type="text/javascript" src="myscript.js"></script>
</body>
```

Next, the myscript.js JavaScript file:

```
function send_alert() {
  window.alert("Hi, there is a sale today! 20% off everything!");
  return false;
}
```

This makes the HTML file shorter and easier to read because the JavaScript functionality is placed in its own file and out of the way of the HTML code.

The next move you may want to make is to change the use of the onclick event handler in the HTML tag. Though valid, it becomes troublesome if you decide to use a function with a different name or decide to make it a normal link without JavaScript, because you will need to update each HTML file to accommodate the change cleanly (you can simply change the script to have the new function use this function name or just do nothing when called, but this could be confusing for those who may need to update the code later). To get this onclick event handler out of the HTML code, you could rewrite the JavaScript slightly and give the anchor tag an id (much like what you have done earlier in this book). First, the updated HTML code:

```
<body>
<a href="#" id="sale">Hi</a>
<script type="text/javascript" src="myscript.js"></script>
</body>
```

Next, the myscript.js JavaScript file:

```
function send_alert() {
  window.alert("Hi, there is a sale today! 20% off everything!");
  return false;
}
var s_alert = document.getElementById("sale");
s_alert.onclick = send_alert;
```

Now the HTML code has no JavaScript commands sprinkled in with it, just a call at the end to the external script. The anchor tag is given an id of sale, which can be used by the JavaScript code to capture the click event on that element. The JavaScript code now uses document.getElementById() to grab the anchor element and then assigns it a function to run when clicked.

The final note here is that the link simply does nothing for those without JavaScript. Since the content of the alert is something you need the visitor to know (so that they will know there is a sale), you will want to be sure that even those visitors without JavaScript can get this message. You can either display it elsewhere on the page, use a set of <noscript></noscript> tags to display the message inline, or code the link so that it leads to an HTML page with the message, as in the following code:

```
<body>
<a href="sale_alert.html" id="sale">Hi</a>
<script type="text/javascript" src="myscript.js"></script>
</body>
```

Then, you can place your message in the sale_alert.html file:

```
<body>
Hi, there is a sale today! 20% off everything!
</body>
```

This ensures that all users can access the message with or without JavaScript.

Enhancing Content

One technique for ensuring wide accessibility that has become widely used is one that provides the content for the viewer first, then uses JavaScript to make the experience more appealing for those that can run it. This is typically called "progressive enhancement" and allows all viewers to use the site while providing a richer experience for those with modern browsers.

This is what you did (on a small scale) with the script in the previous section. By offering the "sale" message when the link is clicked, you made it accessible to all viewers. However, those with JavaScript were able to view the alert without leaving the page and needing to go back, enhancing their experience somewhat.

This process can be simple, as in the previous example, or it can be as complex as adding a lot of JavaScript code to work with various browsers and/or adding server-side scripting to aid those without JavaScript. You can learn more about progressive enhancement at http://developer.yahoo.com/yui/articles/gbs/#progressive-enhancement. Yahoo! has a very detailed and organized system of progressive enhancement that allows the JavaScript code to work with as many browsers as possible, but also provides server-side scripts or HTML content for those without JavaScript.

TIP

For information on accessibility with JavaScript and forms, refer to Chapter 14, which discusses this topic and the use of forms with JavaScript.

Try This 16-1 Make This Code Accessible

```
pr16_1.html
sales.html
prjs16_1.js
```

To practice making JavaScript more accessible, you will take an HTML page and work with it to separate the JavaScript and HTML code as much as possible. You'll also use code that ensures that those without JavaScript can also obtain any additional content.

Step by Step

1. Create an HTML document named pr16_1.html and use the following HTML code for the body section:

```html
<body>
<script type="text/javascript">
function new_win() {
   window.open('sales.html','newwin''width=300,height=200');
}
</script>
<div>
<h1>Sales:</h1>
</div>
<div>
<a href="#" onclick="new_win(); return false;">Click for Sale
Information</a>
</div>
</body>
```

2. Create an HTML document named sales.html and use the following HTML code for the body section:

```html
<body>
<h1>Sales:</h1>
Clothes: 25% off<br />
Electronics: 10% off<br />
Appliances: 15% off (with coupon)
</body>
```

(continued)

3. Make the code accessible and usable for those without JavaScript by making any necessary adjustments and moving as much JavaScript code as possible to a JavaScript file named prjs16_1.js.

4. For an added bonus, try removing the new window from this entirely and placing the sales information in the division that simply has the text "Sales:" in it for those with JavaScript.

5. Save the HTML and JavaScript files and open the HTML file in your browser. The content should now be accessible in any browser with which you choose to open the page.

Try This Summary

In this project, you used your knowledge of accessibility to make a document and script more accessible for the viewer.

Using Cookies

A *cookie* is a small text file that is stored on the end user's computer. It can be referenced any time the viewer returns to your site, provided the cookie hasn't been deleted or expired. Of course, if the viewer doesn't accept cookies, then a cookie won't be able to be set or referenced later. Keep the following points in mind when using cookies:

- Cookies must be 4KB (4000 characters) each or less.

- A browser can accept up to only 20 cookies from a single domain.

- If a number of viewers don't accept cookies, this eliminates any advantages of your cookie(s) to those viewers.

Netscape invented cookies to help users browse your site more effectively. For instance, if you use a script on your main page that sends one or more alerts while the page is loading, you won't want that to happen every time the viewer goes to another page on your site and then returns to the home page. It would likely be so aggravating that you wouldn't have a visitor after it happened a few times.

The alerts pop up each time the page loads, because HTTP lacks state persistence. Cookies fill that gap because they allow the browser to "remember" that the viewer has seen the pop-up alert before and thus not display it on subsequent page visits. With cookies, you can fix problems like these for any viewers who have cookies enabled.

Setting a Cookie

Setting a basic cookie is as easy as giving a value to the cookie property of the document object. The only restriction is that you can't have spaces, commas, or semicolons inside the string.

For example, you can set a cookie that will store a name so that you can identify it if you set more than one cookie later. The following code sets a basic cookie:

```
function set_it() {
  document.cookie="name=tasty1";
}
```

CAUTION

Remember when setting a cookie not to use spaces, commas, or semicolons inside the string that sets the cookie data.

The preceding code sets a cookie with a value of name=tasty1 when the function is called. You can set any delimiter you want, though (or none at all, but setting delimiters allows you to store multiple values like a query string), so the following code would work as well:

```
function set_it() {
  document.cookie="name:tasty1";
}
```

The only problem is that you may need to use a space, comma, or semicolon in your cookie at some point. For instance, you might want to add in some text that tells what your favorite kind of cookie is. Adding the additional information isn't very difficult as long as the value does not need a space, as shown in the following code:

```
function set_it() {
  document.cookie="name=tasty1&fav=Sugar";
}
```

As you can see, the value of the cookie is being formatted in name=value pairs, and each pair is separated with an ampersand (&). Again, you can choose any type of separators you want. The following code is fine as well:

```
function set_it() {
  document.cookie="name:tasty1|fav:Sugar";
}
```

In this case, the names and values are separated with colons, while the pipe (|) symbol separates them into pairs. You can use anything that you are comfortable using.

The escape() Method

If you want to use spaces, commas, or semicolons in your cookie, you need a way to "escape" them so that they are translated into something a cookie accepts.

A cookie will accept character codes like a CGI program often does. They may look like %20, %41, or something similar. To turn spaces, commas, and semicolons into these codes, you must use the JavaScript escape() method. It is a method under the window object, so, as you have seen in previous chapters, you can just use escape() rather than window.escape().

The following code shows how you could use the escape() method to set a cookie with a space in it:

A string literal is created with information to be used in the cookie

```
function set_it() {
  var thetext="name=tasty1&fav=Chocolate Chip"
  var newtext=escape(thetext);
  document.cookie=newtext;
}
```

The string is escaped so it can be used in the cookie

The value of the escaped string is placed into a cookie

The thetext variable is set to include the string you want to use in the cookie. The newtext variable is set to hold the result of using the escape() method on thetext. The escaped text is then used as the string for the cookie, which will now have the code for the space character in it (when you want to use this data, you will need to unescape it).

Allowing User Input

By using the escape() method, you can prompt the viewer for the information, escape it, and then use it in the cookie. The following code shows how to do this to get the viewer's favorite type of cookie:

The viewer is able to enter information into this prompt

```
function set_it() {
  var thefav=window.prompt("Enter your favorite type of cookie","");
  var thetext="name=tasty1&fav="+thefav;
  var newtext=escape(thetext);
  document.cookie=newtext;
}
```

The value entered in the prompt is then added to a string to be used for a cookie

The string is escaped so it can be used in a cookie

The escaped string is placed into a cookie

Now the viewer can help decide the information that will be set in the cookie, and you can use the information your viewers enter on your site on their next visit.

Setting an Expiration Date

Adding an expiration date to a cookie will keep it from being deleted once the browser is closed, or it can be used to expire a cookie you no longer want to use. To set an expiration date, add a little more to your string for the cookie, as shown in the following code:

```
function set_it() {
  var thetext="quote=I have a quote";
  var expdate=";expires=Mon, 30 Mar 2009 13:00:00 UTC";
  var newtext=escape(thetext);
  newtext+=expdate;
  document.cookie=newtext;
}
```

An expiration date is given

The expiration date is added to the text

The cookie is given the value of the combined text and expiration date

Basically, you are adding on another name/value pair that adds an expiration date (notice the name/value pairs are separated with a semicolon). It needs to be in this form:

```
expires=date (in UTC format)
```

In the code, an expiration date for the cookie was added by adding the date in UTC format. Then the result is added to the variable that will be used to set the string for the cookie.

If you want a cookie to last a long time, you can set the date far into the future. If you want to expire a cookie you have decided not to use anymore, set a date in the past and the cookie will expire.

Reading a Cookie

Reading cookies is fairly simple if you have only a single cookie set and want to read it. To read the cookie, you just need to get the value of the document.cookie property from the browser:

```
function read_it() {
 var mycookie=document.cookie;
}
```

However, the preceding code will only give you a long and possibly messy string for the value of the mycookie variable. It might look like this:

```
name=tasty1&fav=Chocolate%20Chip
```

The %20 got in the code when the input for the cookie was escaped using the escape() method. To fix that, use the unescape() method to get the data in a more readable format.

Thus, the following code would provide the string you need:

```
function read_it() {
 var mycookie=document.cookie;
 var fixed_cookie= unescape(mycookie);
}
```

Next, you must find a way to extract the information you need from the cookie. Assuming the cookie contained the string just used as an example (name=tasty1&fav=Chocolate%20Chip), the string would now look like this:

```
name=tasty1&fav=Chocolate Chip
```

Notice that the text is divided in two different ways. The ampersand divides the string into name/value pairs, while the equal signs divide the name/value pairs into their names and values.

Assuming the string name=tasty1&fav=Chocolate Chip is what is now in the fixed_cookie variable from the code, you could use that variable to create a new array by splitting the string on the ampersand character:

```
function read_it() {
 var mycookie=document.cookie;          The value of the cookie
 var fixed_cookie= unescape(mycookie);  property is read
 var thepairs= fixed_cookie.split("&");
}
```

The value of the cookie property is read

The value is unescaped so the string will have readable characters

The cookie string is split into an array on the &

The preceding code splits the string into two array values:

```
thepairs[0] with a value of name=tasty1
thepairs[1] with a value of fav=Chocolate Chip
```

You split each of these into a new array that will have a name and a value. Therefore, you need some code like this:

```
function read_it() {
  var mycookie=document.cookie;
  var fixed_cookie= unescape(mycookie);
  var thepairs= fixed_cookie.split("&");
  var pair1=thepairs[0];          The values of the array elements
  var pair2=thepairs[1];          are assigned to variables
  var namevalue1=pair1.split("=");     The new variables are
  var namevalue2=pair2.split("=");     split on the equal sign
}
```

Now you have all the information you need using the namevalue1[] and namevalue2[] arrays:

```
namevalue1[0] with a value of name
namevalue1[1] with a value of  tasty1
namevalue2[0] with a value of fav
namevalue2[1] with a value of  Chocolate Chip
```

You can use them in any way you like, such as placing them in alerts:

```
function read_it() {
  var mycookie=document.cookie;
  var fixed_cookie= unescape(mycookie);
  var thepairs= fixed_cookie.split("&");
  var pair1=thepairs[0];
  var pair2=thepairs[1];
  var namevalue1=pair1.split("=");            The values obtained from
  var namevalue2=pair2.split("=");            the cookies are used
  window.alert("The cookie's "+namevalue1[0]+" is "+namevalue1[1]);
  window.alert("My favorite type of cookie is "+namevalue2[1]);
}
```

You might want to be sure document.cookie exists before you try to run all the code in the function. Any cookie you set to expire later can be read, but those without the cookie may get an error. By making the check, you can ensure the existence of the cookie or send the viewer to the function that sets the cookie. To do that, add an if/else block around the code in the function, as shown here:

```
function read_it() {
  if (document.cookie) {
    var mycookie=document.cookie;
```

```
var fixed_cookie= unescape(mycookie);
var thepairs= fixed_cookie.split("&");
var pair1=thepairs[0];
var pair2=thepairs[1];
var namevalue1=pair1.split("=");
var namevalue2=pair2.split("=");
window.alert("The cookie's "+namevalue1[0]+" is "+namevalue1[1]);
window.alert("My "+namevalue2[0]+"orite type of cookie is
"+namevalue2[1]);
 }
 else {
  set_it();
 }
}
```

The preceding code assumes that the set_it() function exists and will set the cookie so it can be used. It also assumes that this cookie is the only cookie set from this domain and that it is formatted a particular way. If you plan to use multiple cookies, you will need to do additional testing to ensure you grab the cookie you need.

Try This 16-2   Remember a Name

`pr16_2.html`
`prjs16_2.js`

In this project, you use a cookie to remember a name when a visitor returns to the page.

Step by Step

1. Create a new HTML document that uses an external JavaScript file named prjs16_2.js. Save the HTML file as pr16_2.html.

2. Create an external JavaScript file and save it as prjs16_2.js. Use it for the remaining steps.

3. Create a function named set_it() that will set a cookie. Set the expiration to a future date. Allow the viewer to enter a name in a prompt and then use the viewer's entry in the cookie.

4. Create a function named read_it() that will check whether the cookie exists and, if so, read the cookie and send an alert to the viewer with the name in it, in the following format (replace *<name>* with the name read from the cookie):

   ```
   Welcome, <name>!
   ```

5. If the cookie exists, call the read_it() function. If the cookie doesn't exist, call the set_it() function.

6. Save the JavaScript file and open the HTML file in your browser. Enter your name. Close your browser and open the page again. This time, you should get an alert with your name rather than the prompt.

(continued)

Try This Summary

In this project, you used your knowledge of setting and reading cookies with JavaScript. You created a Web page that remembers the viewer's name when the viewer returns to the Web page.

Working with Images

JavaScript uses the image object to preload images, create rollover effects, and even create slide shows or animations. The image object's properties will help when you want to create such scripts. Table 16-2 lists and describes the image object's properties.

The src property is used the most in this chapter because it allows the source of an image to be changed to create a rollover effect.

Preloading

When you code your Web pages, sometimes you may want to preload your images. *Preloading* an image allows it to be in the browser's cache before it is called in the HTML or JavaScript code in the browser. This way, the image will show up much more quickly when it is called and the viewer will not have to wait for an image to load.

One technique for preloading is to load on your main page an image that will be used on other pages in your site. The image will be in the browser's cache on each of the other pages and will load instantly. For example, you may want your Web site's logo to appear on every page of the site. When it is loaded on the first page, the other pages will load it instantly.

Property	Purpose
name	Holds the value of the image's name from the name attribute
src	Holds the value of the URL from the src attribute
width	Holds the value of the width from the width attribute
height	Holds the value of the height from the height attribute
border	Holds the numeric value of the border property from the border attribute
hspace	Holds the numeric value of the hspace property from the hspace attribute
vspace	Holds the numeric value of the vspace property from the vspace attribute
lowsrc	Holds the value of the URL from the lowsrc attribute
complete	Indicates whether an image has finished loading

Table 16-2   Properties of the Image Object

Of course, doing this with HTML makes sense because you are likely to want the logo to appear on the main page as well as all the other pages. Therefore, when you code the img element, the image is loaded into the cache.

In some cases, you may want to preload images that will appear later on the same page. This practice is common when using rollovers or other scripts that call images after the page has finished loading. In such a case, you don't want the viewer to be stuck waiting on a new image to load, because it keeps the script from working as well as it should.

For instance, if you have set a new image to appear when the viewer moves the mouse over an image, you want the new image to show up immediately. If the viewer has to wait a few seconds for the image to load, it can ruin the intended effect.

With JavaScript, you can create a new instance of the image object and then give its src property the URL of the image you want to preload, as shown in the following code:

```
if (document.images) {
  var pic1= new Image(120,35);
  pic1.src="image1.gif";
  var pic2= new Image();
  pic2.src="image2.gif";
}
```

Recall a similar bit of code in Chapter 9 when the images array was discussed. The first instance (pic1) of the image object defines a width and height for the image. The second (pic2) does not, but it will get those values from the actual width and height of the image.

You don't have to use both methods. You can choose the method you prefer and use it for all of the images you want to preload.

The HTML page with the img elements could look something like this:

```
<body>
<script type="text/javascript" src="preload.js"></script>
<h1>Some Images</h1>
<img src="image1.gif" width="120" height="35" />
<br /><br />
<img src="image2.gif" width="50" height="75" />
</body>
```

The JavaScript code could look like this:

```
if (document.images) {
 var pic1= new Image(120,35);
 pic1.src="image1.gif";
 var pic2= new Image();
 pic2.src="image2.gif";
}
```

Of course, the preloading really isn't serving a purpose in this case. To give the technique of preloading a purpose, you want a script that shows a new image when an event occurs, such as in a rollover script.

Rollovers

Image *rollovers* (also known as hover buttons, image flips, and other similar names) can add some zest to your navigational images. When the viewer moves the mouse over a linked image, the image changes. This change could be anything from a simple color change to a completely different image, which can create more viewer interest in the navigational system.

The effect described in the last two sentences is a simple rollover, but you can also change an image from a mouseover event on another linked image or text link, or even change more than one image at a time.

A Simple Rollover

A simple rollover just changes one image to another when the mouse moves over the initial image. First, you create two images and make the second image different in some way. For example, examine the two images shown here:

Shoe Page

Shoe Page

NOTE

For each rollover effect you create, you need two separate images.

Once you have two images, you can begin working on the code for the image rollover. First, you preload the images so that your rollover won't need to download the second image from the server when the viewer moves the mouse over the first image. Technically, you need to preload only the second image, as the first image will be loaded as the page loads.

```
if (document.images) {
  //Preload image that will show on the mouseover event
  var pic1_new= new Image();
  pic1_new.src="image1_c.gif";
}
```

Notice that the names of the image object begins with pic1, has an underscore (_) character, and uses the word new. By using this naming convention for the image object, you can add more images to the script later with a consistent system that may help you keep track of the images (but is not necessary).

Now, you can code your initial image into your HTML document, giving it an id:

```
<body>
<h1>The image below changes! Move your mouse over it!</h1>
<a href="somepage.html">
<img src="image1.gif" id="pic1" border="0" /></a>
</body>
```

The anchor element is used around the image element so that the image can be used as a navigational link; it is not necessary (in modern browsers) for the image rollover, as you can use document.getElementById() to access the image elements directly.

In your JavaScript code, you will simply need to get the image element by its id and assign it a new value for the src property on a mouseover event. Then you will simply change it back on a mouseout event. The following is the JavaScript code:

```
var im1 = document.getElementById("pic1");
im1.onmouseover = function() { im1.src = pic1_new.src; };
im1.onmouseout = function() { im1.src = "image1.gif" };
```

Notice that the src property is changed to pic1_new.src on the mouseover event. This can be done because a new image object was created for the second image and the src property was set for it at that time (which also preloaded it). You could go back to the preloading script to do the same for image1.gif if you desired, which would allow you to use the property value instead of hard-coding the image URL back into the script. This can be useful if you have numerous rollover images on the page.

Now, go back and use these three files to create the effect. First, the HTML file:

```
<body>
<script type="text/javascript" src="preload.js"></script>
<h1>The image below changes! Move your mouse over it!</h1>
<a href="somepage.html"><img src="image1.gif" id="pic1" border="0" /></a>
<script type="text/javascript" src="change.js"></script>
</body>
```

Notice that the preload.js script is called first so that the second image will be preloaded as soon as possible. The change.js script is placed after the image so that the necessary image element will have been loaded before the script tries to get it by its id. Next, the preload.js file:

```
if (document.images) {
  //Preload image that will show on the mouseover event
  var pic1_new= new Image();
  pic1_new.src="image1_c.gif";
}
```

Finally, the change.js file:

```
var im1 = document.getElementById("pic1");
im1.onmouseover = function() { im1.src = pic1_new.src; };
im1.onmouseout = function() { im1.src = "image1.gif" };
```

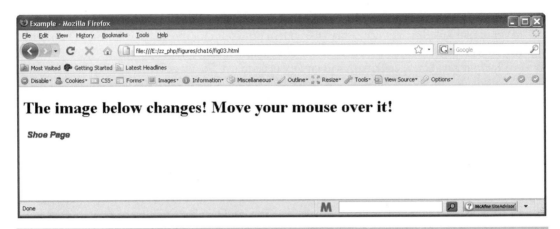

Figure 16-2 The initial image

The closest you can get to seeing the results here is to see a before and after set of images. Figure 16-2 shows the initial image, while Figure 16-3 shows the result when the mouse is moved over the image.

Changing a Different Image

You may decide you want to change a different image from the one the mouse is moved over. To do this, the setup is the same as in the preceding section except that you need to change which element is changed when the mouse moves over the initial image.

You could change the code you have been using to leave the first image static and to change a different image. Thus, you will want to preload the second image on the image that will change. Here is the code for each file, starting with the HTML code:

```
<body>
<script type="text/javascript" src="preload.js"></script>
<h1> The first image below changes the second image! Move your mouse over
it!</h1>
<a href="somepage.html"><img src="image1.gif" id="pic1" border="0" /></a>
<br /><br />
<img src="image2.gif" id="pic2" />
<script type="text/javascript" src="change.js"></script>
</body>
```

This simply adds the new image (image2.gif) after a couple of line breaks. Next, the preload.js file:

```
if (document.images) {
  //Preload image that will show on the mouseover event
  var pic2_new= new Image();
  pic2_new.src="image2_c.gif";
}
```

This changes everything from pic1 and image1 (which will no longer be changed) to pic2 and image2 (which will now be the image that will be changed).

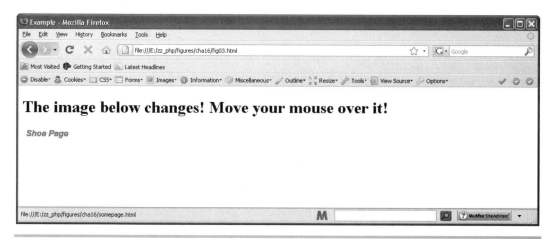

Figure 16-3   The new image appears when the mouseover event occurs

Finally, the change.js file:

```
var im1 = document.getElementById("pic1");
var im2 = document.getElementById("pic2");
im1.onmouseover = function() { im2.src = pic2_new.src; };
im1.onmouseout = function() { im2.src = "image2.gif" };
```

Here, the im2 variable is added to grab the second image by its id (pic2). It is then changed when the viewer moves the mouse over the first image (im1).

Now the mouse can move over the first image and change the second image. Figures 16-4 and 16-5 show another set of before and after screens.

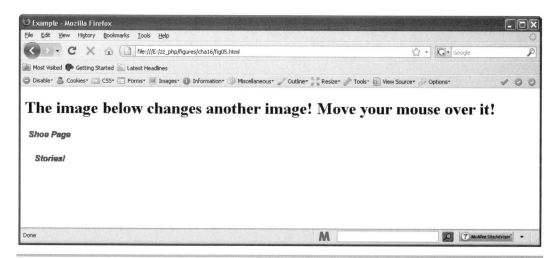

Figure 16-4   The images shown before the mouseover event

Figure 16-5 The images shown after the mouseover event

Changing Multiple Images

To change more than one image at a time, you need to have a set of two images for each image you want to change. For simplicity, the example you will use only contains two pairs of images. The code created will cause a mouseover event on the first image to change both itself and the second image on the page at the same time. The images used for this script are image1.gif, image1_c.gif, image2.gif, and image2_c.gif.

The HTML code will be the same as in the previous example (other than the heading):

```
<body>
<script type="text/javascript" src="preload.js"></script>
<h1>The image below changes itself and another image!</h1>
<a href="somepage.html"><img src="image1.gif" id="pic1" border="0" /></a>
<br /><br />
<img src="image2.gif" id="pic2" />
<script type="text/javascript" src="change.js"></script>
</body>
```

Next, the code for preload.js:

```
if (document.images) {

    var pic1_start = new Image();
    pic1_start.src = "image1.gif";
    var pic1_new= new Image();
    pic1_new.src="image1_c.gif";
```

```
var pic2_start = new Image();
pic2_start.src = "image2.gif";
var pic2_new= new Image();
pic2_new.src="image2_c.gif";

}
```

The major difference is that you are now preloading both images in both image sets (which will help with organization as the script grows and allows you to use the src property later for the starting images). Finally, the changes to the change.js file:

```
var im1 = document.getElementById("pic1");
var im2 = document.getElementById("pic2");
im1.onmouseover = function() {
  im1.src = pic1_new.src;
  im2.src = pic2_new.src;
};
im1.onmouseout = function() {
  im1.src = pic1_start.src;
  im2.src = pic2_start.src;
};
```

This adds the second set of images and changes both of them on the mouseover event to their respective second images, then back on the mouseout event. Notice that you are able to use the pic1_start.src and pic2_start.src properties since the starting images were also assigned as image objects in the preload.js script.

When the code is run, you will see something like the before and after screens shown in Figures 16-6 and 16-7.

Figure 16-6   The images before the mouseover event

Figure 16-7 The images after the mouseover event

JavaScript Security

You may have noticed that when you try to use the window.close() method on the main browser window, a confirmation box appears asking if you really want to allow the window to be closed. This situation is one of the issues of JavaScript security. The browser does not want a site to close a window that the viewer opened without permission from the viewer. If that were allowed, the programmer would have some control of the viewer's computer, which could be a problem.

Another aspect of security is the mistaken belief that you can "protect" Web pages with passwords or keep the source code of the page from being viewed by a user.

Yet another aspect of security is protecting against cross-site scripting, the use of JavaScript to grab information from a server-side application that didn't properly filter user input.

Security and Signed Scripts

To get viewer permission to close the main browser window or to use certain properties or methods in JavaScript, you must use signed scripts. Signed scripts will open up some additional JavaScript features, but you must do some additional work.

Basically, you digitally sign the script using a special tool. The viewer then gets a message when entering the page that asks whether to allow the signed script, with some information about the signed script. If the viewer accepts, then you will be able to use the additional features. If not, you'll need to have alternative code ready to avoid JavaScript errors.

For further information about this subject, go to the Web site www.mozilla.org/projects/security/components/signed-scripts.html.

Page Protection

Many scripts attempt to keep viewers out in some way, such as by using password protection or by using a "no-right-click" script to keep the source code of the page from being viewed.

However, these security strategies are largely ineffective because these "password" and "no-right-click" scripts can often be bypassed by turning off JavaScript or by doing a little extra work.

Passwords

Some password systems are better than others, but none really seems to offer true Web page security. If you don't want someone to view a page, much better methods exist than using a JavaScript system, such as using server-side languages or using certain setups on your Web server.

If you are on a free Web-hosting service, the better methods may or may not be available. However, keep in mind that a JavaScript password system is not foolproof and that you should not protect anything important with such a system.

Hiding Web Page Source Code

Many people would love to hide the source code of a Web page. However, JavaScript isn't going to do the trick. A number of scripts try various means of disabling the right-click. Basically, these strategies don't work because they can be bypassed in a couple of ways:

- If the right-click is disabled, you can always try selecting View | View Source.

- If the preceding method does not work, you can always turn off JavaScript or look in your cache directory on your computer. The browser must have the code to display the page, so a copy of it goes into the browser's cache.

In the long run, these scripts just make viewing the source code more difficult (and they can be annoying). For more information about this topic, go to http://webhome.idirect.com/~bowers/copy/copy1.htm.

Cross-Site Scripting

Cross-site scripting (often shortened to XSS) uses JavaScript code (or other types of code) in a malicious way to obtain information from users of various Web sites with vulnerable applications. With this information, a person can use someone else's cookie or session information and access the Web site as though they were the user from which they obtained the information. This, of course, can lead to big trouble, especially if that user is an administrator in that application or if the application deals with money (such as a banking or shopping application).

While JavaScript is one of the ways used to perform such an attack, the vulnerable application is usually one that is server-side and displays user input on the page. If the user input is not sanitized (validated) in the server-side application, then any number of possible malicious scripts could be entered instead of the expected input.

For example, you might have a form that uses a server-side script to allow people to send comments. The script displays the comment the user submitted back to the user as a confirmation. If the input is not sanitized, it is possible to enter something like this into the comments field: <script>alert("You've been had!");</script>. If someone submits this and sees an alert on the response page, the person will know there is a potential vulnerability and could simply direct a subsequent user to a malicious URL where the user's cookie or session information can be taken. Figure 16-8 shows how a vulnerable application would display such an alert (this one also included some comment text to help disguise the intent of the person submitting the form).

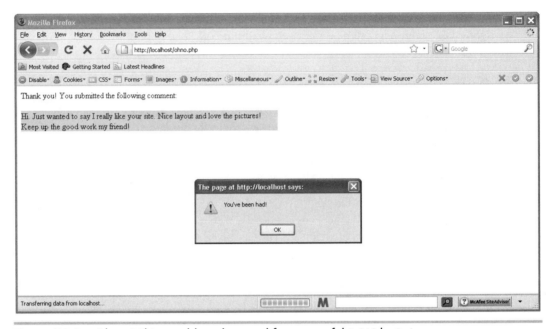

Figure 16-8 Oh no! This would not be good for users of this Web site!

Cross-site scripting has evolved over the years. In the beginning, it was that a bad Web site could load a good Web site in a frame (or in a pop-up browser window) and then access the text boxes, cookies, and other data (user id and password) using JavaScript—thus the name "cross site." It should be noted that modern browsers, within the past four or five years, don't allow this type of cross-site scripting. One domain cannot access the contents of a different domain. Most of the modern cross-site scripting attacks are injection attacks like the example here (though often much more complex).

This introduction just scratches the surface of this type of security issue. The main thing to remember is that when you are using server-side applications, you must sanitize any user input to be sure that you receive the type of input you expect. For more information on this topic, go to www.owasp.org/index.php/Cross_site_scripting.

AJAX

AJAX stands for Asynchronous JavaScript and XML, which is a way JavaScript can obtain information from an XML file without the need to reload a page. For example, a synchronous request to the Web server requires that the current page be reloaded to use the new information. An asynchronous request allows the information to be obtained and used without the need to wait for the entire page to reload.

This type of scripting is useful in progressive enhancement, as it allows applications to enhance the user experience for those with JavaScript enabled in modern browsers. Instead of waiting for a page to load again, the information can be obtained and used on-the-fly.

In JavaScript, an XMLHttpRequest object is created, which can then be used to make HTTP requests to the server in the background and allow the user to continue using the application without interruption.

In-depth coverage of this topic is beyond the scope of a beginner's guide; however, more information on AJAX and how to use it in your applications can be found at the following Web sites:

- https://developer.mozilla.org/en/AJAX

- www.w3schools.com/Ajax/Default.Asp

JavaScript Libraries

There are a number of JavaScript libraries available that can help you write higher-level scripts with less effort than it would take to write all of the code from scratch. Some of these are listed here in case you would like to look into them further:

- **jQuery** http://jquery.com

- **Prototype** www.prototypejs.org

- **Yahoo! YUI** http://developer.yahoo.com/yui

Ask the Expert

Q: **Where can I find free cut-and-paste JavaScript code on the Web?**

A: http://javascript.internet.com
http://webdeveloper.earthweb.com/webjs
www.javascriptcity.com

Q: **Where can I learn more about JavaScript?**

A: https://developer.mozilla.org/en/JavaScript
www.javascriptkit.com
www.quirksmode.org/js/contents.html
www.pageresource.com/jscript

Q: **Where can I learn more about Cascading Style Sheets?**

A: www.w3schools.com/Css/default.asp
www.csszengarden.com

Q: **Where can I learn more about DHTML?**

A: http://webreference.com/dhtml
www.dynamicdrive.com

Chapter 16 Self Test

1. Which of the following lines does not create a JavaScript syntax error?

   A var myvar="cool;

   B function 1cool()

   C document.write("Is there an error?");

   D window.alert "what is this?");

2. Which of the following lines does not create a JavaScript syntax error?

   A var else=3;

   B window.alert("Cool!");

   C document.write("Cool!');

   D function while()

3. _____ errors are often tougher to find because the syntax of the code is correct.

4. _____-_____ scripting might allow someone to obtain information from a user of an application.

5. _____ enhancement provides content for all viewers, but enhances it for those with JavaScript in modern browsers.

6. It's a good idea to remove as much JavaScript code from the HTML file as possible and move it to an external file.

   A True

   B False

7. _____ stands for Asynchronous JavaScript and XML.

8. JavaScript _____ may make some advanced coding tasks easier by making the code easier to write.

9. JavaScript should be used for password protection of important information.

   A True

   B False

10. A _____ is a small text file that is stored on the end user's computer.

11. Which property is used to set and read a cookie?

    A The cookie property of the window object

    B The cookie property of the document object

C The cook property of the document object

D The set_or_read_cookie property of the document object

12. Which property of the image object sets the source of an instance of the image object?

A width

B height

C img_width

D src

13. In which type of script would you want to preload images on a page?

A Status bar text change

B Rollover effect

C Animating text

D Disabling a right-click

14. Is it effective to try to hide the source code of a page using JavaScript?

A Of course!

B Why not?

C No, but it can make reading it more difficult or annoying.

D Works every time!

15. Is JavaScript fun?

A Yes!

B No!

C I was forced to learn this by my boss, so it can never be fun!

D What is your definition of fun?

Appendix

Answers to Self Tests

Chapter 1: Introduction to JavaScript

1. C. HTML

2. A. A Web browser

3. C. JavaScript

4. B. False

5. D. lenient

6. A. True

7. C. LiveScript

8. A. object based

9. B. client

10. B. It can validate the information before it is sent to the server.

11. C. scripting

12. A. True

13. D. The Web browser

14. D. It is added to an HTML document.

15. A. <script> and </script> HTML tags

Chapter 2: Placing JavaScript in an HTML File

1. D. All of the above

2. B. To be sure the browser does not interpret your JavaScript as another scripting language and to ensure the Web page validates in XHTML

3. A. Yes

4. The noscript tag provides **content** for those without **JavaScript**.

5. A. .js

6. B. <script type= "text/javascript" src="yourfile.js"></script>

7. In older versions of HTML, the script tag is not case sensitive. However, with XHTML, the script tag must be in **lowercase**.

8. D. semicolon

9. A. document.write()

10. C. When the script is very long or needs to be placed in more than one HTML document

11. JavaScript comments can be very useful for the purpose of **documenting** or **debugging** your code.

12. C. //

13. A. /*

14. D. */

15. A. close

Chapter 3: Using Variables

1. A variable **represents** or **holds** a value.

2. A. They can save you time in writing and updating your scripts, and they can make the purpose of your code clearer.

3. To declare a variable, you use the **var** keyword.

4. D. =

5. C. var pagenumber=240;

6. B. False

7. A variable name must begin with a **letter** or an **underscore** character.

8. A. True

9. B. var my_house;

10. In JavaScript, the variable values, or **types**, can include numbers, strings, Booleans, and nulls.

11. To denote an exponent in JavaScript, you use a letter **e** right after the base number and before the exponent.

12. C. var mytext= "Here is some text!';

13. D. document.write("John said, \"Hi!\"");

14. **Special** characters enable you to add things to your strings that could not be added otherwise.

15. B. document.write("I like to " +myhobby+ " every weekend");

Chapter 4: Using Functions

1. In general, a function is a little **script** within a larger **script** that is used to perform a single **task** or a series of **tasks**.

2. B. They provide a way to organize the various parts of the script into the different tasks that must be accomplished, and they can be reused.

3. On the first line of a function, you **declare** it as a function, **name** it, and indicate whether it accepts any **parameters**.

4. C. function

5. A. Curly brackets – { }

6. A. True

7. B. False

8. C. function get_text()

9. **Parameters** are used to allow a function to import one or more values from somewhere outside the function.

10. B. parentheses – ()

11. D. Comma

12. D. window.alert("This is text");

13. B. some_alert("some","words");

14. A. var shopping=get_something();

15. A **local** variable can be used only within the function in which it is declared.

Chapter 5: JavaScript Operators

1. A(n) **operator** is a symbol or word in JavaScript that performs some sort of calculation, comparison, or assignment on one or more values.

2. **Mathematical** operators are most often used to perform mathematical calculations on two values.

3. The **addition** operator adds two values.

4. When the increment operator is placed **before** the operand, it increases the value of the operand by 1, and then the rest of the statement is executed.

5. D. $\$\#$

6. A. Assigns a new value to a variable

7. The add-and-assign (+=) operator adds the value on the **right** side of the operator to the variable on the **left** side and then assigns to the variable that new value.

8. C. Compares two values or statements, and returns a value of true or false

9. A. 4!=3

10. D. 4<=3

11. The **logical** operators allow you to compare two conditional statements to see if one or both of the statements is true and to proceed accordingly.

12. B. !(17>=20)

13. B. (4>=4)&&(5<=2)

14. **Bitwise** operators are logical operators that work at the bit level.

15. In JavaScript, the operators have a certain order of **precedence**.

Chapter 6: Conditional Statements and Loops

1. A conditional statement is a statement that you can use to execute a bit of code based on a **condition**, or do something else if that **condition** is not met.

2. You can think of a conditional statement as being a little like **cause** and **effect**.

3. A. True

4. B. if (*y*<7)

5. C. Curly brackets

6. The **switch** statement allows you to take a single variable value and execute a different line of code based on the value of the variable.

7. A **loop** is a block of code that allows you to repeat a section of code a certain number of times.

8. B. False

9. A. for (*x*=1;*x*<6;*x*+=1)

10. A **while** loop looks at a comparison and repeats until the comparison is no longer true.

11. B. while (*x*=7)

12. A. True

13. B. False

14. B. False

15. D. As many times as you like

Chapter 7: Event Handlers

1. A. True

2. Event handlers are useful because they enable you to gain **access** to the **events** that may occur on the page.

3. To use an event handler, you need to know the **keyword** for the event handler and where to place the event handler in the HTML code.

4. C. <input type="button" onclick="window.alert('Hey there!');">

5. The **load** event occurs when a Web page has finished loading.

6. D. The viewer moves the mouse cursor over an element on the page.

7. B. False

8. The **unload** event occurs when the viewer leaves the current Web page.

9. The blur event is the opposite of the **focus** event.

10. A. <input type="text" onfocus="major_alert();">

11. The **change** event occurs when a viewer changes something within a form element.

12. The submit event occurs when the viewer **submits** a **form** on a Web page.

13. A. True

14. C. onmousedown

15. The **addEventListener** method and the **attachEvent** method are two new ways to register events.

Chapter 8: Objects

1. An object is a way of modeling something **real**, even though the object is a(n) **abstract** entity.

2. When you think of an object, you'll probably want to visualize something **general**.

3. Objects are useful because they give you another way to **organize** things within a script.

4. B. dot operator

5. The rules for naming objects are similar to those for naming **variables** and **functions**.

6. You can create JavaScript objects using either a **constructor** function or an object **initializer**.

7. A. True

8. B. False

9. C. Assuming the myhouse object exists, it assigns the value of the kitchen property of the myhouse object to the variable *x*.

10. D. this.cost=get_cost;

11. B. window.alert("You are using "+navigator.appName);

12. C. Assuming the myhouse object exists, the kitchen property is assigned a new string value.

13. In JavaScript, there are many **predefined** objects you can use to gain access to certain properties and methods you may need.

14. The **navigator** object gives you access to the various properties of the viewer's browser.

15. C. appType

Chapter 9: The Document Object

1. The **document** object is an object that is created by the browser for each new HTML page that is viewed.

2. The **referrer** property of the document object returns the URL of the document that referred the viewer to the current document.

3. A. True

4. D. getElementById()

5. B. False (it is added as the last child node rather than the first)

6. C. www.pageresource.com

7. The **anchors** property of the document object is an array that contains all of the anchor (<a>) tags on the page.

8. The **innerHTML** DOM node property allows you to change the HTML content of an element node.

9. The **lastModified** property holds the value of the date and time the current document was last modified.

10. A. True

11. A. True

12. C. URL

13. C. It adds a JavaScript newline character at the end of the line.

14. A. When a form is given a name, the name of the form becomes the property name.

15. B. document.write() and document.writeln() statements

Chapter 10: Window Object

1. A **window** object is created for each window that appears on the screen.

2. A. True

3. The **length** property holds the value of the number of frames within a window.

4. A. True

5. The **name** property holds the name of the current window and also allows you to give the window a name.

6. A. The window object is the default object in JavaScript.

7. The **self** property is another way of saying "the current window" in JavaScript.

8. C. Newer browsers do not allow the window status to be changed by default, so the user would need to change security settings in order for it to work.

9. A. The parent property goes to the top of the current frame set, while the top property goes to the top window of all frame sets on the page.

10. The **alert()** method pops up a message to the viewer, and the viewer has to click an OK button to continue.

11. A. true

12. The **print()** method enables the viewer to print the current window.

13. The prompt() method is used to **prompt** the viewer to enter information.

14. D. yes, no, 1, and 0

15. B. The setInterval() method is used to repeat a function at a set time interval, while setTimeout() executes a function only once after a set time delay.

Chapter 11: JavaScript Arrays

1. An array is a way of **storing** data of similar types for easy access later in a script.

2. In JavaScript, an array is basically a user-defined **object**.

3. B. index number

4. A(n) **associative** array allows access using a string in place of the number.

5. D. soap

6. D. var if= new Array[10];

7. C. cool[4];

8. A. Creates an empty array named s_list

9. A. The length property

10. The **prototype** property allows you to add properties and methods to an object that already exists.

11. The **concat()** method is used to combine the elements of two or more arrays and return a new array containing all of the elements.

12. The join() method is used to combine the elements of an array into a single **string**, with each element separated by a specified character.

13. The **pop()** method is used to remove the last element from an array.

14. C. It sorts the contents alphabetically.

15. D. A string value

Chapter 12: Math, Number, and Date Objects

1. A. Take the square roots and other such values of strings and return a number

2. The **E** property holds the value of Euler's constant.

3. The LN10 property holds the value of the natural **logarithm** of 10.

4. B. False

5. C. document.write(Math.PI);

6. The **SQRT2** property holds the value of the square root of 2.

7. C. absolute

8. The **asin()** method returns the arcsine of a number sent to it as a parameter.

9. The pow() method returns the numeric value of the **first** parameter raised to the power of the **second** parameter.

10. C. var rand_int= Math.floor(Math.random()*8);

11. The **sqrt()** method returns the square root of a number sent to it as a parameter.

12. D. An instance of the Date object

13. The **getDay()** method returns the number of days into the week.

14. B. False

15. B. var weekday= rightnow.getDay();

Chapter 13: Handling Strings

1. The **String** object provides properties and methods to get information about strings or to modify strings.

2. A. Creating an instance of the String object and creating a string literal

3. You can create a string **literal** by assigning a string value to a variable.

4. C. JavaScript takes the string literal and turns it into a temporary String object

5. C. length

6. The **length** property returns the length of a string.

7. B. var the_text= "Look at me!";

8. B. charAt()

9. The **big()** method adds <big> and </big> tags around a string value.

10. The concat() method **combines** two or more strings together and returns the new combined string value.

11. D. The indexOf() method returns a numeric value that is the position of a character sent as a parameter, but only the position of the first occurrence of that character.

12. The **italics()** method adds <i> and </i> tags around a string value.

13. The **toString()** method returns the string literal value of a String object.

14. To replace information in a string, you can use regular expressions and the replace() method of the String object.

15. The **match()** method compares a regular expression and a string to see whether they match.

Chapter 14: JavaScript and Forms

1. Each time you add a set of <form> and </form> tags to an HTML document, a(n) **form** object is created.

2. The forms **array** allows you to access a form using an index number.

3. B. document.forms[3]

4. A. document.forms[2].length

5. C. document.forms.length

6. Using form **names or ids** allows you to name the forms on the page that you want to access later.

7. A. document.f1.e1.value

8. The **action** property allows you to access the value of the action="*url*" attribute in the opening form tag.

9. The **elements** property is an array that allows you to access each element in a specific form.

10. The options property is an array that contains an element for each **option** listed in a select box in a form.

11. The **reset()** method allows you to reset a form using your script.

12. B. true or false

13. When the viewer clicks the submit button on a form, a submit event occurs and can be captured with the **onsubmit** event handler.

14. The **submit()** method allows you to submit a form without the viewer clicking the submit button.

15. D. The selectedIndex property

Chapter 15: JavaScript and Frames

1. Frames divide a window into two or more separate areas, each containing different content.

2. Frames differ from tables because the divisions in a frameset contain separate **HTML** documents.

3. The **<frameset></frameset>** tags are used to create a frameset.

4. A single frame is created with the **<frame></frame>** tags.

5. The **cols** attribute divides a frameset into columns.

6. If you want to have a more complex frameset that includes both rows and columns, you can **nest** one frameset within another.

7. A. The frames array or a frame name

8. A. True

9. C. The number of frames in a window

10. B. The frame should take up any remaining space in the window.

11. A. top

12. B. top.right_side.location="frame3.html";

13. Using a target of **top** tells the browser to use the full window when opening a URL rather than opening the URL in a frame.

14. A. True

15. The **rows** attribute divides a frameset into rows.

Chapter 16: An Introduction to Advanced Techniques

1. C. document.write("Is there an error?");

2. B. window.alert("Cool!");

3. **Logical** errors are often tougher to find because the syntax of the code is correct.

4. **Cross-site** scripting might allow someone to obtain information from a user of an application.

5. **Progressive** enhancement provides content for all viewers, but enhances it for those with JavaScript in modern browsers.

6. A. True

7. **AJAX** stands for Asynchronous JavaScript and XML.

8. JavaScript **libraries** may make some advanced coding tasks easier by making the code easier to write.

9. B. False

10. A **cookie** is a small text file that is stored on the end user's computer.

11. B. The cookie property of the document object

12. D. src

13. B. Rollover effect

14. C. No, but it can make reading it more difficult or annoying.

15. Any answer is correct!

Index

T